A Goldstar Century

Front cover:
'31 Squadron 100 Years' by Ian Wilson-Dick. Specially painted for 31 Squadron's centenary, the picture depicts Tornado GR4s and a BE2c over terrain close to the North West Frontier. Having served with Thirty One as an air mechanic during the 1947 partition of India, Ian is now a member of the Guild of Aviation Artists

Back cover:
Top left: Wapitis high over India. Photo from Bertie Mann's collection
Top right: How we never thought it would be. The author, Ian Hall, greets Hungarian MiG-21 pilots whom he had escorted through German airspace in 1994 to a landing at RAF Brüggen.
Centre left: MiG en route. Following the end of the Cold War, these were the first former Warsaw Pact aircraft to land at an RAF base in Germany.
Centre right: A Tornado GR4 waits in its shelter at Ali al Salem, Kuwait for tasking during Operation Telic (photograph by Thirty One's Corporal Mark Handford)
Bottom: Unusually, a Tornado GR1 is seen with wings fully swept to 67 degrees.

A Goldstar Century

31 Squadron RAF 1915–2015

Ian Hall

Pen & Sword
AVIATION

First published in Great Britain in 2015 by
Pen & Sword Aviation
an imprint of
Pen & Sword Books Ltd
47 Church Street
Barnsley
South Yorkshire
S70 2AS

ISBN 978 1 78340 058 4

A CIP catalogue record for this book is available from the British Library

Typeset in Ehrhardt by
Mac Style Ltd, Bridlington, East Yorkshire
Printed and bound in Malta by Gutenberg Press Ltd.

Pen & Sword Books Ltd incorporates the imprints of Pen & Sword
Archaeology, Atlas, Aviation, Battleground, Discovery, Family History,
History, Maritime, Military, Naval, Politics, Railways, Select, Transport,
True Crime, and Fiction, Frontline Books, Leo Cooper, Praetorian Press,
Seaforth Publishing and Wharncliffe.

For a complete list of Pen & Sword titles please contact
PEN & SWORD BOOKS LIMITED
47 Church Street, Barnsley, South Yorkshire, S70 2AS, England
E-mail: enquiries@pen-and-sword.co.uk
Website: www.pen-and-sword.co.uk

Contents

Acknowledgements   vii
List of Maps   viii
Prologue   ix

Chapter 1   Birth of a Squadron   1

Chapter 2   Peace?   17

Chapter 3   Imperial Air Policing   32

Chapter 4   Forces of Nature   44

Chapter 5   Bomber Transport   58

Chapter 6   Middle East and Africa   67

Chapter 7   Call of the East   77

Chapter 8   Two Years of Hard Graft   91

Chapter 9   Pitched Battle   104

Chapter 10   Drawing Breath   112

Chapter 11   On the Offensive   117

Chapter 12   The End Game   133

Chapter 13   Zipper, or What?   137

Chapter 14   RAPWI   146

Chapter 15   Darkest Days   155

Chapter 16   Aftermath   160

Chapter 17   Job Done   168

Chapter 18   Back to the Frontier   173

Chapter 19   Independence Days   180

Chapter 20   Communications Interlude   187

Chapter 21   Through the Lens   196

Chapter 22   Cold War   216

Chapter 23   Single–Seat   231

Chapter 24   The Fin   246

Chapter 25   Back on Ops   253

Chapter 26   Policing the New World Order   267

Chapter 27   Coming Home   279

Chapter 28   War on Terror   285

Chapter 29   Family Business   299

Chapter 30   *In Caelum Indicum Ultimus*   309

Chapter 31   Crystal Ball   320

Appendix A: 31 Squadron Commanding Officers   322
Appendix B: 31 Squadron Locations   324
Appendix C: 31 Squadron Aircraft   326
Abbreviations and Glossary   333
Bibliography   338
Index   339

Acknowledgements

Individuals too numerous to mention have assisted in bringing this publication to fruition. But I should like to single out and give special thanks to three of my friends: to Mark Dunham for producing the marvellously-professional maps; to Sylvia Coward for her expertise in restoring and enhancing grainy old prints without sacrificing their charm; and to Terry O'Halloran for his work in sorting and digitizing the thousands of 31 Squadron Association pictures from which I have drawn.

The history of a Squadron – a live entity – is a continually evolving story, and this is not the first published history of 31 Squadron. In preparing this narrative I have, naturally, drawn on earlier works. In about 1951 a book was published for, it is believed, internal circulation within the 31 Squadron Association. Its title was *The History of No.31 Squadron Royal Flying Corps and Royal Air Force in the East from its Formation in 1915 to 1950*. This volume's provenance is unknown but it appears to be a near-direct transcript of official records. If the author or publisher should be discovered, I would be delighted to give appropriate credit in any subsequent reprints of this book.

In 1983 a further history was produced, this time for commercial publication. Entitled *First in the Indian Skies*, it was written by Norman Franks and published by Life Publications Ltd. I am most grateful to both parties for their unrestricted permission to draw from this work.

In the final stages of preparing this volume I was lucky enough to have the assistance of editor Martin Derry. For his expert advice I thank him most sincerely.

Finally, my heartfelt thanks go to 31 Squadron Association member Ian Wilson-Dick for painting the picture which forms the basis of the book's cover.

The views and opinions expressed are those of the author alone and should not be taken to represent those of Her Majesty's Government, MoD, HM Armed Forces or any government agency.

List of Maps

Map 1   No.31 Squadron operations on the North-West Frontier, 1915–1941   2
Map 2   No.31 Squadron operations in the Middle East and Africa, 1941   68
Map 3   No.31 Squadron operations in the Burma theatre, 1942–45   78
Map 4   No.31 Squadron Burma operations, rear bases, 1942–45   92
Map 5   No.31 Squadron RAPWI operations in the Far East, 1945–46   147
Map 6   No.31 Squadron operations in northern India, 1946–7   174
Map 7   No.31 Squadron operations during the Indian independence / partition
         period, 1947.   181
Map 8   No.31 Squadron Cold War operations and Germany basing, 1955–2001   197
Map 9   No.31 Squadron operations in the Gulf Conflict, 1991   254
Map 10   No.31 Squadron operations in the Balkans, 1999   278
Map 11   No.31 Squadron operations during the post-Gulf Conflict period and
         the Iraq Conflict, 1992–2003   280
Map 12   No.31 Squadron operations in Afghanistan, 2009–2014   310
Map 13   Tornado operations against Libya, 2012.   315
Map 14   Tornado operations in response to Islamic State activity, 2014–15   318

Prologue

Flight Lieutenant Sasha Sheard of the Royal Air Force's Number 31 Squadron eases her Tornado GR4 into position off the port wingtip of the VC10 tanker one morning in 2013, waiting patiently for the pair of aircraft currently plugged in to complete their refuelling. The whole formation swims as though in a goldfish bowl, the aircraft rising and falling in unison on gentle air currents. The air at 22,000ft above sea level is smooth, but an occasional warning 'beep' from the radio altimeter (radalt) indicates that her aircraft is from time to time less than 5,000ft above the terrain below. Such warnings are not what one would usually expect to hear while refuelling at altitude, but the crews on Operation *Herrick* are used to the extraordinary terrain in the area. As if to confirm the radalt's intelligence, Sasha glances to starboard as a snow-capped peak of the great Hindu Kush range swims into view through the haze.

Each of the pair of Tornados carries two Paveway IV guided bombs as well as three Brimstone air-to surface missiles and a laser target designation pod. They have already been airborne for two hours and have completed an armed reconnaissance detail, transmitting invaluable intelligence on insurgent activity to ground HQ. Once they've topped up the tanks they'll be ready for further tasking if required. In the meantime, Sasha and her weapons system officer (WSO) in the back seat nibble on their in-flight rations, enjoying a relaxing interlude.

The two US Navy Hornets' tanks are full and their pilots pull back and away, leaving Sasha and her wingman to position behind the VC10's now-vacant hoses. With a minimum of fuss, and acting on the silent 'traffic lights' on the tanker's pods, the Tornado pilots nudge their probes into the shuttlecock-shaped baskets on the ends of the hoses and push forward until the two GR4s sit a mere twenty feet behind the VC10's wings, just a little below the tanker's high-set tailplane. Fuel flows, and as the formation reaches the far point of its assigned area the three aircraft turn as one onto a reciprocal heading.

Five minutes later the GR4s' gauges indicate full, and Sasha and her wingman peel away. As they do so, her back seater's screen lights up with data. A distant army unit is coming under fire and is calling by secure radio for assistance. With his cursor, the WSO enters the coordinates of the target's reported position into the aircraft's main computer and, as Sasha receives the new steering instructions on her head-up display, she confirms that the appropriate weapon is selected and armed. Now she is receiving vectors towards the weapon release point, and she swings the jet onto course.

As they leave the tanker behind, Sasha catches a blink of light from far below. Squinting down into the haze she is almost certain that something is moving there, but nothing is showing on the radar warner, and AWACS, the Airborne Warning and Control System, hasn't reported strangers in the area. There it is again though, and now she is sure she can pick out a minute dot moving slowly above the rugged landscape far below. Although she's certain it poses no threat to her current mission, she stores its position for future reference. And as her Tornado gets into its stride in preparation for the coming attack, the distance between it and the unknown contact far below stretches out. But Sasha briefly, nevertheless, senses a connecting tingle of history.

Far below, Captain Colin McDonald of 31 Squadron Royal Flying Corps (RFC) nursed his spluttering BE2c across the barren countryside where the North-West Frontier Province merged into Afghanistan, a blast of air catching him on the cheek as the little stringbag yawed awkwardly. At the Indian field from which he'd taken off it had been stiflingly hot, sucking the already-limited performance out of the machine and making even leaving the ground a questionable event. But high in the mountain pass he was freezing, despite his thick leather coat and fur-lined gauntlets.

An infantry column, moving painfully slowly across the rugged landscape, was signalling its position to him by heliograph; it had hostile tribesmen in sight. The commander had thought to call, for the first time, for this revolutionary new means of assistance – an aircraft. The BE2 rocked again in the turbulence, clawing for altitude in the high, thin air as McDonald gauged whether he'd get through the pass by maintaining his present course – or whether he'd have to circle again to gain the extra altitude he needed. At that moment a shadow flashed across the ground, and he squinted up into the sun's glare. Could there be other craft up there, high above him? He doubted it. His machine was already just about at the limit of an aeroplane's performance in these alien conditions.

He returned his attention to the job in hand, cocking the machine's fixed gun in readiness for the action ahead. His engine fitter, doubling up as an airborne gunner, did likewise with his rear-facing weapon, at the same time checking the box of small bombs between his feet in preparation for throwing them out at ground targets. Satisfied that he was ready, he tapped McDonald on the shoulder and stuck up a frozen thumb.

A couple of mountain eagles, soaring on a thermal just to the right of the nose, indicated to the pilot the position of the rising air he needed, and he altered course towards them. For the time being he thought no more about that shadow, although a fleeting vision crossed his mind of how, one day, his profession might evolve. But the year was 1917 and, for now, he knew that his concentration needed to be fully on the job in hand.

Between those two events – and even before the former and after the latter – 31 Squadron has operated in many of the world's most troubled regions. As well as performing the army co-operation work hinted at in these opening paragraphs, it has served with distinction in roles as diverse as bomber, transport, reconnaissance, strike and attack. It has seen two world wars and countless, more localized conflicts. During this time its service has been virtually unbroken; that it has lain dormant for a mere eight months in the hundred years of its existence places it up among the longest-serving of RAF units. And that it has been stationed overseas for a full seventy-eight of those years is also notable. Its form and composition have altered immeasurably over the years, yet its spirit has endured. It has gained the respect of units with which it has served, achieved the recognition of the nation in the award of battle honours, and maintained the loyalty of its members, both current and past. Through the medium of its active Association, both old and young recall the memories and exploits of their forebears, remember their fallen comrades, and celebrate the Squadron's current expertise and commitment.

This is the story of the people and machines that have kept 31 Squadron Royal Air Force – the Goldstars as the unit has come to be known – in premier place throughout the hundred years of its existence.

Chapter 1

Birth of a Squadron

On 11 October 1915, Captain Colin McDonald, holder of Royal Flying Corps certificate number 220, formed the nucleus of A Flight, No.31 Squadron, at the aircraft park at Farnborough. While other units of the rapidly expanding RFC were preparing to go to France, McDonald was ordered to take his Squadron to India. They arrived in Bombay on Boxing Day, and after journeying on with their equipment to Pir-Pai in North-West Frontier Province, uncrated and assembled their three BE2c aircraft. On 20 January 1916, McDonald took to the air in machine number 4452, becoming the first RFC man to fly in India.

This short, bald paragraph says much, but also omits a great deal of detail. The official record is scarcely more illuminating, its opening paragraph declaring simply that 'the formation of No 31 Squadron commenced in October 1915 when on the 11th inst. an Indian draft … was selected and sent on five days leave.'

McDonald at that time had a grand total of 197 hours flying and, with a tour on the Western Front already under his belt, would have been very conscious of how desperate the RFC was for numbers in that area. So one can only imagine that his new posting must have come as something of a surprise. What an immense task it must have been to assemble all they would need. What an adventure – and what a journey! How much vital equipment must have been delayed or lost in transit? How much must have had to be improvised to enable a flying operation to be set up from scratch more than three thousand miles from home? A contemporary report from Eric Neale, who rose through the ranks to become a flight sergeant with the Squadron, tells a little more – albeit with remarkable understatement:

'On the convoy from Farnborough to Birkenhead we hit very icy roads, and many of the old solid-tyred Leylands finished up in a ditch, causing considerable delay. Otherwise it was a good trip with a night stop at Castle Bromwich. We had a pretty rough passage through the Bay of Biscay in the old Anchor Line SS *Elysia*, and for three days I was the only NCO who could face my meals. We hadn't a clue of our destination until we arrived at Bombay, then five boring days in a special train taking all our planes and equipment to Nowshera. Our camp was at Pir-Pai, a few miles south-west of the city. We got settled in, hangars erected and a few flights made, but shortly afterwards the camp was almost completely destroyed in a sand storm.'

It has often been said that McDonald made the first ever flight in India, but this is not in fact the case. George Eccles, who joined in India as a clerk in the 1930s and later rose to the rank of squadron leader, was both a keen writer and a student of history, and uncovered the following account of the very earliest days of aviation in India. It is

Map 1: No.31 Squadron operations on the North-West Frontier, 1915–1941.

gleaned from the book *The Army in India and its Evolution* published in Calcutta in 1924, an introductory note explaining that 'this book is intended for the information of the general public and also for the use of military officers in connection with their promotion examinations.' It goes on to say:

'In 1912 an officer of the Royal Artillery attended Army exercises at Rawalpindi with an early type of Farman biplane and a French pilot. Both the pilot and the machine had been imported into India at the officer's private expense. The few flights that were made – they were the first flights made in India – ended in disaster to the aeroplane; but they bore fruit in directing serious attention to the military potential of the new arm. Within a short time it was decided to form an Indian flying school … The outbreak of the Great War, however, intervened. It was not possible at that time to foresee either the duration of the war or the enormous demand that would ensue for trained aviators, so the flying school was broken up. The staff and equipment were sent to active service, and the winter of 1915 saw the demise of the Indian Flying Corps as a separate body.'

Understood to be a picture of Thirty One's first take off in Indian skies. Capt McDonald gets airborne from Pir-Pai in BE2c number 4452.

So Thirty One wasn't the very first unit airborne on the sub-continent, but it's probable that it was the first formed, operational, military squadron to operate there. Before going further, we'll look at the background to its arrival and against which it would fly for the next twenty-seven years.

From the earliest days of colonial rule in India, tribes on the North-West Frontier had been a thorn in the flesh of the British. There had been two full-blown Afghan wars in the nineteenth century, and during the Great War another was brewing which would come to a head in 1919. At a strategic level, the British worried about the threat potentially posed to India by Russia. Indeed, the Asian imperial ambitions of Britain and Russia had led to disputes which, on several occasions, had manifested themselves over Afghan territory and borders. The area also came under pressure during the First World War from the Ottoman Empire which, allied with Germany, attempted to take Afghanistan under its umbrella. However, despite accepting Turkish and German missions in Kabul, the country stayed resolutely neutral during the Great War, albeit continuing to delegate responsibility for its foreign policy to India.

Even given this continuing instability, it's not immediately obvious why, given the overriding need for aircraft in France, a Royal Flying Corps squadron was sent to India. The answer seems to lie first in the fact that this novel mode of transport was finding military applications worldwide – which could certainly be exploited on the sub-continent. More specifically though, the imperative for the British in India at that time was to cover a temporary shortage of troops. Because so many Indian Army units had been dispatched to the Western Front, the Frontier area had been left vulnerable to tribal incursions. All in all, aviation's time in the area had, quite simply, arrived.

As it turned out, Sir Hugh Trenchard (later to become Marshal of the Royal Air Force Lord Trenchard, the 'father' of the service which would be formed in 1918 from the air wings of the Royal Flying Corps and the Royal Naval Air Service) had a further vision. One of the missions he envisaged for his embryo RAF was colonial air policing. Perhaps he had seen that his infant service would quickly need to 'find a role' in order to fend off designs by the army and navy to dismember it. But whatever his

Certificate No. 220

ROYAL FLYING CORPS.
(Officers.)

CENTRAL FLYING SCHOOL,
UPAVON, WILTS.

12th September 1916.

CERTIFICATE "A."

THIS IS TO CERTIFY that Lieutenant C. J. McDonald
Seaforth Highlanders
(6 weeks)
has completed a short course at the Central Flying School, and is qualified for service in the Royal Flying Corps.

Captain R.F.
Commandant.

Here insert "First" or "Second."

Colin McDonald's RFC flying certificate.

underlying motive, it had become apparent to Trenchard that a small number of aircraft could exert a level of control over vast areas which would have taken thousands of troops to achieve. And at much lower cost, a factor which, in the difficult financial circumstances of the 1920s, would possibly become the clinching argument. There would certainly be plenty of work in India in the coming years, with a series of 'little wars' which would keep the Frontier pot bubbling between the world wars. So when 31 Squadron departed British shores in 1915 it was almost predestined to remain overseas for many years.

The First Five. Captain Cooper, Lieutenant Fletcher, Lieutenant Taylor, Captain McDonald, Lieutenant Tweedie.

Whether or not that storm at Pir-Pai influenced the decision to move Thirty One so soon after its arrival we shall never know. But we can say with certainty that the primary reason for the RFC vacating the station soon afterwards was that the airfield was found to be

Captain McDonald's log book records with a complete lack of fanfare his 'first flight in Indian skies' on 20 January 1916. A twenty minute flight, 'to test new machine, result good'.

subject to torrential rain, when the ground would become waterlogged. So the Squadron was moved to Risalpur. Before they left, Captain Cooper gave Eric Neale his first flight. This was a great thrill for Neale, who now goes on to describe the move:

'We shared splendid bungalows with the 21st Lancers. But en route we had quite a difficulty transporting the large containers of complete BE2c planes over the pontoon bridge and up the road to Risalpur. I was transport sergeant at the time and we were provided with a large low trailer which could hold the containers, but on the first trip I had trouble with the little cast-iron wheels which kept seizing up on the steel axles and which only had a tiny oil hole for lubrication. I was duly hauled up by my transport officer, Lieutenant Eyre, before the CO next day. I reported that the design was useless and that phosphor-bronze brushes should have been fitted and proper grease caps provided, and I then suggested that whoever designed the trailer was hopelessly wrong. I noticed the CO looking a bit grim, and he then asked if I was aware that Lieutenant Eyre had designed it? A hot moment for me and I was dismissed, but that evening I was transferred to C Flight as engine sergeant.'

Neale's mention of C Flight dates this piece sometime in late spring. The Squadron record shows that B Flight arrived from England early in the New Year on the SS *Benala*, complete with two crated BEs, and travelled up to Risalpur by train to join the Squadron. Both B and C Flights formed at Gosport; C Flight joined in May.

Throughout early 1916 there was much to do. As well as setting up the airfield and flying, there were classes in Urdu and Pashto to attend. In fact what might be described as the colonial administrative aspects of the deployment had been identified in the record from the outset: '[On initial arrival] the flight was met at Bombay by Lieutenant H. Tilley, 1st Batt The Durham Light Infantry, who had been selected for attachment with two NCOs and eight men to instruct the personnel in Indian ways'.

The story of early operations, initially at least, tends to read as a list of obstacles to be overcome. If the first days of aviation were challenging and exciting in Europe, then in India the difficulties seemed to be magnified. Performance of the early aircraft, limited at best, was wholly inadequate in the harsh climate. Their unreliability was made more critical by the nature of the terrain and the hostility of the population; forced-landings usually resulted in crashes, while capture could lead to brutal treatment at the hands of the tribal people. Inadequacies in piloting skills and lack of understanding of aviation, common in the early days, were magnified in the demanding terrain and climate. Supply chains were lengthy and slow, while landing fields had to be scraped from nothing on the unforgiving terrain. Having said that, we do read of polo pitches making excellent runways – although we are left to wonder quite how the resident cavalry regiments must have taken to that solution!

The Squadron's first aircraft type, the BE2c, had entered service in 1914. Twelve squadrons of the machines served with the RFC in France but, being insufficiently armed and not very manoeuvrable, the BE was soon badly outclassed by German aircraft. It was reportedly nicknamed 'Fokker Fodder' and a project to replace it was started as early as the end of 1915. But it remained in service on the Western Front until 1917 before being relegated to training and home-defence duties. This inadequate type was to equip Thirty

One until 1920, but a report dated April 1916 notes that 'aircraft availability stood as follows: five machines on charge of A Flight of which two are serviceable and three repairable. Five machines on charge of B Flight of which one is serviceable, three damaged and one totally wrecked.'

The general staff in India soon began to take a serious interest in the Squadron's equipment, and the following report was compiled for their benefit:

A BE2c

'In cold weather the machine proved fairly satisfactory. A considerably larger landing ground was found to be necessary than is required in England and France. Probably this is chiefly owing to the dryness of the atmosphere. In hot weather it will be impossible to use these machines at all except for two or three hours after dawn, and even then a very much larger landing ground is necessary than most of those now existing in the district. For example on 18 April at about 4.45pm, a machine with pilot and observer and a light wireless set ran 450yd before leaving the ground and then took approximately fifteen minutes to climb the first thousand feet, after which the climbing speed steadily improved. The 90hp engine has proved very liable to overheat in warm weather, and in hot weather it will be quite impossible to run this engine at full power long enough to climb through the hot strata of air on the ground.'

Accident reports came thick and fast:

'Lieutenant V. P. Cronyn, a Canadian, under-estimated his glide approach and landed on the roof of one of the hangars …'

'Lieutenant Leslie Mann, on his first solo in June when the temperature was 115°F, found "little lift in the air that day", and it was very bumpy. He stalled, the BE suddenly dropped 1500ft and went into a spin. He remembers switching off the engine, but his next conscious recollection was of lying amidst a pile of matchwood, bleeding from above his right eye where his goggles had struck. Bending over him was a tribesman who had already taken his cigarette case and was cutting the buttons from his uniform. Luckily he then heard the sound of approaching horses as an Indian cavalry unit came to his rescue.'

Logistic problems required innovative solutions, as the official record shows:

'Experiments were carried out with a view to using camels for the purpose of transporting hangars if necessary. Difficulty was experienced with the tripods and the long poles, and the drivers asserted that these could not be carried on camels. A trial was therefore made, and on one occasion two poles were lashed one on each side of a camel. It was found that when the camel walked, a swaying motion developed in the poles and the latter often came in contact with the camel's head and neck. But, after trials and modifications, the conclusion reached was that "the transport of hangars by camel would be possible if necessary, with the total number required to transport one hangar being eighteen".'

The Squadron was straight into operations, but a necessary step for the aviators was to persuade the army and the colonial authorities of the aircraft's utility. Slowly and laboriously, however, joint operating practices and procedures were developed. In April 1916 a scheme was laid out with Peshawar Division for 'four weeks practice in co-operation between aircraft and artillery. Only three weeks of this practice were completed owing to severe dust storms which wrecked most of the machines.'

This first effort at co-operation gave HQ enough work to carry on with for the next six months, the record noting HQ's efforts as: 'compiling impossible instructions to be carried out by both arms. By the end of the year, however, some sort of working procedure had been arranged, to be experimented with at the next winter camp, to be held in December.'

One of the priorities was to develop communications between ground and air, essential if an 'army co-operation' squadron ('AC' being the formal role designation applied to Thirty One) was to prove really useful. A report from a practice camp conducted at Akora a little later with the 1st (Peshawar) Divisional Artillery demonstrates the various methods which were in use:

'Targets and corrections were signalled by map squares, wireless, Verey lights and klaxon horns. One observer successfully ranged two batteries simultaneously with the klaxon; the system has obvious advantages in a moving battle and worked quite successfully. Corrections were sent from 3,000ft under favourable weather conditions, but would not work so well in the case of a reverse wind.'

During 1916, life began to take on a pattern. Major C. R. Bradley, apparently a handsome man and known to his men as 'Beautiful Braddles', became CO in the summer, with Captain McDonald reverting to flight commander until he left in early 1917. Colin McDonald's legacy will remain unique, and he will forever be remembered as the first RFC man to fly in Indian skies. At the time of Bradley's arrival, by the way, B Flight was commanded by Captain G. L. Hunting, who later went on to found the Hunting aircraft company.

Operations in support of army manoeuvres against restless tribesmen began in earnest during summer '16, comprising reconnaissance, bombing, strafing and artillery ranging. Eric Neale, from whom we've already heard, tells another tale:

'D Flight at Lahore (which, with a number of Thirty One's personnel and aircraft subsequently formed the nucleus of the new 114 Squadron [and moved to] Aden) was suddenly ordered back from detachment to Risalpur, as trouble was developing on the Frontier beyond Peshawar. So our six BE2c aircraft took off pre-dawn. I was with Lieutenant Paddy Travers in an old brown machine which was notoriously slow and always seemed to fly tail-down. Once the sky got light we found we were quite alone, but after an hour or so we spotted two of our machines which had forced-landed. We slogged on against a strong headwind and I asked Paddy how we were for petrol. His reply made it certain we wouldn't reach the nearest diversion, Rawalpindi, and I asked him to turn back to an emergency landing ground we had just passed, and we got down well. A crowd soon arrived from nowhere and I heard that there was a local man with a car a mile or so away, so I set off to see whether I could get some juice. He only had a low grade of petrol but he let me have two four-gallon tins. I discussed with Paddy whether we should risk it, but the alternative was so bleak and it was getting so damned hot that we decided to give it a go and filled her up. She started all right; we had no chocks so couldn't open her up for a test. We taxied to the far side of the small, cup-shaped field and I told Paddy to give it all he'd got. We cleared the mud huts by just a few feet and eventually made it to Risalpur, getting a real strafing from the CO as flying wasn't allowed after 11 o'clock in the summer. Only one other plane arrived that day and it transpired that two others had flown cheerfully south instead of north and landed pretty badly.'

It's noteworthy that the pilot would apparently have been at a complete loss during this episode had it not been for his crewman, whose primary function was ostensibly on the ground. But Thirty One's airmen were versatile people. The air gunners, for example, also aimed bombs, fired signal flares, dropped messages, operated the wireless set, assisted with map reading, took aerial photographs and serviced the aircraft. They were chosen from amongst the groundcrew; despite only being paid a pittance for their flying duties, they were very proud to be members of the aircraft crew and of the winged bullet they wore to indicate their role.

Neale seems to have flown a lot and, as he continues here, witnessed his fair share of accidents:

'On another occasion I accompanied a pilot early one morning on a trip to Peshawar. We were enjoying low flying over the city, seeing the inhabitants still on their *charpoys* and beds on the roofs, when suddenly the engine spluttered and stopped. We made a quick landing on some allotments and ended up on our nose. We blamed the magnetos, of course, but the pilot had forgotten to pump up the petrol from the reserve tank.'

And he certainly wasn't the only one who viewed his pilots with a degree of circumspection. Lieutenant Charles Eastley, an artillery man, volunteered for aircrew duties and joined the Squadron in the autumn of 1916 as an observer. He quickly formed an opinion on the varying degrees of skills he witnessed:

'I flew with a pilot named Taylor, but when taking off he held the tail down and we quickly landed in a rye plantation, where the machine collapsed. Then, on another occasion, Major Steele-Hutcheson took me off without flying speed and we came down – wallop. Neither of us was hurt but, in spite of being insubordinate, I flatly refused to fly with him again. Colin Cooper was a great pilot and used to take delight in flying under the bridge across the Indus River at Attock.'

The intrepid Cooper always seems to have been ready for a jape. On one occasion he was reported as having been dispatched with an NCO to Nowshera

Maybe not the infamous Attock Bridge, but machines nevertheless seem to be queuing up fly under it.

railway station to collect a Crossley touring car which had been received. On arrival he found a two-seater Rolls-Royce standing there, sent by a local maharajah and labelled for delivery to an army unit. They changed over the labels and 31 Squadron was soon the proud possessor of the Roller. Years later, Eastley recounted the story to the air officer commanding, to be told that there was a large file on the incident in New Delhi. Luckily, the AOC seemed to be amused.

Cooper was also known for his pet dog 'Kim', which often flew with him. The hazards must have been obvious, but it apparently took a serious incident to bring them home to him:

'Circling Kohat prior to landing with the mail, a passenger, and of course Kim on Cooper's lap, the large mail bag became dislodged and jammed between the stick, the dog and the fuselage side. The machine lost height rapidly and was down to 500ft before Cooper managed to sort it out.'

Accidents and incidents continued on operations throughout 1916. Typical of early reports was this one from October of that year:

'The Kuki Khel Mohmands commenced to give trouble and threatened the Khyber Pass. Aeroplanes were eagerly sought by the general staff for reconnaissance purposes, and machines from 31 Squadron carried out continuous recce and bombing raids over the area until, to further facilitate operations, one flight was detached to Shabkhadar where a temporary aerodrome had been constructed. In these actions the enemy were apparently armed with a fair percentage of good rifles, their fire was quite accurate and several machines were hit. One cylinder head was shot away and a petrol tank pierced, but the fuel in the top tank enabled the pilot to reach the landing ground. An engine bearer was also pierced. The only casualty amongst machines during the week was the complete wreckage of one on its way back to Risalpur when it came to ground with its engine apparently in perfect order, but the machine suddenly refused to hold the air. No defect in the rigging could be found owing to the wrecked condition of the machine. The pilot and passenger were unhurt.'

Artillery officer Charles Eastley's impressions of his first pilots weren't favourable. But it's interesting to follow him as his aviation career developed. Initially, he commented that he found 'the tuition for becoming an observer mediocre, as was the tuition on the Lewis gun. What one learned was mostly self-taught. Having "qualified" I was put onto instructing newcomers. A case of the blind leading the blind!' Despite that, he then went on to qualify as a pilot. Here's one of his earliest stories in his new trade:

'In January 1918 I did my first solo in a Farman. Because of the wind direction I had to take off towards the hangars. My first and second efforts were flops, for I could not get the brute to unstick. But others had succeeded, so I was determined to do so and I fairly yanked the machine off the ground. Up went her nose, and down I brought it, only to lift it back again to avoid striking the top of the hangar. It was a ghastly machine. What use it could ever have been in service I fail to comprehend. It had been sent to India with a lot of other rubbish discarded by our troops in East Africa.'

Having survived this initiation he went on to enjoy further piloting adventures:

Demonstrating the field of fire from a Farman.

'At Landi Kotal parade ground I took off for Risalpur. Owing to the direction of wind, an Avro (the most manageable and lovable of machines in those days) had taken off across wind left wing down, and I did not see why I should not do likewise in my BE2. Having become airborne I had the feeling that somebody had taken me by the seat of my pants and was forcing me toward the roadway on my right, along which there were a number of soldiers marching up towards the Khyber Pass. I might have killed the lot! So I gave a violent kick to the right rudder and landed up against a concrete pylon marking the edge of the parade ground. No injury, barring a scratch. Mechanics who rushed up told me that a "dust-devil" – a small whirlwind – travelling far faster than I was, had caught my rudder, rendering me helpless. A bit of luck if you like!'

And then later:

'I was heading for Parachinar at the entrance to the Powai Kotal Pass through which, years previously, Lord Roberts had made his famous march from Kabul to Kandahar. I encountered strong headwinds and much cloud. In despair I decided to land at the next white circle (which marked our emergency landing grounds) which manifested itself through the clouds. I did so, and was lucky enough to find myself at Parachinar.

'On checking the sump I found only a teaspoonful of thin, black liquid; the engine had been on the point of seizing. So I sent to Risalpur for another one.

'This took several days to reach me. Meanwhile, I lived like a lord in the mess of the Khurram Militia. Beautiful food – asparagus, strawberries, cream, etc. In return I volunteered my services to the general, and spent the time replenishing stores. It was an interesting experience, visiting villages with an Indian political officer, commandeering supplies. The courtesy I received from tribesmen was amazing.

'When the new engine arrived we installed it with the assistance of some Indian soldiers. On taking up the machine on test it seemed that the rigging had become distorted. I was assured by my mechanic that it had not, so I took it up again. This time the wind was blowing from the mountains, which necessitated taking off with an uphill gradient. I got into the air all right, but a sudden downdraught from the said mountains caused me to pancake very suddenly on the uneven ground – and that was the end of the machine. So I had to return by road; altogether a most unfortunate excursion.'

By now, it seemed that Eastley was thoroughly into the swing of piloting, accepting both its hazards and its wonderful moments:

'At about 7,000ft the engine cut out and I chose as an emergency landing ground what looked like a beautiful green field near a village. It was not until I had flattened out to land that the field turned out to be undulating, and so after a couple of jumps after landing the centre section went off like a pistol, which was the end of the machine. The villagers came out, and I *"salaamed"* the headman. Explaining was difficult, as he didn't speak English and I had no Baluchistani, so we both struggled with indifferent Hindustani. After securing the wreck we were taken to the nearest station on the railway. Here, having woken the station master and being given tea, we sent a telegram to Lahore to report the disaster. We were turned over to the policeman, who insisted on our partaking of his *Arak*, which looked like water, smelt like varnish, and tasted like hot coals.

'We were looked after royally. Once the rescue party had arrived and dismantled the aircraft we were given a bullock cart for the engine, the wings were strapped to camels, while the fuselage was towed by another bullock. I wish I had been able to do something to reward that headman and his retinue – wonderful people.'

Notwithstanding Eastley's pleasant encounters with the local population, a serious concern was that many of the tribesmen were very hostile and, it was believed, merciless. Colourful and horrifying tales circulated, describing what not only the tribesmen but also their womenfolk were reputed to do with their knives to captured British military personnel. And falling into enemy hands was a real and present danger. Not only could hostile action bring an aircraft down, but unreliability was at least as great a problem. The solution lay in the system described by Mark Tomkins in an article in *Air Mail*:

'Aircrew carried "goolie chits" promising a very substantial reward if the crews were helped to return to base. But it was with somewhat black humour that Kipling wrote:
   "When you're wounded and left on Afghanistan's plains
   And the women come out to cut up what remains
   Just roll to your rifle and blow out your brains
   And go to your Gawd like a soldier".'

Tomkins went on to remark that as 'the very large majority of tribespeople were illiterate, goolie chits were of scant comfort, and any uneven engine noise was reason for concern both as to where to force-land (parachutes were not issued until the late 1920s) and how subsequently to survive.'

He was undoubtedly right about the cause for concern, but goolie chits were nevertheless known to have been successful. Lieutenants Barker and Hoare, for example, were captured on 14 May 1919 having force-landed in the Bazar valley while on a recce sortie. They were successfully ransomed 'by the good offices of the chief commissioner NWFP and his agent Sir Abdul Q'ayum from Afridi tribesmen for 30,000 rupees.'

Flying Officer Donald Hardman commented also that 'goolie chits, written in Urdu and Pashto, certainly worked in the case of Foster and Ridley, although they had a rough time.' He went on to explain gleefully that 'there was also a story of a chap with red hair who was reputedly kept by the Wazirs for stud purposes.' The author has been unable to verify that particular tale!

We shall come to other, related stories in due course, but there certainly seem to be no records at all of 31 Squadron aircrews being tortured or killed by tribal people. So perhaps this indicates the success of the goolie chit system. The possibility of brutal treatment must, nevertheless, have been a constant fear, and puts into context the type of courage it must have taken to have operated such rickety machines over hostile terrain and peoples. A story from the record illustrates the point:

> 'In March 1918 Lieutenant Travis took off alone with orders to bomb the village of Kahan. Despite a strong wind his first 20lb bomb hit the corner of the village, causing about two hundred people to start to leave by gateways. Travis then dropped a 112lb bomb on the crowd, and a later report noted that fourteen had been killed. Two days later, Travis again flew alone to the village, dropping ten 20lb bombs of which four landed in the bazaar, causing casualties. On leaving Kahan, Travis was forced down by engine trouble, landing beside the Sibi-Lahri track. Walking to the village of Tarri, Travis obtained a horse and rode to the 81st Pioneer Regiment's camp at Lehri, collected an officer and twenty-one men to guard the machine, and wired the results of the raid and his whereabouts.'

One can only wonder at the thoughts which must have gone through the man's mind as his engine began to splutter. Just what might have been the consequences if he had been brought down in the vicinity of the village he'd just bombed?

Late in 1916 the Squadron was inspected by General Salmond, commander of the Middle East Air Brigade. (Sir Geoffrey Salmond, who was subsequently to become AOC the RAF in India, and later chief of the air staff. Not to be confused with his brother Sir John Salmond, also later to become chief of the air staff, and whom we shall shortly also meet). He was given a flight around the border in order to get an idea of the terrain in the North-West Frontier Province.

It must have been useful to be able to brief a senior, air-minded officer, and the army was soon finding that this new and novel military arm had a role to play, not just in pure operations, but also in the demonstrations and ceremonial which served to bolster the political prestige of the Raj. As shown earlier that year when two machines, flown by Captain McDonald and Lieutenant Gordon-Dean, flew to Peshawar for a *durbar*, a formal conference complete with parades, demonstrations of cavalry charges, and the like. This particular occasion was headed by the chief commissioner North-West Frontier Province, Sir George Roos-Keppel, and all the chiefs of the trans-border tribes attended. A report later commented:

> 'It was most interesting to watch the faces of these chiefs – hardy old warriors – at their first sight of aeroplanes in flight. They said that the machines were only large birds and that no human being could possibly be inside them … but when they witnessed the machines land and Sir George, whom they knew so well, enter a machine, go for a flight and land safely again, their wonder and awe was indescribable. One remark was to the effect that "the day of the Robber and Murderer was at an end in the Raj, for *Sirkar* [the government] could get behind them and see all their doings".'

The report betrays the colonial authorities' willingness to exploit the local people's complete unfamiliarity with aviation, and a story from 1919 confirms this:

'On 14 July a determined attack was made on Bannu aerodrome by local tribes. This attack was beaten off by the guards, but many bullet holes were found in the hangar roof. The political agent subsequently reported that the tribesmen had purposely fired up there as they were under the impression that the machines would be roosting in the roof.'

It's easy to dismiss these local populations as primitive and uncivilized – to scoff at their gullibility. But even sophisticated Europeans had, a few short years earlier, found early aviation almost beyond belief. In India, both sides played mind games, and the colonial authorities soon learned to apply the psychological effect of air operations as well as the physical. These aspects are well illustrated from both sides in this report from 1919:

'Lieutenants Keeping and Cox landed at Miranshah to refuel, and crashed when taking off. At this, a local *mullah* announced that he could cast spells over flying machines. In consequence, 31 Squadron sent a machine to bomb the area, the effect of this raid being to produce gifts of sheep, milk, eggs and fowl to the British.'

It wasn't necessary to convince only the local people of the various characteristics aviation could bring to the mix. Further extracts from the record serve to reinforce the importance accorded to getting the senior British people on-side:

'The first landing in Amritsar was successfully accomplished by Lieutenants Thomas and Kirk, an emergency landing ground having been marked out on the polo ground. Various notabilities were taken for short flights, and a civic welcome was accorded the two officers.'

Then, later:

'On 7 April 1917 His Excellency the Viceroy of India, Her Excellency, and all the viceregal staff, accompanied by the chief commissioner with his staff, paid a visit to the Squadron, inspecting the aircraft park, workshops and sheds, and witnessing flying. The Hon. Joan Thesiger, the Viceroy's daughter, was taken for a flight.'

The chaps clearly already knew how to impress a girl and where their priorities lay! Another fine example of 'winged diplomacy' appears in the record a couple of years later as follows:

'A crew participated in a review of his troops by the Maharajah of Dhar. The machine arrived at Dhar while the parade was in progress and did a little stunting, finally flying low along the parade ground and saluting the maharajah. This obviously made a hit with the great man, for on another occasion a machine landed at Dhar at the maharajah's invitation and was inspected by him and his household. The CO and three other officers were invited to dinner, when a silver cup was presented to the officers of the Squadron

The Viceroy's daughter, ready to be thrilled by her pilot.

and another to the CO to commemorate the occasion of the first aeroplane to fly over Dhar.'

As already hinted, throughout those early years the Squadron did not confine itself to flying the BE2c. By 1917, Thirty One also had on strength the Farman F27 and the FE2b. There was also at least one BE2d (dual controls) and a number of BE2e machines (identifiable by shorter lower wings). One of the Farmans (possibly ex-RNAS aircraft, as there is little record of the RFC using the F27) was also fitted with dual controls with a view to using it for training. As far as is known, neither the Farman nor the FE was found to be a particular improvement, although the FE2b was noted at one point as 'behaving better than the BE2c in the bumps caused by the hot air.' Nevertheless, the BE continued to be, in all forms, the main equipment.

An FE2b outside the hangar.

Gurkhas guard a couple of Farman F27s.

A report from the following year shows the stock to have grown to a surprising size: 'At the end of the year the Squadron had a strength of 64 machines, of which 26 were BE2c, 34 Farmans, 3 BE2e, and one FE2b. The total engine inventory was 79.'

Given that the officer strength of the Squadron reached a maximum of about forty during the period (although we cannot tell how many of those were pilots), it must be questionable whether all those sixty-four aircraft were in flying condition. It's likely that a proportion could have been wrecks being used for spare parts.

Preparing a Farman for action.

In May 1917 a large raiding party was threatening the landing field at Tank, so all the BEs had to be manhandled at close of play each day a mile or so to be housed within the perimeter of the garrison. The operation to counter this threat continued for a few weeks through the height of the summer, the heat severely limiting aircraft performance, but air and ground forces pressed on together. A Waziristan Field Force column then ran into serious opposition from the Mahsud tribe:

'Lieutenant Boyd, reconnoitering high ground, dropped bombs successfully on villages in advance of the column and fired into a party of men near Darsheli, causing about 100 casualties. Lieutenant Robinson, with Captain Kitson as observer, discovered about a hundred Mahsuds holding a ridge in a very strong position. Coming down to a hundred feet he flew three times up and down the ridge using his machine gun, causing many casualties and forcing the enemy to retire, thereby allowing our troops to advance. Many other small bodies of the enemy were scattered later by machine-gun fire. Lieutenant Robinson's machine was hit five times by rifle bullets, but the enemy's shooting was apparently very erratic. On 25 May, Captain Fletcher, who was up solo with bombs and a Lewis gun lashed to the side near the pilot's seat, successfully bombed two villages and scattered a small party of the enemy which was following our own troop column. The following day, Captain Fletcher with Lieutenants Robinson, Boyd and Rankin, bombed Makin and Marobi, getting direct hits and doing considerable damage. All four machines returned safely. Makin is the second largest village in Mahsud territory and is built in terraces on the hill side at an elevation of 6,400ft. From Tank to Makin is about forty six miles. There is practically no ground upon which a machine could make a forced landing, the whole country being mountainous and intersected with steep ravines.'

And in another related report it was noted that: 'On 19 June Captain Fletcher, having dropped his bombs, observed seventy to 100 Mahsuds in the fields and hedges. This body was dispersed by flying low and firing his revolver at them.'

A wire received on the 27 June reads:

'The GOC [General Officer Commanding] Waziristan Field Force congratulates the RFC on the successful raids in Mahsud territory. These raids have had a great effect, and this morning a messenger arrived from Kangrim asking that they might be stopped while peace terms were being considered. He says that one bomb killed twelve men, wounded another and destroyed some cattle. If the Mahsuds come to terms, a full share of the credit will be due to the Royal Flying Corps'.

He followed up even more enthusiastically: 'On account of the wonderful morale effect and usefulness of aeroplanes, the GOC WFF has asked for details of buildings necessary to house one flight at Tank.'

And in August, even the commander-in-chief felt impelled to join in: 'For the first time, the tribesmen of this frontier have felt the power of the Royal Flying Corps, which carried out its duties with the dash and daring to which the army has been accustomed.'

Waziristan would become very much the Squadron's home territory for many years. No sooner would one uprising or tribal raid be dealt with than another would arise. Never a 'war' but, conversely, never an area at peace; the pot continually bubbled. The extract below offers a succinct description of the area and its people, which were the focus of Thirty One's attention for so long.

'Waziristan consists of a tract of independent territory lying between the North-West Frontier Province and Afghanistan; in shape it is a rough parallelogram with an average length of 110 miles from north to south, and an average breadth of sixty miles. In the north-west and on the slopes of the mountains are thick forests.

'The inhabitants of Waziristan are all more or less of Afghan extraction and are divided into two main divisions, these being the Mahsuds and the Wazirs. The former have always been our most formidable enemies on the Frontier. They are a typical highland race and in many respects they resemble the mediaeval Scots. The tribes are divided into clans and again into sections and sub-sections, every chief having his stronghold. Personal bravery is accounted the chief virtue, and compared with other tribes the Mahsuds are of a frank and open disposition, although they are past masters in the art of deceiving an enemy.

'The country is a difficult one for aerial operations. Tribesmen on the ground can get excellent cover among the rocks and are almost invisible from above, while in many cases they can fire down on to machines from above. The great heat and the height of the ground also present difficulties and, owing to the rocky and precipitous nature of the country, forced landings are fraught with much danger.'

Regarding the 'independent territory' mentioned, the North-West Frontier Province was actually separated from Afghanistan by a line of areas occupied by the Mahsuds, the Afridi and the Wazirs. These were collectively known as tribal areas or, sometimes, the 'buffer states'.

The record notes that, from September onwards, 1917 was taken up with 'training in wireless, photography, reconnaissance, pigeons, formation, stunting, gunnery, cross country flying etc.' Pigeons? That sounds incongruous, but of course birds were a time-honoured means of military communication – which had been adapted for air operations.

Sad to relate, the airman had their first recorded lesson in airframe fatigue on 6 December of that year:

'Lieutenant Robinson and Air Mechanic Cameron, in a Farman, were involved in an accident over the aerodrome. The machine had just completed one loop and was entering another when the starboard mainplanes were seen to fold back along the fuselage. The machine came down in a spin and, on crashing to earth, burst into flames. The pilot and mechanic were killed instantly.'

This was particularly poignant in the case of Robinson, who had been one of the leading players in the Waziristan operation. In fact he, along with Captain Fletcher, was awarded the DFC for 'gallantry and distinguished service'. Regrettably, in Robinson's case the medal had to be awarded posthumously.

Chapter 2

Peace?

D espite the continual operations, military formality still had to be observed. Annual inspections came and went, with the report from 1918 showing 31 Squadron to be achieving a state of maturity:

'Physical appearance satisfactory. The men are well turned-out and are well disciplined. Musketry has just been carried out. Economy and internal condition of the Squadron are in all respects satisfactory. The Squadron is ably commanded and well officered. The personnel are keen and efficient. The Squadron regularly proves its ability and a very good tone exists, as should be the case in the Royal Flying Corps.'

Number 31 Squadron was fully occupied in its own limited world, with events on the Frontier tending to maintain a momentum all of their own. Significant happenings in the wider world were noted in what seems, to today's reader, to be a curiously detached way, as in this bulletin, published on 18 November 1918 by the CO:

'Special Routine Order No 17 dated 13/11/18 by the Director of Aeronautics in India is republished for communication on to all ranks: "The following message has been received by Lord Weir from His Majesty the King. 'In this supreme hour of Victory I send greetings and heartfelt congratulations to all ranks of the Royal Air Force. Our Aircraft have been ever in the forefront of battle. Pilots and Observers have consistently maintained the offensive throughout the ever changing fortunes of the day, and in the War Zones our gallant dead have lain always beyond the enemies' lines or far out to sea. Our far flung Squadrons have flown over Home Waters and Foreign Seas, the Western and Italian Battle lines, the Mountains of Macedonia and Gallipoli and Palestine, Rhineland and the plains of Mesopotamia, the forests and swamps of East Africa, the North-West Frontier of India, and the Deserts of Arabia, Sinai and Daruf. The birth of the Royal Air Force with its wonderful expansion and development will ever remain one of the most remarkable developments of the Great War. Everywhere, by God's help, officers, men and women of the Royal Air Force have splendidly maintained our just cause, and the value of their assistance to the Navy, the Army, and the home Defences has been incalculable. For all their magnificent work, self sacrifice and devotion to duty, I ask you on behalf of the Empire to thank them.'

'"The following reply has been sent to the Air Ministry. 'Your telegram dated 12th instant conveying His Majesty's gracious message received. All ranks RAF in India profoundly stirred, their devotion to His Majesty remains ever imperishable.'"'

From 22 November until 1 December a holiday was granted by the commander-in-chief on the occasion of the armistice. And that, as far as the climax of the 'war to end wars' went, was apparently that. India's remoteness from those events must, of course, have been a factor, and it was also true that 'peace' never lasted long on the Frontier. In fact operations in theatre continued pretty well as before.

BE2 ready for action.

The reader may also have noted in the King's message the passing reference to the formation of the Royal Air Force, which had occurred on 1 April 1918. As far as can be discovered, the mention in the bulletin above, written in November, is the first in Thirty One's written history referring to the emergence of the new service. Perhaps because this, too, seemed to make little difference initially. Indeed, the record up until as late as the end of 1919 still lists all the Squadron officers with army ranks.

An impressive line-up

But by 1920 the final transition from RFC to RAF was being implemented. The comment then was that 'the days of many and varied uniforms came to an end. The service dress and mess kit uniforms were finally settled and officers were ordered to obtain these by the end of December.'

As always with bureaucratic processes, there was a sting in the tail:

Presented by His Highness the Khan of Kalat.

'In June 1920 a new rate of pay was brought in for RAF officers in India. On reading the official pamphlet on the subject, one was led to believe that owing to the "increased cost of living" the new rate would be beneficial to all. Quite rightly, observers were to be paid the same as pilots. But when the rates were published it was found that all except the most senior officers had suffered to the extent of 100 rupees or more. Married officers were now in a desperate plight.'

In 1919 the routine of tribal skirmishing on the Frontier began to be supplemented by something altogether different, namely general unrest among the local populations, directed against British rule. The first major manifestation was a series of riots at Amritsar. These were clearly major events although, as hinted at in the record, reported at the time with considerable circumspection: 'Full details are unobtainable as they were never made public. Even the official résumé is very brief and leaves a lot to the imagination.'

But the 'Amritsar Massacre' was most certainly significant, later acquiring a degree of notoriety and being commonly quoted as hardening Mahatma Gandhi's opinions (which had hitherto tended towards peaceful protest) with regard to Indian nationalism. And plenty of information has become available since, not least from a speech on the matter by Winston Churchill in the House of Commons. This became widely recognized as a milestone in his political career – forming the turning point of the debate and saving the government of the day from defeat. So it's important to summarize the events as they unfolded.

Following unrest in Amritsar, the holy city of the Sikhs, a British woman missionary was assaulted. The colonial authorities responded by imposing what were widely regarded as unjustified and cruel reprisals. Many of the local population attended a protest rally on 13 April in a confined square in the city, during which a British army unit apparently fired into the defenceless crowds. In all, 379 Indians were killed and 1,500 wounded.

For Thirty One's part, the Squadron was ordered to send two aircraft to Lahore on 10 April as tension rose, and the pair of them were airborne over Amritsar that same evening. Their recce report noted buildings on fire, including the railway station, as well as a crowd of locals assembled in the square. Later, a night reconnaissance sortie was launched, of which it was said that: 'Because it was not carrying parachute flares, it could only provide negative information.'

But with the situation becoming more serious, an entire flight of aircraft was dispatched to Lahore the next day. The general staff was out of contact with its force in Amritsar and retained two 31 Squadron aircraft on standby for the sole purpose of conveying orders to the garrison and returning with dispatches. To facilitate this, Air Mechanic First Class George Haynes was dispatched to Amritsar landing ground with orders to form a guard to protect any aeroplanes which might land. Having looked around, he is reported to have assembled a force comprising 'an American jute merchant, an old Armenian and an elderly local man.'

On 13 April, a large column of reinforcements was supported by four Squadron aircraft as it entered the city. The pilots' brief was to bomb targets which the army indicated, but although the aircraft were airborne for over two hours their services weren't called upon.

Following the Amritsar incident, unrest spread and five districts of Punjab Province had to be placed under martial law. Three machines were dispatched to Gujranwala to aid the civil power in dispersing rioters. Bombs were dropped and crowds strafed, but this appeared to be the last significant action of these disturbances.

Incidentally, the above mention of 'night recce' is the first known record of Thirty One having any such capability.

No sooner were these riots calmed than rumours arose of an impending Afghan war. Afghanistan's largely neutral stance throughout the Great War, despite attempts by the German / Ottoman alliance to bend the administration in their direction, had been maintained. But following the war Afghanistan aspired to look after its own foreign affairs. Although this strategic aim was initially denied, change within the ruling family led to a belief among Afghans that they might be able to take advantage of unrest in India such as that at Amritsar. On 3 May, information was received by the British that

Afghanistan was about to declare a *jihad*, being inspired by false reports as to the internal situation in India.

There then began a campaign of cross-border raids during which Afghan forces captured a number of Indian towns and cities. On 4 May, 31 Squadron received orders to keep two machines ready to take part in the suppression of any aggressive movement by troops assembled on the border. Hostilities were formally declared on 6 May 1919, the date marking the start of the Third Anglo–Afghan War.

On that day, a reconnaissance was requested of the Afghan side of the border, with three machines being employed. The enemy's distributions were located and reported on. Machines reportedly 'received a very hot reception and came back with many bullet holes.' Enemy forces were located in the heights of the range bordering the Khyber Pass, apparently based on Loe Dakka.

No work was requested for the next two days, but on 9 May a striking and effective bombing raid was carried out on the enemy's base at Dakka. All available machines, sixteen in number, made as many visits as possible and the enemy was remorselessly harassed from morning until late in the evening. Numbers of casualties reported by agents amounted to some 600 men, and the record reports that, 'the destruction of two elephants constitutes a unique record in the annals of aeroplane bombing history.'

It was later ascertained that the Afghan commander-in-chief's brother, a *mullah* and a *malik* were among those killed. On this day the record tells us that:

'No less than a ton and a quarter of bombs were dropped, 1,151 rounds of ammunition were fired into the enemy, and 14 photographic plates were exposed. The total day's flying reached 60 hours 10 minutes. Three machines were brought down on our side of the lines. Of these Captain Carberry in the Squadron's only Armstrong-Whitworth F.K.8 forced-landed and crashed, and Lieutenant Keeping got a bullet in the sump of his engine which caused a forced landing. An extract from the military résumé of operations tells how: "The employment of aeroplanes, which were of the BE type at the commencement of operations, was in part limited by the mountainous nature of the terrain. Machines received a hot reception, due partly to the intrepidity [sic] of the pilots and partly due to the good marksmanship of the Afridi tribesmen".'

On 17 May, Lieutenants Oddie and Villiers had an experience which fortunately ended in comedy. After a forced landing, Villiers saw some troops which he took to be hostile and walked towards them, revolver in one hand and ransom chit in the other. A voice came from behind a boulder in broad Somerset tones: 'I hope you ain't 'urt, Zur?!'

Information received indicated the almost complete demoralization of the Afghan troops and tribesmen:

'Jalalabad was deserted by its population, and messages describing the destruction

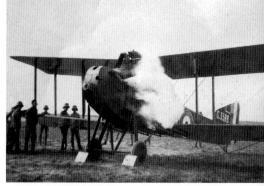

As far as is recorded, C3588 was the Squadron's only Armstrong Whitworth A.K.8.

of the city were reported to have had a great deal to do with inducing large enemy forces to retire from the Dakka front without taking any offensive.'

A few days later, in response to rapid moves by the Afghan commander to enlist the sympathy of most of the southern tribes of the buffer states, as many as nine machines were dispatched to Kohat – which was a large, Frontier military station. According to the record, 'The energy with which the pilots set about their task effectively deprived the Afghan general of the support of these tribes, who lived in dread of aeroplanes.'

In late May the town of Thal was in a state of siege, with a detached flight at Kohat carrying out intensive bombing and strafing attacks said to be designed to 'shake the enemy's morale.' Messages were also dropped to the garrison to the effect that relief would not be long delayed and, on 1 June, four machines successfully co-operated with the relieving column, attacking targets out of the infantry's range and directing the artillery. Lieutenant Kirby had a race with an armoured car to be first into Thal at 8.45am. This he won by two minutes but was forced to take off again after coming under the fire of hostile guns and rifles. By 10am, though, Thal was relieved.

The official record continues:

'Between 15–18 June, Lieutenants Vincent and Curry carried out bombing and recce over Wana. On the first of Vincent's raids, great surprise and effect on morale was caused by gliding down from 6000ft and dropping seven 20lb bombs in the fort, which was packed with men and animals, causing many casualties.'

And aircraft continued to find innovative employment, with commanders and aircrews learning to appreciate the diversionary capabilities of the force at their disposal. Another anecdote from the record:

'In June 1919, A Flight was operating from Tank to assist the Waziristan Force against the Mahsuds. The transport for this detachment had had a long and trying journey, with day temperatures reaching 123°F and no ice available. A great deal of heat-stroke and prostration were experienced. Lieutenant Vincent, on a recce, read a heliograph message to the effect that the Jandola garrison was under siege and running out of water. Vincent dropped a message informing the garrison that he would return to bomb and strafe the tribesmen and that, while they were distracted, those under siege should obtain water from a stream some 200 yards away. He was as good as his word and, after landing to re-arm, returned to inflict several casualties on the tribesmen. While this was going on, the fort obtained a fifteen-day supply of water without a shot being fired at them. Previously they had been unable to show a finger outside the fort.

'Three days later the garrison was relieved, the hills having been picketed under Lieutenant Vincent's protection. It was estimated that there were between two and ten thousand Mahsuds in the surrounding hills. He was the first to land at Jandola, entering the fort while the relieving column was still a mile away.

'Following these operations, the GOC Royal Air Force (Brig Gen MacEwan) conveyed his "high appreciation of the excellent work during these operations. He realizes the strenuous and difficult conditions … and that the excellent results could only have been brought about by continuous and conscientious work on the part of the WOs, NCOs and AMs under very trying weather conditions".'

The Afghan conflict was still bubbling and, at about this time, reinforcements arrived on the Squadron in the form of a heavy bomber. Captain 'Jock' Halley, a Great War veteran with a DFC, together with Major MacLaren, had flown a Handley Page V/1500, the 'Old Carthusian', on the first flight from England to India. This four-engined bomber had taken off from Suffolk on 13 December 1918, arriving in Karachi on 15 January.

Halley, having received an AFC for his part in this epic flight, was ordered to Risalpur on 13 May with a view to taking part in the Afghan campaign by bombing Kabul in another Handley Page. However, before this O/400, a twin-engined machine, could be used it was wrecked by a storm as it stood on the airfield.

Not to be discouraged, the staff ordered that the V/1500 be launched instead. It needed modifying, and racks for 112lb bombs racks were borrowed from Thirty One's BEs. Bombs would be aimed using a sight fitted in the front cockpit. A further sixteen 20lb bombs were stacked in the mid cockpit, to be dropped through the bottom doorway by crewmembers when they saw the 112lb bombs being released. Halley took off at 3am on 24 May, with Ted Villiers his 'volunteer' observer. He reports:

'The route lay towards the Khyber Pass and, as the clearing height was about 3,000ft above take-off, this meant flying around for about an hour to gain height before going over the ridge. As daybreak came we reached Jalalabad, but to my horror I saw water leaking from the base of the second cylinder of one of the engines. I called Flight Sergeant Smith up to me and, with engines throttled back, we hurriedly conferred on the course of action. The leak came from a rubber hose but it was not possible to judge the extent of the water loss. Kabul was still ninety miles distant, and then we would still have to get back. We decided to press on, and through the precipitous mountains I could see the Jagdalak Pass high above me. Chancing all I hauled back on the stick and just cleared the top. Even now I can see the look on Villiers's face! On the other side I could see our target ahead, spread out over a vast fertile plateau. With a population of 300,000 I was not surprised by the extent of the city. Still nursing our leaking engine we made the bomb run and our missiles achieved good results. If that didn't frighten the inhabitants, many of whom would never have seen an aeroplane before, the sound of 'Old Carthusian' just a few hundred feet up with four engines roaring must certainly have done!

'On the return flight we again scraped over the Jagdalak Pass, helped by a lightened aircraft and a following wind. Finally the leaking engine's temperature rose so I had to close it down. But by now we weren't far from Risalpur, where we landed safely after six hours in the air, all greatly relieved.'

Jock Halley received a bar to his DFC for the raid, which was yet another nail in the régime's coffin and helped force an end to hostilities in early June. Whether either the aircraft or Halley could have been said to have ever officially been on 31 Squadron strength is doubtful, although Scotsman Halley's words showed that he, at least, was quite clear about which side his bread was buttered on:

'During my time in India I was a freelance, only taking orders directly from the AOC in Delhi. However, I'd heard that officer personnel received an extra 100 rupees a month for serving in theatre ...'

Eventually Afghan aggression was repulsed, and the armistice signed on 8 August 1919 marked the end of the Third Anglo-Afghan War. Afghanistan agreed to respect the border with India, so Britain could be said to have 'won'. However, in exchange Afghanistan would look after its own foreign policy in future. And, given that a virtually continuous series of tribal skirmishes continued afterwards, those who were serving on the Frontier barely noticed the war's end.

The conflict served, though, to crystallize Trenchard's ideas on how the Frontier could better be policed by air forces. But attitudes on combat operations were entrenched and, according to Michael Barthorp in his book *Afghan Wars and the NW Frontier, 1839–1947*, it was not until 1937 that it was agreed that 'In the event of a further Afghanistan War or in the event of a major tribal uprising, air would take the offensive with the army primarily looking after defensive aspects.'

The V/1500 raid had been an epic in its way, with aircrew getting most of the glory. But there had been, as noted, mechanics on board, and groundcrew continued to play at least as big a part in developing frontier operations – although not necessarily receiving the consideration due. Here's a good illustration, taken from the pages of *First in the Indian Skies*:

'Dakka airfield, which had been heavily bombed and shelled during the war, was now to be taken over by the British. George Haynes, who had just been released from hospital in Risalpur following a bout of heat fatigue and fever, was detailed to be the engineer who would make it ready. He would proceed by air and, having clambered into the observer's seat of a BE, his assigned pilot, Captain Butler, took off for the Khyber. They had only covered twenty miles when hot soot and oil began to spew back into their faces. Haynes's advice to the pilot was that they should return to Risalpur and, on landing there, it was discovered that the spare oil tank had inadvertently been turned on which had resulted in the engine becoming flooded.

'The machine was fixed but evidently not properly, for the engine stopped as they climbed through 300ft following their second take-off. The BE hit the ground and its undercarriage was smashed, but both men were unhurt. Taking to the air for a third time in another BE, Butler made his way up the Khyber Pass but found that he was unable to coax the machine over the mountains. After making four or five attempts, each time the BE falling away in the thinner air, Butler gave up and flew to the landing ground at Peshawar where a tyre exploded on touch-down.

'Had they made the attempt in the cool of the morning, as intended, they'd have cleared the terrain. To lessen the weight, Butler flew on alone to Dakka, leaving the crewman to continue by road. Haynes completed the journey by lorry the following day, only to collapse on arrival owing to the extreme heat. But having recovered he was given a tent to pitch just outside Dakka army camp. He was the only airman in the place, the garrison comprising the Somerset Regiment plus Gurkhas, Punjabis and Sikhs.

'Getting to work the following day with the assistance of twelve local troops, Haynes embarked on the three-week task of levelling the cratered 400 yard strip, in the process diverting the nearby river to dampen down the eternal dust.

Throughout, local hill tribesmen sniped at the workers, while a nearby mountain battery fired creeping barrages up the hillsides. At night Shinwari tribesmen would tiptoe down to the camp to steal food and equipment. George's isolated tent was vulnerable so he was given a companion from the Somersets. This chap reputedly awoke on the second night to find tribesmen in the tent but, believing his throat would be cut if he was found awake, he feigned sleep. For some nights following, George slept in a nearby trench, but later returned to his tent, this time with a guard of six Indian troops.

In the early days crashes were regarded as part of the routine.

'Meanwhile the landing ground, having been irrigated by the river, slowly turned to a verdant green, and Haynes focused his attention to erecting two steel and concrete hangars. With the help of two local lads he had them up and ready in two days. A tribute to the versatility and inventiveness of airmen on the Frontier!'

At about the midpoint of the Afghan War the record returns, inexplicably, to Risalpur, where, apparently,

'The usual programme of training was being carried out. Flying had been curtailed in order that machines might be overhauled and personnel given a rest, pending possible heavy demands should hostilities recommence. All ranks that could be spared were sent to the hills. At the same time airmen were selected to take part in the peace celebrations, and for demobilization on extreme compassionate grounds.'

Stretching the glide!

Even after reaching the landing ground they had trouble stopping ... although something soft in the way – such as the campsite – always helped.

All in all, a confusing report. Training, right in the middle of the Afghan War? Were these 'peace celebrations' belatedly being held to mark the end of the First World War? We cannot tell. Nor do we know what 'proclamation' was being announced in the following extract:

Given the shortage of aircraft and spares, salvaging the wreckage was important. All available means were employed, including this gun carriage cadged, no doubt, from a co-located artillery unit.

'On 30 June one machine was detailed to drop proclamation leaflets on Kahi and Peshbolak, but it had to return owing to engine trouble. Another machine was dispatched to drop leaflets on villages. The pilot reported a big parade at Jalalabad of about a thousand troops with two thousand civilians looking on, full dress uniform being worn. The pilot came down very low and dropped propaganda. The troops did not scatter but the civil population ran in all directions. When they saw that no hostile action was intended, they got quite excited and waved frantically, finally fighting among themselves for leaflets.'

It's possible that the 'proclamation' was simply a warning that the village was later to be bombed – for it was a common practice at the time to attempt to spare women and children from attack.

The same couldn't necessarily have been said for livestock, though, and the reader cannot fail to have noted the recurring – and somewhat incongruous, to our current-day eyes at least – mentions of attacking animals. This brief piece offers some insight into the rationale:

'The grassy uplands of Waziristan afford excellent grazing for the flocks and herds, which are the most valued possession of the tribesman. It is these which are the principal targets for machines operating over tribal country. The tribesman is adept in the art of concealing himself and it is seldom that a good human target is found for bombs and machine guns. These flocks and herds, however, offer an ideal target, and the strafing of these eventually persuades the bellicose tribesman to listen to reason, and to return to more peaceable pursuits than raiding and the cutting up of pickets.'

New aircraft, in the form of Bristol Fighters, were beginning to appear on the Squadron, and the first operations in which they took part were leading up to an army campaign known as the 'Waziristan Expedition'. But a 'Brisfit' was soon forced to land in the Bazar Valley, with Lieutenants Wells and Winstanley being taken into captivity. However, they were treated well and, after negotiations, were returned. A heavy ransom was paid for them. Extracts from Wells's vivid report give us a good picture of the whole incident:

'On the morning of 13 September I flew over the hills to the south of the Bazar Valley in order to view the approaches from that side. I heard a shot or two and later found boiling water coming back into my face. I glanced at the thermometer, which registered well over boiling point, and immediately turned back, being a little way west of Chora. Later, smoke commenced to issue from the cowling and the engine dropped revs, eventually seizing up completely. I made up my mind to land in a green patch of cultivation about a mile east of Chora. This was as far as I could glide. It turned out to be terraced and walled. Finding that I had slightly overshot I dipped the right wing to the ground. The undercarriage was swept off and the machine then rolled over to the right. Winstanley was thrown out of the cockpit and landed on his shoulder, fortunately only bruising himself. Beyond this, neither of us sustained any injuries. Winstanley immediately went to his cockpit to get a pigeon for release. He got hold of the pigeon box and his revolver and had just turned away when a Pathan slipped in and relieved him of both. We then found about six to eight Pathans by our side. Their approach was entirely concealed by the maize. They pointed to a *nullah* just below us and said *"Chelo"*. After crossing the nullah, in which there was a great deal of water, we went westwards.

'The following morning we moved on at about 6.30, arriving at a summer camp at about 11am. There were no buildings, only rude branch shelters. We were told that we were going no further. We remained until the evening of 15 September when, after a big *jirga* [assembly of elders], they removed Winstanley to the valley. I remained in the hills for three days, then I was also moved down, about two hours march.

'The Maliks of the Khyber had been sent out by the Political Agent to arrange for our release. A settlement was finally come to on the morning of 20 September. Within an hour we were moving towards the village of Karaman, or Karani, where we were put up, and the following day arrived at Landi Kotal. During the whole of our time we were well treated by the tribesmen, many of them in fact being ex-soldiers, and moreover, latterly, there was nearly always a political messenger present.'

A happy outcome, and the report reveals no hint of the crew being in any doubt that they would be released. But one wonders whether it was compiled sometime later when they'd recovered their *sang-froid*. For it's hard to believe that they didn't feel a degree of anxiety on initially being captured by tribesmen.

Later in the month, Lieutenant Devonshire was killed whilst on reconnaissance in the Chora area. The following report of his death was received later from the political agent of the Khyber:

'Devonshire was flying very low over the retreating Lashkar, causing considerable damage with his bombs and a great deal of confusion. As he passed from north to south across the plain close to Chora Fort, a single man stepped out from under a tree and had the extraordinary luck to hit Devonshire just below the right eyebrow and he must have been dead before reaching the ground. His body was unfortunately never recovered.'

The conclusion of this particular round of Waziristan operations was marked by what was becoming the usual flurry of appreciative telegrams, not least one from the chief of the air staff, Air Marshal Sir Hugh Trenchard: 'Hearty congratulations to all ranks on satisfactory reports of operations and maintenance of RAF units on Indian Frontier.'

Soon afterwards, the Squadron learned that it was to move to Mhow in April 1920. Once again, the record's account of the logistics of the transfer is illuminating:

'The whole Squadron left by rail, taking with them three Bristol Fighters. The move was accomplished with two trains, and was completed in two days in spite of the fact that the Bristols had to be packed in BE cases, and that machines, stores and troops had to be trans-shipped at Rutlam onto the narrow-gauge railway. The last leg to Mhow was completed by road.'

By all accounts Mhow was not a successful location, the officers' mess being a mile from the barracks and the aerodrome being two miles from both. More importantly, the landing field was reported as being composed of 'black cotton soil which became soft and boggy in wet weather'. Luckily Mhow was only to be a temporary home, pending a move to Cawnpore later the same year.

The harsh Indian climate – temperature, monsoon, humidity and dust were all factors to a greater or lesser extent according to season and location – always caused problems. And still the performance of the aircraft continued to produce some hairy moments:

'Atmospheric conditions were a source of interference to our aeroplanes over the hilly country of the Frontier. Dust storms were a problem and, from the end of May, when temperatures had got up, it was almost impossible to leave the ground after 9.30am. To illustrate the difficulties, Lieutenant Vincent was flying over the Kohat Pass at about 10'o'clock one morning in June in an 80hp le Rhone Avro. Owing to air disturbances the machine sank to the road, which runs at about two thousand feet above sea level, even under full power. Vincent had to fly along the winding road for about half a mile, bouncing his wheels at intervals, until eventually the machine climbed a little.'

A good job the road happened to be there. And perhaps it was just as well that, by 1920, the last of the BE2s was dispatched to Lahore. Although still recorded as retaining a couple of Avros (including the underpowered beast mentioned above), 31 Squadron was now almost fully equipped with Bristol F.2B Fighters. The 'new' aircraft (which actually first saw service in France in 1917) were recorded as having a top speed of 123mph with upwards of 5,000, of various marks, being built. At one time or another thirty-nine RAF squadrons operated the type; with modifications to the cooling system, it saw a great deal of colonial service. These aircraft were generally liked, looking a good deal more solid than their predecessors and also being regarded as a little 'racier' than earlier equipment.

Brisfit.

But logistic considerations still loomed large, and things were not to improve as economies began to assume uncomfortable proportions. A further dip into *The Army in India and its Evolution* confirms the situation:

'By 1920 the RAF had eight squadrons in India, comprising two bomber/recce, four army co-op, and two scout/fighter. But almost immediately the new organization began to suffer the effects of post-war financial stringency and the scout squadrons disappeared. In other respects also, the air service was affected by the government's financial difficulties, and major economies followed. Notwithstanding the formation of the independent Royal Air Force in 1918, C-in-C India retained control – with the air force budget incorporated within the army estimates.'

Despite the success of Trenchard's 'imperial policing' role, the RAF in India was struggling without control of its own purse strings. In February 1921, No.31 Squadron was inspected by Field Marshal Lord Rawlinson, the C-in-C himself, the record confirming that:

'This heralded the beginning of a great economy campaign throughout all arms in India. This was carried out to such an extent that it was with great difficulty that machines were kept serviceable. On one occasion a machine was flown with rope on one side of the axle instead of shock absorber, as this was unobtainable in the country, and machines had to be returned as unserviceable owing to a lack of split pins.'

And in 1922 it was said that:

'Owing to the shortage of spares and the age of the machines, the Squadron was now decreasing in strength on account of the many engine failures and forced landings, and this became so acute that paragraphs appeared in the papers about it and questions were also raised in the House. Only to be answered in the usual manner of politicians!'

Flying Officer Donald Hardman was less than impressed:

'We were equipped with an old model of Bristol Fighter and soon after my arrival were plunged into a punitive war against the Mahsud tribe in Waziristan. Our unserviceability was so high that the three squadrons on the Frontier were only able to put six aircraft on the operation. I wrote a report and we were subsequently re-equipped with a later model of Bristol.'

In February 1921, Squadron Leader A. T. Harris had taken over the Squadron from Flight Lieutenant Neale. Neale had been in command for a year but had now reverted from squadron leader, being quoted in the record as 'being too young, under the new regulations, to retain his rank.' Whether this was a further economy, a consequence of the post-war contraction of the military, or because the RAF rank structure was not exactly equivalent to the army's we cannot tell. Whatever the cause, we must hope that his reward would come later.

However, the new CO was clearly just the man for the situation, not being afraid to speak his mind. On the Squadron's new location (a base with much history), he commented:

'Cawnpore was a pleasant station, although lacking practically everything that an air force squadron would regard as essential for maintaining its aircraft. Because we were under the army vote, we got little of everything and much of what we got was useless.'

Harris also felt that the accommodation provided at Cawnpore for his men was pretty grim:

'When I complained to the CO about the conditions, he seemed most incensed, saying "Don't you know that these barracks were the ones defended during the Indian Mutiny before all the defenders were massacred?" To which I made the obvious retort that "at least you might have whitewashed them since!" '

He seemed to revel in confrontation, telling a story of an early meeting with his superior officer, who happened to be a gunner:

'A battalion of newly enlisted young infantry soldiers arrived and, as far as I recall, over twenty of them died of heat stroke within the first few weeks. The station commander pointed out that I was infringing station standing orders because my airmen were working in the open throughout the morning and sometimes the afternoon as well. He asked me if I didn't realize that, during the hot season, the men were not allowed out of their barracks during the heat of the day. I pointed out that I had had only had one case of heat stroke on my Squadron, while the

Squadron Leader 'Daddy' Harris with his men. Seated in the centre of the front row, leaning forward, he would later become Air Chief Marshal Sir Arthur 'Bomber' Harris.

infantry men were going down like nine-pins. Probably because my men had plenty of essential work maintaining aircraft to take their minds off the malaise affecting the soldiers – who had nothing to do but lie around all day on their beds wondering who was going to die next!'

Harris later reported:

'We were called to an advanced landing ground called Miranshah where more trouble was brewing. A rather unpleasant type of army officer came up to me and said words to the effect that we were not likely to be required to take action for several days while the army got on with the job themselves. The army were always jealous of the air force doing them out of a job! I said "Fine, in that case I will take my few remaining aircraft back to Peshawar until they are wanted." The general then, in a rather sarcastic tone, said "Oh, I suppose the air force can't exist for a few days away from their base supplies." This annoyed me into replying, in view of my lack of every conceivable spare part thanks to our being under the army vote, "Yes sir, it is essential that we get back to our ball of string".'

Magnificently blunt speaking, and the reader will probably not be surprised to learn that this CO, known on Thirty One as 'Daddy' Harris, was later to achieve great eminence. He was of course the same man who, as Air Chief Marshal Sir Arthur 'Bomber' Harris, would lead Bomber Command through its most gruelling and demanding period during the Second World War. While commanding Thirty One he returned several times to his theme of an under-resourced RAF:

'Some time later we were inspected by the then Prince of Wales (later to become King Edward VIII) who was outspokenly sympathetic to our somewhat forlorn condition, especially as he recognized Coryton as "the fellow who taught our Bertie to fly".'

'Bertie' was the future King George VI. And the 'Coryton' in question was a flight commander who would later, as Air Chief Marshal Sir Alec, present Thirty One with its first Standard.

Harris was later quoted as despairing of 'the more or less hopeless task of trying to keep aircraft functioning safely under the thumb of the army in India.' But he was delighted to note later that, in consequence of a letter to *The Times* from Lord Montague of Beaulieu describing the disgraceful conditions under which the RAF was working, Lord Trenchard would send Air Vice-Marshal Sir John Salmond (the other brother) to India to enquire into RAF affairs. Following his report, a speedy reorganization resulted.

Perhaps the CO's outspoken comments were also a sign that the embryo RAF in India was beginning to assert itself. Flying Officer Noel Moreton, apparently known as 'Egg', recounts an example which occurred during the rehearsal for the Prince of Wales's visit mentioned above:

'We were on the left of the line and marched past after the Supply and Transport Corps and their mules. We had given them plenty of space so that we could see what they had left behind! The parade commander afterwards complained about our spacing to our wing commander on the telephone. I happened to be in the room and he went red with rage, saying "Next time we'll take twice the distance, and we'll arm our men with dustpans and brushes." Slamming the phone down, he said "Colonel H thinks the sun shines out of his bloody arse!"'

Moreton also has something to say about Cawnpore, the base:

'It was hot – very hot. We're brought tea and toast at 4am, before going off on bicycles or motor bikes to get on parade for 5. Then do our day's work, followed by brunch at 11.30. Then back to bed, brought more tea followed by games. Dinner, always in mess kit, with the big question being whether to wear one's tie inside or outside the high, done-up collar of the jacket. Inside was considered correct by our senior flight commanders. The loyal toast was to "The King Emperor", and we had all sorts of strict rules about dress, including the wearing of field boots. Until our AOC, on one of his visits, had to be cut out of his!'

Indeed Moreton always seemed to see the funny side of senior officers' visits:

'General Birdwood, the GOC, came to inspect us. I was one of three officers waiting in the duty pilot's office as the parade was falling in. Suddenly someone called "He's here – get on parade!" He was half an hour early, and the CO and our other senior officers hadn't arrived. I darted out and took up my position as supernumerary on A Flight. When Birdwood reached me he did what apparently was his usual greeting and put his arm round my neck! When he had gone on to B Flight, someone whispered to me "Slip round to take command of HQ Flight where there are no officers!" This I did without being noticed and, when Birdwood arrived, pulled them up to attention and saluted. Birdwood again put his arm around my neck and said "My boy, where have I met you before?"'

Chapter 3

Imperial Air Policing

Later in 1921, Thirty One moved to Peshawar, the capital of North-West Frontier Province and situated at the Indian end of the Khyber Pass. The record's description of the farewell social events followed by a slightly chaotic journey tells something of the spirit of the times:

'Machines were made serviceable, stores were packed, train and landing ground arrangements were made, and the advanced party was sent off. Before leaving, a farewell dinner and dance was given by the members of the Cawnpore Club to the officers of the Squadron. The evening was a great success, and many touching but slightly bemused speeches of farewell were made. The sergeants also gave a farewell dance at the King Edward memorial hall, at which no time or energy was spared by them to make the evening a complete success.

'The first formation left at 6.30am the following morning for Peshawar, the machines having all been tuned up, repainted and generally beautified. The flight met with nothing but misfortune during the whole of the trip. At Agra at the end of the first stage, Flying Officer Vosper overshot the aerodrome and turned the machine on its nose, but was luckily not seriously injured. Flight Lieutenant Watts was also delayed there for several days with a broken fuselage fitting. The remainder of the formation reached Delhi the same afternoon and were entertained by the Leicester Regiment to a guest night.

'Next morning the formation left for Ambala in a rainstorm, and in the afternoon ran into a dust storm near Lahore, which was of such intensity that it was impossible to see the ground from over three hundred feet; only by following the railway could the pilots find their way to Lahore. Flying Officers Robinson and Jackson missed the railway and were forced to land on the first available open space. Jackson, landing in a recreation ground, crashed, whilst Robinson landed in a field of maize, managing to get off again the next morning. This stout effort on the part of Robinson saved the dismantling of the machine and the further delay of the formation. Flight Lieutenant Coryton and Flying Officer Playford continued the journey alone the next morning and arrived safely, via Jhelum, that afternoon.'

The second formation had a similarly bad trip; suffice to say that, with the added complication of picking up the pieces of the first formation, it was almost a month before they were safely at Peshawar. The personnel, stores and all ground sections moved up in two trains and had an altogether less eventful journey, arriving without a hitch after forty-eight hours of travel. As the record comments, they were greeted with due ceremony: 'The troops were met at the station by the band of the West Yorkshire Regiment and were marched into barracks.'

The social side of Service life in the Raj intermeshed nicely with operations:

> 'On the evening of 6 April 1922, when the officers were in the thick of a dance at the club at which the Squadron jazz band was playing, orders were suddenly received to the effect that the Squadron would fly to Tank at dawn on the following day for further operations. Preparations for this went on the whole night, and the band kept on until four'o'clock in the morning, when the officers who had been playing had just time enough to get back, change, and reach the aerodrome in time to load up their machines and get away.'

And, during the Prince of Wales' visit to Peshawar, 'there were several dances and a garden party at Government House, to which the officers were invited.'

There were other lighter aspects to life. Pilot Officer Gerald Combe, Thirty One's first RAF College graduate, recalls:

> 'We operated over pretty frightening territory in single-engined, not very reliable aircraft, so the teamwork between aircrew and fitter/rigger was of prime importance. Each pilot had his own aircraft, and esprit de corps couldn't have been better. I remember the officers had "luncheon jackets" made – a symbol of Squadron unity. On one famous occasion we held an egg eating contest to see who could eat the most at one go. It was won by our signals officer who chose prairie oysters, but he had to be pumped out afterwards to get rid of the Worcester Sauce. We also had the "rumbling club". Pilots were fined one rupee if they used their engine when coming in to land – i.e. if they'd misjudged their glide approach.'

Remaining in lighter vein we'll take the opportunity of having a customary chuckle at the 'grocers' – the suppliers. Far from home and living in primitive conditions Thirty One might have been, but the record was still moved to comment on the inappropriateness of the 'machine-like quartermaster's stilted language' in one particular invoice from the stores section: 'Please remit to this office the sum of rupees forty-nine on account of the value of one coffin, large, supplied for the late Sergeant C. An early settlement is required.'

Following the Squadron's move to Peshawar, work continued on developing army co-operation tactics and on convincing ground forces of the value of air power:

> 'A large amount of infantry co-operation was also carried out, even in the mountainous districts of the Khyber, with the greatest success. The director arrow, the Popham panel [a ground-to-air signalling device which had become well established during the Great War] and the wireless were brought into play for this purpose, and owing to the great keenness and energy of the officers of the Squadron, led by Squadron Leader Harris, the other services were gradually convinced of the enormous value of the assistance which could be rendered by aeroplane co-operation. On one occasion a machine-gunning and bombing demonstration was given before an Indian battalion, which astonished them greatly. On another occasion during a contact patrol show near Nowshera, the officer commanding the column with which the aeroplane was co-operating received so much information as to the enemy's dispositions and his own troops' progress, in the form of situation maps, that he exclaimed "How many more of those is he going to drop?"'

Further operations in 1922 illustrated how the military intermeshed with the political:

'Two machines flew to Lucknow to demonstrate at a meeting which was being addressed by Mr Gandhi, the leader of the Non Co-operation movement. The pilots, acting under the instructions of the civil authorities, circled over the meeting and dropped pamphlets containing the Duke of Connaught's speech [he being an uncle of the King's, visiting India performing royal duties]. It was ascertained afterwards that the machines attracted far more interest than Mr Gandhi's speech, and he had considerable difficulty in making himself heard above the roar of the engines.'

And there was no shortage of exciting action throughout the year, as shown by this report from Flying Officers Chadwick-Brown and Jackson:

'Arrived Wana and dropped eight 20lb bombs on encampments and flocks to the west of Wana Fort at the foot of the hills. Three direct hits observed, a fourth bomb failed to explode. Then came down to 800ft and fired 100 rounds of Lewis gun ammunition at flocks of sheep in the same vicinity. The starboard side of the engine then cut right out and the revs dropped to 1,250. I headed for Wana fort, but was forced to land about two miles to the west. We immediately came under fire so abandoned the machine and ran for the fort. After we had gone for about five minutes, another machine spotted us, and coming down to within about 50ft, dropped a message to us in a piece of "four by two" weighted by an orange, telling us that the fort was straight in front of us and finishing up by saying "run like hell". Two men then came up on horseback making friendly signs and, making us mount their horses, led us to a ruined rifle butt near the fort. Wazirs then commenced coming in from all directions, firing, and the Khassidars, who had come from the fort to our rescue on seeing us land, returned the fire.'

The machine which had assisted them was flown by Flight Lieutenant Coryton, with the CO in the back seat, and it now turned out that the fort was too closely surrounded by Wazirs for the rescue party to attempt entry. So, to cut a long story short, friendly forces led the airmen to safety by a circuitous and rugged route, taking until the following day.

The CO, Harris, also has something to say about this operation:

'We got involved in a typical, small Frontier war in Waziristan. Lashkar tribesmen had come over the Afghan border and laid siege to Wana fort. This was defended by a company of Khassidars, a type of tribal militia whose loyalty rather depended in any dispute on which side happened to be winning. Incarcerated in the fort was an Indian deputy political agent, a rather diminutive Punjabi. By means of runners and eventually a telegraph line much further away, he was sending messages to his boss, the political agent, who unfortunately happened to be away on leave. The agent's *babu* [clerk] carefully filed each message for his master's return, and when the PA did get back he was able to read right up to the last report which pleaded that "tomorrow my throat will be cut, but I do not require the Indian government to sympathise with my family."

'As a consequence, the PA rang us up in the middle of the night, and the following morning we took our last four aircraft to Tank, bombing and shooting up everything we could see around the fort. We then took the PA to Wana, landing alongside the fort, and there he held a *jirga* with the Khassidars and the Punjabi – luckily still alive.

'While this was going on, a sniper started shooting at us from a nearby hill. Not particularly appreciating that form of attention, I got into the back of a waiting Bristol, turned the Lewis gun on the hill and sprayed it up and down. Whereupon the deputy political agent, about whom this had all been, ran over to me saying "Sir, please, no shooting. Somebody might get killed, and then there will be trouble!"'

Several more raids on Wana followed, on all of which Harris flew as observer to Coryton. He was quoted as saying that he much preferred the Lewis gun work to bombing, which perhaps explains his readiness to deal with the sniper in this way.

The length of the logistic chain has been very apparent throughout this story, and it's easy to imagine just how remote the characters we've already met must have felt from their homes and families back in Britain. In these days of mobile phones and internet we can but marvel at a five-year overseas tour during which letters sent by sea were the sole means of communication. And, while thinking about that long journey, we may also imagine what an indelible impression the troopship must have made on young airmen posted 'out east' for the first time. This story, from George Eccles, is of his trip in the 1930s, but must be typical of many similar ones:

'India was beckoning. There was kit to be collected, examined, inspected, certified fit and complete, embarkation leave to be enjoyed and, best of all, a series of inoculations and vaccinations to be endured to make me immune from all the horrible diseases that were awaiting my arrival in the mystic east. I remember the final injection as if it were yesterday; the upper part of my left arm stiffened into a lump of wood. Then, final checks before I was put on the train to London – eventually to report to Waterloo Station where a special train was awaiting to take us down to Southampton to board that well known and popular cruise ship of the period, His Majesty's Troopship *Dorsetshire*. When I saw this gleaming white vessel, I thought "Gosh – all this for me! The skipper needn't have gone to so much trouble." It was all very friendly, I thought, as I was greeted by a host of RAF policemen, army redcaps and jolly embarkation staff, all jostling to relieve me of my kitbags and escort me below. I was herded with the rest of the guests down into the bowels of the ship to what was euphemistically known as the troopdeck. There, at right angles to the ship's bulkheads, were rows of tables, each one seating fourteen to sixteen men. There were hammocks, and hooks from which to sling them.

'The table to which I had been allocated became my home for the next three weeks. It was a situation of elbow-touching intimacy, with almost everything about our living seeming to happen there. Two of us each day collected food from the galley and this was distributed as evenly as we could to the other occupants of the table. Whatever food was contained in the meal all appeared on the same plate, whether it was kippers or custard. Hammocks were slung above the table, but not before trumpet call after supper, and we slept in a mixture of human smells and stale food. There were "rounds" every day, which usually comprised the ship's adjutant, the medical officer, the orderly officer, the ship's warrant officer and the orderly sergeant. We lesser mortals were given self-supporting fatigues such as "captain of the heads", which meant an introduction to the mysteries of the ship's sanitary arrangements. Ugh!

'Although we single fellows were not concerned with families, their accommodation I learned was not exactly cruise-ship style either. The open troopdecks were partitioned off by canvas screens dividing the space allotted to one family from that of its neighbours. Nor did the officers fare so well. In a cabin reported to be approximately eight feet by six were one wardrobe, one wash basin, and four bunks. As mess kits were required every night, it was all achieved by agreeing a roster for dressing. Hard luck for the first; he had to start at about 5.30.'

Unsurprisingly, not all found the journey congenial, especially later conscripts during the Second World War. Because the Mediterranean was by then so dangerous and the Suez Canal not usable, many of those had to take the longer route around the southern tip of Africa. For them, conditions were, if anything, worse than they had been a century previously.

George, though, was a volunteer and eager to travel – as his continuing notes show:

'Port Said, the Suez Canal, Aden – all very exciting. And the warm nights across the Arabian Sea were marvellous, although the moonlight made you realize that there was still something or someone missing with whom to enjoy the romantic atmosphere to the full. The dockside at Karachi was all hustle and bustle. Our troop train was already drawn up on the quayside, and the sights were an eye-opener for a young fellow. Snake charmers, gulli-gulli men, Indian rope trick performers, fortune tellers. But best of all a fried egg sandwich which will surely go down as a meal to remember. From that instant I took to India like a duck to water.'

The Squadron continued, between operational tours, to develop tactics and to take on new roles. In 1925 an experimental air-mail service was set up, with similar arrangements being made in future years on occasions when flooding or landslips interrupted surface mail.

Also that year, night bombing was commenced, firstly in a practice environment. Later, in operations from Tank, night attack under parachute flares was said, not surprisingly, to have caused considerable consternation among the hostiles.

Then in 1926, front and back seaters were finally able to speak to each other in flight without shouting above the din of the engine, when Gosport speaking tubes and earphones were adopted. And at the beginning of 1928, experiments were made in the dropping of supplies from the air, presaging some of Thirty One's most stirring exploits during the Second World War. The containers were, according to the record, 'slung below the mainplane and parachuted down from a height of 500ft whilst the aircraft was flown at an airspeed of 90–110mph.' In October an opportunity came to enable these supply-dropping trials and experiments to be put to the test when

'… a patrol of armoured cars and lorries became stranded on the Toba plateau owing to a breakdown of one of the vehicles. Headquarters Western Command, anxious as to the position of this convoy, requested that aircraft should endeavour to locate it. The convoy was duly found, supplies were dropped, messages were picked up, and it was maintained generally from the air for several days before it was able to proceed.'

And the following piece from an unknown reporter paints a good picture of how the whole gamut of air operations was being expanded. Although we have already read of the use of wireless, the article reports its use by 31 Squadron as though radio had, perhaps, not previously been known to the general public:

The heliograph party.

'The 1927 RAF display at Delhi was performed in the presence of HE the Viceroy and his staff and in front of thousands of spectators. Aircraft from 5(AC), 20(AC), 27(B), 28(AC) and 60(B) Squadrons, equipped with DH9As, Fairey IIIFs, Siskins and Victorias demonstrated message picking up and low-bombing, aerobatics, air combat, parachuting and airlifting of troops. There was an inter-squadron relay race, and the display concluded with a fly-past of all the squadrons. 31 Squadron gave a demonstration of air drill by radio telephony – something entirely new and here used for the first time in India. The Viceroy gave orders to the Bristol Fighter leader who relayed them to his five formation members. In the grandstand was broadcasting apparatus lent by the Indian Radio and Telegraph Company, the transmitted orders being clearly heard by the spectators.'

Sad to report, accidents continued to occur with monotonous regularity. Indeed they seemed to be accepted as almost routine. Leading Aircraftman George Brown, a photographer who joined the Squadron in 1920, has so many tales to tell that one

The Squadron's pigeon loft – homing birds carried by the observers in boxes, to be released with messages in the event of incident or accident.

Message pick up by hook – here demonstrated by a Wapiti.

wonders whether he had developed a naive faith in his immortality. Certainly, he could almost have made a special note in his log-book of the trips which ended safely!

And finally, they graduated to radio. Parties were dispatched on operations with the ground forces, and here Corporal Sherwood demonstrates the equipment.

'I was with Flying Officer Waller on a recce sortie from Ambala. Having already all but collided with the Kaisir-I-Hind bridge while I was photographing it, Waller later drew my attention to a ragged tear in the leading edge of the port lower wing. We had struck a bird and, as I watched, the tear grew bigger. We pressed on toward base but prepared for a forced landing. The nearer we drew to base, the bigger grew the rent. Soon the loose fabric wrapped itself around a bracing wire, but our luck held. As we touched down, the fabric split the whole length of the wing. Poor Waller, I was not to fly with him again. The following night he misjudged his height on landing and was fatally injured.'

Brown would already have been wary of flying with Waller, for they'd crashed while together on a previous occasion:

'Following a rough passage, we were dropping towards the 'drome at Peshawar when a sudden air pocket caused the machine to crash into some telephone wires with a terrific crack. A wing broke away and I was flung out of the cockpit. By a stroke of luck I came down squarely on the severed wing which broke my fall, but I was taken to hospital with two pieces of steel in my leg and my right arm skewered with a splinter. I had visions of a lovely long time in bed recuperating, eating egg custards, chicken and other succulent morsels. But alas there was a shortage of photographers and three days later I was on my way back to resume duty. I spent the following sixty days doing my work with arms bandaged and leg in splints!'

'Shortly after Waller's death, Flying Officer Findlay, one of our best pilots and one with whom I'd flown many a time, took the political officer from Delhi up for his first flight. The plane collided with a church spire in Delhi. Findlay's body was found in the wreckage but the PO had been thrown out and had crashed through the church roof. He was found right in front of the organ – which was poetic in a way, for it subsequently transpired that he had been the organist of that church.'

'We had hardly got over the shock when we had a series of night-flying accidents. Flying Officer Ridley landed with a terrific crash and overturned, being killed outright. The next night Pilot Officer Gay was badly injured in much the same way, and on the third night Pilot Officer Walters turned over but escaped with bruises and a petrol bath.'

Then the Squadron had a particularly noteworthy near-accident. In October 1927 the Viceroy, His Excellency Lord Irwin, visited Fort Sandeman, and Thirty One was given the honour of conveying him by air. The record notes that the Squadron *dherzi* (tailor) was asked to make a pennant appropriate for a viceroy and this was fixed by cords to the port mainplane's outer rear strut. Flight Lieutenant Kirby began his take-off run but, as he gathered speed, the Bristol swung violently to port, Kirby just managing to avoid crashing into the rugged ground at the edge of the aerodrome. The flag had fouled the 'gap wire' connecting the top and bottom ailerons, making lateral control impossible. The flag was hurriedly removed and the flight continued without further incident. There is no record of Lord Irwin's reaction to this near miss.

The flag which nearly brought down a Viceroy – now amongst the Squadron Association's collection of memorabilia.

None of this seemed to put the intrepid Brown off flying, and he continued to log hair-raising events:

'I had orders to take photos of Landi-Kotal at the edge of the Khyber Pass. Everything went smoothly until we were overhead the 'drome again when the engine went off duty. The pilot glided but I could see bungalows ahead and it seemed an even chance whether we would clear the roofs. We didn't. There was a crash, away went our undercarriage and – wallop – we landed upside down on the 'drome. But we both crawled out unhurt.

'A few days later I happened to be on the 'drome when a replacement machine arrived. Our test pilot asked whether I would care for a flip. No need to ask me twice, and we climbed to eight thousand feet. Then we went into a power dive with the wires screaming and I thought the gun ring would cut me in half. The pilot pulled the joystick back and I had a confused vision of the earth disappearing under my feet and then reappearing over my head with the sky being under my feet. I had experienced my first loop! Then the pilot looped, rolled and spiralled until I didn't know whether I was on my head or my heels. The final and worst experience was when we flew upside down, following which the pilot gave up trying to make the plane fall to pieces and headed for home. The most exciting forty-five minutes I had ever had.'

We can sense in those words the pure love of flying which must have been etched into the consciousness of many who served on the Squadron in those demanding early days. But although this history has concentrated very much on the working and operational side of life, in the harsh Indian environment the airmen certainly needed some rest and relaxation as well. The debilitating effect of the summer climate was well recognized; indeed, much of the government, together with both army and air headquarters staffs,

Whilst the aircrew flew to forward operating bases or summer camps, the poor groundcrew had to make their way by other means, sometimes being 'made to march even though lorries were available.' Good for body and soul, no doubt!

However, travelling in lorries such as these doesn't look a great deal more comfortable.

There was first-class for the officers!

moved up to Simla in the foothills of the Himalayas each summer to get away from the heat of the plains. To provide a cool break in hot weather, a hill station was established at Lower Topa in the beautiful, wooded Murree Hills on the road to Kashmir. An officer was appointed to take each party up to the resort, this naturally being a much sought-after duty.

The military being what it is, however, even the journey was used as a form of training – as evidenced by one airman's rather plaintive comment: 'Although lorries were available the men were forced to march the fourteen miles from the railhead at Rawalpindi.' No doubt this was all very character-building, not to mention good for the men's physical conditioning.

Many families also decamped to hill stations, while in May 1922 the Squadron itself is reported as 'having deployed to the hill station of Parachinnar, leaving behind a detachment of two flights.'

Baggage parties utilized camels.

Trains were fine, but usually terminated miles from the desired point. Here is shown the Darjeeling railway.

Some had their own exciting off-duty adventures. George Eccles, an enterprising man determined to make the most of his time on the sub-continent, recalls a memorable holiday to Kashmir during 1938:

'I was to travel with Tubby Mills, a happy-go-lucky lad from Manchester. From our weekly pay of 15 rupees (£1 at the exchange rate of the day) we would save 10 rupees. This meant I had 5 rupees left per week to pay the bearer, furniture wallah, char wallah, dhobi and cycle wallah. However, I had recently sat my trade test for reclassification to leading aircraftman, so the extra cash was a godsend.

'We booked two first-class seats on the post bus. Well, they were called "first class", but this only meant we sat up beside the driver. In order to start our journey, we took the overnight train to Rawalpindi. As it was June, the temperature was at its fiercest. However, we arrived safely enough and organized a *tonga* (pony and trap) to take us and our bedrolls and trunks to the post office. We didn't know quite what to expect, but we didn't bargain for an assortment of locals waiting for the bus, men women and children complete with tied-up bundles and what appeared to be enough livestock, in the shape of various poultry and a goat, to stock a small farm. With the sort of miracle we had come to expect in India, all the baggage and crates of birds were securely loaded on to the roof of the bus – the goat stayed inside – and off we went. With the significant drop in temperature and humidity as we climbed, prickly heat thankfully began to disappear. It was a splendid feeling. Hairpin bend followed hairpin bend and it soon became evident that the bus would have to stop at some point as the engine had reached boiling point and steam was spouting furiously. Meanwhile, buses would go clattering by on the downward journey, grossly overloaded and swaying wildly at corners.

'Past the summit there were, if anything, more twists and hairpin bends than on the earlier ascent. The road surface, which had been good, became broken and full of potholes. When we dared spare a glance, there were splendid views of the River Jhelum several thousand feet below. We had been warned to expect landslides and there was plenty of evidence of earlier disasters. It wasn't long before we encountered our very own landslide. It happened on one of the narrowest parts of the road between two craggy hillsides. Boulders everywhere, which we negotiated after some delay.

'It was mid-afternoon when we arrived at the post office in Srinagar and we were relieved to be met by the *khitmagar* [bearer] from the houseboat, all ready to greet us. In no time it seemed we and our luggage were on our way down the Jhelum to Nagin Bagh, eager to board the good ship *King's Bench*. The boats were real Victoriana, ornately carved and furnished, as the Kashmiris were excellent wood carvers. Baths, tin of course, and thunderbox were in the stern. There was a separate cook boat moored alongside, complete with *khitmagar*, his family, cook, and sweeper. Each houseboat had its own *shikara* [pleasure boat] propelled by paddles shaped like lotus leaves, this was very useful for our own explorations around the lakes.

'A favourite trip was across the lake to the garden at Shalimar Bagh, the "Garden of Love", laid out four centuries ago by the Mogul emperor for his queen. As well as sitting on the veranda admiring the Himalayas and the stunning scenery, resisting the blandishments of the travelling salesmen, fortune tellers and the like, there was plenty to do and see. There was also a club which was the social centre for the *burra sahibs* and their *me'msahibs*, which had two tennis courts. It took some time to convince the manager that we airmen did not wish to avail ourselves of the full facilities of the club, only to use the tennis courts. In the end he agreed and we took very good care not to give any cause for the privilege to be reversed.'

One has to smile at George's description of the Indian bus driver. In another of his writings he refers to another expedition, this time with a professional RAF driver. This character, rather disconcertingly, was known as 'Crasher' Smythe. So perhaps driving competence in India wasn't overly high in those days – regardless of the driver's nationality!

Noel Moreton also visited Kashmir, recalling that:

'We were allowed three months leave, and many of us taking a houseboat on the Nagin Bagh hired punts in which we laid at great ease while half a dozen boatmen paddled us about the lakes. The maharajah lived in a marvellous palace and one of his idiosyncrasies was cricket. He would field a team against the British and, when he went in to bat, he had to make fifty runs before you were allowed to get him out. If by sheer luck the ball hit the wicket before then, the umpire would call "not out!" '

A slightly different perspective on bus travel comes from Flying Officer Bertie Mann:

'One of our number went missing after visiting his sister who was at a Frontier station some two hundred miles distant. He had travelled in an Indian bus, and of course it was regarded as disgraceful for an officer, or an airman for that matter, to travel with the locals in their rattletrap vehicles. The drivers had a fixed and tense expression; they were suicidal and incompetent, tearing along in a cloud of dust and weaving through the bullock carts and pedestrians, an overflow of luggage and passengers on the roof.'

The man concerned was located and recalled immediately – and, readers will be relieved to learn, he was unharmed. Bertie Mann, by the way, rose through the ranks. Although he lost touch with Thirty One for a while after leaving the Frontier, he was delighted to re-establish contact with the Squadron Association seventy years later, not long before his death in 2009. In his last years he wrote a series of descriptive memoirs into which we shall dip in due course.

Having mentioned the Association, now would seem an opportune moment to say a few words about the wider 31 Squadron family. 'Old boys' organizations are, of course, common in the military, but Thirty One is lucky in maintaining a particularly active Association. The first records of such an organization tell of 'No 31 Squadron RFC and RAF Old Comrades Association, 1915–1919'. Little is known now of its activities, except that our erstwhile pioneering Captain McDonald was one of its vice-presidents, but we can say for certain that the remnants were eventually absorbed by an organization formed post-Second World War for the benefit of veterans of that later conflict. Nowadays, a single Association embraces all eras, and is lucky enough to be able to draw on young blood from the current unit. So there's a strong link between past and present, and this helps to keep the organization up to a strength of several hundred. This narrative will return to the subject from time to time as Association interests touch operational work, but for now let's move back to the business of the 1920s.

Following eighteen months at Peshawar, 31 Squadron moved in 1923 to Dardoni/ Miranshah in Waziristan. This was far into the Frontier where, as Noel Moreton describes, 'We carried out a lot of punitive raids on villages that gave trouble. These wild Wazirs and Mahsuds all had rifles of sorts – and it was a dangerous place.'

Donald Hardman saw both good and bad in the new location:

'We were there for a year. We lived in a barbed wire encampment with a section of armoured cars and a Gurkha Company. The aircraft had to be towed out of the encampment every morning and towed back behind the wire each evening. Being far from the fleshpots, we had nothing to do but to become the most efficient Squadron in India. This was acknowledged by the AOC who, having inspected us, absolved us from the following year's annual inspection. I think the airmen were happy at Dardoni. We played endless games of soccer, hockey and cricket – inter-flight and with the soldiers.'

Perhaps the AOC didn't fancy visiting Miranshah too often! George Brown certainly seemed to agree that the place had its limitations: 'For the next twelve months we stagnated there. It was a good life in an austere fashion, our only relaxations being sports, comic football matches and camp concerts.'

The next stop, in 1924, was Ambala, a station the Squadron occupied for two and a half years. Located in the Punjab, Hardman described it as being 'civilization' after Miranshah. But George Brown still seemed to concentrate on the downsides:

'Ambala was a thickly-populated place as far as the bazaar went but, owing to an outbreak of bubonic plague, it was out of bounds to troops. The camp cinema was a flimsy wooden affair, the seats were backless benches, the films were of 1918 vintage and the film never broke down more than six times per performance. The orchestra consisted of a pianist if available; failing that, the background noise of the audience cracking nuts had to suffice. It was always crowded – once I saw as many as eight people there. Alas the whole place was "accidentally" burned down one night.'

Chapter 4

Forces of Nature

From 1926 to 1935, Thirty One's base was Quetta. This was a strategic point and the home to a huge military garrison, including the army staff college. Keith Luhman, who was a driver with the Squadron from 1931 to '36, describes some of the background:

'The Bolan Pass is situated at the southern end of the Quetta Plain and leads to the plains of the upper Sind and the Punjab. The governments of the day still feared that Russia might make a move against India. Once through the pass, there would be no stopping an invading force. The jewel in the crown – Karachi – would be vulnerable. Hence the very big military presence in Quetta.

'Being nearly six thousand feet up, Quetta had a very pleasant climate. We didn't have those drenching monsoon rains, just blue skies and a gentle breeze all summer, with a little rain and snow during the winter. During the summer months we would, as the mood took us, sleep outside on the veranda, under the stars and open to the wide, wide world. The attitude of the Quetta people and of those in the surrounding villages was not at all hostile, perhaps largely because of the vast – and I mean vast – military set-up there which provided much-needed jobs. Small wonder that it was known as the Aldershot of the east.'

Sergeant Norman Clarke, a signaller who joined the Squadron in 1933, adds:

'The town was about three miles away by *tonga* pulled by scraggy ponies. There were two sleazy cinemas, a racecourse and a golf course, whose greens were actually "browns" – rolled cow dung, mud and straw. All ranks were allowed to play, but only officers were allowed membership of the club. The "Quetta column" was always on standby and 31 Squadron was part of its support.

'Christmas in Quetta was very special, with a week's unofficial holiday being enjoyed. Each bungalow was decorated to a theme and open house was declared. A number of beds were kept spare in each bungalow so that anybody passing out could be coped with without problem. Often one woke up in a bungalow other than one's own!'

Christmas was, incidentally, the only time of the year when airmen in India were permitted to drink spirits.

Flying Officer Michael Dwyer recalls detachments from Quetta:

'To the Makvan (that part of Baluchistan between Iran and the Arabian Sea), to airstrips in the Poona area, to Jubbulpore and Secunderabad (Hyderabad State). These detachments were great fun with just four aircraft under a flight commander. We lived in tents and were hundreds of miles away from our parent unit. Work was combined with sightseeing tours, picnics, swimming, fishing, shooting etc., while we fielded scratch cricket, hockey and football teams against locals, both civilian and military.'

Throughout the Squadron's time on the Frontier, the challenging nature of the terrain and the unreliability of the aircraft meant that groundcrew needed to fly on many trips. We have already had a few stories from those stalwart men, and now Corporal Benny Watts contributes. He was associated with Thirty One for many years, actually serving on the Squadron as a fitter from 1943–46 but having earlier memories of flying on the Frontier:

'I would initially fly in the rear seat to our first landing at one of the many forts, from whence my place would be taken by an army officer for tribal *jihad* observations. My primary reason for being there was to check for possible damage to the aircraft on landing in such rough areas. On one occasion I was sent out with the assistance of an army Urdu speaker to secure an aircraft that had forced-landed. We found ourselves in a time warp – in an area so backward it had not changed since times we think of as biblical. We had to cross a fast-flowing river, and some villagers arrived with an inflated buffalo skin with leather handles. Perhaps stupidly, I felt I ought not to show fear and clung on for dear life across the torrent. The interpreter followed, and later paid the head man, assuring him we did not intend to return the same way.

'Razmak – now that was a place. It was a small fort in tribal territory, and we often had to fly a political officer up there to attend a *jirga* with the Wazirs. As they were overnight stops with a rough terrain landing, a fitter was always required for the daily inspection the next morning. There were only four British officers there, who, with viceroy-commissioned officers, were in charge of the garrison of local conscripts. The first time I went there was with a sergeant pilot. Even though we were just NCOs they put on a dining-in night complete with silver – they didn't often have guests. After dinner, they invited us to a sporting game of snooker – with just a few rupees on the side, "just for fun!" Sergeant Wright explained that he had paid his mess bill just before coming on the trip and was broke – so I lent him ten. In the corporals' mess at Peshawar we had a first-class table, but I recalled that the one at Drosh fort had had a cement bed. And I was right to be worried. Nothing could have prepared me for what I saw in Razmak's billiard room. Full sized tables – nice cushions, although worn – and no baize at all on the bed. Just three slate slabs.

'We were invited to break off. The white ball jumped every crack in the bed, hit the cushion after missing the cluster and came back like a rocket. "Bad luck old boy," said the old colonel. "That's four away," said the scorer.'

Hard rules! George Eccles also comments on Razmak, which had a strip known for its particular difficulty:

'The landing ground was some 6,800ft above sea level, it had about a one-in-sixteen gradient, and was only some 500yds in length. You landed uphill, with no overshoot and facing into a big black mountain, and took off downhill with no second chance.

The air gunner or passenger had to pivot the aircraft by one wingtip at the top of the strip, and then run with all speed to his cockpit as the pilot opened up. Only experienced pilots need apply! One of these described Razmak as the most treacherous strip he'd ever used. Surrounded on three sides by high mountains, it was also the habitat of hostile tribesmen whose joy in life was to snipe at aircraft on the strip. It also had a tendency to flood and for aircraft to bog down.

'Notwithstanding all this, it lay on the border between Wazir and Mahsud tribal areas so was an ideal place for a garrison. The place grew to house the Razmak Brigade – strictly all-male and occupying what came to be known as "the largest monastery on the frontier". The men were confined to barracks throughout their tours. On the positive side, because of its altitude Razmak had a reasonably equable climate compared to some of the lower stations, albeit prone to snow in winter and dust in summer. All in all a desolate spot and a difficult airfield. Landings often resulted in two burst tyres. So it was then the pilot's job to gather hay to stuff into the tyres.'

And Noel Moreton adds memories of getting there: 'To get to Razmak we had to fly up the Narai and over the pass. We always felt we wouldn't make it but somehow we always did; there was always a surge of wind up the valley that carried us over. Coming back from a raid with only half an engine was quite an experience!'

By the beginning of the 1930s another change of equipment was long overdue. The Bristol Fighter had been regarded with some affection, as evidenced by this little tribute gleaned from another Mark Tomkins article in *Air Mail*:

'With her tyres like sinews tautened and her tail-skid's jaunty twist;
  Her grey-cowled snout juts grimly out like a tight-clenched boxer's fist;
  She leans at her place on the tarmac, like a tiger crouched for a spring;
  From the arching spine of her fuselage line to the ample spread of her wing.'

But the aircraft was becoming extremely long in the tooth, and it was something of a relief when, in February 1931, the first Westland Wapiti Mk IIA, powered by a Jupiter VIIIF engine, was received. By June the Squadron was completely equipped with this type and the faithful 'Brisfit' passed into retirement.

It was said that the first Wapiti prototype 'exhibited poor flying characteristics which took considerable modification to correct.' Only later was it discovered that the prototype had inadvertently had a two-foot section of fuselage omitted.

That must have taken some explaining! Apparently, though, the impromptu modification was so successful that the missing section was not reinstated – at least until the later introduction of the Wapiti Mk V.

Bertie Mann had a word or two to say about the 'new' equipment:

'Contact!' Wapiti starting up.

'The Wapiti Mk IIA was a "general purpose" aeroplane (a specification which has often plagued the Royal Air Force in peacetime), and this old lady was certainly not ahead of her time. The drive for economy was with us in the late twenties too, and the "Wap" was designed to use up the remaining mainplanes and many other left-over spares still held for the de Havilland DH9, which had been its predecessor on most of the squadrons in India. It travelled with dignified grace at a steady 85 to 90mph.

'Like all biplanes of that era, the Wapiti was a mass of wires, turnbuckles and stitching. Bell-crank levers and bungee rubbers were essentials to the integrity of her construction; and rigging the aeroplane to ensure that the incidence of the flying surfaces was true and symmetrical was a demanding item in the servicing schedule. The practical measures to achieve this, called "boxing the mainplanes", were learned, and hopefully understood, by all young pilots.

'She was excellent for the work we were doing, and held in deep affection by all who flew in her or attended to her.'

During this relatively settled period, the Squadron was able to turn its attention to improving its expertise in the various disciplines of the army co-operation role, as well as to developing its tactics and operational capability. The record in March 1933 showed that 'Thirty One conducted a test to ascertain the length of time to photograph an operational area, return to the unit, develop, print and deliver the photographs. This took several hours from receipt of task to delivery of fifty-four prints to the army.' Very much the type of work – if not the timescale – with which Thirty Oners would, many years later, become involved at Laarbruch in Germany. And in another link between the two theatres, the Squadron won in 1933 and 1935 the Salmond bombing cup which was competed for by the India-based army co-op squadrons. Years later, in Germany, the Salmond competition would again be the 'one to win'.

A Wapiti makes an early attempt at supply dropping.

Army and air force habits of all sorts had to be harmonized if co-operation was to reach its full potential. An illustration comes from the story of when Flying Officer 'Duke' Mavor (later to become Air Marshal Sir Leslie – an early, and much-loved, president of the 31 Squadron Association) was drinking in the mess with an army captain. Mavor was on beers, the other chap on pink gins. It emerged that Mavor was flying an escort sortie to a convoy up into the mountains that afternoon, and he agreed to the captain's request that he should go along as a passenger. After flying for some time, Mavor felt the call of nature and, having no receptacle handy, just relieved himself on the cockpit floor. Shortly afterwards the captain called from the rear cockpit that he had discovered some liquid seeping into his area. He was able to reassure the pilot that 'It's all right, it's not petrol – I've just tasted it!'

A Brisfit demonstrates casevac ops, with the casualty strapped on top of the rear fuselage. Might the remedy have been more painful than the injury?

All in all, Quetta life was good. Keith Luhman again:

'Work ceased every day at 13.30, and with the pleasant climate at that altitude is it any wonder that some of us signed on to extend our service? Thursday, by order of Queen Victoria, was a day off for all members of the British armed forces in India, so some of the more energetic types would engage in what we called "dogs and sticks". We were allowed to keep one dog in each bungalow, so with dogs and walking sticks we would set off to walk to the Murree brewery situated at the foot of one of the many mountains which surrounded the Quetta Plain. About an hour's walk it was. Upon arrival we would be served with a free large glass – a little less than a pint – of beer which we consumed sitting on the stone wall in front of the brewery. The brewers claimed that the sparkling stream tumbling down the mountainside made their beer quite special.'

Sadly for everybody in the area, and not least for members of 31 Squadron, this Quetta idyll was disrupted on 31 May 1935 by a massive earthquake, later estimated to have measured approximately 7.7 on the Richter scale. Huge structural damage occurred, with the RAF suffering 160 casualties, including 52 fatalities. Practically every building on the camp was destroyed, many airmen being buried beneath the debris. Number 31 Squadron lost twenty-two men, while a total of between 30,000 and 60,000 people were estimated to have died in the surrounding region. Much has been said and

Quetta was a huge station. This picture hardly does it justice, but nevertheless gives an idea of the camp's apparently well-ordered permanency.

written about the disaster, but we can do no better than quote from eyewitness reports and letters. First, Keith Luhman:

Then at 3am on 31 May 1935 came the earthquake.

'The quake occurred at 3am on a moonless night. Those of us who got out quickly could not do much in the dark to help those still under the wreckage. Our bungalows were built of mud bricks, with corrugated iron roofs on a wooden framework. All we could do was pull the rubble away – just couldn't do much to open up those collapsed iron roofs.

'[In the days] after the earthquake we slept under canvas on the football pitch alongside our old quarters. It was thought there was a danger of looting, so the GOC ordered a tank to patrol our lines. What sort of night's sleep could you get with a tank engine starting up every half hour and then the vehicle trundling round our lines!?'

A letter written from Karachi in June by one of Thirty One's airframe fitters, Walter Locke, tells a little more:

'Dear Mother. You can see we have got away from Quetta and we are only too thankful. I am well and nerves much better; I thought I could never sleep in a building again. The majority are quite fit, and some of the sick are going home very soon. I managed to rescue most of my kit, but only one pair of boots which hurt my feet. I also lost some private stuff, all correspondence, trinkets, souvenirs and sports kit. So I'd be grateful if you would send me out £3 to get me a little straight again.

'Sorry to report another death in my bungalow on the day we left Quetta. A fellow died of pneumonia, making seven in all on B Flight. You have read all the details in the papers, obviously. On the Thursday night I went to bed as normal. The next thing I remember was being half awake and rocking from side to side. Then a rumble of other buildings falling, so I tore at my mozzie net to get out, and while doing so our bungalow began to fall. I fell on the floor waiting for death, a fatalistic feeling, all the time there was a terrible row going on of falling bricks and so on. Our ceiling had pinned me to the floor and there followed a deathly silence – black with dust – and I thought myself the only one alive. I struggled to get free and then the injured started calling – the fellow next to me yelled blue murder.

'I got out and for a while could do nothing – just sat, deathly cold. After a minute though I joined others in getting the trapped free. There is no need to tell you the details of what I did and saw. Remember, I had never seen a dead body before, and now they were my friends I was seeing. Of the many deeds of heroism, I can tell you of a medical orderly with a broken shoulder dosing himself with morphia and carrying on dressing the injured for hours. A sergeant who talked cheerfully throughout the seven hours it took to dig him out then died, his will to live gone.

A friend was just stepping off the end of a veranda when it fell on him. He died of a broken back and legs two days later.

'The next few days were engaged in manual work which was probably good for us. We got the undamaged machines away and salvaged stores and kit.'

By the afternoon of the day of the earthquake three aircraft were available to fly reconnaissance of the area and to establish communications with Simla. Aftershocks hampered the efforts, including a particularly severe one on 3 June. It was decided to re-group the Squadron at the aircraft depot at Drigh Road, Karachi, the survivors all being in place there by 8 June. They

Many died, with much of the camp's infrastructure being reduced to rubble.

were honoured by a visit from His Excellency the Viceroy, who inspected the Squadron and addressed them as follows:

'Wing Commander Slessor, Officers and Airmen of Number 3 (India) Wing. I am very glad to have this opportunity today of paying my tribute to you all in my position as Governor General of India for the way in which you faced your recent terrible experiences in Quetta. I deplore very deeply the heavy casualties suffered by Number 3 Wing and I sympathize with you sincerely in the loss of your comrades.

'Notwithstanding the nerve-shattering experience in which your branch of the service suffered more heavily than any other, the way in which you met and overcame the effects of the catastrophe was magnificent. I have been told of the rapidity with which you set to work to extricate your comrades from the ruins of their quarters and subsequently to save property from the wreckage.

'The speed with which you got your damaged aircraft into action again was remarkable and proved of the greatest value. The Government of India are truly grateful for the splendid service which the aircraft in Quetta gave in reporting the conditions of outlying districts immediately after the earthquake, in flying emergency equipment to Quetta, and in evacuating casualties.

'Let me express to you all in conclusion my admiration of the fine spirit you have displayed throughout the disaster, and warmly congratulate you on maintaining to the full that spirit of courage and initiative which has always been a tradition of your service.'

The scene of devastation.

The following Thirty Oners are recorded as having died in the tragedy: Flight Sergeant L. Powell, Sergeants D. Fincham, H. Grant AFM, Corporals H. Herring, H. Knowlton, G. Easton, T. Livermore, C. Seymour, Leading Aircraftmen J. Arthur, M. Bond, A. Cronk, S. Evans, B. Nicholls, T. Penwarden, G. Scrafton, T. Smith, Aircraftmen First Class F. Bailey, J. Clayton, R. Curtis, W. McGill, T. Somerford, R. Verey.

With a couple of omissions, the names of Thirty One's lost men are recorded, together with those of the other dead, on a splendid memorial which stands today in the city of Quetta. A tablet in the station church at RAF Halton also commemorates the tragedy. Signs of the severity of the Quetta earthquake, in the form of violent rifts in the terrain, remain visible today in the surrounding countryside, and it still ranks in the top thirty earthquakes ever recorded in terms of casualties. None of those who lived through the terrible event will ever forget it.

The Squadron resumed limited operations on 14 August, working from a tented encampment on the perimeter of Drigh Road Airfield. But life would never be quite the same again, and personnel didn't find Karachi altogether congenial. Norman Clarke tells of the new station:

> 'The climate was less pleasant for one thing. High humidity made the heat seem worse, and there was sand everywhere, being on the edge of the Sind Desert. It was not so easy to keep up "Squadron spirit" in such a huge community as the depot. The Drigh Road types were inclined to look down on we scruffy Squadron airmen, who came in for *tiffin* in working clothes.'

But people got used to managing the circumstances, as noted by Flying Officer 'Blanco' White, who joined in October 1937 as equipment officer:

> 'Drigh Road was a very sandy and dusty affair. But it was a cheerful outfit and all personnel put up with the rather uncomfortable working conditions. I had a very happy time with 31 Squadron – a very cheerful crowd.'

The groundcrew's part in operations continued not only to be on the airfield and in the cockpit but also, as Norman Clarke illustrates, sometimes in close proximity to hostile tribesmen:

> 'I was on the wireless section, and always seemed to be attached to other ground and army units. Following our evacuation to Karachi, one flight was stationed at Fort Sandeman in tribal territory where the political agent lived. I was posted there on the advance party. By that time the Faqir of Ipi, Harji Mirza Ali Khan, had declared a holy war against the British. This eventually escalated into the Waziristan Operations of 1936/7 in which the Squadron was engaged in close army support – and I was seconded on signals liaison duties. We never caught the crafty old Faqir, but did manage to put down the rising of his followers.
>
> 'On one operation, the army column to which I was attached was commanded by a rather portly brigadier. He had his personal equipment, including a large tin bath, carried on two camels. My mode of transport was foot slogging, and I slept on the open ground with one blanket – very cold. Fortunately my wireless, carried on a mule, behaved itself.

'The Squadron's Wapitis carried a gunner who would also operate the wireless set. If wireless contact failed, though, we had the facility to drop or pick up messages from the ground. The latter depended on a hook at the end of a stick mounted underneath the rear cockpit, and needed very skilful flying by the pilot.'

'It didn't add to our comfort, when attached to these columns, to see on occasions a dozen tribesmen suddenly appear from behind rocks and stand about fifty yards away, watching us intently. Most were armed with the inevitable rifle and bandolier.'

The 'Faqir of Ipi' referred to by Norman is a name which crops up time and again in Frontier history. And usually, it seems, with the suffix 'the wily old'. He led, for well-nigh twenty years, a guerrilla force which, although poorly equipped, nevertheless managed to be a continual thorn in flesh of the British. Never captured, he was afforded a kind of grudging respect.

The 'hook' method of picking up messages had first been trialled in 1917. Now another wireless man, Aircraftman First Class Tony Evenett, enlarges on the airborne side of communicating, and also has some perceptive comments to make on the relative places of officers and other ranks in those days:

'During message picking up the occupant of the rear cockpit had to turn around, wedge his shoulders between the fuselage cross-bracing wires, pull the hook up and retrieve the message. For all the wireless exercises, the transmitter HT voltage was provided by a wind-driven generator mounted on the leading edge of the starboard mainplane. The revs of this generator were kept fairly constant at 3,600 by the Mortly Sprague slipping clutch. Should wireless not be wanted for a sortie, the propeller would be tied up to avoid volts appearing at the control box at the right-hand forward side of the rear cockpit, for contact with the unscreened brass terminals could cause an unpleasant surprise.

'Now, all pilots are frustrated fighter pilots. Sorties were normally of 45 minutes duration, but the front seater would usually try to complete the job well within this time and then turn and ask if it was OK to fling the aircraft about. They would then perform every aerobatic possible, which was sometimes fun, but not if you had your feet on transmitter LT batteries, receiver LT and HT batteries, and a box or two of spare valves – in addition to having to stay away from that control box.

'Sometimes a flight of four aircraft would visit an out-station. Three would be crewed by officers and the fourth by a pilot and a wireless operator. The officers would be met by the local political agent and whisked away to lunch, while the WOp [wireless operator] would be left with the unexpended portion of the day's rations, usually bully and biscuits. In addition, as the local Indian caretaker at the airfield was too feeble to hoist up the four-gallon petrol cans to the upper

Ferocious terrain. (*From the archive of Bertie Mann*)

centre section, this job fell to the wireless op, and petrol flowed down and under the armpits to the more sensitive parts of the lower body. Great fun!'

Bertie Mann paints a complementary picture of the operations described a little earlier by Norman Clarke:

'The duties of the flight were mostly reconnaissance of the roads in south Waziristan, particularly the road from Wana to Manzai, a small perimeter camp on the boundary of the North-West Frontier Province. The garrison provided a proportion of the troops and the supporting services used to protect and keep open the vital supply route. This was (and probably still is) a winding military road passing along the floor of a succession of valleys. There were no villages or habitations on the route or even at Wana itself, only a sizeable army outpost in some of the most barren, rocky and hilly country in creation. Along the road were three forts – Sarwekai, about a third of the way along the road, Jandola, two thirds along and Sorarogha, a little to the north – built on high cliffs at the confluence of two rivers, usually dry. This was a most picturesque and dramatic sight, in its very appearance embodying all the story-book romance of the North-West Frontier. The forts, manned permanently by the South Waziristan Scouts, and the two camps at Wana and Manzai, all had landing grounds.

'Operations mostly concerned the maintenance of safe transit by road of troops and supplies, but frequent patrols (*ghashts*) were mounted to discover and chase hostile tribal incursions, and to investigate or quell any local uprising. On "road open" days, air support was important. A Wapiti, with loaded guns and sixteen 20lb bombs would take off from Fort Sandeman at 7am, fly sixty miles or so to Wana then along the road on reconnaissance all the way to Manzai at about 1,500–2,000ft. It would check the signals of pickets already in position, who would display two white ground-strips indicating their position to supporting aircraft. Strips forming a cross said "OK, no opposition". An inverted V-shaped signal with the point towards the enemy meant "engaging hostiles". Thirdly, a T-signal, crossbar towards the direction of the threat and additional bars to show distance in hundreds of yards; this indicated "in serious difficulty and in danger of being over-run. Situation requires immediate air support".

'The recce pilot would also check that all bridges and culverts were intact, for the tribesmen regularly brought them down. A favourite trick of the rebels was to fill an empty 50 cigarette tin (discarded by the British in large numbers from issue cigarettes) with wet picric acid explosive and bury it in the sand where troops would pass. The explosive dried in the hot sun and the makeshift mine was ready to blow a soldier's foot off.'

It's quite extraordinary, really, how Bertie's description of recce and IEDs [improvised explosive devices] would find echoes in Thirty One's operations in the same region seventy years later. Perhaps even more vividly, he continues:

'Having examined the entire road and the area on either side, the recce flight would land at Manzai, report to the brigade major in his operations room, and stand by for further orders at the landing ground. If things were quiet, there might be another recce or perhaps no more action before a return flight to Sandeman at the end of the day. On the other hand things could get very exciting. On one of these missions I took the first offensive action of my career.

'I was on the morning recce flight followed by landing at Wana. While on the ground, an urgent request came through for a further look at an area close to the road near Manzai, where a large number of armed tribesmen had gathered who were advancing towards the camp with menace and taking pot-shots. I managed to locate our own defending troops who were displaying their "V" signal to indicate the direction of the enemy, but this also showed they were in no danger at that time. Having failed to see any sign of the opposition, there was no point in an attack from the air so we landed at Manzai to refuel. A little later, I was summoned for an urgent briefing, for the pickets were now in serious danger of being over-run. We arrived in the area to see two or three emergency "T" strips displayed which converged to give a fair idea of where the enemy were hiding. A few low swoops over the boulders and scrub were enough to flush them out.

'Clothed in grey cloth from head to foot, Pathan tribesmen are very difficult to spot even when they are running away in swarms, but we now had a proper target (within the regulations) and made two or three "VBL" attacks (Vickers/Bomb/Lewis gun) – front gun on the run in, bombs when overhead, then a turn to bring the rear gun to bear. As the rout proceeded, having dispensed our load of sixteen twenty pounders and a few hundred rounds of gun ammunition – from what I was told later had been a dangerously low level – we circled around for a bit and saw them still running and shaking their fists at the hated *hawai-jehaz* ("fire bird" in the vernacular). There was no sign of any casualties nor any of them even limping in the retreat! We then flew back to the pickets, by then on their feet and waving, with their groundstrips restored to the peaceable "X", and returned to Manzai for debriefing, a meal and more fuel. As soon as we had become engaged in the battle, another bombed-up Wapiti had been called up from Sandeman, but he was disappointed as the battle was already won. That made my day; we were 7hrs 35mins in the air before lunch – I remember it like yesterday. The whole incident was real life *Boys' Own Paper*/Kipling/Bigglesworth, as were all Frontier operations at that time in history. The army had not changed its system or its tactics for a century, and our little air force joined in and kept pace with it!'

Clifton Stephenson, who spent six months as a pilot on the Squadron at this time, adds a little more and also offers further insights into relations with the army:

'The Wapiti was a wonderful aeroplane and it never let you down, which was just as well when you were staggering over the 10,500ft pass on the way to Chitral with perhaps a couple of hundred feet to spare and the pine trees soaring up to the sky on either side of you. It was rumoured that the engines that pulled

The Wapiti carried a decent bomb load. (*From the archive of Bertie Mann*)

them along were already on their fourth set of tolerances, which says a great deal for the standard of maintenance in those days.

'There wasn't much love lost between the two services in those days, however, though it varied a lot. The army tended to regard the air force very much as an upstart, johnnie-come-lately arrangement. It was understandable, perhaps; some of the old-established Indian Army regiments were almost family affairs. I once had to stay a couple of nights at Drosh, in Chitral. The CO, after greeting me, handed me over to a very young officer telling him to look after me. Over the mess fireplace was the regimental coat of arms, inscribed "11th (Rattray's) Sikhs". "Didn't the colonel call you Rattray?" I asked the young officer, pointing to the coat of arms. "Yes," he replied quite naturally, "my grandfather!"'

In 1937 Thirty One received its own official Badge, signed by King George VI and the Chester Herald of Arms. This was a full twenty-two years after the Squadron's formation but, according to the RAF website, 'It wasn't until 1935 that the post of Inspector of Royal Air Force Badges was introduced to advise the Air Council on matters armorial, and to control the design and issues of these devices.'

The centrepiece of Thirty One's Badge was described as being 'On a wreath of laurel, a mullet.' The mullet – in heraldic terms a straight-sided star – was probably based upon a star symbol known in the local area. There are many references to the 'Star of India' but little that is substantive – and efforts to ascertain the precise derivation have foundered. That an identical star may be seen on the helmets of both the current-day Pakistan and Indian cricket teams confirms, however, a connection with the region.

The motto chosen, '*In Caelum Indicum Primus*' must have virtually suggested itself – 'First into the Indian Skies'. And the unit title was proudly formalized as being 'Number 31 (Army Co-Operation) Squadron'.

Perhaps unofficial insignia were carried earlier, but the first photograph of an aircraft wearing a star is of a Wapiti. It's undated but, curiously, Thirty One's five-pointed star is mounted within a six-pointed star resembling the Star of David. This larger emblem was, reportedly, carried by all army co-op squadrons in India.

Now we return to Bertie Mann's memoirs, which also offer illuminating descriptions of domestic life on the Frontier:

'It seemed to me that life in India for officers had been unchanged for at least a century. [Generally] the only contact with the local population took place in daily business with personal and mess servants, tradesmen, shopkeepers, office clerks and "runners", the "*munshi*" (teacher of Urdu and interpreter), and the odd "box wallah" who was a visiting trader in clothing, wood carvings, pictures, *gewgaws* etc. Accommodation was in spacious bungalows at most

The first airborne shot of Thirty One's 'Star of India' insignia is of this Wapiti. The external, six-pointed star was the India Command logo of its army co-operation squadrons.

stations; others had single officers' quarters near the mess. Washing and bathing facilities were primitive – a bare room in the bungalow or adjoining one's quarters called the *gussle khana* (literally bath room) had a concrete drain in the floor. There was a large tin bath, a wash stand and a "thunderbox" for obvious purposes. The latter being a large square wooden throne with a lid and an enamel container within – disposal was performed by an operative called the *bhisti* (or "sweeper"). Cold water came from an outside tap; hot water was brewed up on a wood fire by the bearer in a *ghee* tin (a universal four gallon cooking-oil tin). Except in large hotels and expensive residences in Bombay and Calcutta, I never saw a flush lavatory in the whole five years I was in the country. Rooms were well furnished with locally made chairs, chests and wardrobes; the bed was, of course, a *charpoy*, a basic Indian necessity diagonally strung with hemp surmounted by a straw-filled palliasse, and strangely comfortable. On arrival, one's bearer took it upon himself to go out and purchase, on the master's behalf, a thin quilt, a tea set, and if necessary a mosquito net which he would rig on the bed; no resting or sleeping without its protection. He also arranged for the purchase of a "bog wheel", the essential bicycle, and invariably had a friend willing to sell one.

'An important health safeguard was drummed into us – never lie naked and sweaty under a fan; always cover the tummy with a towel to ward off the serious consequences of a chill. Usually bearers would remind the new arrivals on the dos and don'ts – wearing of hats out of doors in the sun, no short trousers after 5pm, and many others – otherwise the old *koyhais* (old timers) would dispense their advice in earnest and in no uncertain terms!

'I met my bearer the instant we docked in India. Not knowing what to expect after the brief formalities of arrival, it was a surprise to be met by a deputation of bearers from our new stations who were to be our personal servants. I don't know who allocated them, but mine, name of Ismail, spoke almost no English. I later heard that his last employer had been a Greek shipping agent. He was full of confidence, however, and was quite sure he knew what was expected of him and got on with it. But I drew the line firmly when he tried to bath me. All in the day's work when employed by his Greek master, I expect!

'The messes were very comfortable, cool and well run by a large staff, usually Pathan tribesmen. They were highly trained and very long serving, father and son, completely loyal and respectful but losing none of their pride and fierce character. Your own bearer served you in the dining room as well as in his duties of personal attendance in the living quarters, shopping and running messages – a true factotum! He would travel anywhere with you, by air at times, but more often in a dusty bus (sometimes through hostile territory). Together with all locally employed staff he showed tremendous devotion to duty, the staunchest loyalty and never a murmur of complaint. For this continuous, devoted hard work these men were paid a standard rate of Rs40 (about £3 sterling) per month. It was forbidden to pay more. It became clear very quickly that they considered it an honour to serve, and they made no bones about it.

'Work started at 7.30am and stopped at 1pm. In the hot months one took to one's *charpoy* each afternoon to prepare for energetic tennis at teatime – but there was lots of flying interspersed with tiresome duties such as running pay parades.

'There was no wine – it didn't travel. The food varied but was usually good in the officers' mess. Water was impregnated with chlorine, ice made with boiled water, and vegetables were washed in solution of permanganate of potash – *pinky pani*. Nonetheless, tummy trouble was rife.

'A few married officers lived with their families in some fairly luxurious and spacious bungalows in the cantonment. New arrivals were required to leave visiting cards at the station commander's residence, and at the households of senior married officers, various government dignitaries and others on a strictly specified list. If you failed to do this within a fortnight of arriving, you heard about it! In all cases, the lady of the house mounted a "not at home" box next to the entrance which indicated her wish to be visited or not. There was a sliding panel showing "at home" when she was happy to be called upon, and you would be admitted to leave the card and accept the offer of tea. If the "not at home" sign was displayed you dropped your card in the box and beat it.

'The dodge was to tour the cantonment armed with your cards during the heat of the afternoon when all the *me'msahibs* were resting on their *charpoys*, indicating "not at home". This was perfectly acceptable and pleased everyone – no tiresome visitors or formal cups of unwanted tea. Then, a few days later the lucky caller would probably be invited to tennis, drinks, or dinner.

'Social life was not hectic, but it was very formal and occasionally directed kindly towards the single. There were some daughters of course, and an annual influx of young ladies known as the "fishing fleet" who came out for a few weeks each year, during the cooler months as a rule, to see if there were any prospective husbands about.

'Flight lieutenants were very aloof towards pilot officers who were usually just about tolerated by flying officers but hardly ever addressed by anyone else except at their place of work. To start with, you could not escape the feeling that you were "under the eye" all the time. No talking at breakfast; not even "good morning". We actually had an aged ex-Indian Army colonel in the mess (who somehow was the station education officer) and he sat glowering over his newspaper. The story went that a new arrival greeted him one morning, and he replied with seven "good mornings" on the trot, muttering loudly, "That will do for the week!" Drank nothing but neat gin with onions in it (later on I got to like this a lot!)'

It seemed as though it had always been that way in India, and perhaps always would remain so. Thirty One would fly army co-operation sorties and the pilots would land back for tiffin. From a scratch start in 1915, the Squadron's aircraft had become an indispensable part of the Indian scene.

But changes were in the offing, and the Frontier would never be quite the same again. Storm clouds were gathering over Europe and the Pacific, and Thirty One would, before long, be plunged into the maelstrom. They would eventually emerge at the other end and continue to play a part in the various new orders which would evolve on the sub-continent and adjacent lands. But before the Squadron left India on its original tour of duty, there was to be an unexpected change of role.

Chapter 5

Bomber Transport

It was now 1939, and Bertie Mann's antennae were humming with rumour:

'Before B Flight left for one particular detachment there was a murmur that Thirty One was soon to change its role to that of a "Bomber Transport" Squadron, and as the time drew near for us to return it became apparent that this was already afoot. A Flight was converting onto the aircraft of the old BT [Bomber Transport] Flight, which had been based at Lahore for many years, and the CO of that unit was now our squadron commander. Then, as we gathered up our gear to go back, a Valentia arrived, driven by the other flight commander, to collect the B Flight groundcrew. So a bunch of pilots trained and experienced in army co-operation flew the dear old Wapitis back home, and we were apparently about to "change our spots".'

This was clearly more than rumour, and on 1 April 1939 the BT Flight disbanded, with its Wing Commander Read moving to the helm of Thirty One. The apparently unholy mixture of 'bomber' and 'transport' roles seems unimaginable today, presumably stemming then simply from the type of work that could be performed by 'big' aircraft.

Additional machines were inherited from Egypt-based 216 Squadron, a move typical of the times in the sense that equipment, and sometimes personnel, often seemed to move further and further east as they aged. Some of these airframes were flown into India, while others came in crates by sea before being re-erected at Drigh Road.

Bertie Mann wasn't keen on his new employment:

'At Lahore things had changed. Our Wapiti flight remained for a while, but before long we all commenced conversion to the "flying pig". This was my first experience with more than one engine. The Valentia (with two Bristol Pegasus engines) was unwieldy and underpowered, being a plywood and fabric development of the Vickers Vimy which Alcock and Brown had flown across the Atlantic. I'm sure it was designed in good faith with the best of intentions, but it rumbled along on the ground and lumbered into the air by the skin of its teeth; then wallowed in a slow, horizontal spiral at 75mph. It was impossible to synchronize the engines for long, so they gave out a long, continually undulating, low-pitched, sing-song with the tips of the airscrews a couple of feet from your ears. The fabric flapped and creased under the strain, and if you stood up in the open cockpit to look backwards down the fuselage you could see the box tailplane twisting about. I found it impossible to fly properly and, although that might have been my own fault, quickly became very unhappy.'

The cultural difference between the two tribes was immediately apparent to the new CO, who put his viewpoint:

> 'In 1938 I was posted to command the Bomber Transport Flight which later absorbed, or was absorbed by, 31 Squadron. It was my job to convert them all from single-engined Wapitis to Valentias, and from Army Co-op to Bomber Transport. It would have been hard to find a more disgruntled, bolshie-minded crowd – until they realised what fun and variety BT work afforded!'

Wild and inhospitable terrain. From Dudley Burnside's collection, a picture of a Valentia over the Frontier.

Relating the aircraft to the Vimy was, in fact, a little unkind, for the Valentia actually derived from the Vickers Victoria of 1922. Some of the Squadron's aircraft were new-built as Valentias, while others were Victoria conversions.

A converted example was JR8232, which originated as J8232, a Victoria Mk III procured under Air Ministry contract 707156/26 at a price of £9,000. It had originally been issued to 216 Squadron at Heliopolis. In early 1935 the aircraft was reconditioned and modified. Changing the engines from Napier Lion XIBs to Bristol Pegasus IIL3s increased its top speed from 110 mph at sea level to 130 mph at 5,000 ft. The modification brought the aircraft to Victoria Mk VI standard, while the reconditioning warranted the change to a 'JR' serial number.[1]

But before the full power of the Pegasus engines could be utilised and the all-up weight increased from 18,000lb to 19,500lb, certain structural improvements had to be made. Most notably, the undercarriage was strengthened, pneumatic wheel brakes were added, and a tail wheel replaced the skid. With all this completed, in May 1935 the aircraft became a Valentia.

But by 1939 the design was undeniably antiquated. An anachronism, really, by that time – an open-cockpit biplane bomber transport with a fixed undercarriage. Like dignified steam locomotives, the BT Flight's aircraft bore brass nameplates on the nose, reputedly reflecting the cities and rajahs who had funded the aircraft: *City of Calcutta; City of Delhi; Sirmur;* and *City of Lahore.* It all seemed rather stately. No wonder many of the Wapiti pilots didn't fancy the idea.

---

1. It is worth nothing that upon conversion from Victoria to Valentia some J- and K- serialed aircraft had the additional letter 'R' added to their serial numbers to become 'JR' or 'KR' followed by four numerals. Largely an administrative tool, this somewhat unusual measure served to distinguish a converted Victoria from the new-build Valentia which began to appear from 1934 onwards, although few actually had the additional 'R' applied to the airframe itself. Occasionally, however, photographs do surface to prove that at least some aircraft of the period, including other types, did indeed carry the additional letter – on their fuselage at least.

Regardless of preferences, the Squadron went through a rigorous training period with its 'new' aircraft, taking on additional crewmen for the larger machines. This took until well into the year, by which time the unit had moved to Peshawar.

Squadron Leader Dudley Burnside joined the Squadron from the BT Flight as Valentia flight commander. He was to have a successful association with Thirty One for nearly three years, and remembers:

> 'Many bombing sorties against the villages and caves of the Faqir of Ipi had been made by the BT Flight and these continued after it was absorbed by 31 Squadron. For example I have an entry in my log-book of a bombing sortie in the Madda Khel area for the night of 3 April 1939, when twenty 20lb bombs were dropped on caves and villages after leaflets warning the villagers of the bombing had been dropped some hours before.
>
> 'Again on 2 October: "Self and Mavor, Valentia K1312 – precision bombing in Madda Khel area, four 20lb, four 250lb and two 520lb bombs. Direct hit with 250lb bomb on tower of Faqir of Ipi's HQ which was destroyed".'

So much for bombing, but the Valentia also performed sterling transport service on the Frontier. Wyndham Dark, a Leading Aircraftman engine flight mechanic (and later a pilot) joined early in 1939:

The Valentia's bomb load. 'Tony' and 'Alfie' were, in all probability, the armourers, while 'Uncle Ubee' was the CO.

> 'I was allocated K2342 "V" for engine maintenance, and I kept this aircraft all the time I was with the Squadron, travelling everywhere it went. The locker in the aircraft's nose carried a comprehensive range of spares. If the machine developed a snag, we set to and fixed it where it stood.
>
> 'Travelling by Valentia might not have been much fun for the poor British servicemen stationed at, for example, Razmak – the a***hole of the Empire, or at least one of them! But think of the alternative. Usually, when a garrison needed to be relieved, the army units had to march all the way, with graves dug in readiness to bury casualties shot by snipers along the route.
>
> 'While Thirty One was at Peshawar it was decided and sanctioned by higher authority that experimental defensive armament would be fitted to a Valentia. At the rear end of the cabin roof a circular hole was cut so that a Scarfe gun mounting could be installed to take a Vickers "K" gun. Stops were fitted to prevent the gunner hitting the main and tail-planes. Next a gun mounting was installed in the cabin doorway. There, two stirrups were fitted for the gunner's feet, one on the trailing edge of the port mainplane for his right foot and one on the fuselage for his left foot. He was to sit on the cabin floor with the gun between his legs, the

arrangement guaranteeing cold feet! A third gun was to be mounted to fire through the nose door aperture, normally used for stretcher access.

'With all the drag from its struts and wires, the Valentia's performance was already in the low-speed area. And the post-modification air test found a further decrease – especially, as I recall, when the front gun was fired. So the idea was not pursued.'

Despite Wyndham's initial belief, when we get to the Iraq operation shortly we'll see another mention of Valentia guns. So it might be that aircraft were individually modified. Anyway, he continues:

'I do remember an aircraft crashing on take-off from Risalpur, the engines having stopped due to a fuel problem at about 50ft. The aircraft had sufficient speed to

The local people's latrine receives a direct hit.

carry on for a while until the *dhobi* house got in the way, at which point it came to rest in a flying attitude. The undercarriage demolished the front wall, the wings ending up supported by the side walls, and the rear fuselage resting inside the building. The slats on the upper port mainplane operated, indicating a near-stalling speed. A ladder was fetched to allow the crew to descend to terra firma, and no-one was hurt in the incident. The aircraft letter was "C for Charlie" which was probably the "City of Calcutta", one of the original three Valentias of the Bomber Transport Flight.'

And Bertie Mann's gleeful description of that same event displays more than a hint of *schadenfreude*:

'There was some welcome light relief one day when a veteran of the old BT Flight tried to overshoot, stalled and flopped his Valentia onto the native latrines from where a number of occupants were seen running and pulling up their nether garments. Could have been a nasty disaster, but the pilot's pride suffered the only injury.'

But bomber transports did have some advantages over short-range aircraft. Mann continues:

'All was forgotten in early summer when there was promise of a trip up the Persian Gulf to Iraq. The remaining Wapiti boys were to take the second pilots' seats and we were to convey crews from the bomber squadrons on the frontier to collect Blenheims on re-equipment. My captain

The aircraft was the 'City of Calcutta', seen here in happier circumstances. (*From the archive of Bertie Mann*)

was to be Brian McMillan, a steady, quiet type of New Zealander who had been in the BT business for some time. We left Lahore in company with another Valentia on a route via Drigh Road, Jiwani, Sharjah, Bahrain and Shaibah to Habbaniya; a somewhat marathon voyage for the old lady, but she sailed along merrily and we got there in one piece.

'On the Bahrain-Shaibah leg we encountered a headwind, not particularly strong, but it took us 5hrs 40mins to fly some 300 miles. We returned from Habbaniya to Lahore by the same route. No sign of our Blenheims on the way but all arrived at their stations except one. We heard that he had dozed off while flying along the Baluchistan coast in the dark – lost altitude, and came to a gentle halt on the beach!'

Stops at Gulf stations always seemed to evoke interesting images. On another landing at Sharjah, Leading Aircraftman Kenway tells of the 'honour guard' which met the aircraft on the apron: 'They were smartly dressed in black head-dress, white robes, cartridge belts, rifles and swords. Our captain was invited to inspect them, performing the ceremony with due solemnity in spite of his non-ceremonial dress of khaki shirt and slacks.'

And at Abu Dhabi on a later date, Sergeant Mike Vlasto mentioned that, as the crew were laboriously refuelling their Valentia from four-gallon drums, the local sheik arrived and started measuring the wings with his umbrella. When asked why, he said that he was going to make one of his own!

Indeed, as Wing Commander Read indicated earlier, such 'fun and variety' was by no means uncommon in BT flying – along with considerable tension. Here, recorded in a letter sent to his parents in spring 1939 by Flight Lieutenant James Chapple on the headed notepaper of Royal Air Force Depot Aboukir, Egypt, is a description of a quite hair-raising event. It concerns a flight from India to Egypt to collect three additional Valentias destined for 31 Squadron; the crews for the 'new' aircraft were travelling in the hold as passengers. We join the skipper as he crosses the Arabian Sea, fearing he might be about to lose a good proportion of the Squadron's aircrew:

'I was forced lower and lower by weather until we were only 300ft above the sea in driving rain, and could actually see sharks swimming about. Still twenty miles from the rocky coast of Oman, I was sitting in my cockpit in about two inches of water, soaked and blinded, while the machine was being thrown all over the sky like a feather. It was completely out of control twice! We RAF pilots only send out calls for assistance when it is a case of life or death, and at last I had to do this through my wireless operator. Then I told all the chaps (the crews for the three returning Valentias) to put on their life-saving jackets and be prepared to "take it" if I hit the water. I don't think I'm a coward, but I knew real fear at that moment, especially with all the helpless chaps sitting in the back relying on me to win though. Thank god I made the shore, but here a fresh danger threatened – the mountains. I could not get over them owing to clouds and lightning, and they rose sheer out of the water to 5,000ft.

'Eventually, with only half an hour's petrol left, I did the only possible thing – I ran down the coast towards Muscat. Here, as dusk was falling, I found a sandy beach and risked a forced landing – it was successful! It was near a village called Kalba, and soon a crowd of heavily armed Bedouins arrived – would they be friendly was the general question? Luckily they were, and the Sheikh – one Hamid Ben Abdullah – insisted on sharing his house and food with us for the night. I have never experienced such hospitality as these simple desert folk extended to us. We sat around in a circle, and forty-seven dishes of queer food were placed on the ground before us. Luckily the Sheikh's brother spoke Urdu and I could converse with him. After two hours we took ceremonial coffee and cigarettes, and the Sheikh told us that we could retire – which we did gratefully.

'I had got through by wireless to Habbaniya and told them we were safe, so next morning petrol was brought from Sharjah by plane and we took off after much "salaaming" and rifle shooting by the Bedouins. Eventually we arrived here (Egypt) after forty-one hours of gruelling flying from India.'

Back at base, Bertie's mind turned to more strategic matters:

'At Lahore war loomed ahead of us, although there was no excitement about it. Everything was going on as usual and we were still able to get down on our *charpoys* in the afternoon. We settled back to our ordinary routine until a day or two before the actual declaration of hostilities.

'I happened to be orderly officer on the evening when a signal arrived from air HQ which asked for the names of two officer volunteers for posting to 28(AC) Squadron, by then at Kohat on the frontier. Handing this to the squadron commander, I was first in the queue. I enjoyed myself dropping bombs on the king's enemies, but I was an AC pilot, and the BT business wasn't really my kettle of fish. I felt disloyal and a bit sad about leaving Thirty One.'

Unbeknown to Mann he would yet have reason to be grateful to 31 Squadron's Valentias – as we shall see in due course.

Soon the last of the Wapitis had gone, and with them the Squadron's army co-operation role. But that role would nevertheless return, ironically in the area in which the Squadron originally learned its trade. But not until after the millennium, so for now the story returns to the business which lay immediately ahead.

In late 1939 the long-foreseen conflict with Germany started. The period from the declaration of the European war in September through to the point in May 1940 when the Germans marched into the Low Countries is often referred to as the 'Phoney War'. And the same could be said of the situation in India – in the sense that nothing changed immediately. Not that there was no activity, for tribal skirmishing continued much as it had for the preceding fifty years – albeit at a fairly low intensity.

Naturally there were over-reactions, as reported by Corporal 'Skilly' Skilton:

'On the declaration of war with Germany, half a world away, we were ordered to black out all lights and intern all German nationals. Then the telephone system broke down and the only person who knew enough to service it was a German technician – who we had to release to do the job!'

Just as during the Great War, though, there were strategic considerations. George Eccles enlarges:

Marvellous cloudscapes.

'When the Second World War broke out, Russia was still perceived as a threat to the Frontier. In reality, though, she was far more interested in her western border than in pursuing her expansion into Asia. However, the Axis powers had been meddling in Afghan affairs for some years; now their object was to remove the neutral Amir Zahur Shah and replace him with the previously-deposed Amanullah who was living in Italy. Suspicion was that the Axis had made a clandestine approach to the Faqir of Ipi, offering him money and arms to raze Waziristan; their aim was to keep British and Indian forces occupied there when they could be better employed.'

In fact George, at the time on the Group HQ staff in Peshawar, was pleased in a very personal way to be involved in the war preparations:

'The HQ was without an operations room so one had to be set up. The only available place was the AOC's residence, which had a room to spare. We clerks were required to man it and, joy of joys, we found that the residence boasted a flush toilet. This was the first I had seen since setting foot in India two years previously, so we luxuriated!'

Forces in situ over the period continued with routine. During 1939 and 1940 the Valentias made a number of flights over the foothills of the Himalayas to Gilgit, and a notable event was the participation of ten aircraft in the 'Chitral Relief'. Leslie Mavor remembers:

'Relief of the Chitral garrison was simply a routine change-over, but 1940 was the first time it had been carried out by air. On all previous occasions the relieving garrison had to foot-slog its way from Peshawar / Risalpur to Chitral, before the relieved garrison slogged its way south thereafter.

'The Lawarai Pass, the main obstruction in our path, was rather higher (10,400ft above sea level) than the more tired of our old Valentias could reach in still air, so to get through the pass one had to circle in a convenient thermal up-current (circling

'Please have your boarding cards ready!'

vultures gave one an indication) and then, with some 2,000ft extra in hand, head for the pass. If the height was dissipated before one got through, then it meant a steep turn away and a search for another thermal.'

All in all, some 500,000lbs of payload, including 1,600 or so men, were carried from Risalpur to Chitral and return, the operation being completed in under three days. Mavor continues:

'I remember one incident on the operation. We had to carry the battalion pay for a year, mostly in rupees. A Bank of India official tried to make me sign a receipt, but I refused and a heated argument took place. Finally I said that the official could come along on the trip, sitting on the boxes. Naturally he refused in turn. It was just as well we did not sign because, on arrival in Chitral, the money was loaded on mules and one of them fell into the river and was carried away with its burden.'

Some warlike operations were flown but, as always, they were against dissident tribesmen. Wyndham Dark recalls:

'We started bombing against the Amedzal and Bhittani salients, and we moved stores to various detachments, then some more bombing from Miranshah. From March to May 1940 my machine was used for training Indian Air Force navigators at Risalpur, the aeroplane having seven desks installed. I flew 370 hours with the Squadron, not bad for ground staff.'

In due course, rumblings from further afield resulted in movements. For example in February 1941, with preparations beginning in the Far East for defence against possible Japanese attack, the entire Squadron was mustered to move the ground personnel and equipment of two other units which were being sent as reinforcements. A Flight transported 27 Squadron to Singapore, while B Flight moved 60 Squadron to Rangoon. The operations took a week, and one can only imagine the state of the passengers after travelling seven legs – twenty-three hours – in the roaring bellies of the convoy of Valentias. Not to mention the state of the flight crews in their open cockpits.

These strategic flights signalled, in a way, the beginning of the end of Thirty One's first long association with the Frontier. It had been an incredible episode, summed up neatly in his memoirs by George Eccles:

En early example of casualty evacuation. *Film still courtesy of the Trustees of the Imperial War Museum*

'If I was going to join my first squadron, I couldn't have joined a better one than Number Thirty One. I finally left the "Grim", as the North-West Frontier Province was known, after three and a half years. You either hated it or loved it. Work played a very important part, and although it was "peace time" there was no peace on the Frontier; only an almost unbroken period of operations. There were no peace-time squadrons, only operational squadrons constantly being re-armed and bombed up by hard-working ground crews in hot and very uncomfortable circumstances; flown almost round the clock by young pilots and their crewmen. Close friends and acquaintances were lost and death was just around the corner. It was this common factor of dedication and selfless support that, perhaps more than anything else, brought personnel of all ranks together. It was very special, and a period in one's service from which all who served on the Frontier can be very proud.'

We must hope, for the appendicitis sufferer's comfort, that the door was airtight. We know he survived his ordeal, for the surviving family of the pilot, Flight Lieutenant James 'Jimmy' Chapple, have in their possession a silver mug presented to him in 1941 on his wedding day by the very man. It is engraved: 'From a Grateful Patient'. *Film still courtesy of the Trustees of the Imperial War Museum*

From 1915 until 1941, 31 Squadron had taken air power in India from zero to a mature state. It had played a substantial part in implementing government policy in that most difficult of regions, and had been awarded a series of battle honours in recognition: North-West Frontier 1916–1918; Afghanistan 1919–1920; Mahsud 1919–1920; Waziristan 1919–1925; and North-West Frontier 1939.

But the influence of the Second World War was being felt increasingly far afield, and now it was time to move on.

Chapter 6

Middle East and Africa

In March 1941, with the threat of rebellion brewing in Iraq, the entire Squadron moved to Karachi to be closer to possible action. From there, both A and B Flights carried out two return flights to Shaibah in early April, transporting personnel of the 2nd Battalion, the King's Regiment. At least that's what the Squadron record called them; other reports, which would seem to be in the majority, have them as the 1st Battalion the King's Own Royal Regiment. Crews averaged ninety-two flying hours each during those eight days of transit, which must have seemed like a lifetime in open Valentia cockpits.

Those flights presaged Thirty One's first combat involvement in the 'big' war, so we must now look at how the Iraq of the time fitted into the picture.

The mandate which Britain had held over Iraq since the post-Great War settlement had ended in 1932, but Britain still maintained staging and overflight rights, as well as an interest in oilfields.

Following an uprising led by Raschid Ali el Gailani (various spellings reported) in 1941, the Regent, Abd al-llah, fled, to be given refuge in a Royal Navy warship. Although Raschid Ali's faction was technically non-aligned, it sympathized generally with the Axis powers. In view of Britain's overwhelming involvement elsewhere, the rebels might have expected a quickly negotiated settlement.

At least that's the conventionally held view. Air Vice-Marshal Tony Dudgeon, however, in his entertaining book *Hidden Victory,* suggests that there might have been more to it than that. Citing sources as diverse as Winston Churchill and official German records, he concludes that the episode was not so much a minor rebellion as a calculated attempt by Raschid Ali, in cahoots with Germany, to initiate a pan-Arab movement that would eventually oust Britain from the Middle East. Which would consequently have allowed the region's coveted oil resources to fall into German hands. He goes on to surmise that, without Iraqi oil, Britain would, in the first instance, have been unable to defeat the Germans in North Africa. And if that had happened, the future course of the war could have been very different.

The 'what if?' possibilities are limitless, so further speculation is fruitless. But the fact was that the rebels in Iraq were able to call upon small numbers of German and Italian aircraft – and even Vichy French fighter-bombers launched from Syria. So it was a serious military operation. In the end though, British troops reached Baghdad by 31 May to force an armistice – and Raschid Ali's forces were defeated.

And the RAF's part in all this? Well, the highlight was the heroic part played by Dudgeon's Number 4 Flying Training School, with its untrained pilots and its training aircraft hastily modified for combat. But Thirty One's contribution was also substantial and significant. The Valentias were dispatched, and before long were heavily engaged in trooping and casualty evacuation. Their 'bomber' function wasn't called upon as far as we know, but there were still a couple of exciting stories, and Dudley Burnside leads off:

		31 (B.T.) SQDN:- LAHORE.			ATTACHED	BASRAH.	

| YEAR 1941. | | AIRCRAFT | | PILOT, OR | BASRAH. | DUTY | |
MONTH	DATE	Type	No.	1ST PILOT	2ND PILOT, PUPIL OR PASSENGER	(INCLUDING RESULTS AND REMARKS)	
—	—	—	—	—	—	— TOTALS BROUGHT FORWARD	
MAY	2	Douglas D.C.2	D.G.473	S/L BURBURY	3 PASS	LOCAL FLYING.	
				F/L MACKIE	SELF	(R.A.F. AND CIVIL AERODROMES)	
"	2	Douglas D.C.2	D.G.473	F/L MAVOR	4 PASS.	LOCAL FLYING.	
				SELF	—		
"	2	Douglas D.C.2	D.G.473	F/L BISHOP	4 PASS	DUAL.	
				SELF	—		
"	4	VALENTIA	K3600	SELF	CREW	KARACHI - JIWANI.	
				SGT. VLASTO	11 PASS.		
"	4	VALENTIA	K3600	SELF	CREW	JIWANI - SHARJAH.	
				SGT. VLASTO	11 PASS.		
"	5	VALENTIA	K3600	SELF	CREW.	ENGINE TEST AT SHARJAH.	
				F/SGT. DAUPHIN	—		
"	5	VALENTIA	K3600	SELF	CREW	SHARJAH - BAHREIN.	
				SGT. VLASTO	11 PASS.		
"	5	VALENTIA	K3600	SELF	CREW	BAHREIN - SHAIBAH.	
				SGT. VLASTO	11 PASS.		
"	5	VALENTIA	K3600	SELF	CREW	SHAIBAH - BASRAH.	
				SGT. VLASTO	—		
"	6	VALENTIA	K3600	SELF	14 PASS.	BASRAH - SHAIBAH.	
				SGT. VLASTO	CREW.		
"	6	VALENTIA	K3600	SELF	14 PASS.	SHAIBAH - HABBANIYA.	
				SGT. VLASTO	CREW		
"	7	BLENHEIM	?	?/L ?	SELF	RECCO K.3 LANDING GROUND.	
				F/O ?	CREW		

GRAND TOTAL [Cols. (1) to (10)]
1590 Hrs. 50 Mins.

TOTALS CARRIED FORWARD

Dudley Burnside's logbook records the drama of forced-landings in his ancient Valentia during the Iraq campaign.

'On 6 May I was leading a flight of three Valentias, each full of armed soldiers, on the last leg of our flight from India, and had taken off from Shaibah for Habbaniya. However, near our destination we ran into a severe dust storm. We could not see the ground, so missed Habbaniya by some eight or ten miles.

'When the storm cleared we found we had overshot and were rapidly running out of fuel. Seeing a small strip below, I landed my Valentia on it and the other two aircraft also approached to land.

'On landing, my aircraft was fired upon and hit in a few places, with one of my groundcrew, Corporal Bradley, being wounded. I immediately took off again down wind and tried to prevent the other two from landing. For one it was too late; he landed and was hit in the petrol tank. All the crew and passengers ran for shelter behind the sand dunes. The other, captained by Flight Lieutenant Chapple, saw what was happening and overshot.'

IRAQ OPERATIONS.   MAY – 1941

	SINGLE-ENGINE AIRCRAFT				MULTI-ENGINE AIRCRAFT						PASS-ENGER	INSTR/CLOUD FLYING [Incl. in cols. (1) to (10)]	
	DAY		NIGHT		DAY			NIGHT					
	DUAL	PILOT	DUAL	PILOT	DUAL	1ST PILOT	2ND PILOT	DUAL	1ST PILOT	2ND PILOT		DUAL	PILOT
	(1)	(2)	(3)	(4)	(5)	(6)	(7)	(8)	(9)	(10)	(11)	(12)	(13)
	50.25	90.45	-	-	10.30	140.25	176.45	8.35	64.55	16.50	49.30		
							.35				.35		
							.35						
						.25							
						5.00							
INTER COMMAND						6.15							
TROOP						.15							
						6.05							
CARRYING						4.30							
						.20		SQUADRON ATTACHED TO BASRAH OPERATING FROM BASRAH AIR PORT.					
TROOP CARRYING.						.20							
FORCED LANDED ON ENEMY LANDING GROUND K.3 RECCO. OF ENEMY LANDING GROUND TO FIND CREW AND PASSENGERS OF VALENTIA K3604.						7.55		AIRCRAFT DAMAGED BY GROUND ACTION. CPL. BRADLEY (CREW) WOUNDED. 1.00					
	50.25	90.45	-	-	10.55	171.05	177.20	8.35	64.55	16.50	51.05		
	(1)	(2)	(3)	(4)	(5)	(6)	(7)	(8)	(9)	(10)	(11)	(12)	(13)

A. F. (L) 414.

George Wetherburn, a wireless mechanic who served on Thirty One from 1939–41, takes up the story:

'I was the WOp on Valentia JR8063 on the day in question. At Haditha (K3 Pipeline) as we prepared to land I saw through the port window that two Vals had already landed. One was burning, while the other was preparing to take off in great haste. Instead of landing, we left K3 airspace, as did the escaping Val. We then landed briefly at desert spot 1, before pressing on. At spot 2, we saw the escaping Val on the ground; he had run out of fuel so we landed and transferred some of our petrol to him. We then got airborne again together, before both finally running out of fuel and landing at spot 3. There we waited, protected by a Blenheim of 203 Squadron circling overhead, until another Valentia (of the Middle East Comms Flight) landed and transferred enough fuel for us all to continue, by night, to Habbaniya.

'The captured crew of the Val that was shot up at Haditha, which included an engines sergeant and a fitter by the name of J. Wall, were taken by the Iraqis to Baghdad where they were interned for a month, only being released when the

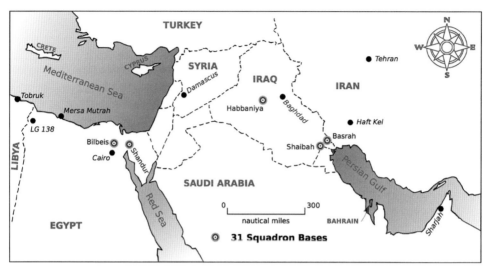

Map 2: No.31 Squadron operations in the Middle East and Africa, 1941.

rebellion was put down. I have no idea whether they ever rejoined Thirty One, but I seem to recall they were initially repatriated to the UK on their release. While imprisoned, their diet apparently consisted of soggy *chupattis*. The story was that they used to fling them at the hot wall where they stuck fast and dried in the sun. Eventually, they'd drop off and could be eaten as biscuits!'

The record talks of a happening on 18 April which is so similar as to suggest the two reports could refer to one and the same event. In the official account it is mentioned that the captured captain was Sergeant Chalk and second pilot Sergeant Tommy Farr. Farr had, apparently, urged restraint in returning fire in case it provoked the Iraqis, but had himself ended up being wounded by gunfire. Further, two members of Burnside's crew in the Valentia which managed to escape by taking off again (one being Corporal Bradley) were also wounded.

The passengers, fifteen soldiers of the KORR, were captured along with the crew. This particular version of the incident concludes by saying that when the prisoners were finally released and returned to the Squadron, Farr told the boys that the soup they had been given to eat had had cats' eyeballs floating in it!

Transport aircraft were at a premium during this operation, with five civilian Armstrong-Whitworth Atalantas being seconded to Thirty One to supplement the Valentias on the initial deployment. But the record for April 1941 also contains a report which, although short on detail, is nevertheless long on significance. It states simply that 'the period 12–15 April was spent in converting B Flight to the DC-2, and on the sixteenth both the Valentia and DC-2 Flights carried out further reinforcements to Shaibah, where they remained as a detachment.'

There were four DC-2s initially, and this conversion is certainly worthy of greater comment, as it took Thirty One into the modern era. It also heralded the end of the Squadron's short interlude in the 'Bomber Transport' role, for the DC-2 was a pure transporter. So before going on with the story of the Iraq operation, let's say a little about the new machine.

In the 1920s a number of American airlines had been looking to open up their continent to regular, scheduled operations. They needed an aircraft which was quick, comfortable and reliable. Boeing was first, in the early 1930s, with its model 247, a ten-seater of unheard-of luxury. But by 1933, the Douglas DC-1 prototype was airborne. It showed such promise that Trans World Airlines immediately ordered the first of the 211 DC-2s which would follow. The production DC-2 was a fourteen-seater and would later pave the way for the fabulously-successful DC-3. We should also add that the DC-2 was known in RAF service as the DC-2K. Wyndham Dark recalls the arrival of the first aircraft:

'I was on a fitter course when the first DC-2, DG477, arrived at Karachi by sea from the USA. The fuselage was towed by road, tail first, to Drigh Road where it was to be prepared for military service. The wings followed in further Queen Marys. This journey was not without incident, the aircraft proving too wide for the level crossing gates at the railway, so those had to be dismantled. The machine had come as deck cargo and was covered with grease as protection against water and salt spray. This had to be removed, following which the interior had to be stripped from its passenger state and converted to cargo configuration – seats, carpets, racks and galley had to go. There was no suitable tool kit, the machine being built to American standards. So my working party of student fitters were detailed to manufacture tools. Every nut and bolt was measured with a vernier gauge and we made the spanners. DG477 was said already to have tens of thousands of airframe hours on arrival, having originated with TWA.'

In fact 477 is actually reported in Arthur Pearcy's *Dakota at War* as having been the very first DC-2, serving with TWA from 1934 as NC13711.

As the following passage from Flight Lieutenant Tiny Howell shows, the odd pilot seems to have skipped the Valentia stage and moved straight to the DC-2 – with occasionally quite exciting results:

'I was converted from Wapitis by Flt Lt Bishop, the conversion consisting of a few circuits at Karachi. During one circuit Bishop went back to spend a penny. Bumbling around on my own I was interested to see a couple of red lights appear on the co-pilot's panel, which I pointed out to him on his return as if to say "See how observant I am!" He jumped up and down with excitement, his hands flying about the flight deck. Not having had the technicalities of the DC-2 explained to me, I only then learned that they were fuel low pressure lights and that the engines had been in imminent danger of stopping.'

Four more DC-2s joined at Shaibah, being delivered directly by civilian pilots, and before long the full complement of both types was busy with the operation. The detachment moved to Basrah on 19 April and continued to fly men, stores and equipment to Habbaniya daily. The record continues with further stories of the brief Iraq campaign:

'About 29 April, the Germans began using Messerschmitt Bf.110s and Heinkel 111s based on Hinaidi and Mosul, so all subsequent flying had to be carried out at night. During this period many evacuees and casualties were flown out of Habbaniyah.

'Ferrying men and material continued throughout May, although one DC-2 was knocked out during a strafing attack on Habbaniya by Bf.110s. The detachment used six DC-2s and six Valentias throughout, the groundcrews putting up a most magnificent show working all hours of the day and night under the most difficult conditions and in great heat. The Valentias in particular were extremely difficult to maintain, and all major inspections were dispensed with.'

Indeed throughout the operation, as in earlier days, groundcrew also played their full part supplementing the airborne crew. Leading Aircraftman Les Sumption, who would remain with Thirty One for many years, confirms the terms on which he and his fellows shared the operating hazards:

'I joined 31 Squadron as an engine fitter about the middle of 1941. My introduction was very precise and to the point. The CO said, "Come with me Sumption" – so Sumption duly went along, and the boss took me to a DC-2 standing on the tarmac and said, "This is your aircraft, Sumption, and where this goes, you go, You will have to act as a dispatcher, get yourself a log book, and you will be paid an extra one and fourpence a day flying pay. You will not get a parachute, as we have none on the Squadron. Good luck Sumption".'

And George Wetherburn confirms the dedication of the team:

'On one occasion I was doing a temporary cable repair on a DC-2, it had been severed by a stray bullet. The job was done at 0200 hrs in darkness illuminated by another Habbaniya airman holding a torch. The aircraft was required for a flight at first light. From Karachi, I did two trips to Iraq. On the second, I stayed over in Bahrain for four or five days awaiting a spare engine.'

George Bush, an armourer with the Squadron who doubled as an air gunner, also has a tale to tell:

'When we arrived at Basrah from Karachi we were allocated tents in the grounds of the airport hotel. One morning, Lummie Lord [Sergeant David Lord, of whom much more later] invited me to go with him on a short trip to Shaibah. We overstayed a little and my pilot became concerned. He started the Valentia's starboard engine, but the other refused. I tried the port engine with the magneto starter but without success. The only other method was with the bag and rope and, as this took three men, I grabbed a couple of airmen. Although one of them fell on his face, the engine started.

'There were very few facilities at Basrah, so after a while we gave way to the army and moved to Shaibah. On my first visit to Habbaniya I was emerging from the hangar when, without any warning, I saw three German aircraft in close formation bombing the depot. A lone Gloster Gladiator challenged but was quickly shot down. The single Lewis gun mounted in the rear of the Valentia did not offer much protection. So, now that we knew of the proximity of the Germans, we stuck to night flying.'

The Squadron's main 'customers', army personnel being ferried into action, were never shy of commenting on the remaining Valentias' antiquity, even at one point being overheard suggesting that their aircraft had been overtaken by an elderly nomad on his camel. However, the army also had its own old-fashioned ways. Not only did the Iraq campaign feature what became accepted as the last-ever British cavalry charge, but there were further curiosities. At a post-war reunion at the Victory Services Club in London, Benny Watts encountered a soldier who had also been engaged in the Iraq action. In conversation it emerged that the gentleman's original deployment had occurred while he was attached to either Skinner's or Hodson's Horse (Benny couldn't be sure which, but both were cavalry regiments originally raised on the Frontier). At any rate the point was that not only did the unit travel into combat with its horses, but also its pack of foxhounds for R&R. So one might say that allusions to the Valentias as antiquated were sometimes a bit rich!

With the Iraq business dealt with, the DC-2 detachment, now commanded by Wing Commander Ubee, moved to Habbaniya on 1 June to operate in the Syrian area.

Following the post-Great War Middle East settlement, Syria and Lebanon had come under the French umbrella. Now there were fears that their colonial administrations would provide facilities for the Germans. Indeed the Vichy French governor of Syria had declined to give any assurance that he would not permit German use of, for example, Syrian airfields. Increased German presence could easily have affected adjacent Turkey, unbalancing her neutrality.

Hidden Victory also suggests that the Italians, as well as supplying equipment to the Iraq campaign recently concluded, were advocating a push via Cyprus towards the Levantine coast. Thus it seems clear that any Axis advance into the Middle East was expected to come through Syria – hence the British resolve to nip the problem in the bud.

A substantial Allied force was assembled, including Free French units. Thirty One's task, as described rather inadequately in the record, was 'evacuation of casualties, operating many trips into the Middle East.' Among the Syrian strips used by the aircraft were Deir ez-Zor, Hassetche and Kamechlie. Little news was broadcast about this operation, as the British leadership knew that combat against French forces would be perceived badly at home. An earlier instance of similar difficulties had followed the sinking by the Royal Navy, in 1940, of French ships in Algeria. But the fact remained that the Vichy French had signed an armistice with Germany, and the additional irony in Syria was that the British would now find themselves in combat against Vichy forces equipped with American armaments.

Operation *Exporter* lasted for a month from mid-June, with British air involvement including Hurricanes, Blenheims and Swordfish. As an example of the confused nature of the fighting, Christopher Shores's *Dust Clouds in the Middle East* reports that an RAF recce pilot was 'shot down by Allied AA as he attempted to drop [his report to his own ground forces]. He force-landed but was shot dead by Free French colonial troops as he left the aircraft.'

As it happened, German attention switched at about that time to their newly opened Russian front. Nevertheless Operation *Exporter* was successful, with Free French leader General de Gaulle being recorded as visiting the area after its conclusion to thank the British.

Work in the Middle East would continue to occupy Thirty One for a while longer. Now the focus switched to Iran, where the operation was, in common with that in Syria, of a pre-emptive nature. It was conducted by Britain and its new Soviet friends – the Russians having joined the Allies following the German invasion of the Soviet Union.

The Shah's kingdom was widely suspected of leaning towards Germany, and the need to

Down in the desert during the 1941 Iraq uprising.

keep open a route from Russia to the Persian Gulf, with its warm-water ports and oilfields, was seen as a priority. Additionally, Iran itself had oil. So in August the Allies invaded Iran with the aim of neutralizing its small military forces and damping down any possible opposition. Soviet troops went in from the north while British forces advanced from the Gulf coast. The combat phase of Operation *Y* commenced on 25 August and lasted barely four days. After encountering minimal opposition, the two allied forces met one hundred or so miles west of Tehran in mid-September, with the whole episode being successfully completed by the end of that month. The record has little to say about it except that A Flight, operating from Shaibah, lost two Valentias, but with no casualties.

One of those losses occurred on 25 August. Six Valentias flew in formation to Haft Kel, each machine taking fifteen Indian troops with the mission of protecting the oilfields there and evacuating dependents. Dudley Burnside led the flight and the order was to land in formation, disembark the soldiers and be off again within two minutes. However, the last aircraft to land did not have sufficient room, hit a ditch and '… seemed to disappear in a cloud of red sand.' Pilot Officer Bill 'Flash' Kelly, in one of the other aircraft, saw it happen, and also saw Tommy Farr (of 6 May fame) 'catapulted out of the cockpit to do some very spectacular somersaults as he flew through the air.' Kelly waited behind and picked up Farr and his crew.

The Iran operation was the Valentias' swansong on the Squadron, following which the aircraft were transferred to the Air Landing School in Delhi. There, each had a large hole cut in the fuselage floor as an exit for paratroop trainees. And with that modification completed, the dinosaurs headed off into the sunset.

Even at the time it must have been hard to believe that such an incongruous antiquity could have survived for so long. A biplane bomber transport with the crew perched outside in the airflow, it had somehow completed every modern war mission asked of it: from strategic trooping to the Far East to tactical resupply of garrisons on the Frontier; from bombing caves to making opposed landings at hostile strips in the Middle East; and all at ninety miles per hour. Of course the development of aviation had been compressed to an unimaginable degree by two world wars, so it was perhaps hardly surprising that relics from the early days should still have been in service in 1941. But the Valentias had served Thirty One well, and many on the Squadron would look back with affection on their days with the old lady.

By September, the whole team was back in Lahore. But not for long, as in October eight DC-2s under a new CO, Wing Commander Jenkins, were ordered to Egypt.

While covering relatively minor (in strategic terms) events in Arabia we've neglected the bigger picture. So now, let's just summarize how the European conflict had relentlessly spilled into the Mediterranean area.

In June 1940, Italy had entered the war, armies in her north-African colonies immediately threatening British forces based in Egypt. Although the Italians were forced back to positions west of Benghazi by the following February, there was more to come when Germany's *Afrika Korps* entered the fray in spring 1941. Throughout that year tank battles ebbed and flowed across the North African desert − and would continue to do so during 1942. The British would hold Tobruk throughout 1941, while German forces would reach their furthest eastward point in the El Alamein area by May '42. At that point the Eighth Army would begin its ultimately successful counter attack.

Meanwhile, the British had reinforced Greece in March 1941, only to be ejected by advancing German forces weeks later. Most of those British troops were evacuated to Crete which, in turn, fell to a German airborne invasion in May.

The Mediterranean was now a hostile sea, with British shipping to Egypt and the Far East having to be diverted via the time-consuming Cape route. Together with stretched North African supply chains as British army units advanced from their Egyptian bases, this put a premium on the limited air transport available. It was during the build up to one ground push, Operation *Crusader* in late 1941, that India Command received the call to reinforce the North African theatre – and Thirty One was dispatched.

The first of the DC-2s. They bear Indian identities given to them on handover from the US, as well as the RAF serials which they received on subsequent transfer.

Jenkins sets the scene:

'On arrival in theatre with eight aircraft, we were based at Shandur on the edge of the Nile delta between Ismailia and Cairo. We were in tents, sharing the airfield with 117 Squadron, also newly converted to DC-2s.

Dakotas, now camouflaged, and Valentias together.

'After a trip to Khartoum at the beginning of November to collect stores, we started operating to the western desert, flying supplies out and casualties back. Our main fuelling point en route was Mersa Mutrah, where they had an efficient ground party to look after us. Minefields round the airfield were an encouragement not to over or undershoot!'

The Squadron was now operating in full-scale combat, the operation's objective being to lift the 1941 siege of the British garrison in Tobruk. Following the Valentia experiments with defensive armament, the DC-2s had a new breed of crewman to assist, Leading Aircraftmen 'Butch' Burgess and Kenway being two of eleven airmen who had volunteered for air gunner courses. Kenway in fact joined having completed a gunnery course prior to being posted in, and he tells his story from the time of deployment:

'Our DC-2s were adapted to take a mounted Lewis gun to fire through an opening in the fuselage near the door. I was a part-time air gunner, and was headed for the Middle East. My aircraft, flown by Flight Lieutenant Howell and Flight Sergeant Lord, left Karachi on 23 October. Our take off was delayed because an accompanying aircraft, "S", crashed and burnt out at the end of the runway.

'We were in Egypt for two months. All the air gunners flying with the Squadron were leading aircraftmen, probably among the last aircrew below the rank of sergeant. None of the aircraft, by the way, carried parachutes for the crews.'

The crashed aircraft referred to was being flown by Mike Vlasto, who would stay with the Squadron for many years. On this occasion he was with a pilot from the embryo Indian Air Force on conversion. Vlasto explains the accident:

'We were loaded with ammunition for Iraq. Of course, being heavy, this looked a very small load – so somebody had put in another load as well. With a dawn take off nobody noticed in the gloom, and we ran off the end of the strip into the dunes and went up in smoke.'

Jenkins continues with the story of operations in Egypt:

'On 8 December, Lummie Lord, with Flight Lieutenant 'Tiny' Howell as second pilot, was shot down over the desert. Tiny was wounded in the shoulder, but they managed to get the aircraft down without anyone else being injured (although one passenger had been killed in the attack). This aircraft loss was made up by one of our pilots picking up another DC-2 which had been shot through the main spar. We flew this to a maintenance unit where I knew the CO, and they repaired it in exchange for a DC-2 passenger seat!

'The shoot-down of DG475, "X", occurred when the crew were carrying supplies to landing ground LG138. Ten miles north-east of their objective they were attacked by three German Bf.110s. After landing in the desert the crewmen walked to LGl38, and were flying again the next day.'

Operations continued, with several longer-range trips, including to Cyprus and, on one occasion, to Russia. But, although the Allies would not finally secure North Africa until May 1943, another crisis was developing. Thirty One's presence was urgently required elsewhere.

Readers might well have found this information on the Squadron's Middle Eastern and North African adventures somewhat thin. Part of the explanation may be found in the operational record for the period which opens, rather confusingly, with the following paragraph:

'At the beginning of 1945 notification was received from the Air Historical Branch at the Air Ministry that "… no historical record existed in respect of 31 Squadron for the period September 1939 – March 1942." The newly-formed Historical Branch at HQ Air Command South East Asia was therefore obliged to make an attempt at repairing the past sins of omission and the following narrative has been compiled from the meagre information available in 1945.'

This could, understandably, account for the ambiguity regarding the identity of the regiment transported to Iraq; it would have been well-nigh impossible for personnel who hadn't been present to verify such details. So some doubts inevitably remain. One such concerns the Squadron's location in Egypt, stated by Jenkins to have been Shandur, but by the retrospective record to have been Bilbeis. An authoritative source, *The History of the Mediterranean Air War, 1940–45* by Christopher Shores, is of the opinion that Thirty One was never based at Bilbeis, although reporting that they did spend some time at another field, Ma'aten Bagush. Very probably the Squadron operated from several locations, some perhaps for very short periods.

What we can say for certain, though, is that 31 Squadron left the Middle East having been awarded three proud battle honours: Iraq 1941; Egypt and Libya 1941–1942; and Syria 1941. These related, officially, to campaigns during the following dates: Iraq, 2–31 May 1941; Syria, 8 June–12 July 1941; Egypt, 10 June 1940–6 Feb 1943.

Chapter 7

Call of the East

The day before Howell and Lord were shot down in Egypt was 7 December 1941, on which date the war took another turn. As well as bombing Pearl Harbor and thus bringing the USA into the conflict, Japanese forces swarmed through Indo-China, threatening British interests in Singapore, Malaya and Burma. Allied units were urgently required to reinforce the area, and Thirty One would soon be recalled – first to India, and thence onwards and eastwards.

Britain had an immediate crisis on its hands, with her people in Burma being overwhelmed by the forces of the Rising Sun. Personnel, many of them casualties, urgently needed evacuating. At that time India Command was desperately short of airlift capability, having only two of Thirty One's DC-2s available and serviceable. These were immediately flown by Squadron Leader Burbury and Flight Lieutenant Bengree from Lahore to Mingaladon, Rangoon, from where they plied backwards and forwards to Calcutta carrying urgently needed supplies in and casualties out.

Oh – and we mustn't forget those Valentias. In mentioning dinosaurs a couple of paragraphs ago, the author was careful not to add the word 'extinct'. Because such was the shortage of air transport and the urgency of the situation in the Far East as 1941 moved into '42 that the dear old aircraft were pressed back into operational service one more time. They are recorded as 'flying to Burma, and then making repeated trips, grossly overloaded, from Akyab to Dum Dum. During the emergency it was a matter of "anything that could fly would fly." Apart from the Valentias and the couple of Daks, available transport aircraft could be counted on the fingers of one hand.'

The assumption is that those Valentias were from the Air Landing School, and there is no information as to whether any of Thirty One's people were involved. Although, by coincidence, former flight commander Dudley Burnside (now Wing Commander) was the station commander at Akyab, Burma, during that desperate period, and his log book records that he not only flew Dakotas, but also Valentia K3613 on 18 March to 'recce a satellite landing strip known as "Old Angus".'

We also have anecdotal evidence of passengers being grateful for the presence of the old aircraft. Remember Bertie Mann from Frontier Wapiti days? He thought he'd escaped the 'flying pig', but he now had reason to eat his uncharitable words. We shall, therefore, give him the last say on the subject:

> 'Having been posted to 28 Squadron I subsequently fetched up in command after the Japs took Burma. But after a "Nip" shot me in the foot, I was evacuated from Rangoon, and then from Akyab to Calcutta – in a 31 Squadron Valentia!'

So Thirty One's glorious association with the Far Eastern theatre began in the chaos of a rearguard action being hastily and desperately mounted. The Burma campaign would be

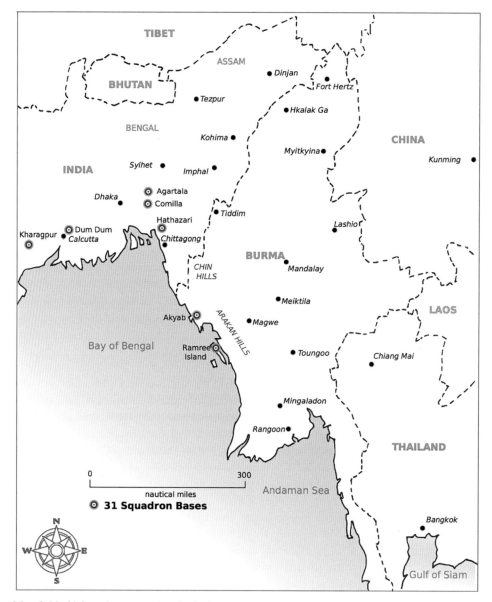

Map 3: No.31 Squadron operations in the Burma theatre, 1942–45.

complex, ebbing and flowing for three and a half years, so before we get down to detail, a couple of minutes outlining the strategic whole would be time well spent.

To many in the West the war in the Far East began on 7 December 1941, with that 'surprise' Japanese attack on the US Naval Base at Pearl Harbor, Hawaii. But the root of the problem went back much further. The Japanese had had designs on China for years, as long ago as 1931 annexing the province of Manchuria. The main line of Anglo-US support to the Chinese nationalists thereafter, especially following the Japanese military build-up in the western Pacific, was via the Burma Road, with Rangoon being the chief port of entry.

In 1940 Japan took advantage of France's weakness by occupying French Indo-China (Vietnam, Laos and Cambodia). Then in July 1941, following further acts of Japanese aggression, the US and Britain froze Japan's assets worldwide and placed an embargo on supplies of oil to Japan. Basil Liddell Hart, in his noted *History of the Second World War*, commented that 'In taking that last action it had always been recognized by the Allies that such a paralyzing stroke would force Japan to fight.' So from that moment on – still five months before the attack on Pearl Harbor – both Britain and America knew that the likely Japanese response would be military action. Hence, probably, that earlier British reinforcement, including the deployment of Nos.27 and 60 Squadrons by Thirty One's Valentias.

But the RAF build-up was constrained by demands in other theatres, leaving inadequate numbers and obsolete types available for the Far East. When the Japanese strike against the Americans eventually came it was accompanied by virtually unopposed military advances through Thailand towards Rangoon, as well as on the Malayan Peninsula. On 15 February 1942 Singapore fell, and by May the British had been chased out of Burma and into Assam. In passing, it's worth noting that Java and the rest of the Dutch East Indies – to which we shall return much later in this story – fell to the Japanese during the same period, fulfilling a further enemy aim of acquiring valuable oil production facilities.

For the next three years the timing of the land battles in Burma as the Allies attempted to recapture the country was governed by the annual monsoon period. There would be a pause each year from April onwards, with the fighting resuming in October.

But even when in static positions during the monsoon, the armies needed resupplying. With Burmese ports in enemy hands and the land option closed off, it was the air transport force which continued the year-round work during some truly awful weather conditions. Air supply to China also continued across the formidable 'Hump' of the eastern Himalayas throughout most of the period.

In December 1942 the British army made a push southwards through Burma's Arakan Hills, with a main aim being to regain airfields, both to shorten the supply line and to facilitate an attempt to gain air superiority. But this advance was rebuffed, once again leaving the Japanese in control of the whole of Burma and condemning the RAF to continuing its resupply operation from bases in eastern India.

Although probes were conducted by specialist infiltration units, the Chindits, into Japanese territory during February to April 1943, the Allied command intended its next major counter-attack to be during the dry season 1943–44. To this end they amassed forces beforehand, preparing airfields in Bengal and Assam from which to operate more modern types. But the Japanese forestalled this. Hitherto, their forward line had remained on the Chindwin River – not far off the Burmese-Indian boundary – a line sufficiently advanced to fulfil their aim of choking off the route to China. But now they crossed into India as far as Kohima and Imphal, which would become the scenes of epic and bloody battles.

The Japanese were successful in causing the postponement of the main British operation for a full year, but, after the 1944 monsoon, the Allied advance southwards at last commenced. The airfields at Akyab and Ramree were retaken in early 1945, permitting RAF aircraft to move forward again, and the Burma Road was reopened in

April, allowing land resupply once again to reach China. Rangoon fell to the Allies in July, its recapture more or less completing the eviction of Japanese forces.

Number 31 Squadron deployed to Burma in strength in February 1942. Despite the obsolescent equipment around them, they were now up and running with the DC-2, which was well suited to the massive task ahead. One of the original two airframes was quickly lost, destroyed on the ground at Mingaladon, but the Squadron as a whole was now working from Akyab on the Burmese coast. With its full complement of aircraft back from the Middle East, it got down to the job of evacuating forces from Burma during February and March. Things were chaotic, though, as J.H.Smith describes:

'I flew with Squadron Leader Burbury as his fitter. One day a DC-2 was u/s at Rangoon and I was sent with some spares. Burbury managed to get me a lift in an Indian Air Force Lysander. The pilot got lost between Toungoo and Rangoon, ran out of fuel and crashed. We never made Rangoon, which was taken by the Japs the same day. But we got back to Magwe and hitched a lift back to India on the last DC-2 out of Burma. On the way back my Indian pilot told me it was his second crash in two weeks, which explained why his foot was heavily bandaged!'

It was a tense time, with another adventure befalling a crew which included Les Sumption. Their goal had been Rangoon but they'd been unable to land as the Japanese were in the vicinity. On the way back, one of the engines developed a mag drop so it was decided that a landing on a known airstrip would be wise. But having got down they found that nobody was home – the British had retreated. The aircraft couldn't safely get airborne until the fault had been repaired. Looking around, Les came across a crashed Brewster Buffalo, still with its dead pilot nearby. As luck would have it the Buffalo had the same type of engine as the DC-2, so he stripped it of its magneto.

Meanwhile, the WOp had picked up a news item which indicated that the airstrip they were on had been captured by the Japanese. There was no enemy to be seen or heard, so the mag was fitted and the engine ground run. By this time it was too dark to take off, but the aircraft was taxied to the end of the strip in preparation for an emergency getaway should it be necessary. Not surprisingly they all spent a sleepless night. As soon as dawn broke they made a relieved escape.

With the rapid Japanese advance through Burma, Akyab quickly became untenable and Thirty One was compelled to fall back to RAF Dum Dum, Calcutta. Wing Commander Jenkins, the CO, continues the story:

'My first flight into Burma was on 25 February, to Magwe and Mingaladon on a recce. Mingaladon was at this time being attacked by Jap aircraft day and night. We operated initially into various dispersed landing grounds in the area – "John Haig", "Cascade" and "Highland Queen" – but after this we were mainly used on the run from Akyab to Magwe. We took a British battalion in and casualties and evacuees out.

'I later landed with Lummie Lord at Chittagong in a cross-wind. We swung and damaged our undercarriage on an anti-airborne-attack obstruction. Thanks to an American engineer with the China National Airways Corporation, who also had DC-2s, we got the aircraft patched up and back to Calcutta.'

Having withdrawn to India, the Squadron continued to be heavily involved flying supplies and reinforcements into Burma, to Shwebo and Mandalay in particular, returning with wounded soldiers. Each evening at dusk one aircraft landed at Akyab, now merely a forward staging post, until the port finally fell into Japanese hands.

All the aircraft were by this time in a very poor state. Because of the emergency and the acute shortage of transport aircraft in Burma, inspections had had to be skimped – a backlog building up because aircraft were flying six to ten hours each day. By the end of March, total strength on the Squadron was just eight DC-2s. They were all old machines; when Thirty One took them over the airframes had already accumulated between 8,000 and 17,000 flying hours, with engine usage varying between 2,000 and 10,000 hours each.

What with the lack of spares, too, it is remarkable that so many aircraft were kept operational. All credit must go to the ground crewmen (many of whom had to double up as aircrew) under Flight Sergeant Leeder. Jenkins confirms the type of measures necessary: 'One machine (AX755), flown by Flight Lieutenant K. F. Mackie, was lost on 13 April on one of the last Akyab night-stops when it ran into a bomb crater. The machine was a write-off, although the engines were salvaged'

Relief was at hand, for in April 1942 the first DC-3 arrived, and by the end of the month three were on strength. Thirty One, increasingly, was getting the aircraft it needed for the task.

Having already looked briefly at the origins of the DC-2, now is an opportune moment to tell a little more of the story of how the Douglas masterpiece developed. In the mid-1930s a larger and longer-range version had been demanded, which would permit the US to be routinely crossed in fifteen hours. This airframe, by 1936, was being produced in two versions: the DST (Douglas Sleeper Transport); and the twenty-one seat DC-3. The latter became the standard, with production eventually running to over 13,000, while a derivative with strengthened floor and a cargo door was procured by the military as the C-47. All versions in RAF service were known as 'Dakota', and typical performance on a tactical mission with a full load of 7,000 pounds was a radius of action of about 250 nm.

A further sub-division, commonly referred to by the Squadron's people, differentiated between 'Dakota III' and 'Dakota IV'. The 'III' was in fact the C-47A, while the 'IV' equated to the C-47B, the principal difference being that the IV's engines were fitted with two-speed superchargers, improving performance.

Thirty One is known to have operated at least nineteen DC-2s from April 1941 onwards, while upwards of ten DC-3s were on strength from April '42. Additionally there was a DST adapted to carry fourteen passengers, while the first of many C-47s arrived in June 1942. By the following year, the Squadron's complement comprised entirely C-47s.

It has been said that the name 'Dakota' was originally an acronym derived from *Douglas Aircraft KOmpany Transport Aircraft*. Maybe that's true. What is indisputable, however, is that the aircraft became an icon, with many examples continuing to fly well into the twenty-first century. US General – later President – Eisenhower neatly summed up its contribution by including the Dak as one of the primary elements in the winning of the Second World War. His list, variously reported, was commonly reckoned to have had as its top four the Jeep, the bazooka, the atom bomb and the C-47.

Much of that would be for the future, and Jenkins returns to the early days:

'On 27 April I took over the first DC-3 (LR233) from a US pilot at Delhi. The DC-3 carried twice the payload of the DC-2 and was the easier aircraft to fly. We now moved a detachment to Dinjan, a newly opened station on the Assam−Burma border, flying into Myitkyina to evacuate casualties. There was no mess and we were accommodated with tea planters in the area, which was very welcome. Number 5 Squadron, flying Mohawks, was also based a Dinjan. An

Gurkhas boarding.

attempt was made to provide us with fighter escort, but the Mohawks had poor instruments, and one went down after losing contact in cloud with the DC-2 it was escorting.'

Dinjan certainly wasn't popular with everybody. Austin Cullingworth was a corporal fitter who, joining Thirty One in early 1942, relates the tale of a flight to join the Dinjan detachment:

'After doing a thorough inspection of the DC-3, it being the first one I had ever worked on, we set off in G-George carrying spare DC-3 wheels and tyres plus five 31 Squadron ground crewmen. It was late evening when we landed, and the crew and passengers dispersed to their billets or to the cookhouse leaving me to check the DC-3 over. Having done this I grabbed my bedroll and walked to the accommodation. But being a complete stranger, I didn't know where Thirty One's billets were, nor where one went for a meal or to wash. So I put my bedroll on an empty *charpoy* on the veranda of the nearest billet and slept for about ten hours. When I awoke and went to the main runway I found G-George had disappeared and so had the rest of Thirty One.

'This is surely never going to go through that tiny opening!'

'Just about made it!'

'So I walked to where I could see aircraft in the distance. There was an American P-40E Tomahawk (Warhawk), but the crewman working on it didn't seem talkative – perhaps he was fed up with Dinjan too! It certainly was the most god-forsaken place I had ever seen. Then C-47s and C-46s began landing, and later some 31 Squadron Daks. Each taxied up to a large Red Cross bamboo *basha* where I helped move evacuees and wounded from the aircraft. We were kept busy all day, as each aircraft would be off again as soon as it had been refuelled. The next day I was flown to Tezpur, thankful for getting away from all the desolation of Dinjan.'

In fact the records tell us that 'G for George' was the Squadron's sole DST, so Cullingworth might have imagined himself bunking down on board amidst memories of the aircraft's more gracious times. It was destroyed not long after by a bomb attack.

Certainly, Dinjan had much of the atmosphere of a remote outpost, where almost anything could happen. Eric Brown remembers it being set amid tea plantations, which was pleasant. But he also comments:

'The intelligence and enemy warning system was practically non-existent. For instance one morning a yellow Verey light was fired to warn of possible air attack and, almost simultaneously, twelve aircraft landed on the strip, three of them crash landing. They turned out to be Republic P-43 Lancers of the Chinese Air Force en route to somewhere − and lost.'

Despite the desperate situation in Burma, the poor state of most of the Squadron's aircraft meant that Thirty One's main base had to be withdrawn to Lahore [see map 4] in June 1942. There, the DC-2s went in for complete overhaul. But Squadron Leader Burbury, commanding the remaining Dinjan detachment with three DC-3s and one DC-2, continued to operate at high pressure throughout the monsoon. Les Sumption, like many other groundcrew, continued to fly:

'In May I was off again on detachment to Dinjan on supply-dropping missions to British and Indian troops, and to refugees fleeing from the Japanese in the vicinity of Myitkyina. As was usual throughout the Burma campaign, fitters and riggers used to fly with their aircraft and perform the task of pushing the food, medical supplies etc., out of the aircraft over the dropping zones – usually just small clearings in the jungle. I clocked up some 500 flying hours on these missions, and although we were promised flying pay I don't remember ever receiving anything!'

There was certainly no doubt that the Squadron was well and truly in a shooting war. Les continues:

'Returning from a successful supply drop over Myitkyina we were cruising quite peacefully back to Dinjan. Suddenly, in the distance off our port quarter appeared two fighter aircraft, radial-engined monoplanes heading in our direction at a fair old lick. I thought this must be a couple of 5 Squadron Mohawks who occasionally escorted us. A bit late catching up with us, but a welcome sight nevertheless. I watched the gap diminish at an increasingly alarming rate – until it suddenly dawned on me that these bleeders were a couple of Zeros, which at a distance looked remarkably like Mohawks.

'I went up to the pilot, Pilot Officer Williams, who very smartly slung the good old Dak into a dive heading for a most convenient bank of cloud, hoping to lose the following Zeros. We did, for about five minutes, then either due to good anticipation by the enemy or due to sheer luck the Nips showed up again astern of us and catching up fast. All this time I stood by the opening where the door would be (we normally flew with them off for supply dropping) holding a Thompson machine-gun – our only armament. Quite what I intended to do with it I do not know. However, Williams found another cloud bank and this time, although losing a lot of height, and getting well off course, we finally lost the Nips.'

Always, seemingly, in the thick of the action, Les continues:

'About this time I was engaged in a night operation to rescue eleven British soldiers stranded on the Island of Akyab in the Bay of Bengal. The Japs were expected to take the island in a matter of days. Unfortunately my pilot got the runway mixed up in the dark and put us down in the middle of a bomb crater. The aircraft was a write off and we, the rescuers, were now in need of rescuing. The following day, Japanese bombers came over and gave us a real pasting, and as I was heading for a dugout alongside the runway I was very much aware that a Zero was chasing me at almost ground level, and bullets were kicking up the dust just a foot or so to my right. I made the dugout in double quick time! Eventually, two days and more air raids later, another 31 Squadron Dakota flew in at night, did a quick about turn, and got us all safely away.'

Mention of Zeros looking like friendly Mohawks prompts a word to the effect that those 'Zeros' were, in all probability, 'Oscars'. The two Japanese types looked similar and, whereas the Mitsubishi A6M Type Zero was a naval aircraft, the Nakajima KI-43 'Oscar' was land-based and operated by the Japanese army. In fact it was, indeed, often known as the 'Army Zero', so throughout the narrative the term 'Zeros' is left in quoted pieces. Both Zeros and Oscars were, needless to say, more than a match for the Dakotas.

Wednesday 6 May 1942 brought drama. Planned early operations were delayed because of poor weather. En-route forecasting during the campaign was always sketchy, so 'probe' aircraft were commonly launched to check the conditions. On this particular day Squadron Leader Burbury and Tiny Howell in LR231 'E' and Squadron Leaders Withers and Mackie in LR230 'D', took off to test the weather. This proved variable, but the next pair, David Lord and Sergeant Howser in LR233 'H' and Pilot Officers Williams and Coughlan in LR235 'J', were ordered to proceed.

As the first two landed at Myitkyina, near the Chinese border, enemy aircraft were heard overhead. It was thought the raiders were recce machines, so loading proceeded. But as Withers started his take-off run, a bomb fell in front of the aircraft destroying the port wing and causing his Dakota to swing and crash. Moments later a second bomb fell some five yards to the right side of Burbury's taxiing machine, shrapnel puncturing the wheel on that side. Other bombs exploded on the airfield, then Japanese Army Type 98 dive-bombers made a low-level strafing attack. The two Dakotas were rapidly abandoned. Wing Commander Jenkins, a passenger in 'E', scrambled out of the rear door carrying a wounded Indian soldier to a nearby bomb crater, while Burbury and Howell left by the pilots' hatch, Howell grabbing a Tommy-gun as he went. The bombers made several runs over the airfield, the last being extremely low. Howell opened up with his gun and appeared to hit one plane. It staggered away over the trees and was thought to have force-landed in a nearby river bed, but there was too much going on at the time for the Squadron to be able to gather evidence of the 'kill'.

Two women had been killed in 'E'; a child had also been killed, while two army doctors had been seriously injured and others had slight wounds. But the runway was still usable and, by now, the two other Dakotas had landed. While 'J' was being loaded, another alarm was given and 'H' immediately took-off. 'J' eventually left, piloted by Burbury and Williams, who took Howell and Flight Sergeant Cook with them. Jenkins, Mackie and Withers remained to organize affairs and clear the runway for the evening landing. Further enemy aircraft attacked during the afternoon and set the damaged 'E' ablaze. 'J' returned later, and all RAF personnel were flown out that evening by Howell and Williams. It is said that sixty-five passengers were crammed onto this flight – which was not bad for an aircraft designed to take twenty-four. Jenkins recalls this action:

> 'In the chaos of the attack I had armed myself with a Verey pistol – the only weapon available. The next day, a recce of Myitkyina reported Jap aircraft on the ground. The position of enemy land forces in north Burma being uncertain, we did no further flights to this airfield, but some supply drops on the route out to Assam continued until the middle of May.'

Wing Commander Jenkins left the Squadron that month, later receiving a DFC for his work with Thirty One. Bill Burbury who, along with Mackie, had collected a DFC for his part in the Myitkyina evacuation missions, now took command on promotion to wing commander, a most popular appointment. The aircraft count was now two DC-2s, ten DC-3s and four Lockheed 12As – a total of sixteen. Of these, five were grounded awaiting engines and spares, while five were still undergoing major inspections.

So the situation was still parlous, which perhaps explains the appearance of those Lockheeds on the list. Whether they were ever formally on the strength is not clear, but at any rate their attachment was brief. On 8 June, they left to form the Air HQ Communication Unit. Many of its personnel were drawn from Thirty One's C Flight, depleting the Squadron's strength by two officers and twenty airmen.

And in another reorganization later in 1942, Thirty One would sire a new squadron. Number 194 was formed at Lahore with one of Thirty One's flight commanders, Squadron Leader 'Fatty' Pearson, appointed as its first CO. This was initially a Lockheed Hudson unit, although subsequently converting to Dakotas. Before they did so they lost one of Thirty One's pilots; on 15 December at Tezpur, Flight Sergeant Foot, who was attached to No.194 training new crews, failed to return from a supply-drop mission. One member of the new unit was Flight Lieutenant Douglas 'Chota' Williams, who subsequently became chairman of the 194 Squadron Association. He recalls:

> '194 owed a great deal to 31 for its smooth introduction to supply dropping and the later conversion to Dakota aircraft. During the height of the Burma campaign a healthy rivalry developed between the two squadrons to the ultimate good of air supply. The only difference between 31 and 194 in my view was that, whereas 31 seemed to emanate the rigid atmosphere of the old Imperial Airways, 194 enjoyed a more relaxed attitude in its daily life.'

An interesting perspective! The author has never heard any other reports of Thirty One's war efforts being conducted in a particularly formal atmosphere – but we'll not trouble to challenge 194's viewpoint. However – and this might explain things – we can add that 194 became in time known as 'The Friendly Firm'.

The Japanese had now reached Lashio and cut the Burma Road. Then Mandalay fell and all hope of holding northern Burma was abandoned, following which the British army began its final withdrawal into India. The RAF had already air-lifted 8,616 people out of Burma, many being women and children. Of these, Thirty One had flown out some 4,000.

As well as airheads there were other groups and locations receiving supplies and support, including evacuation columns. One rather different drop was made from Dinjan, when Mike Vlasto and Sergeant Vic Lazell flew in LR234 to Hkalak Ga, dropping stores and packages each containing 500 rupees in silver currency. This money was to be used to gain co-operation from the locals in aiding a relief party led by a Polish officer who had established a receiving centre. Information was later passed from the army that 'the pilot who dropped money on 19 July did some good shooting – nine packets out of ten were collected, although they bounced hundreds of feet into the jungle.'

After Myitkyina fell to the enemy, the only base in Burma remaining in Allied hands was Fort Hertz in the far north, which maintained a small party of British personnel including some women. These people had retreated before the advance; now, without food, arms or spare clothing, they could only be helped by air. On 9 May the Squadron dropped supplies, and this support continued until 13 June when aircraft managed to get in and evacuate the remaining twenty-three people.

Fort Hertz was soon to have another use. The Americans were now making regular flights over the 'Hump' from north-east India into China. It was decided that the field should be developed into an emergency landing ground and outpost along this route. On 24 August the first of many such landings was made there by one of 31 Squadron's aircraft. By 10 September, 197 troops and airmen had been flown in, and thereafter this garrison was entirely dependent upon air supply carried in by the Squadron's Dinjan detachment.

Although those formidable runs were initially an American (civil, then USAAF) responsibility, Thirty One's crews also played a substantial part. Here, Max Taylor, an Australian WOp from Victoria, relays some vivid memories:

'Early in our second tour, George Hanson and I were detached to Dum Dum to facilitate regular access to Kunming, China. Terrain and weather in the region were rugged; on a good day, it was possible to get through the passes at 10,000ft, although the wreck of an American aircraft lay at the summit of one as a caution to those who might have been tempted to take liberties with the downdraughts on the lee side. When weather closed in it was necessary to push the Daks up to 18,000ft to be sure of clearing the mountains. Flying time in each direction was of the order of nine hours. The majority of those China runs were done by the Americans who, post-war, maintained their memories by forming the very active 'Hump Pilots Association'.

'Some of those trips were very rough; on one occasion we recorded a drift angle of 45°! On another, a wild-weather ride, we made it across, although no fewer than eleven American aircraft did not. Glimpsed one nearby – he had cut three of the motors and they were getting ready to jump. Luckily, on our twenty-two trips over the Hump, we were never faced with that fearsome prospect.

'Overnight in Kunming we would be accommodated at the British Embassy, sharing it with the staff of the resident "China watchers" who maintained our presence there. Quite a treat dining at the long refectory table with those learned gentlemen.'

'On one occasion, 19 March 1944, among our passengers was the noted war artist Feliks Topolski. He was British, although born in Poland, and was known for his sketches and murals, most notably his *Memoir of the Century* which was painted on viaduct arches on the south bank of the Thames. At the time he flew with the Squadron, he was en route to London, returning from a stint on the Russian front. He was kind enough to do a sketch for us.'

The Squadron had formed another detachment at Tezpur. Austin Cullingworth, who had been nicknamed 'Jeep' by his pals, says this of the place in the early days:

'On a fine day one caught a glimpse of the snow-covered Himalayan peaks in the distance. Conditions differed from Dinjan. As soon as a Dak landed it was taxied into a jungle clearing and unloaded. The lads had acquired machetes, others had Gurkha kukris. We would set to and chop long lengths of bamboo so as to prop them against the leading edges of the mainplanes. It was very hard stuff to cut, and due to the heat the leaves on the cut bamboo soon died, so it was often necessary to replace it. Sometimes camouflage netting was used as well. This business was considered essential, as Japanese recce aircraft paid frequent visits to the area.'

There was indeed always a chance of meeting Japanese aircraft, and the Tezpur detachment twice had aircraft chased by fighters in November. David Lord, now commissioned as a pilot officer and flying LR235, had an encounter with the opposition on 1 December, spotting a twin-engined aircraft and later being chased by a biplane. But Lord was able to outdistance the latter, no doubt grateful he was no longer flying the Valentia. Incidentally, it has been said that the Dak was the first of Thirty One's types to be faster than the Squadron's original BE2c!

Ten days later, Pilot Officer Smeaton and Sergeant Perry were heading for Palal with supplies when their Dakota was spotted by an enemy aircraft. Smeaton managed to escape, dropping his cargo over Tiddim instead.

The picture by Feliks Topolski as presented to Australian WOp Max Taylor. The caption reads 'To the Kunming-Calcutta crew.' Max is on the left; the others are Morris Green (nav) and Peter Salveson (pilot).

In June 1942 the first of the specialized military DC-3 derivatives arrived, MA928 and MA929 being flown from California by USAAF crews. In fact some sources, including Gordon Smeaton's log book, record these two aircraft as being C-53s (known to the USAAF as 'Skytrooper') rather than C-47s (the more common 'Skytrain'). Whilst the RAF received only a handful of the former, which were distinguished from C-47s by lacking floor reinforcement and the wide cargo door, it is known that a few did serve in India. At any rate, both variants could carry thirty fully-equipped troops, and now the Squadron was really into its stride.

But the machines were taking punishment from the conditions in which they operated, and quite often aircraft had to return to Dum Dum for spares and major repairs. These trips offered welcome relief from the jungle, and Cullingworth remembers one such, with pilot Flight Lieutenant Baugh and fitter Ken Carr:

'On landing we were driven into Calcutta, stopping on Chowringhee near to Dharamatola Street, but we were a spectacle! Our pilot in smart, clean khaki drill with peaked cap, Ken in KD shirt and slacks, brown suede shoes and no hat, and me in stained KD, sawn-off Betty Grable shorts, oil-stained shirt, battered pith helmet cocked at an angle over the left eye, short socks and Indian sandals. A determined-looking redcap sergeant spotted us but our pilot explained our operational position to him.

'It was hard to obtain spares through the usual channels but we had an arrangement with the China National Aviation Corporation (CNAC), who had a fleet of DC-3s flown mostly by Americans. Unlike Thirty One's aircraft, which were finished in a dirty olive colour, theirs were in beautiful polished metal.'

Trips to Dum Dum often seemed to have odd aspects. Benny Watts:

'I recall one time when Horace Welham and Les Sumption were sent to attend to a Dak which the crew had left there with an engine problem. Together they stripped the engine down. But, having no time to complete the rebuild that day, they went off to their digs in the city, leaving the engine parts laid out in replacing-order on a cloth under the aircraft. Returning next morning they began reassembly, but soon found that they were short of a connecting rod. They split up to ask for information of people seen near the aircraft overnight. On his round Horace spotted locals attempting to unblock a drain with the missing rod — and quickly dispossessed them. The two friends soon wiped the rod clean and refitted it. Being confident in their work, they of course insisted on flying on the air test and thence back to base.'

The shortage of spare parts and mention of CNAC prompts an explanation of that airline's position, also cueing a couple of tales of what might be termed 'two-and-a-halves'.

Until Pearl Harbor, the American position vis-à-vis Japan and China had officially been neutral. Although they actually favoured China, they preferred to exercise air-related assistance through the ostensibly civil medium of CNAC. But in reality the line dividing the airline's civil and military activities was blurred – and as we've already seen there was also a degree of co-operation between it and the RAF. Indeed CNAC had assisted with the British evacuation of Hong Kong when the colony had fallen.

At about that time Thirty One had created a hybrid aircraft, as described by George Parkinson, one of the Squadron's first Canadian WOp/AGs:

'I was on the crew when DC-2 DG477 was ferried on 24 January 1942 from Lahore to Bangalore for installation of larger, DC-3, engines. After weeks of delay we finally did the air test with Mike Vlasto at the controls. The port engine caught fire as soon as we left the runway so we circled back to land. The aircraft was eventually fixed and flown back to Lahore. It was fast, but was never liked. Then one day it was side-swiped there by a Hudson doing a ground loop. Mike subsequently commented that he was so happy to see the 'two-and-a-half' written off that he could have kissed the Hudson pilot!'

Not to be outdone, CNAC also improvised another 'two-and-a-half'. A bomb-damaged DC-3, urgently required for transport operations and needing a wing, was reported as receiving the available spare, a DC-2 wing. Despite the replacement being considerably shorter than the original, the hybrid flew adequately. An amazing example of make-do-and-mend, typical of the times, and undoubtedly a huge tribute to the Dakota's robustness. The report of this comes, by the way, from Zygmund Soldinski's *Wings Over Asia*.

It was hard to celebrate festive seasons in the traditional way while at war, but driver Eric Honeyman recalls the valiant lengths to which the boys went in 1942:

'As Christmas approached, we MT lads in Lahore decided to decorate an empty room at the barracks, and much time and effort was devoted to making it as gay as possible, my contribution being to paint the Squadron crest and greetings. We were a long way from home and, in determined effort to create a good party atmosphere, a well-stocked bar was set up with plenty of goodies such as nuts, apples, oranges, etc. In the afternoon I went to a little Indian whisky shop with a couple of friends – after we had partaken of our Christmas dinner. There we consumed ten tots of Indian whisky. I finally left because, as I remember, it was having no further effect on me! Not bad, I suppose, as I was not and still am not, a spirit drinker.

'Came the evening, and the long-awaited party got under way. I remember being there till about 7.30pm, consuming a variety of drink, feeling ill, staggering outside, giving vent to my feelings and then lying down for half an hour. I took two aspirins and woke up next morning feeling perfectly refreshed and healthy – which, judging by the groaning sounds of distress, was more than could be said for the rest of the MT section in my barrack room! Strangely, the hour I spent at that party is clearly etched in my mind, yet I can remember nothing whatever of the next three Christmases spent in the Far East.'

From the moment Burma fell, British commanders recognized that anything the army could achieve by way of counter-attack would be entirely dependent on air resupply. There were no ports available, and lines of communication in the country were so constrained by jungle and geography that any land resupply would be extremely difficult. Despite these handicaps, the British launched a limited offensive through the Arakan in December 1942, but without defensive air cover or naval support it had petered out by May '43. In the long term, the ability to resupply by air would be the defining difference between the Allied and Japanese forces in Burma, but this particular Arakan operation had come too early.

Still one of the very few transport units in the theatre, Thirty One's contribution continued to be prodigious; during February 1943, for example, they dropped almost 178 tons of supplies. That month they moved the main base briefly from Lahore to Palam. From there the Squadron continued to operate several detachments. One outstation was Agartala, which before long became the main base. Another was Dhubalia, in the middle of jungle seventy miles from Calcutta, and here the men initially lived in tents before being housed in a more permanent camp over two miles away.

One of the famed 'goolie chits' carried by aircrew on the north-west frontier.

This much later notice is from the Burma theatre.

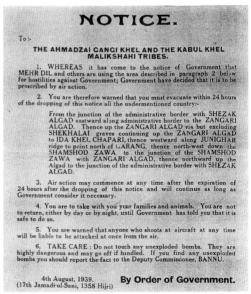

An example of leaflets which, from time to time, were dropped to pre-warn frontier villagers of imminent attack in a bid to encourage evacuation and lessen collateral damage.

Chapter 8

Two Years of Hard Graft

That same month, Thirty One began dropping supplies to Brigadier Wingate's 'Chindit' raiders who were on their epic first deep raid from Assam into the Japanese-held areas of Burma – Operation *Longcloth*. Les Sumption enlarges:

'Each Chindit column would have attached to it an RAF wireless operator. When the column commander had decided on a venue for a drop, usually nothing more than a clearing in the jungle, the wireless operator would radio our base with the column's requirements: food; medical supplies; arms and ammunition, etc. The loads were normally mixed. The free-fall items, such as sacks of rice etc, would be pushed out flying at tree-top height. Medical supplies, arms, etc needed a parachute drop, so we would go in at 600ft. The time over the dropping zone was usually about twenty minutes or so. On several occasions the operation had to be aborted due to enemy interference.'

And Squadron Leader Peter Bray had a similar story to tell at a location known as 'Blackpool'.

'The enemy had it under siege. We got in seven drops, the aircraft all over the place and bullets whistling past. Then through the windscreen in the pouring rain I could see smoke from shells exploding on the DZ itself. It was under attack; our chaps couldn't get out to the packs we'd dropped and there was a real chance the Japs would get them. That was always a risk with air drops – the white chutes were like a magnet to the enemy. So the ground controller sent up a red Verey light, terminating the drop. We didn't push our luck any further. It was throttles open, flaps up and back through the downpour to base – all in the pitch black, of course.'

Agartala was often the launching base for these missions. By early April 1943 the Chindits were on their way back from behind the Japanese lines, but still had a long way to go and much jungle to hack through. They were still in enemy-held territory when David Lord was flying one of their resupply sorties. He located them and made his drop, but saw the words 'PLANE LAND HERE' written on the ground in strips of parachute silk. Lord tried to get down but found it impossible owing to the small size of the jungle clearing.

Back at base, Lord told Burbury that a landing could be made if the Chindits marked out a runway over firm ground and cleared away further obstructions. Soon, the Squadron learned that there were a number of wounded and sick Chindits there, who were unable to walk out through the remaining 200 miles of jungle. They would simply have to be left behind, and their only hope was for Thirty One to pick them up.

A message was sent to the men on the ground, who hacked away vegetation, tested firm ground and, again using parachute silk, marked out a landing area. Two Dakotas

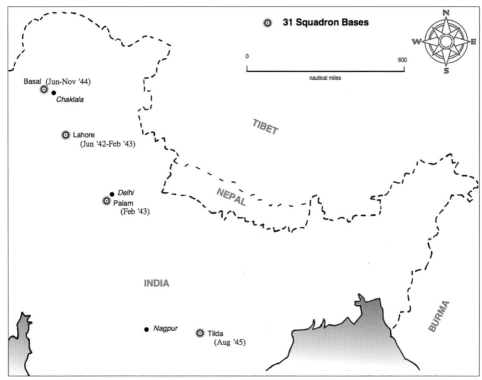

Map 4: No.31 Squadron Burma operations, rear bases, 1942–45.

took off to make the pick-up, being escorted by Mohawk fighters. It was anticipated that the Japanese might by now be aware of the Chindits' position. Not far from the strip, a radio message was received that the number of soldiers to be picked up was fewer than predicted, so one aircraft turned back.

The crew of the remaining Dak was Mike Vlasto (by now commissioned, and a flying officer), Sergeant Frank Murray from Jamaica as second pilot, Sergeant Jack Reeves, a Canadian WOp, and Sergeant Charles May, flight rigger. Reaching the clearing, Vlasto could see the message 'Land on white line. Ground there VG.' Circling, he first dropped his load of supplies, then came in for a landing. The strip was only 800 yards long, 400 shorter than he'd have liked, and a strong wind was blowing up the strip towards the tall teak forest edge.

'What about it?' asked Vlasto. 'Here's hoping,' said the co-pilot. 'Plane landing,' yelled Vlasto to the crew – and in he went. The Dakota touched the rough ground and Vlasto braked hard, pulling up right at the end of the strip. He was on the ground just twelve minutes, but long enough to take aboard seventeen wounded or sick Chindits. The remainder of this particular Chindit column finally reached Fort Hertz three weeks later to be flown back to India. It was a courageous piece of flying, duly recognized by the award of a DFC for the captain.

It's instructive and humbling to hear the story also from the ground side, and here's an account by Major Walter Scott, the Chindit column commander:

'On 22 April our last mule, which was carrying our large wireless set, collapsed and had to be shot. Before smashing and burying our wireless set we signalled airbase and arranged two supply drops. The first drop was to be on or just after 25 April; as we had not received a drop since 17 April when a Hudson dropped us rations for four days for each man, most people were by now out of food, other than some rice we had foraged.

'Spirits throughout the column were somewhat low, due in part because, prior to recrossing the Irrawaddy, we had had to leave behind two of our comrades, who were both seriously wounded and were unable to walk. They had been carried for many days on makeshift stretchers until finally they asked to be left in a Kachin village – the Kachins were very friendly and always helpful. They both knew that they were going to die, but did not want to die in the jungle. This occurrence cast a deep shadow over the whole column and brought home to us all the reality each one of us accepted. This we all dreaded, particularly the one to be left behind but secondly by the one who had to make the final decision. I had never felt so alone and depressed, even knowing that those concerned could never survive the arduous journey back to friendly territory.

'I knew in my heart that there were twelve to fifteen men with us who would never survive the long and arduous journey to the Chindwin and beyond. So when the head of the column walked out onto a vast open area, there was a desperate hope that, in spite of having no wireless set, the dream of air rescue could well become a reality. It was this hope that inspired our attempt at signwriting. And 'PLANE LAND HERE NOW' was the request that 31 Squadron so nobly answered.

'This air rescue undoubtedly pioneered the air evacuation of wounded and sick from deep inside Burma during our second Chindit campaign in 1944. It also set the pattern for all future campaigns. Before General Wingate left for Quebec and the Allied conference there, he told me that the air rescue carried out by 31 Squadron was an acorn, and that one day I would see the oak tree. He kept his word, and from then onwards air recovery of the sick and wounded took place during all subsequent campaigns in south-east Asia.

'The inspired attempts of Lummie Lord and his crew and the final magnificent effort of Mike Vlasto and his crew set the seal on the outstanding performance of 31 Squadron, who throughout our campaign supplied all our needs. Even beyond the Irrawaddy, in terrible weather and flying conditions. At times we gave

On a supply dropping mission, Lord ventures back from the flight deck to the apparent chaos of the fuselage. After leaving 31 Squadron, he would win a posthumous VC at Arnhem.

the Squadron some frightful dropping areas, varying from mountain tops to deep valleys and river banks. But they always met our requests. I remember one of my corporals said "Thank God for the RAF", and as the Dakota disappeared back towards the west, another of my lads said "Yes, but in a couple of hours those so and so's will be able to have a cold shower and a hot meal!" But they more than earned it. I only hope that someday I can thank them.'

It was Lord who initially spotted the Chindit patrol's desperate plea for help 'Plane Land Here'.

While there were many tales of bravery in the air, we mustn't forget those on the ground. In March 1943 a refuelling truck containing 800 gallons of petrol caught fire, threatening the whole fuel dump. Corporal Norman Bowers was on hand and backed a fire tender to the blazing vehicle before towing it 50 yards to safety away from the dump. He also got the driver and an assistant, both burned, to hospital and removed petrol drums, with the help of some Indian workers, to a safe distance. For his actions he received a command mention from the AOC-in-C India.

Talk of injury prompts a comment that, despite the conditions in which both air and ground crews had to live and work, the health of the men was generally reckoned to be good apart from dysentery and minor

But it was Mike Vlasto, another long-serving stalwart, who won a DFC for making the subsequent rescue.

complaints such as prickly heat. At least we, at some distance from the event, may categorize prickly heat as a 'minor complaint'. But of course those who lived with it found it an on-going hell. Corporal Horace Welham was a fitter on the Squadron, often flying as a cargo dispatcher as well. On one occasion he went sick with prickly heat and went to the medical officer (MO). When he explained his ailment, the doc lifted his own shirt and showed Horace his version of the ubiquitous problem. His only comment was to ask Horace, if he found a cure, to come and let him know!

That would accord with the recollections of many ex-servicemen, who well know that military MOs were seldom chosen for their bed side manner. J. H. Smith confirms this with a story:

'There was an airman at Agartala who said he'd been bitten by a snake. He ran all the way to the sick bay, where the MO simply said he shouldn't worry because if he'd run all that way with poison inside him he'd have been dead by now!'

Despite the hazards and discomforts, the snakes and the scorpions, Thirty One's personnel continued to make the best of their jungle existence. Corporal Ron Hanscombe, an electrician, recalls a story or two of his period with the Squadron:

'We had a u/s aircraft at Palal, which at the time was under siege from the Japs. Personnel were sleeping on the strip as the enemy were constantly making raids on the domestic camp, killing many people. Gurkhas were brought in to cope with this, which they did most excellently, bringing in many ears as proof of their prowess. Under these conditions, Lawrie Wynn from our electrical section was sent out. He effected a repair on the strip under mortar fire, but was astonished at seeing his aircrew running up and down with a rugby ball practising passes – and dodging the mortar shells. Must have been 'King' Levin, 'Pappy' Reeves and the others from their crew. Pappy, as I remember, had a mynah bird without whom he would not set foot in his aircraft. He would rush into the mess kitchen before a flight for some porridge for his good-luck pet!'

Sport was, rightly, one of the main off-duty diversions, a distraction from the daily round, the heat, the monsoon, the ants and the dysentery. The rugby players, including the aforementioned Sergeant 'King' Levin, a staunch South African and a devoted fan of the Springboks, could put out a quite presentable team. But there was always a call for more players – as Taff Mills, a ground wireless operator, noted the day he joined the Squadron:

'An airman came into the billet and asked "Is there a Welshman just joined the Squadron?" I admitted I was that man, and he said "Then I want you to play rugby!" And I did: on a nice grass pitch at Kharagpur; on solid concrete at Chaklala; and in inches of water at Ramree.'

And the footballers weren't to be outdone. When 31 Squadron played 36 Squadron in Krishnada, the local inhabitants turned out in force to watch. Football newcomers were also vetted on arrival for their sporting prowess, as Benny Watts recalls:

'On arrival I was met at the guardroom by Bert Thomas. The first question was "Do you play football?" I was not deemed good enough for the Squadron team, but always played in later days for B Flight.'

Local leisure activities were vital. During those long overseas stints – four years in many cases – the occasional and much-needed rest sometimes took the form of being sent up into the mountains for a week or two, just as had been the case during Frontier days.

Trips like these led, on occasions, to great things. Flying Officer John 'Jacko' Jackson was a WOp/AG who served a little later on the Squadron. Following 500 hours of operational flying he took his two weeks R&R climbing in Kashmir with Len Ayres and Bobby Finberg. There, he says:

'I first looked into the great Himalaya range. North of me, line after line of snow-covered peaks stretched far away. I was reminded that, in a few days, I would once again be flying over the Chin Hills of Burma. Even those jungle-clad hills stirred my mind in similar fashion. Both areas were, perhaps, places where man had never trod, and for me there was a strong pull to the heart; I longed to trek them. That was the effect of seeing the Himalaya for the first time, and I knew immediately I must return.'

And return Jacko did. At the end of his tour he was posted to the RAF aircrew mountaineering centre in the foothills, a unit whose mission was to get aircrew fit physically and mentally, and also to prepare glider and para troops for particular missions. He eventually became the chief instructor there, opening up a life of serious climbing. Indeed he was a reserve in 1953 for the team which made the first-ever ascent of Mount Everest and, in 1954, led a *Daily Mail* expedition in search of the Yeti – the 'abominable snowman'. We have no record of his finding it! But in 1955 came his own personal 'high' when he was a member of the team that reached the third highest spot on earth, the 28,205ft peak Kangchenjunga.

Mention has been made of Gurkhas, and Squadron members saw much of these doughty fighters in Burma. So much so that many Thirty Oners would retain a life-long connection with and affection for the Nepalese. Indeed Squadron Association members, for many years, contributed substantially to Gurkha welfare funds. Flight Lieutenant Allan Coggon, a Canadian pilot who later recorded a good deal of his wartime experiences in the form of memoirs, had this to say on the topic of Gurkhas:

'If there was one thing the Japanese feared far above anything else it was a silent, night attack by Gurkhas, those fearsome, kukri-wielding warriors. I was once briefed for a drop of some of 254 Gurkha Parachute Brigade. As I recall, it was to support one of the Wingate-type columns. I had twenty of them on board, plus their subadar-major, and we had a bumpy ride in rain and clouds. I left the cockpit and went aft to see how my passengers were doing, and was surprised and assured to see them acting like well-seasoned flyers. They were cheerfully knitting socks for themselves, these not being an issued item. I asked what operational experience the group had, learning that this was their third operational drop. A short time later we received a recall by radio, and I set about organizing that.

'Later, when I returned to the cabin, I expected to see an even happier group. They most certainly were not! The officer explained: "Ah yes, saah … you see, saah," he revealed, "it's because we have never landed in an airplane before, saah!"'

'On another occasion I feared a court martial. After landing at Toungoo I was asked to take back some patients to hospital. A medical sergeant held out a folded paper that I grabbed and stuck in my waist-band as we hastily climbed on board. As I made my way to the cockpit through and around the patients I noted that they were a doleful-looking lot, more like refugees than fighting men. By their appearance they were all Asian, their clothes in tatters, devoid of any military identity, not even a hat or cap.

'As I was taxiing in after landing I happened to notice something tucked in the waist of my shorts. Curious, I extracted a soggy piece of paper, wet from sweat. It was my manifest. As I noted the content, fear struck my guts. I knew I was in trouble. I should have asked about the passengers, or read the manifest before leaving Toungoo.

'I had departed without a guard, we had twelve POWs on board; four Japs and eight JIFs (Indian National Army, supporting the Japs), plus five Gurkhas. Quickly

I told Jerry to take over. Immediately I opened the door I could see my fears were justified. Just the five Gurkhas were there, looking up at me, smoking. I asked: "*kishnay* (where) Jap? – *kishnay* JIF?" They just stared at me. I angrily repeated the question. Two of them, with innocent gesticulations, replied: "*Nay mallum sahib.*" (I don't know what you are talking about) The devils had tossed them all out!

'I was responsible for the loss of twelve prisoners. Immediately there would be hell to pay, at least on the surface. The army would be upset because they wouldn't have the opportunity to interrogate them. For several days I worried. But I heard no more about it.'

With US forces entering the war zone, new problems emerged, the most significant of which was that there were instances of Americans attacking British aircraft, apparently mistaking the red in the latter's national markings for the Japanese 'rising sun'. The solution arrived at was the adoption of revised colours for RAF machines in the area – a blue outer roundel with either a white (initially) or very pale blue centre. Unsurprisingly, Squadron troops took a somewhat jaundiced view of this, asking 'who was here first, us or the Yanks?' But nevertheless the problem was real, and revised roundels were applied.

Other developments consequent on the new, joint operations included the formation, in 1942/3, of an Anglo-American organization known as 'Troop Carrier Command' – at the head of which was an American general. Then, around the turn of the years 1943/4, 'South East Asia Command' – SEAC – was formed. Despite the perceptions of the men in the jungle airstrips, the Allies were indeed working together.

Nineteen forty-three's monsoon was felt in earnest in mid-year, reducing to some extent the Squadron's flying activities. But only by a little, for there were still army units in the jungle which needed resupplying. So, monsoon or not, the Dakotas still had to be got into the air, sometimes in the most fearsome weather. Wyndham Dark, who had started the war on Thirty One as groundcrew but had later returned to India as a pilot, tells a hair-raising story of one such flight:

'We were a crew minus a co-pilot that set course for base. The weather at the height of the monsoon was atrocious, but I spotted a break in the clouds and spiralled down from our cruising altitude of 12,000ft to about 1,000ft above sea level before proceeding towards Akyab. Over Hunters Bay we were in radio contact with base, who warned us to stand off because of a violent storm overhead. This we did until they called to say that conditions had eased, at which point we set course for base. But the storm now lay between Hunters Bay and Akyab, so we remained below cloud. Rain formed a curtain of water under the storm, and suddenly the airspeed disappeared, with the needle on the zero stop. At the same time the vertical speed increased to max climb, and the altimeter started winding upwards. At 12,000ft the aircraft rolled inverted and spun; needle and ball were max over, my head was on the ceiling, and the crew were hanging from their seat belts. Now plummeting downwards, the speed increased to 270kts – although much of this must have been from the updraught. I recovered the situation, although almost immediately a zero-speed climb to 13,000ft recommenced, followed by a further spin. After three full sequences, I was becoming a bit nonplussed as to what to do – so I lowered the wheels and flaps. This action did them no good at all, but nevertheless we came out of the storm at about 1,000ft, between the 1,500ft hills of the Baronga Isles, about thirty miles from Hunters Bay. "Climb, you'll kill us all," shouted the nav. I didn't want to put any more strain on the Dak, and certainly didn't want to go back into the cloud. Hence my response: "If we've lived through that lot, we'll live through anything." Shortly afterwards, we landed.

'Seeing the state of the aircraft, I was struck dumb. I recall lighting a cigarette and sitting down in the pouring rain. My flight commander came along; "What's wrong with you – get up you bloody fool!" I pointed to the remains of KN227 and I will not repeat his remarks. Windows out, strips torn off the fuselage, tailplane twisted, wing fillets gone, etc, etc. I have subsequently read so many tributes to the Dakota, but my own experience is enough for me. After the storm and the condition it was in, it should not have flown another mile.'

In commenting on the monsoon, one Thirty Oner described it like this: 'Before you could run three yards it was as if someone had emptied a swimming pool on you!'

The violent turbulence when flying was incessant; drenching rain and mud made ground operations a misery. And there was worse; in June 1943, LAC Harry 'Butch' Crutch, an instrument specialist, was at Tezpur. On this particular day he was awaiting a weather report before an aircraft was due to take-off for Dinjan. Low, black clouds, right down in the valleys and on the hills, were scudding by. Suddenly there was a tremendous clap of thunder and Butch was struck by lightning. It flung him into the air, and he landed heavily on a concrete area, concussed. Blood was trickling from his nose and ears, and those about him thought he was gone. However, he was alive, and an American medical aide drove up and gave him an injection of digitalis. Several hours later he woke up in an Indian field hospital, where he reportedly heard a voice say, 'OK son, you're all right, you've been hit by lightning,' whereupon Butch rapidly passed out again!

It was a mystery that he had no visible injuries and it was decided that he was saved because he had been wearing gum-boots. He was kept perfectly flat, with his head between two sandbags and was then given a soft mattress, a fact which did not go down too well with other patients, all army types. Butch eventually rejoined the Squadron several months later, although he was far from fully fit. For some time he suffered from deafness, and if he looked up the world would spin and he would fall down, but at least he had survived.

The Squadron's base at Agartala was east of the Ganges delta and close to the operational area. And now at last they had a full complement of aircraft. In August, the ground crews managed to provide an average of over eleven aircraft per day. But a recurring problem was still that new Dakotas were often received minus the aircraft's toolkits – which had mysteriously disappeared en route. So Thirty One's stock of American tools was low. With this, and considering the often primitive conditions in which work was carried out, plus the monsoon, the serviceability rate was very creditable. One who could take much of the credit was Pilot Officer Leeder, the former flight sergeant having been commissioned.

Continuing the statistical theme, in September 1943 the tonnage dropped was 468 in 182 sorties – roughly 1,000 flying hours. The effort was now mostly in support of the new campaigning season, drops going down on Fort Hertz and in the Chin Hills. But the daily round in the Far East with 31 Squadron was never routine. Two incidents are recalled by J. H. Smith:

'During a Jap raid on Agartala we were out at the aircraft dispersal point when a bomb dropped very close, so we flung ourselves on the ground. I was in the bottom of a ditch; in a moment there was a squeal and I found myself on top of the pile as people had worked under me. The next minute a petrol bowser blew up.

'We were detailed one night to ground-run a u/s aircraft ready for early morning supply drops. An army officer arrived in his Jeep and told us a tiger had been reported on the prowl. Being very brave boys on Thirty One, we slept most of the night in the aircraft!'

Dakota 'W', FD791, out of Agartala on 7 October and en route to Tiddim, encountered a Japanese aircraft, but Flight Sergeant Murray and Sergeant McGreevy managed to shake it off. FD793, though, didn't have the same luck; Warrant Officer Colin Lynch, a navigator, tells its sad story:

'For months Tiddim had seemed the only place to visit – from June to September I flew eighty-seven sorties there, including three on each of the first three days of July. All these were supply drops, mainly without serious incident. I remember that over this period the crew felt as if we were just flying to "the office" each day; any strain seemed to be from the monotony of the daily routine.

'For the supply drops there were bags of grain, para packs of rations, rolls of barbed wire, ammunition, grenades, primers, toilet rolls – the mind boggled on occasions. And let's not forget the landings behind enemy lines with Jeeps, mules, troops, special forces and heavy weapons. Leaflet runs and evacuations – if lucky the odd mail run. But we didn't need too many days like the fateful 28 November.

'On that date we took off at 7.20am and headed off yet again. Once in the drop circuit we noticed that the only other aircraft on the circuit was a Dakota flown by Flight Sergeant Richards and crew.

'We lined up behind him as he approached the DZ. Suddenly we heard a series of cracks and recognized them to be anti-aircraft fire – simultaneously three Japanese dive bombers escorted by four fighters attacked their target – our DZ. Before we could blink, three of the fighters peeled away, banking into the classic line astern position and opening fire on us from behind. We heard repeated bursts of fire, and bullets shot past our aircraft on both sides – but not one hit us! The three Jap fighters flashed past and we then saw that Richards's aircraft, directly ahead of us, had been hit. All this seemed to be happening in slow motion. The other aircraft burst into flames and veered out of control across the valley of the Manipur.

'Simultaneously we banked down low towards the river in an attempt to lose the fighters. As we did so we saw Richards's aircraft hit the cliff across the river and blow up. We flew as low over the river as we dared in our attempts to evade the fighters. When test firing our VGO machine guns, one jammed, and I spent a few minutes clearing the jam after removing eight bent rounds from the action. I then fired another testing burst, the result of which was the plane behaving very violently. Rushing into the cabin I discovered that Flying Officer Larsen had thought the burst I'd fired meant we were being attacked again and had taken evasive action!

'That night took on a strange silence in our *basha* because Richards's bed lay empty and his cheerful Scottish voice was no more. For the first few days after the crash we had Hurricane escorts. Then it was back to normal.'

Richards's second pilot was Flying Officer Hopkins, with Sergeant McKee the navigator and Warrant Officer Low and Sergeant Yates the two WOp/AGs. Together they comprised what was, as far as is known, 31 Squadron's only all-Scottish Dakota crew.

It's easy to understand how melancholy the atmosphere was in camp when crews didn't return. Flight Lieutenant Arthur Delaney, a New Zealand pilot who spent eighteen months with the Squadron, remembers one particular aspect: 'the auctions of the belongings of killed crews, and the high bidding by some who had owed money to those who did not return.'

Warrant Officer Duncan MacLean joined the Squadron in September 1943 for a tour as WOp/AG that lasted fourteen months. He was introduced relatively gently, as Thirty One tried to do with all newcomers, with routine shuttles:

'At first I went onto flying the mail runs from Dum Dum, flying almost all the trips with Squadron Leader Bray. In December I was sent to Agartala for supply dropping, and now I was on Squadron Leader Honeyman's crew. As he was often busy with paperwork, I was the first person he thought of when another crew was short, so I flew with almost all the pilots on the Squadron. Some I try not to remember!

'Once, when taking off with Honeyman from Agartala, he gave the wheels up sign to the navigator, Flight Lieutenant Brockbank, who unlocked and whipped up the lever. The cabin immediately filled with smoke. He got such a shock, thinking he had done something wrong, that he instantly rammed the lever down again, locking the wheels in the down position. It is just as well he did, as it was not smoke but hydraulic oil. A pipe had burst. Since we were fully loaded and had no flaps available, we flew up and down the edge of the runway, dumping three tons of supplies out. You can imagine the army dispatch team boys were not amused when they had to pick it all up and reload another aircraft.'

Those dispatch teams, mostly Royal Army Service Corps people, were perhaps the most unsung of the heroes, seldom getting a mention. What a job they did, though, in the most appalling of conditions – up to their knees in glutinous mud at primitive airfields, ensuring that the requested loads were placed, in correct dropping order, in each of the aircraft. Back-breaking work – a Jeep plus a towed howitzer might have to be man-handled in through the fuselage door. It's quite remarkable in the circumstances that, by and large, the right loads were delivered to each DZ. The unseen work put in by those teams contributed hugely to the respect developed by the troops in the jungle for the Squadron – a respect which grew throughout the campaign.

Japanese bombers made one of their rare offensive appearances in December 1943 when ten aircraft raided Thirty One's base, destroying the instrument section and all its tools. But the Squadron closed the year by chalking up another supply-dropping record, a total of 901 tons going down on the various DZs. Average serviceability was now thirteen out of eighteen Dakotas, and the Squadron had gained much experience and expertise over the year. The war still had far to go, but Thirty One, now more than ever, was ready to face new tasks and overcome continued hardships.

A few days into 1944, however, FD802 was reported by the army to have come down. There were survivors, some injured. Then the No.221 Group mail run from Kharagpur to Calcutta for 28 January, FD811, crashed only minutes after take off. Flying Officer Tom 'Chota' Townley, plus his crew of Warrant Officer Thompson, Flight Sergeant Wallis and Aircraftman Miles, all died. Other Thirty One personnel flying as passengers were Flying Officer Beswick (nav), Flight Sergeant Knight (WOp/AG), Corporal Parry (WOp), plus four Americans.

The Squadron had been based at Kharagpur for a spell in the second half of 1943 but was now back on familiar territory at Agartala. 'Jeep' Cullingworth recalls life there in 1944:

'Under 'Chiefie' Leeder, the Squadron workshop constructed a marvellous tea-brewing and boiling machine – from 40 gallon drums, pipes and valves, plus much welding and brazing. The contraption provided tea and also hard-boiled eggs for sandwiches.

'There was also nature study for those interested. In the nearby jungle one could hear but seldom see the golden oriel, with its marvellous voice, bamboo beetles, so called because of the colour of their wings, also beautiful crimson and black swallow-tailed butterflies. Several kinds of lizard, the most common being iguanas, could also be seen. Local people would bring large turtles to the village in their canoes to sell at the market. These were "snappers", so called because they could bite through a half-inch thick branch with little trouble.'

Taff Mills also saw the good side of Agartala:

'There were all sorts of strange plants over the camp. At one time I even had pineapples strung up on the walls of our billet. Much better to suck a slice of one of those than drink the usual chlorinated water.'

And Colin Lynch ventured to explore the local night spots:

'The village of Singabil was a longish walk from Agartala. We had heard rumours about "entertainment" there, so one afternoon a group of us trudged off to see what was on offer. There was a single street with a few bamboo huts on stilts. Oh, and a Chinese cafe – sort of! Also, near the water's edge, a blacksmith and boatyards. Several of us occasionally used to walk there for a local breakfast or the Chinese-style duck-egg omelettes with trimmings. Maybe also a boat ride for a fishing trip. The blacksmith was a dab hand at making swords and knives out of suspension leaf springs of old lorries. I could not resist getting him to make me an oversized, customized kukri with scabbard. As for the "entertainment", we dared not stay late enough to find out, for the street took on a "dodgy" atmosphere after dark. You know what I mean?!'

Most of all, it was 'Jacko' Jackson who always saw camp life in a positive light. Some viewed snakes and the other assorted creepy-crawlies as simply pests to be killed, but Jacko was a great man for the beauty of nature – for the flora, the fauna, the scenery – finding fascination even in the 'pesky termites'. Here he describes an early 1944 flight to an isolated DZ far into Burma on Operation *Phylis*. This was deep into enemy-held territory, dropping supplies to small, intelligence-gathering patrols of locally trained people led by British officers who had previously served with the Burmese forestry commission. Once settled in the cruise back home following the drop, Jacko had time to record his unique take on the scenery:

> 'By now, down in the dark and deep-cut valleys it was already night, but at 12,000ft the sun still shone, lighting up the clouds that, in this cooler part of the day, were forming along the ridges of the mountains. Katabatic air currents caused their silvered surfaces to curve and flow into huge, greying streamers of mist like gigantic waterfalls, their veils of spray pouring down into the jungle. Over in the east the sky was darkening to a deep Prussian blue with a base of yellow greens and lilacs, whilst in the west the sun sank to the horizon, changing from gold to a blood-red orb, rapidly being consumed by the devouring earth. At first the propellers and wing leading edges held a glint of burnished copper, followed by a fiery red that was finally quenched. Very high cirrus clouds still caught the sun, whilst inside the aircraft a blue fluorescent glow from the instruments provided small pools of light. Following the burst of furious activity over the DZ some fifteen minutes previously, we all worked quietly now, content with the success of the mission – pleased that, in the Burmese jungle, men would be cooking nourishing meals over tiny fires because of what we had done.'

One never knew with whom one would be sharing the jungle, for as Jacko reported later, that particular day was to contain yet more interest:

> 'On return to Agartala it turned out not to be the end of "just one more day" on the Squadron. As we left the briefing room to return to the *basha*, we could hear the beat of drums so loud and insistent it broke through the ever-present cacophony of cicadas, mosquitoes, and the many other sounds of Indian night life. It reminded me of Kenya, and the drums beating across the east African veldt. We went exploring, and it turned out that the 81st West African Division had arrived while we were airborne and were now camped little more than quarter of a mile from the Squadron huts and cookhouse. Though so late, they were now relaxing before turning into their bed tents, and were clearly pleased that we had gone over to meet them. From there on, we and the 81st had many evenings together sitting around camp fires and listening to the drums. They eventually left Agartala early in 1944 to go down to the Arakan forward area. When we saw them again it was from the air. We dropped supplies to help them break out of the Japanese ring during the Battle of the Arakan. Those were really satisfying operations, for they obviously knew who we were and waved back enthusiastically when we waggled our wings at the end of each drop. But all that was in the future. On that first night, we – the crew of FD823 – returned to our *basha*s happy with the meeting and merry on their generous offerings of army-issue rum. My last thought before sleep was that it had been a full and varied day – and a good one.'

'Hump' runs were still continuing, and Mike Vlasto puts some more flesh on the bones of those extraordinary missions:

'After I'd done about 1,000 hours with Thirty One I was sent for training on the 'Hump'. I flew a dozen return trips with CNAC pilots, who were mainly Americans; they seemed to us at that time grossly overpaid, but they didn't seem to have any trouble in getting rid of it! I flew mostly with Captain Robertson, who had been a stunt man before the war. He chewed tobacco, which he spat out of the window, so that the port tailplane of his aircraft was stained red. Flying with these old sweats, after a very sound training with the RAF, prepared me well for flying the Hump.

'At about the same time the USAAF was starting intensive flights into China, and the CNAC pilots were amused by their countrymen's excited chatter over the R/T. They had a poor opinion of their military cousins' training for that sort of flying, and their fears were somewhat borne out by the USAAF's rather heavy losses.

'I started regular Hump crossings in August 1943 with a New Zealand co-pilot, Flying Officer King. The early radio beacons and controls were installed by CNAC, and these were considerably supplemented by ATC, who now had a massive flow of traffic over the Hump. Our call-signs were pre-fixed "Limey", and that stuck even when our initial one flight per week went up to daily at one stage.

'Shortage of petrol in Kunming made it necessary to leave India with enough fuel to get back. On one return we encountered a head-wind that reduced our ground-speed to 82mph and we had to land and top up at the American base at Yunnanyi.

'I was posted away from 31 Squadron after two years and nine months, but put in about a hundred Hump crossings all told – first with 31 and then with 353 and 52 Squadrons. We suffered the loss of only one aircraft and crew – Flight Sergeant Collard (an ex-London policeman), who disappeared without trace. He might well have encountered a Zero, although fortunately the Japs were hard-pressed elsewhere and could not spare many for our front.

'A special thank you goes to our excellent ground crews who kept the aircraft in first class condition, often under difficult circumstances. I never had an engine stop involuntarily, though one did behave strangely after a bird had started to build a nest in its air intake. On another trip I arrived at our aircraft in Kunming to find one elevator up and the other down – a C-46 had got stuck in the mud behind us and its slipstream had done the damage. The passengers were quite peeved when I told them that they would have to wait a bit. The Yanks repaired the damage very quickly and off we flew: but on return to Kharagpur our riggers were horrified to find the control cables were crossed twice, so that, although the elevators worked in the right sense, the cables were frayed and had to be replaced.

'There was a fair-sized British colony in Kunming, mainly with the military mission or the ministry of economic warfare. Most of them had stills dripping away in their bathrooms and they were extremely hospitable, so that one sometimes arrived for take-off with rather a sore head, but a few good draughts of oxygen usually put this right!'

Vlasto referred, by the way, to enemy fighter opposition being no more than occasional. But earlier, it was known for Oscars operating from Myitkyina to trouble aircraft on the Hump runs.

Chapter 9

Pitched Battle

The year 1944 started at a furious pace. British army units were creeping down on the Arakan once again in preparation for a new offensive. On 4 February, however, the Japanese pre-empted them with their own attack. Three days later, Japanese troops overwhelmed the British divisional HQ, the commanding general managing to escape to join administrative troops positioned in a narrow defensive area at Sinzweya which became known as the 'admin box'. This had a difficult DZ, measuring only 200 yards by 60 yards, surrounded on all sides by enemy forces.

Number 31 Squadron flew ten sorties on 8 February, three to Tabual and seven over the Arakan. They had dropped about half of their cargoes over the 'box' when six to eight enemy fighters came on the scene. One got onto the tail of Flight Sergeant Jackson's Dak, FL556. He took evasive action as directed by his gunner, but then the Japanese aircraft appeared to be hit by ground fire, dived into the jungle and exploded. Hawker Hurricanes came to the rescue, although Flight Sergeant Odlin, the captain of FL574, saw a Hurricane fall in flames and crash after being engaged by two Japanese. The Hurricanes claimed one enemy fighter destroyed with four more damaged.

Flight Lieutenant Walker, a Canadian, was last seen flying north in his Dak with a fighter on his tail, and failed to get home. Johnnie Walker's crew was Warrant Officer Young, Flying Officer Baptie (nav), Flying Officer Gould (WOp/AG), and Flight Sergeant Smethurst (WOp/AG). But the good news was that Nat Gould survived the crash, and 'walked back' through enemy lines. Then Flying Officer Larsen's Dak, heading low towards base, was hit by AA fire from a 'friendly' MT park. Luckily nobody was hurt.

It was a truly vicious battle, although we can't leave it without mentioning a possible success for the Squadron's air gunners. Jacko Jackson tells the story:

> 'Oddly enough there were two Flight Sergeant Jackos on board FL556 that day. I was known as 'mark 2' while my pilot, a New Zealander, was 'mark 1'. Anyway, the AA gunners and the fighter escorts reported that I had shot down one of the Zeros. I myself believed that the AA had done the job, and said so in my report.'

Given that Dakota airborne 'kills' were as rare as hens' teeth, it seems a shame that Jacko was so modest. Anyway, the next day sixteen aircraft flew to the 'box', but enemy air activity prevented seven drops. Six aircraft were damaged, two having petrol tanks hit and another having its instruments shot away. The action was so intense that, by 12 February, all flights had to be made by night. Frequently, crews landed at Ramu to take on casualties for evacuation.

While the Arakan affair was under way, the Squadron continued to be busy with the second Chindit expedition, Operation *Thursday*. Delaney's diary recorded his crew's share of the action:

'1 March. We practised night landings with a loaded aircraft – obviously we were being prepared for something!

'4 March. A Flight went on detachment to Sylhet in Assam – on the way up with a full load of ground crew we hit a vulture at 8,000ft. It went through the starboard windscreen and was flattened on the bulkhead – terrific stink! Warrant Officer Wilson, who was at the controls, just ducked in time. We unloaded at Sylhet and took the damaged aircraft back to Agartala – a most uncomfortable and cold ride. There, Flight Lieutenant 'Chiefie' Leeder fixed up the windscreen and we returned to Sylhet that night.

'5 March. Left Sylhet at midnight for a DZ deep in Burma for a Chindit group. Had a disastrous trip; we found out later that we had passed over the Chindwin River in cloud, and then when we crossed the Irrawaddy we thought it was the Chindwin. We continued on for about an hour with a strong tailwind but we were obviously hopelessly lost. Our subsequent calculations had us over the Chinese border. On top of it all our radio broke down. Despite Warrant Officer Robinson dismantling it on the floor, he couldn't revive it. We headed back to Assam, accepting that the headwind might prevent us from reaching base. We all put on our parachutes, took off the back door and the arrangement was that, when the engines stopped, I would get down the back as quickly as I could and we would all jump, hopefully ending up together. However, in the moonlight we saw a landing strip and, still with our full load of supplies, we landed, keeping both engines running as a Jeep came out to meet us. Fortunately it was a British officer who told us that we were at Tamu, just a mile or so inside the front line and that his men were in retreat and we should get off quickly. We finally arrived at Sylhet with a few gallons of fuel left.

'Each night until 15 March we did four-hour trips to various parts of mid-Burma to supply the second Chindit expedition, and on the ninth we took as an observer Brigadier Marks, who was Wingate's second in command.

'On 19/20 March, A Flight was involved in transporting the 5th Indian Division from the Arakan to the Imphal valley – about 300 miles. On each day our crew did two round trips, Agartala–Dohazari–Tullyhall (Imphal)–Agartala. Fifteen hours flying altogether and we carried in total three Jeeps, forty-three men and tons of equipment.'

Very few drops were straightforward. On 21 March, for instance, two Daks had to retain 3,000lbs of equipment when the parachute attachment wires broke, while Flying Officer Davies's crew was forced to jettison part of the load when a sack fouled the tailplane.

The actual business of dispatching the packs was both back-breaking and dangerous. Crew members were not

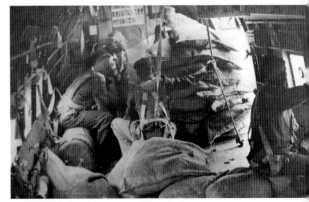

The 'kickers' are ready, waiting for the green light.

normally established for the job, with co-opted groundcrew – commonly volunteers – supplemented by the co-pilot or other flight crew, regularly being responsible for getting the supplies out of the cargo door situated to the rear port side of the Dak. They were known as the 'kickers' – or sometimes 'chuckers'. The usual method was to stack the sacks around the door, with one man lying against the starboard side of the fuselage. On the signal, he would kick them out, his legs going like pistons as two other men dropped further sacks in front of his feet by the open door. Rarely if ever was any form of safety-harness used by these 'kickers'. Not surprisingly, there were many hairy moments. Flight Sergeant Sheppard, a WOp/AG, recorded:

> 'On one sortie, the chute cords caught in the door and the container was swinging under the aircraft. Jock Jamieson lay on the floor and, with myself clutching his feet under my armpits, he reached out of the door and cut the chute free with a knife.'

Certain loads caused the 'kickers' to curse more than usually – not least, and for obvious reasons, barbed wire coils. And Flying Officer Brian Stanbridge can add a tale guaranteed to strike horror into any aircrew:

> 'Dispatching large pieces of timber required to build a bridge, I was terrified to feel the control column snatched out of my hands during the drop. It turned out that this had been caused by the parachutes getting caught in the aircraft door with the timber swinging up and hitting the tail and elevators. The dispatchers managed to cut it away and we just made it over the ridge.'

There were 'special' loads, too, as Horace Welham recalls:

> 'Some packages, reinforced by bamboo, we'd check out in the air by feeling inside them. Occasionally, in packages intended for the HQ people, we'd find bottles of rum or the like. Our Thirty One boys would take those out and put them in the later packages intended for the ordinary troops. These loads usually weighed 56lbs, and to stop them bursting on impact they were put into double sacks. After the end of hostilities we even put live chickens in – although they tended to lose their feathers in the slipstream!'

And there was more substantial livestock, too. Army forces in the jungle employed pack-mules, and from time to time replacements had to be flown in. Not a pleasant or an easy load to carry, as Ivor 'Chota' Bentley tells:

> 'On one occasion a particularly stubborn animal just would not be moved and stood firmly at the bottom of the ramp. Finally a local handler came forward and whispered something into the mule's

Loads included assorted wildlife. The USAAF aircraft in the background reflects the joint nature of SEAC ops.

ear, whereupon it shot up the ramp and into the Dak with no other assistance whatsoever.'

Writing to his wife about mules and donkeys, Ivor said that 'They would kick seven bells out of the aeroplane as well as making it smell like an old toilet!'

In fact out-of-control beasts had been known to wreck Dakotas, and mixed loads including mules were, unsurprisingly, unpopular with human passengers.

In an extract from the diary kept by Leading Aircraftman Johnny Boardman, who had been on the Squadron as a fitter since Lahore in 1942, we hear of a two-day trip into Burma – again in connection with the second Chindit expedition:

'2 April 1944, 12 noon. I hear that I am to accompany Flight Sergeant Simpson 250 miles behind the lines into Burma to survey one of our machines which has crashed.

'We arrive at 6pm and I must admit I feel a bit scared. The army blokes here have long beards and some are in poor condition – they are having a tough time. Simmy and I, after inspecting the damage to the crashed aircraft, get to work. It cannot be repaired so we are taking as many spare parts as we can; we need them! The port engine and undercarriage are in a hell of a mess so we decide on the starboard engine. We work until 10.30pm with the aid of a couple of torches. All the time transport aircraft are landing and taking-off.

'When we have removed the most urgently needed parts we load them aboard one of our machines going back to Agartala. We will stay another day and get some more parts off. I have slept in some queer places since I joined the RAF, but that night beat the record. We managed to get two stretchers, so bedded down in the machine – rather uncomfortable as the tail was stuck 30ft in the air. We had not brought any blankets and all we had was a monsoon cape each. I think I got about one hour's sleep that night, what with the cold and the noise of aircraft coming in and out.

'In the morning we awoke to find the Yanks, who had been working all night on their machines, had pinched one of our tool-kits and also a few parts from one of our engines. Did we curse! For breakfast we had bread, cheese and cold tea. It was very quiet all day as it is too dangerous for our machines to land in daylight. We are told that the air raid warning is given by a machine gun giving off a few rounds. This warning went three times during the day and the third time, at 6pm, ten Zeros came over and circled. Our ground defence opened up and Simmy and I ran like hell for cover. Luckily for us the Jap machines did not open fire. They were trying to catch our aircraft which were due any minute, and barely ten minutes later the first American machine hove into sight, circled and landed. I expected the Japs to put in another appearance but they didn't.

'The transports were coming in every five minutes now, and at 9 o'clock three of our 31 Squadron machines landed. We loaded our equipment aboard and I gave a sigh of relief when we left at 9.30pm. I was very tired, dirty, needed a shave, and my hands were all cut and bruised from working in the dark the previous evening.'

Landing strips were being bulldozed out of the jungle (the bulldozers first being taken in by gliders as soon as rudimentary landing spots were usable) and pressed into operation the very next day. 'Broadway' was one such, and Peter Bray gives us a flavour of it:

'There wasn't much room between the jungle and the strip so we came in just above stalling speed with full flap – hanging on the props so to speak – and dropped her in. At first it was a rough old landing run but the engineers kept at it – filling in the water buffalo holes and cutting down trees – and before long even Spitfires could get in and out.'

'Aberdeen' was another, with Colin Lynch recounting a tale which, by the sound of it, could have been the precursor to the story we've just heard from Boardman:

'When we got there it was dark and the strip was flooded. On landing we overshot and ran into a rocky mound at the end, colliding with a crashed American Dak that had hit the same mound the previous night. Our Dak was wrecked – both wings broken, engines torn off and fuselage snapped in two. We were trapped there until a rescue team arrived and got the wounded out. At two in the morning, as we were trying to get some sleep in the wreckage, there were shots – and we were on the end of a full-scale Jap attack. People were killed on both sides, but somehow they missed us. It was too dangerous the next day for anybody from the Squadron to fly in because of the danger from enemy attacks, and it was not until the following day that we were taken out.'

As the April fighting in the Arakan petered out it became apparent that the Japanese had failed in their immediate objectives. The admin box defence had lasted seventeen days, a heroic and desperate effort. But Arthur Delaney's final reference, above, to 'transporting a division to Imphal' presaged what were to prove the really big ones – the Japanese attack on and siege of Imphal and Kohima. Both would call on all the reserves of courage and endurance the army and the supply droppers could muster.

Just as in the Arakan, a planned Allied offensive was pre-empted there by Japanese action. Having watched the huge buildup in Assam, the enemy had correctly deduced that a full-scale push southwards into central Burma was being prepared, and had opted to counter this by themselves moving northwards across the Chindwin River. Those reinforcing Allied troops just mentioned, the 5th Indian Division, were flown to reinforce Imphal, but the Kohima garrison was cut off. With only 1,500 men in place, it came under siege by massive Japanese forces.

The battle of Kohima began in April, the garrison of the surrounded town having to be supplied totally by air. There is no better way to hear about the action than from the diary of Wing Commander Bill Burbury, back in command after a brief interlude during which Wing Commander Olivier had been at the helm:

'Prior to the desperate situation at Kohima the Squadron was not only keeping the Chindits supplied but the whole Imphal garrison on a round-the-clock operation. While most of the supplies for the garrison could be landed on the Imphal strip, which was still held, vital supplies had to be dropped to our troops engaging the Japs on the periphery of the Imphal plain.

'Perhaps the most crucial battle of the Japanese offensive was fought at Kohima. This was a small civilian station perched high on a mountain ridge overlooking the Assam valley in the neighbourhood of Sylhet. It normally housed a deputy commissioner of the Indian civil service who administered the district and the local

Nagas. It was, however, a key point on the only road leading down to the Assam valley and the railway to Calcutta. A small force, consisting mainly of a much under-strength battalion of British infantry, had been rushed by air from the Arakan front to Sylhet, and thence by road to Kohima before the Jap offensive had rolled past Imphal. Subsequently the Japs cut the road to Sylhet, and this small garrison was all that stood between a Japanese division and the road to Calcutta and India.

'The force was hemmed in by the Japs in an area little bigger than two tennis courts – indeed their position was in the district commissioner's garden where the tennis courts had originally been laid out. They were short of everything – food, water, mortar shells, hand grenades and small-arms ammunition. They were subjected to continual attacks by the Japs by day and night. Their situation was desperate, and on their ability to withstand the Jap onslaught hung great issues. By 12 April the Japs had completely encircled their position and a supply drop was ordered the next day for desperately needed water, mortar shells and hand grenades. This drop was carried out by another squadron – no names, no pack drill. It was a complete failure and the great bulk of the drop fell into Jap hands – the Japs, it must be remembered, also being short of hand grenades and mortar shells. The drop also resulted in the loss of two Dakotas and crews to Japanese ground fire.

'I received an urgent cypher signal that evening. The desperate situation at Kohima was recorded, as was the complete failure of the supply drop that afternoon. I was told to consider that 31 Squadron's exclusive task until further notice would be to supply the garrison at Kohima. It was an accolade, no doubt, but it was going to be an onerous task.

'The two principal difficulties were, first, the very tiny area onto which supplies had to be parachuted or free dropped. The penalty of a mis-drop was two-fold. Firstly the garrison, to survive, had to have the supplies and, secondly, it was to their great disadvantage if the Japs got the supplies instead. The second difficulty was that, in order to obtain the greatest degree of accuracy, we had to drop from a very low altitude and this made us extremely vulnerable to ground fire. The latter was intense and involved everything the Japs could bring to bear – rifles, machine-guns and even mortars.

'We made our first drop on 14 April using ten aircraft. After dropping, I watched the operation from above and it appeared to be successful. While we encountered heavy ground fire, we lost no aircraft. On the other hand, our ground crews had an all-night task patching up the bullet holes and ensuring that no vital parts had been hit. I received a signal [from HQ] that night which confirmed that the drop had been a complete success.

'We evolved a technique which possibly reduced the ground fire. Each aircraft had to make several runs over the DZ – usually from eight to ten – to drop the two-ton loads. Every so often – perhaps twice in a drop – instead of dropping supplies we would go in even lower and open fire on the Japs with our Vickers guns. Each Dakota had two Vickers, one firing to port and one to starboard through the escape hatches. While this armament was not very effective against attack by an enemy fighter – the field of fire was severely restricted by such vital structures as the tailplane and the mainplanes – against ground targets it was reasonably effective.

'The Japs, though dug in, were plainly in view from the air and very close – not more than a hundred yards. Whether we scored many hits I do not know but our tactic had, at least, the merit of keeping their heads down. Since they could not tell whether we were coming to drop supplies or to open fire, we introduced an element of surprise. We continued, of course, to be raked by ground fire but, I am glad to say, we lost no aircraft.

'The Kohima garrison held out until 7 May when it was relieved by a column which opened up the road from Sylhet and brought heavy artillery fire to bear. We continued to supply them throughout. Without a shadow of a doubt, the Battle of Kohima was an epic in the annals of British military history. It was also, I believe, a turning point of the war in Burma. The Japanese 31st Division was decimated and, I have heard, was never again an effective fighting force.

'By the end of May the whole Japanese offensive had petered out. Imphal no longer required to be supplied with such intensity and the Chindit columns were, for the most part, safely back. Towards the middle of June, I was ordered to withdraw my Squadron to northern India.'

It had been an extraordinarily intensive period of operations. Flight Lieutenant Francis Hallinan was Thirty One's MO from April 1944 to September 1945, and of course he knew everyone. So his comment on the Squadron at the time is relevant:

'I shall never forget the total commitment of everyone from the CO down to the humblest airman in the task of winning the war in the air or on the ground, under most trying conditions. Everyone took such a pride in his work. This most efficient fighting unit played such a major part in the defeat of the enemy in the Far East.'

The intensity and hazardous nature of the operation had been hair-raising at times. On 23 May, during a night mission, three aircraft flew from Agartala to Sylhet and dropped supplies near the Irrawaddy. However, FL576, flown by Sergeant Bell and Flight Sergeant Gibbs, failed to return. The other pilots reported seeing the aircraft in the circuit and signalled that its load had been dropped, but no trace was ever found. It was that crew's third mission of the night.

And Peter Bray adds a further, graphic perspective on the battle:

'The ghastly thing was that we could see it all as we went in on our runs. There were our lads, dug in just a shovel's length from the Jap trenches. Dead bodies lying all around, and wounded crawling back from no-man's land. What these men suffered didn't bear thinking about. I'd never seen anything so dreadful and I never want to see such things again.

'It was tricky making the drops on that road. As well as the hills and the blinding rain, the slopes above and below it were at forty-five degrees. The only way we could get the ammo in was to drop it practically slap bang into the gun pits. You could see the road from Dimapur snaking up the valley and at the top, at 5,000ft, there's the Kohima Ridge, not quite a mile long. Where the road runs off the ridge and down to Imphal there's a whole lot of hillocks. In the middle of those you could see the Kohima hill station – or what was left of it.'

There were still further casualties. On 26 May, five aircraft were detailed to drop supplies. FL574, 'E', in which Arthur Delaney had come under fire ten days earlier over Hmuntha,

The stacked load as seen from the outside. The peace-time wing roundels, by the way, give this picture away as having been taken in post-war India.

'There they go!'

took off at 3pm but crashed north of Kumbhirgram. Flight Sergeants Hill and Jamieson, with their four crewmen, were all killed.

So the Battle of Kohima ended. There certainly might have been, as Bill Burbury hints at, a strategic Japanese plan to move into India. Indeed the Japanese propaganda machine was reported, according to Roger Annett's *Drop Zone Burma*, to have announced that 'The march on Delhi has begun'. Japanese bombers had attacked Calcutta early in 1943, and some historians believe there might even have been an aspiration to link up with a possible Axis push eastwards down through north-west India. But, given that the Germans had, more than a year earlier, already begun to retreat from their furthest advances into Egypt and the Soviet Union, this seems unlikely. Moreover, events would subsequently prove that the Japanese had already reached the practical limit in

A typically tight DZ.

terms of length of their supply chain. Many later commentators agree that their immediate aim was limited in any case to keeping closed the Allied land route to China, and this was indeed achieved, for 1944 at least, by their Assam incursion.

But the CO was spot on in observing that Kohima would forever be regarded as an epic in British military history. Not for nothing has the *Kohima Epitaph* become the centrepiece of the Royal British Legion's annual Remembrance Day events:

'When you go home – tell them of us, and say
For your tomorrows, we gave our today.'

Thirty One Squadron may be very proud of its part in the operation, and many of its ex-members have for many years afterwards participated with their army comrades in commemorations held by the Burma Star Association. In recognition of the Squadron's efforts, it was awarded a battle honour which would, in time, be proudly emblazoned on its Standard. It reads 'Manipur 1944', Manipur being both a river and the Indian state in which Imphal and Kohima lay.

Chapter 10

Drawing Breath

Thirty One was withdrawn from the front line so that it could recuperate and regroup. Its aircraft were reallocated to 52 and 353 Squadrons, and the move was completed by late July 1944. During the preparations, operations were still flown; sadly, on 5 July, another Dakota and crew were lost – FZ585, Sergeants Storrie and Carden being the pilots.

Arthur Delancy wrote this of the interlude:

'We moved about 1,700 miles to Basal, a newly constructed and previously unoccupied station forty miles from Rawalpindi. It was a most enjoyable period. For the pilots there was glider towing, formation parachute dropping from Chaklala, low-level formation flying by day and formation by night. The WOps did jumpmaster courses and, to complete their education in paratroop dropping, were invited to volunteer for one jump each. After much debate and beer they all agreed to jump, and our crew dropped twenty-seven of them on 17 September. Army instructors with megaphones were at the DZ and were able to give advice to the men as they came down. However, much of the 'advice' was reputedly returned with interest! There were no casualties, although Flying Officer Gould's back-to-front landing was horrible. It was of small concern to him, though; his chute had opened and he was down in one piece.'

While at Basal, many took leave, with houseboats in Kashmir echoing earlier times. Jack Rock, a storeman, recalls:

'I joined Thirty One at Basal after a horrendous journey from my previous unit in Bengal, I found half the chaps were on leave – and the other half were about to go away. My brother, who had been instrumental in getting me the posting to the Squadron, arranged with the SWO, Dusty Moore, for me to join my new colleagues in Kashmir. Not a bad beginning, although the posting cost me a promotion. As a leading aircraftman at my previous unit I had been recommended for corporal, but had been posted before it had been promulgated. I remained unpromoted til demob, but considered the sacrifice well worth accepting for the privilege of being on Thirty One!'

Delaney continues:

'I was sports officer there. We had a concrete cricket pitch but were a bit short of equipment. Our understanding CO authorized a 'resupply' flight on 8 August, and with Pilot Officer George Webb I flew the 150 miles to Peshawar and collected as much cricket gear as we could from 223 Group. From that date on there was a daily cricket match. We had some talented cricketers too – Squadron Leader Honeyman being a consistent scorer, Peter Dymond, Jack Varden and Ginger Buckland. It was easy to set up matches – sergeants v officers, marrieds v singles, aircrew v groundcrew, pilots v navs, and so on. On 20 September we took two rugby teams to Chaklala, and it was strange flying back in rugby shorts, bare feet, with plenty of advice from thirty-odd passengers.

'25 October was a great day for the Squadron. Our soccer team had made the final of the area trophy and again Bill Burbury showed his complete understanding – twelve aircraft took virtually the whole Squadron, flying in formation to Peshawar. We watched a great game but lost to 151 OTU by 3–0'

Corporal Stan Johnson remembers both game and flight:

'Bill Burbury had put up a notice for names of would-be supporters. 300 appeared, but Burbury came through, and every available Dak was crammed full of personnel. He put it down, I believe, as a formation flying exercise! There were aircrew, groundcrew, admin types, Indian bearers, char wallahs, sweepers-out, the lot! The Daks flew in formation led by the CO. Arriving over Peshawar they circled, still in formation, then proceeded to do a slow beat-up of the town.'

Benny Watts had been away on an NCOs' course and just happened to be at Peshawar following a bout of tonsillitis and sand-fly fever:

'I think the people of Peshawar thought war had come at last when a squadron of Dakotas flew in. The most they had seen before were light aircraft on a Battle of Britain commemoration flight! The Squadron lost the match but was not disgraced. As a Group HQ, Peshawar had call on any professional footballers posted to their area and they had a strong team – including a professional referee.'

All dressed up with nowhere to go.

Thirty One's brief period of recuperation cues a couple of 'off-duty' stories concerned with variety shows. In a moment, we'll get to the real thing, but first let's drop in on a home-grown effort. The Squadron had been based at Kharagpur for a couple of months in 1943, and no effort and expense were spared with the show there. Horace Welham sets the scene:

'Kharagpur had a thriving British community that boasted a beautiful club and sports ground complex. Its racial discrimination was most obvious, while the rank and file of the British forces were just about tolerated.

How the boys envisaged themselves on their occasional R&R trips to the cities. From a postcard of the day.

The club boasted a bar, with draught beer available in unlimited quantities. To the members of 31 Squadron it was utopia after continuous operations living rough – and I mean rough – for months on end at desolate airstrips.

'Now, we had a rebellious character by the name of Jack Slinger, a Mancunian who professed to having "trod the boards" and to having been on the fringe of the big time. He suggested that he should partake in and produce an Xmas show to entertain the lads, and activity started with a bang. I had just come back from detachment at Tezpur and Dinjan, and was immediately roped in to audition for a barber's shop quartet, together with about twenty others. Slinger had now affected dark glasses, a cravat, and would have smoked a cigar had they been available. After a number of rehearsals and with the candidates down to five, he took me aside. "Welham," he said, "your bell has a crack – sorry old chap. Mind you, I could do with a stage manager, and you are the ideal man for the job." I accepted.

'Our auditorium was a large bamboo *basha* with a concrete floor and boasted a raised concrete platform at one end. My first tasks were to fix curtains that drew open and closed and to box in the sides to make an enclosed stage. This I managed by purloining some sections of a storm-damaged *basha* and some hessian that was hanging around, some camouflage paint and a spray gun. Jack grudgingly said it would do, and now had another problem for me to sort out. Seeing as most of the acts were vocal, we needed just a small item – a piano.

'Two days prior to the opening night another problem developed. The CO had informed Jack that he and his officers would like an invitation to the show. How could we – or dared we – refuse? Seating was now required. Ask them to do the same as everybody else – bring their own? No way. I think of Ram Bhopal's furniture emporium in bazaar in town outskirts. Problem: bazaar out of bounds to Brit ORs. Still, in for a penny, in for a pound. Take *tonga* into area and am greeted with many, many salaams and gestures of goodwill. Am assured that "Emperor King George very good polo player, very good sahib indeed." Escorted into emporium and assured that "my most excellent requirements, whatever they might be, will be most satisfactorily dealt with in an honourable and speedy contentment." The compound reminded me of a typical English back yard on 5 November. After a cat-and-mouse session of professional bargaining, settled for the one-day hire of five assorted, stuffed armchairs, two three-seater settees, and a horsehair-covered drop-end sofa – all at the magnificent cost of five rupees. Another round of bargaining then began with Ram Bhopal's second cousin removed, who just happened to be the proprietor of the most efficient removal firm in the area! Finally settled for the hire of two bullock carts plus handlers, at the nominal sum of four annas per cart.

'A last-minute demand for a spotlight was soon solved by purloining a landing light and batteries from a cannibalized Dakota. On the big night the auditorium was packed out, the audience in terrific mood bolstered by generous tots of Dhow's Canadian dark ale, Carew's and Hayward's gin, backed up by Indian whisky and 100 per cent issue rum. Officers were booed and hissed for being late, to loud singing of "Why are we waiting?"

'Show opened with Dougie Gordon, a reputable crooner, singing *The Girl of My Dreams* plus two encores. This was followed by rude jokes and ditties, e.g.

There was a Young Lady from Ealing. Arthur Ball, Charlie Worral and myself as the "Brummegem Bullring Buskers" rendered our versions of *The Man who Invented Beer* and *Any Old Iron.* Barbershop Quartet followed and were brilliant. Then Jock Easton, a Scot with a good singing voice. More Scots, then someone played the trumpet. Paddy Hamilton wanted to sing *The Sash His Father Wore* and threatened to fight those who preferred *Kevin Barry.* The audience was getting very merry by now, and it was also noticed that the front row of officers appeared to be restless.

'Just in time, Jack Slinger closed with his impression of Norman Evans in *Over the Garden Wall*, climbing up the wall with his false teeth out and his mosquito-netted wig in paper curlers. He brought the house down, and I still maintain he was far better than the real Norman Evans – who appeared for years on the Royal Variety Concert.

'The remainder of the evening was left to a very popular officer pilot known to all as "Flash" leading the audience in community singing of all the famous ribald overseas songs. As always, the climax was *There's a Troopship Leaving Bombay.*

'I was later baffled by Flash's spluttered comment on the front row performance: "Good show Horace, but bang goes your chances of promotion or being mentioned in dispatches." All was revealed the next morning on sick parade. It turned out that the all-India flea Olympics must recently have been held in Ram Bhopal's emporium. Hence the officers' unrest! The following week, I was crewed on a Dakota destined for the Dinjan detachment again.'

So much for the amateur effort. But most Second World War troops had the benefit of some form of entertainment from ENSA concert parties, and for men away from home and far from the more familiar comforts, ENSA proved very welcome. The initials stood for 'Entertainments National Service Association', although the organization was often irreverently (albeit affectionately) referred to as 'Every Night Something Awful'.

One memorable visit to Thirty One occurred in May 1944 when the 'forces' sweetheart', the great Vera Lynn, came to the jungle. Doc Hallinan recalls her visit to Agartala: 'Shortly after joining Thirty One I had the pleasant duty of conducting Vera Lynn, who was in a visiting ENSA party, around our sick quarters to greet airmen of all ranks. I still have an old diary with her autograph entered for the date 10 May 1944.'

Eric Honeyman also remembers the visit:

'It was a big occasion. For most of us, this was the first time we had seen a white woman for up to two years, and I still recall the tremendous burst of laughter which greeted a remark by one of the officers. It seems most of the Squadron were queuing up for Vera's autograph,

The picture which every Thirty Oner of the era carried in his wallet until the end of his service. The great Vera Lynn captured all their hearts in 1944 with her performance in the jungle at Agartala. After the show she poses with her adoring boys in the jungle.

and a little pushing and shoving was going on. An officer seated at the table with Vera looked up and said irritably, "There's no need to push, you'll all get what you want!"'

Tommy Trinder was another who devoted much time to the forces. Here, he visits Thirty One in Java.

We can only imagine the morale boost amongst the men, far from family and loved ones, homesick, and existing in primitive conditions and an alien climate. But the later Dame Vera was clearly well aware of the huge value of her war work, making tours to the most remote locations. Unsurprisingly, it was the irrepressible Horace Welham who finished up with the most tangible memento of Vera Lynn's visit, for she left her sunglasses in the Dakota she flew in. Horace carefully 'looked after' them for many years thereafter.

After the shows it was always back to business, and there was a sobering postscript to Horace's story of his production:

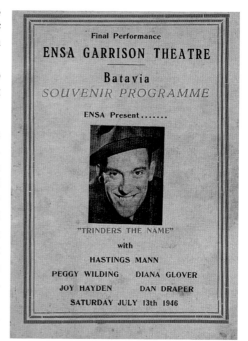

Final Performance

ENSA GARRISON THEATRE

Batavia
SOUVENIR PROGRAMME

ENSA Present.......

"TRINDERS THE NAME"

with

HASTINGS MANN
PEGGY WILDING   DIANA GLOVER
JOY HAYDEN   DAN DRAPER
SATURDAY JULY 13th 1946

And the programme.

'At Dinjan we were flying two long trips a day in often very bad weather conditions. I'd been watching a cut in a tyre, which we suspected as having been caused by sabotage by Indian National Party members. Eventually the cut widened to the point where, in consultation with the pilot, I decided that any overweight landing would be dangerous. Therefore I declared the plane u/s and we returned to Kharagpur for a new tyre.

'On arrival there I reported sick; I had been in agony for weeks, being covered from head to foot with hundreds of red spots. "Prickly heat," said the MO; "Excused duties for seventy-two hours." I have often wondered whether it was prickly heat or septic flea bites. Anyhow, I went back to the *basha*. There I found that I had been crewed on the mail run the next day. But I was excused duties.

'Thus it was that I was asleep the next morning when the mail plane crashed on take-off. All aboard were killed.'

Chapter 11

On the Offensive

By the middle of 1944 new aircraft began to arrive at Basal and, by the end of August, eighteen Dakotas were on strength. Training continued until November, when the Squadron was to return to operations. The Allies had already started south across the Chindwin River on what was to be their decisive push, and it was to be Agartala again for Thirty One. Canadian Pilot Officer 'Howie' Sharpe sets the scene:

'The ground situation at this time found the Japanese retreating from their defeats at Imphal and Kohima. General Stilwell's forces had recaptured Myitkyina, making possible a more southerly air supply route to China. General Slim's Fourteenth Army was on the offensive and planning to advance into the central plain of Burma. They were also planning to push the Japs back down the Arakan coast so that air bases could be established again there. This would shorten supply lines to forces which would then push south through Burma towards Rangoon. Tiddim fell in mid-October, and by the time Thirty One returned the enemy was retreating into the Kabaw Valley.

'Thirty One was now one of four RAF transport squadrons operating in the area. The DZs were all marked with code letters to prevent the enemy from setting up their own DZ and receiving the supplies. Japanese fighter aircraft attacked every now and then, after which we would be escorted by Hurricanes. This would last about two weeks before they would be withdrawn until another Jap attack occurred. Then the procedure would be repeated.'

Immediately Thirty One recommenced operations they were in the thick of things. Fourteen Dakotas took off at around 7.30am on 8 November with loads for various DZs. Aircraft returned at intervals after 11am but two, flown by Flying Officer Stanbridge (FD949) and Pilot Officer Taylor (recorded as FL512), failed to get back. The Dakotas had been attacked by Japanese Oscars. No trace was ever found of Taylor's machine. With its crew of Sergeant Brown, Flight Sergeant McLaren, and Warrant Officers Butley and 'Dougie' Douglas it was simply swallowed by the jungle.

FD949 had been forced down into a paddy field three miles south-east of his DZ. Stanbridge, later Air Vice-Marshal Sir Brian and a much-respected president of the Squadron Association, tells the story:

'It was only my third operational sortie after joining the Squadron in August when it was on rest at Basal. I was dropping supplies at Honiang in the notoriously unfriendly Kabaw Valley when I was attacked by three Japanese fighters who formed up in line astern on me while I was on a dropping run at about 400ft. The first I knew of it was when a hail of bullets rattled through the aircraft, some breaking the windscreen. My navigator, Pilot Officer Howard Ward, came forward to tell me the port engine was on fire. I rapidly realized there was no way I could evade further attacks. With a severely crippled aircraft with one engine on fire there was no going back over the Chin Hills to the nearest friendly airfield even if I had managed to put out the fire. The only thing I could do was crash-land as soon as possible; I did not relish this thought, being surrounded by heavy jungle country. But I suddenly saw a patch of paddy fields in which I managed to make a wheels–up landing. Ward, who flew with me many times both before and after this event has since told me that this was the smoothest landing I ever made!'

Sergeant Len 'Hawk' Ekers picks up the tale from the perspective of those in the cabin:

'We were dropping the first load when gunshot came through the aircraft. Ward picked up the ammo for the VGO and was attempting to put it on the gun when it was shot out of his hands. That was that! Fire was coming back from the engine past the door. I got my parachute and had a look out, but we were too low. I could see we were going to come down so went to a crash position. Stanbridge did an excellent job getting us down. I had lost a lot of blood, but the army came out for us and got Armstrong and me on to stretchers.'

Stanbridge again:

'The aircraft sustained little damage during the crash but by then it was burning pretty furiously. We evacuated it rapidly, carrying the wounded with us, while the Oscars circled overhead and then disappeared. We had ended up between the lines but, fortunately, some West African Division troops in the area sent out a patrol to recover us before the Japs did!'

Of the downed crew, Flight Sergeant Armstrong subsequently died, while Ekers survived despite having been hit repeatedly. Stanbridge, Ward and Flight Sergeant Hill escaped unscathed.

Getting clear of the burning Dakota, Hill and Ward helped the two wounded men through the paddy field. Leaving Hill to tend to their wounds, Stanbridge and Ward set off for help. Locating a village, they also found British troops.

With the help of the troops, they got the wounded to a nearby airstrip. Stanbridge was flown to Yazagyo in a Tiger Moth, there arranging air evacuation for the others.

One who luckily escaped the whole business was Warrant Officer Roberts. A Canadian member of Stanbridge's crew, he had gone down with malaria almost as soon as they had arrived in India; a blessing in disguise. Once he was fit and well again, he recalled flying with Stanbridge and having the crash site gleefully pointed out!

And nav Howard Ward has a postscript to the event:

'Once our rescue had been sorted out I had the job of getting back home. Japanese shelling had damaged the strip too much for any further ops, but I got a ride on a truck to a nearby USAAF glider strip. From there I had the interesting experience of being on the end of a 'snatch' glider pick-up. The idea, developed for Burmese jungle clearings which were too small for powered aircraft to land, was that a glider and its load would first be towed to the overhead and released to land. Later it would be pulled off again with a new load by a tow plane. The glider would stand at one end of the strip with its tow rope laid out in front and looped up between two posts. The tow plane would fly in on full throttle with a hook deployed below. With luck it would snare the glider tow rope and away you would go.

'My particular glider was filled with wounded Gurkhas for the return trip, but I was lucky enough to be given space. The pick-up was successful — acceleration 0–120mph in no time. Very exciting!'

Howard's trip back to base continued via an intermediate landing at Imphal where he transferred to the tow plane. This was an American aircraft, which proceeded to its base at Sylhet. Following a signal message to the effect that 'Lucky Ward has arrived here', he was returned to Agartala.

Several members of Thirty One were themselves trained at one time or another in 'snatch glider pick-up' ops, but there is no record of the Squadron ever having performed the role in anger.

Ekers later remarked that: 'My next trip wasn't until Christmas Day, by which time I was getting behind in my flying hours in relation to my friends. 700 hours was a tour and it took a bit of argument with the MO to get back to flying.'

The question of tour length was a regular topic of conversation in the *bashas*. Colin Lynch, for example, had this to say:

'When I joined 31 Squadron in 1943, a tour of ops was 500 hours and we were expected to do two tours. Later, a single tour was changed to 700 hours, and we only had to do one tour before being entitled to rest, posting or repatriation. By the time the rule was changed, I and several of my contemporaries had already completed over 700 hours, but by some weird reasoning we were still expected to complete our 1,000 hours under the original rules. Such was life!'

Arthur Delaney left in January 1945, having completed 289 operational sorties, which must have amounted to about 1,500 hours. Nevertheless, he had good memories:

'Of the intense but friendly rivalry between several of the crews and in particular between Stan Pedley's and ourselves. The competitive spirit extended from how short we could land through how few circuits over the DZ to dispose of 7,500lbs of supplies, with accuracy of drop being paramount, to the lowest height at which the first turn was made after take-off, it being immaterial whether there was a full load or empty!'

Together with tour length, 'going home' was always the primary topic of conversation. At times the men felt almost unbearably remote from their loved ones. And in the Squadron's predominantly all-male existence in the jungle there were precious few 'happy family' stories to relate. But here's one.

Australian Flight Lieutenants Dick Ridoutt and Alan McEwen were good friends. They had left home together in 1941 to train in Canada, and had been together ever since. In their previous squadron elsewhere in India, Alan had met and become engaged to Sister Harriet Hadnett of the Queen Alexandra's Imperial Military Nursing Service, and when they were married on 18 March 1944 Dick should have been best man. But he'd been posted away to 31 Squadron. Later, Alan had followed him; Harriet was expecting their first child by then and later recalled:

'We had a very wonderful nine months until December 1944 when I knew and told Alan I was pregnant, and he told me he was posted to 31 Squadron. I still had to go on working, and he went to Thirty One. I thought I would be very lonely, but quite a few doctors and RAF officers took me out to dinner, the club, and the pictures, and they seemed quite happy to have drinks and dinner at the sisters' mess. Alan and I missed each other very much and we wrote every day. He became much happier when he was billeted in a room next to Dick Ridoutt. On our first wedding anniversary the officers at Chaklala sent telegrams which I sent on to Alan. Then it was time for me to stop work. I was sent to Murree at the end of June due to the heat and friends used to visit me from Rawalpindi. Our baby daughter was born on 8 August 1945 and Alan came to see me, unshaven and dressed in his dirty jungle uniform. He'd had no trouble in getting to Calcutta but from there it had been difficult. But luckily Alan ran into an ex-patient of mine, who offered him a trip to Delhi and help to get to Chaklala. Next day he brought some of our friends to see little Maureen and eventually Dick Ridoutt got to Murree and they went out to buy me an eternity ring. But they could only get a pair of gold wings with "RAF" worked on them and gave them to me with great enthusiasm. I still treasure them.'

Back to ops, and Operation *Nickel* sorties were flown in November and December 1944. Howie Sharpe explains:

'A *Nickel* raid was the term for a leaflet-dropping flight. Two crews were chosen for these raids, presumably the extra crew was to provide back-up should trouble be encountered. The Wing briefing was complete in every detail, a description being given of the Burmese tribes over which the flight would pass, and their friendliness or otherwise towards the British or Japanese. Money belts were provided with the type of money that would be accepted by each tribe. This was for the purchase of guides and food in the event of being shot down. A briefing grim enough to scare the crews into thinking this was their last flight! The night chosen had a full moon so that the various villages could be seen, and there were five or six different leaflets to be dropped. Some were for the Burmese and some for Japanese soldiers.

'Full of apprehension the crews took off for their flights into enemy territory, on a night so bright they felt conspicuous. The first couple of villages were located and leaflets pushed out to float down. Then the pilots, looking down, saw a dark outline of a twin-engined plane. Japanese night fighters were twins, so they altered course hoping that they had not been seen. But the dark plane did likewise. Again they turned and so did the other machine. Completing a 180 degree turn and still seeing the other dark machine, they eventually realized they had been chased by their own shadow!'

Although this report is written in a light vein, the hint of danger shines through. Not surprising, for Japanese treatment of downed airmen was reputed to be extremely harsh. And Benny Watts reports other hazards:

'I returned to B Flight 9 December and was welcomed by the instrument repairers who had a spare *charpoy* in their small *basha*. This was at the far end of the camp right under the edge of the jungle. It was common to hear various jungle denizens drop onto the roof. We used to freeze in our beds until all was clear, for tigers were often reported in the area!'

The turn of the year brought the customary thoughts of festivity and home – but, as Benny continues, the even more customary continuation of the task:

'Christmas was a bit of a letdown. My mail was following me around, and the food was poor at the time. We had agreed to boycott the mess, but sense of occasion and hunger got the better of us. We were given two bottles of beer and we cracked a bottle of Silver Fizz gin. The occupants of the *basha* had a group photograph taken dressed in our best. It included Gerry Greenstone – who was later to be murdered in Batavia.'

The season always made everybody feel especially far from home, but every year the mess staff managed to pull out all the stops.

Nineteen sorties were flown on Christmas Day 1944, to the Lushia Brigade in the Myittha Valley, while others were flown to drop supplies to XXXIII Corps at Thetkegyin. Two other Dakotas carried special loads of Christmas rations to isolated army units north of Gangaw. Many DZs had messages such as 'Merry Christmas to the RAF' laid out in strips of old parachute silk. The men flying the Daks attached similar greetings to the packages they dropped.

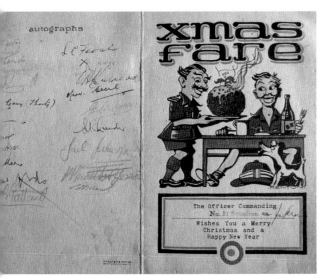

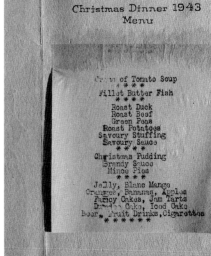

The years in India ticked by; here we see menus from Lahore and Agartala.

The aircrews on that Christmas Day were to have New Year off, and some officers kept tradition by serving Christmas dinner in the airmen's mess. But one man who particularly remembered his festive meal was Sergeant Ken 'Taff' Evans, a WOp. He was in the mess *basha* enjoying soup and looking forward to the main course when he was summoned urgently to operations for briefing. No time for food, he was told, so off he went. At the flights he waited around for nearly an hour until his pilot and navigator arrived. 'Where have you two been?' asked Taff. 'Finishing our Christmas dinner,' came the reply. 'Officers!' thought Taff.

They found their DZ after some searching, for it was no bigger than the size of a tennis court, and out went the soldiers' Christmas cheer. Some of it overshot, but the RAF men were sure the troops would sort it out. Taff, however, never did get his yuletide dinner.

December 1944 ended for 31 Squadron with a happy (and seemingly surprised) note in the Squadron record book: 'No casualties and no cases of VD on the unit.'

Howie Sharpe takes us into 1945:

'On 1 January the Squadron moved again, this time southwards to Comilla. The new camp was of the usual bamboo construction but it did have one convenience – a shower of sorts. A hand pump was placed on a raised platform, and a pail with holes punched in its bottom hung on the pump.'

The work from the new base continued much as before, including supply dropping and leaflet raids. But an event that will forever remain etched in the memory of all who witnessed it was the infamous Comilla fire. Reputedly caused by two electricians trying to start their primus stove with petrol – inside a *basha* – it rapidly spread out of control. Stan Johnson recalls the images:

'Several of us were being driven back to the living area from the airfield when we saw the fire in progress. Someone said it was the officers' mess, which raised a cheer. Then another said no, it was the sergeants' mess – more cheers. Then – "Christ, it's our quarters!" And, foot down, we raced to the fire. As it spread, each *basha* seemed to explode into flames, the heat being so tremendous.'

There were no injuries, luckily, but one significant loss was the Squadron's official Badge, which had been signed by King George VI and presented in 1937. The admin office caught fire and the Badge was never seen again. Well, not for a long time, at least. Happily, it did reappear more than twenty years later – as we shall recount in due course.

Staying with ceremonial, Benny Watts puts an airman's typically wry view on other events at Comilla:

'The qualifications for campaign stars were announced at that time and we were suddenly joined by a surprising number of staff officers from Calcutta, Poona and Delhi, who requested observation trips. These, surprise surprise, would qualify them for the Burma Star!'

Flight Lieutenant Mac McClauchlan, a pilot, remembers this story of 'routine' Comilla operations:

'On 9 January I was taking off in stream formation from Kangla, in number three position. The aircraft developed a slight swing to starboard and I reduced power on the port engine. But on opening up again I realized that I was not getting full power and was now heading for a large monsoon ditch and embankment. At 60–70kts I decided to use all available power in an attempt to clear those obstacles, which we did but crashed into a paddy field. This took care of the undercarriage and we came to an abrupt halt. I glanced to port to find the engine was on fire, so then it was everybody out and well away. Nobody hurt, although the aircraft was completely burnt out.

'I handed in my report next day, the outcome of which was an interview with my flight commander, Squadron Leader Bray, for whom I had great respect. His opinion was that, despite the loss of power, an average pilot should have done more to prevent the crash. He didn't say how! The engineering officer said he could not explain the power loss. So I was found guilty of gross negligence and my logbook endorsed to that effect.

'Months later, on 2 July, I was taxiing out at Ramree. Approaching the take-off point, the starboard engine cut out. I managed to get the aircraft to an unused dispersal, but all attempts there to restart failed. Returning to the Squadron, I left the aircraft with the groundcrew.

'At next morning's briefing, one of the groundcrew came up to me. "My god, you were lucky," he exclaimed. "We drained forty gallons of water from the main tank!"

'A different aircraft, but I guess a perennial problem in the climate out east. Could that have been the cause the first time? We all know that flying is full of ups and downs – but perhaps in my case swings and roundabouts. Nothing more was said officially, although I'm pleased to say that the "gross negligence" endorsement was subsequently expunged!'

Wing Commander Burbury left on 6 February 1945. He was succeeded by Wing Commander Altman, who had previously commanded 271 Squadron – and his arrival brought a sad and significant connection.

David 'Lummie' Lord had left Thirty One at the end of 1943 after four years with the Squadron during which he flew both Valentias and Dakotas. He had risen in the process from sergeant to flight lieutenant, and had been awarded the DFC that July. With 271 Dakota Squadron in England he had flown during the D-Day landings, and then, in September, had flown at Arnhem. On 19 September 1944, his was one of a number of Daks trying to get supplies to surrounded British troops when his aircraft was hit. Despite intense ground fire and his machine being ablaze, he continued his drop. When the job was done, he ordered his crew to bale out, but before he could get out himself the Dak's starboard wing broke away and the machine went in. Only Lord's navigator escaped, to be taken prisoner. Lord's old friends on Thirty One were much saddened to hear of the death of such a popular and respected comrade.

After the end of the war in Europe, and once the nav had been released from captivity, he was able to tell the full story of his pilot's cool heroism under fire. David Lord was subsequently awarded a posthumous Victoria Cross, Transport Command's only one, and his memory is still held dear by all on 31 Squadron who had known him.

On 6 February the Squadron was on the move again, this time to Hathazari, an airfield with an all-weather strip of steel mat construction. New records were set that month, for in those 28 days 1,703 sorties were flown to drop over 2,230 tons, landing another 1,385 tons and 1,046 troops. Thirty One flew to every part of the Burma front, from the Singu bridgehead north of Mandalay to the Ru-Ywa roadblock in the Arakan.

Howie Sharpe, once again concentrating on the washing arrangements, recalls of Hathazari that 'the camp had new bamboo huts plus the convenience of a bath house with a concrete floor.' But Benny Watts remembers another aspect:

> 'There, we were joined by the Americans. They dug in on the other side of the strip, spent days flying in supplies, and erected a large hoarding with their unit name on it. We were allowed to visit their cinema providing we took our own five-gallon drums to sit on. But we were sat behind the screen, which thus showed us the film back to front!'

Thirty One's boys often came into contact with Americans, and were always astonished at the amount of equipment and luxury items they brought with them. Within hours of taking up residence, they invariably had their refrigerators and ice cream machines working, things that the RAF never saw. Those meetings often provoked swift reactions from the more enterprising airmen on the Squadron, with, as always, tool sets providing the trigger. Horace Welham remembers one such story when Thirty One and the Americans shared a base:

> 'Very quickly, single tools, then whole tool boxes, were "liberated" from them, so much so that eventually the Americans said that they would gladly share all their tools with the RAF boys. They had to; the RAF lads had more, in the end, than the Americans!'

One could almost believe that tool ownership must have been one of the Second World War's biggest issues! Anyway, Horace was now onto another dodge, for when an American mess tent went up the smell of good food drove Thirty One's men mad. In no time at all he had fixed himself up with bits and pieces of an American uniform and, with a large bucket, had swaggered into their mess, saying 'yep' and 'hi' to all and sundry, removing everything he could lay his hands on. He returned to his own lines with a bucket full of steaks, potatoes, bread, doughnuts, ice cream – all, reportedly, covered in maple syrup.

The Americans didn't play football, (soccer, to us of course) but Thirty One's own team went from strength to strength. In a 4–1 win at Chiringa, all the goals were scored by Horace. Two days later the team, under its captain Leading Aircraftman Jimmy Broughton, soundly defeated 900 Wing 3–0. Horace again scored all the goals in a 4–0 victory over Chittagong. It's not surprising that, as well as being a fixer extraordinary, and later a leading light in the Association, Horace played professional soccer after the war for, among others, Wolves and West Bromwich Albion.

Many remember Hathazari for the cyclone of 12 April, with the newly built officers' mess and guard room being blown down. Horace recalled that event, if for no other reason than that he had been playing blackjack with some Americans shortly beforehand – he had relieved his hosts of over 100 rupees. When the cyclone hit, Horace was back in his *basha* and the gale was threatening to raise the bamboo roof. He continues:

'Arty Ball had just arrived, saw the roof start to lift, jumped up and grabbed one end from the inside. He then proceeded to go up and down, his legs continually disappearing from sight. In an attempt to save the hut, we threw ropes over the roof and tied six 40-gallon fuel drums to them, filled them with water, then tightened the ropes as they stretched in the wet. But it proved too much for the whole structure, the ropes and drums eventually causing it to collapse.'

As a rule there was huge respect between the RAF and the other services. But just occasionally things didn't go quite so smoothly. Warrant Officer Gordon England, an observer, has a story to tell:

'I was on an 0330 hrs take-off to Meiktila to collect casualties. At Comilla, the crew were met by a REME major who invited us to breakfast (our first having been eaten, of course, at 0200 hrs). He took us in 'his' Jeep to 'his' personal *basha*, whose walls were lined with coloured silk parachutes. The servants were dressed in white uniforms and there were white tablecloths on the tables. We were offered fresh lime juice, tinned Australian bacon, sausages, eggs etc. We could guess where the provisions had come from – and we were not impressed.'

One can see Gordon's point, but on the other hand the Squadron's usual diet wasn't so lavish that they could afford to turn down the occasional treat. And Dick Ridoutt, with his Australian appetite, enjoyed another encounter – in the jungle at Toungoo with a Cameronian officer: 'He was a great chap and treated us to a lunch of boned turkey, salmon, green peas, peaches and cream, plus a whopping Scotch apiece. The hell of war in the forward areas!' No wonder Dick enjoyed that lunch, for the routine diet clearly didn't appeal to him; his diary, somewhat depressingly, elsewhere records 'lunch today' as being 'omelette, tomatoes and prunes.'

Inter-service rivalry was further evidenced by an encounter involving the ever-combative Horace Welham. An army sergeant had told Horace that his unit was going to take over Thirty One's rather pleasant billets. Our hero protested, and a never-promising relationship quickly deteriorated to the point where the sergeant demanded to be taken to see OC 31 Squadron with a view to having Horace put on a charge. 'Where is he?' blustered the brown job. Spotting a Dak landing in the distance, Horace quickly pointed. 'There he is!' 'What's his name?' came back the sergeant. 'Trenchard,' said Horace. 'Marshal of the Royal Air Force Lord Trenchard!'

And Allan Coggon recalls an incident which upset both sides:

'The 20th Indian Division began massing in strength for a river crossing. At the 11 February briefing, there was nothing unusual mentioned for our trip when we took off from Hathazari on the second sortie with three tons of mule feed. We went across the mountains at 13,000ft and, letting down into the haze, we found ourselves in the midst of a crossing of the Irrawaddy River at Myinmu. In reality, this activity was a feint to draw attention away from the real crossing due to start the next day at Ngazum, but there was a lot of action going on; artillery fire from both sides, burning villages, dive-bombing, and the works.

'After stooging around looking for the DZ, the nav directed me to a new strip (which had just been taken the previous day) for landing. As we taxied to a stop and shut off the engines I could see that we were the only ones there. That is, until out of a small dust storm in the distance there emerged a very anxious, dusty and impatient brigade major in his Jeep. We had opened the rear cargo doors and were standing in the doorway. He peered in at our load and demanded, "What's that stuff?" "Mule feed," I tersely replied. He blanched, so that it was difficult to tell his face from his dusty clothes, then angrily yelled. "Where in hell are my artillery shells?" He jumped into the Jeep and faded away in the same cloud of dust from which he had appeared. We dumped our mule feed there on the earth and took off for our base. I instructed the navigator to report to dispatch what had happened, for I was too embarrassed to do so. We had landed at the wrong strip.'

Although the Japanese army had started its southward retreat, it was still fighting hard. Some of Burma's fiercest combat had taken place around Meiktila – and was still doing so. Thirty One flew in much-needed cargo, returning with casualties. Japanese small-arms, mortar and machine-gun fire was encountered constantly in the landing circuit and whilst unloading on the ground. Such was the crossfire that aircrew were instructed to shelter in slit tranches during unloading. One aircraft actually landed, unloaded and was back in the air in less than nine minutes.

Flight Sergeant Rowland 'Ron' Burton, a pilot, had a fright flying in. There would usually be a white cloth out in the landing area, but this day there was none. He circled several times and decided to land nevertheless. Cutting the engines he heard gunfire, so he and his crew jumped out and ran for cover. It turned out that the Japanese had taken the strip, but the army were just in the process of taking it back. Bullets kicked up the dirt all around the RAF boys. The long grass parted behind WOp Bob Webster's head. They thought their time had come but it turned out to be a Gurkha.

Meiktila was said to be 'a place of ordered confusion', which was probably a fair description. As the Dakotas approached, a radio commentary would be given by the flight control officer, describing Japanese ground activity. Sometimes even in a humorous way, as he himself was often surrounded by the enemy and under fire. But he carried on undaunted. If, on occasion, the field was in enemy hands or it was too dangerous to set down, the supplies would be dropped at low level as they ran the gauntlet of ground fire. Brian Stanbridge recalled:

'The strip there was taken over every night by the Japs and retaken every morning by our troops (including the RAF Regiment) so that we could use it. We could never be sure who was in control of the landing field, so each morning we would look carefully at the troops on the side of the strip during the landing run. If they had slant-eyes, we would overshoot and return to base!'

Alan Coggon remembered a particularly exciting trip there:

'The weather at Meiktila on that morning was marginal at best. There was a low overcast of a few hundred feet with a reduced visibility of half to one mile in moderate rain. We had a lot of difficulty in finding the Japanese-built north airport. All of southern Burma was reporting similar weather conditions. Since this condition was forecast, only loads that could be free-dropped were dispatched. The area of the airport we controlled was not long enough for landings because of the strong Japanese pressure.

'I had a three-ton load of steel rails and coils of barbed wire for perimeter defence. There was one aircraft in the circuit when we arrived; an additional one joined us before we completed our drop. Fortunately, seasoned and cautious pilots were flying them, as a very tight circuit was required in such minimal visibility. Each circuit required us to fly over the Japanese forces at such a low height that we all were very real targets for their small-arms fire. Thanks to providence we were not hit, although the possibility did increase the pucker factor during our six circuits. While we were directly over the runway on our drop the Japanese would launch small, black grenades from their knee-held launchers. If they missed the airplane, as most all of them did, they would damage the runway, or items that we had dropped. Additionally they had a mountain gun and a couple of anti-tank guns that were used sporadically.

'As usual during the drop, Jerry, my co-pilot, was at his station near the open unloading door. Even with the windshield wipers going at full speed, the forward visibility was blurred in torrential rain. I had my side window open and used the opening for most of my visual clues, with rapid, alternating scans of the instrument panels. At certain ground references, I had to turn on the green light to signal the crew by the door to "start dropping", then the red light to "stop dropping". On the fourth circuit, just after I signalled "start drop", four things seemed to happen at the same instant. First, a loud explosion took place just outside my open window. Then the port wing started lifting, followed by one of the engines quitting. To cap it, a warm, bloody mess struck me on the left side of my head and face.

'We were perhaps fifty feet above the ground. Instantly, I was busier than the proverbial one-armed paperhanger. My head and face didn't hurt. With my left hand I shoved and wiped the bloody mass off my face so I could see properly, while keeping the aircraft under control with my knees (under the wheel) and my feet. At the same time with my right hand I turned fuel valves, boost pumps, by-pass valves, propeller and throttle controls and "all-the-above" to keep the "dirty side down, and the shiny side up". This episode took no more than several seconds, but to the four other people in the aircraft it must have seemed far longer. As soon as I had the aeroplane straight and level, Jerry came forward to the cockpit and helped me. The engine failure was entirely my fault; I had failed to turn the starboard engine's fuel selector to the fullest tank before starting the drop. The engine had simply run out of fuel.

'During those critical moments I had allowed the aircraft to veer some sixty degrees to the right, and in that short time had travelled some miles away from Meiktila. In those flight conditions of dangerously low ceiling and lousy visibility, we lost about twenty minutes, until we found where we were and arrived back in the circuit to complete our drop. And what was that bloody mess that came through the window and dammed near caused us to crash? I hope that it was a part of a wandering bullock which had been hit by a shell of the Japanese mountain artillery. My mind will not permit me to think of the alternatives.'

The worst of the fighting at Meiktila was over by 30 March, its capture enabling Mandalay to be taken in April. Following this, General Slim signalled a congratulatory message to the Fourteenth Army, and it was heartening to note that it contained the following appreciative paragraph:

'There could not have been any victory without the constant, ungrudging support of the Allied air forces. The skill, endurance and gallantry of our comrades in the air, on which we have learnt so confidently to rely, have never failed us. It is their victory as much as ours.'

In order to keep the pressure on the enemy, the airfield at Toungoo, with its metalled runway, was captured before it could be destroyed. This became the busiest airfield in Burma, a steady stream of transport aircraft constantly coming and going. As Taff Evans again reports, it was now possible to station Dakotas so far forward they could see the whites of the enemy's eyes:

'It was decided that 31 Squadron's range would be extended considerably if an aircraft were stationed immediately behind the front line. This would enable supplies to be dropped far into Siam [Thailand]. One machine and groundcrew were, therefore, sent forward to the airstrip near Toungoo. When we arrived we found a little knoll that gave a wonderful view of the battlefield. We were able to see the operations of our host squadron and were fascinated to see their Thunderbolt aircraft take off. They immediately went into a steep dive to bomb the Japanese positions, five minutes later landing ready to be refuelled and re-armed for the next sortie. We could not help comparing this with our Dakota operations, which took hours of flying.

'We were accommodated in tents on the edge of the airstrip, and one morning we woke up to the news that the Japanese had invaded our camp. This caused us some concern, for we could have been slaughtered in our beds. Later in the morning we found out that we had not been invaded by crack Japanese troops, but by some poor youths who were in bad condition. They had been caught in the food store trying to steal our rations. Our concern turned to anger. We did not mind if the Japanese fired at us or bombed us; this was part of the game of war. But to sneak into our camp at dead of night and steal our grub was an outrage and typical of the perfidious Japanese. We felt strongly that this should be outlawed by the Geneva Convention!'

One of the goals the Allies had been aiming towards was finally achieved in May 1945. When an airfield on the Burmese coast was at last recaptured, the Squadron wasted no time in moving in. The place was Ramree Island, which had previously been garrisoned by 1,000 Japanese troops. During the battle to capture it the cornered Japanese force was rumoured to have lost many men to huge, salt-water crocodiles which inhabited its swampy areas, so it doesn't sound the most salubrious of locations. Indeed it took the advance party, led by Alan McEwen, a full eight days to hack anything like a level site out of the undergrowth. The garrison engineers would have their work cut out to provide operational facilities so, as always, the main party resorted to self-help. Corporal Peter Walker reported that 'We were digging trenches around our tents in the 130°F sun. The monsoon poured, the tents leaked – the only consolation was that our water barrels stayed full.'

Howie Sharpe tells us a little more about Ramree:

'We built our own huts. On the day of the move we were still fully employed on the usual supply runs to the Fourteenth Army. Instructions were given to dig drainage ditches around each tent and sandbags were also provided as the monsoon was about to strike. Ramree was reputed to receive 200 inches of rain during the monsoon period.

'The runway and dispersal were made of steel matting on sand, and pools of water as much as a foot deep formed along the runway. This made taking off in a loaded Dakota somewhat touchy, for they could slow an aircraft by as much as 20mph, so speed had to be gained in a series of bursts between them. Water would be splashed at least 20ft to completely soak the wings and rear part of the fuselage. On landing, groundcrews did a tremendous job keeping aircraft serviceable in spite of the rain and not having a hangar to work in.

'Spare parts were always in short supply and it was not uncommon to have several instruments out – but the crew flew an aircraft as long as the basics were operating.'

Flying Officer Bill Ashmore, a nav, also recalls the weather and the wet runway:

'I joined the Squadron at Ramree during the monsoon. I well remember one of my first flights into Burma, to Toungoo. I was acting as second navigator to get familiar with the conditions. Luckily the pilot was very experienced – Flying Officer Colville, on his last trip before going on leave. We took off, but the runway was so much under water that it came right over the aircraft. On the return trip we were in ten-tenths cloud over the coastal mountains, and the turbulence was so bad that we seemed to fall and rise hundreds of feet at times and the aircraft was being tossed about like a paper kite. It seemed to go on for ages with the pilot struggling to keep control (and the navigator wondering where he was). When we landed, even the experienced lads were looking a bit grey.'

Flight Lieutenant Norman Currell, an English pilot who later emigrated to Canada, remarks on the airfield as well as on the storms and the limited means the airmen had of avoiding them:

'They'd built the runway with a two-foot layer of sand and on top of this had laid a series of steel planks. But the sand was undermined by the drenching rain, then the weight of a Dakota would bend the planking and the ends would stick up. When this happened we'd have to circle in the murk while the groundcrew made running repairs.

'We found that the radio compass on board was the best indicator of the location of storms. If it was set to a certain wave-length – I've forgotten just what that was – it would point directly to the storm centre. If the centre was lying straight ahead, we would veer off some thirty degrees from our given course and work our way around the storm. This way we usually avoided the worst of the build-ups.'

Benny Watts recalls that 'the strip was so wet that, on landing, water came up over the centre section of the mainplanes, making one imagine that one was on a speed boat. It was difficult to distinguish the races that made up the inhabitants and it was found at a later date that two Japs were quietly working among the locals employed in the sergeants' mess!' This proved to be a harbinger of the situation the Squadron would meet in a few months' time.

The one thing that could be said about the weather was that, as described by navigator Steve Brown, the area to the east of the Irrawaddy River was in the lee of the Arakan Hills: 'That region was usually in the rain shadow. We would map and stopwatch from a prominent initial point and could, as a rule, find our way to the vicinity of the DZ.'

Dick Ridoutt, now B Flight Commander, describes the daily routine:

'The programme for the average crew was two sorties a day, the first around dawn, the second concluding around late lunch time, duration over three hours each. Next day would be a single afternoon sortie. If one was not on the early morning flying roster, there would usually be some groups ready to try the available grog. I think we had a ration of one bottle of Scotch, one English gin per man per month – no beer at all. For the rest it was probably Carew's gin – known as "Mad Carew's", which went down well with rain water and a drop of lime.'

Taff Evans offered a Welshman's typically poetic view of the new base:

'When we came to Ramree Island we were accommodated in tents, and by their very nature they were not soundproof, so it was possible to hear every sound from your neighbours. As I lay on my bed I could hear the preliminaries of a male voice concert. We had arrived on Ramree with the alcohol ration, so this had been used to lubricate the vocal chords and the choir was in fine voice. They sang about the invention of a piece of steel machinery. It obviously had a rotary action because it had a great big wheel which went round and round. Unfortunately, no brake mechanism was fitted so the machine just kept running and eventually blew up into pieces. The concert ended on a religious theme as the choir broke into a rendition of the hymn "What a friend we have in Jesus" except that the words had been changed so that it became a paean of praise for life in civvy street.

'A churl would argue that what we heard that night on Ramree was just a drunken orgy. I do not agree; it was fine singing with all the fervour that we Welsh call "hwyl", but above all, the 31 Squadron male-voice choir had wit and originality – and a repertoire that was unique.'

Pilot Officer Hugh Lester, a South African pilot, put a slightly melancholy slant on the daily grind:

'Fifty per cent of the trips remained supply drops, as my logbook tells me. They were usually solo journeys to remote and almost unfindable spots in the hills, where unsung heroes had been left to sort out the forlorn but still-dangerous enemy. Often, after dropping, we landed in some bumpy hideaway for a load of exhausted 2nd Division soldiers. I felt almost ashamed by these haggard and ragged campaigners, and largely remained up front, concentrating on flying. How frightful it would have been to do something stupid to them at the end. They seemed too weary for anything, and we passed each other by, often at night.

'Back at 31 Squadron, apart from the trips on alternate days there was really no routine, except sleeping under our nets. No enlightening lectures, only badminton between the *bashas* and futile efforts to shoot pigeons around the camp. Flying in our unfailing Dakota IIIs and IVs was only threatened by the often devilish weather among the frightening Arakan hills, Perish the thought of what would have happened if either of our Pratt and Whitney Twin Wasps had failed, for we carried undumpable loads of fuel, howitzer ammunition and lengths of interlocking steel for making temporary runways in the interior. I'm sorry to say, too, that we didn't spend enough time with Sergeant Smith and the "erks" of A Flight. Wonderful people, who I never bothered to befriend, to my lasting regret.'

The fighting wasn't over yet, and the Squadron lost another Dakota on 22 May. FL594 'Z' took-off from Ramree at 6am on a supply drop to Pegu and was not seen again, despite a search by the Squadron. 'Z' was crewed by Flight Sergeants Bennett, Cumming, Aubrey, and Moore, Flying Officer Wenning and Warrant Officer Miller.

Then there was another loss. Sergeant Furlong, flying KKI67, 'X', landed at Toungoo on 8 June with a cargo of tinned food. He took off again with his crew, Flight Sergeants Condon and Saunders, Sergeant Stevens, and Warrant Officer Schur. They failed to return. The usual search flights were made, but it was HQ that reported a crash at Luang-Chaung, eighteen miles east of Ramree.

Later a team was sent out under Allan Coggon to confirm the identity of the aircraft and crew. He recalls:

'The weather in June had been getting progressively worse. Individual storms became more intense and closer together. Flying from Ramree on 8 June, we arrived in the drop area to find the ceiling varying between a hundred and two hundred feet. There was near-panic going on. The radio was jammed with the RAF types calling for "QBB" and the Americans for "VDF" steers (courses to fly to home to one's destination). The weather strained my ability to cope with it. My aircraft, which would later be flown by Furlong and his crew, was declared missing that evening.

'The CO sent me out with John Vorthan, our engineering officer, on a jungle expedition in search of the crash site. The next day a gharry took us to pier five where we boarded a landing craft with a Burmese interpreter, a police sub-inspector, a Burmese sergeant boatman as guide, one engineering type and a couple of other RAF guys. At midday we met a local man who guided us to the crash site in the mangrove, and then we went to the nearest village, staying in the village elders' hut. We were told we were the first white men to visit since the time of the "great white mother".

'We were up at daybreak, packed our kit, had a cup of char and left for the crash site. We had to work at low tide, inspecting, probing and searching. There was a crater made by the colossal force of the twelve-ton impact, but it had already been largely filled by soft mud. So there was obviously no chance of discovering the cause. We buried what remains we found before erecting teak crosses that we made with the help of the locals. The villagers watched us pay our last respects to our comrades as we conducted, from the Anglican Book of Common Prayer, the order of the burial of the dead.

'Jack Furlong and his crew had performed their mission and were only eighteen miles, or seven minutes, from the safety of their island home. We thought of them – who had died so frightened yet so valiantly, in a land very far away from their loved ones. It could have been us.'

One pilot who particularly remembered the Furlong incident, again because of the weather, was Dick Ridoutt:

> 'We became uneasy when aircraft disappeared and were prone to blame the weather. One June morning I suffered one of the major surprises and frights of my tour through believing what lay on our direct track to Toungoo was a moderate strato-cumulus layer of cloud. We had in fact barged into violently developing cumulus, and suffered a completely limp control column, the sound of rushing wind, violent shuddering, and a feeling that large parts of the airframe were disintegrating. It seemed a lifetime to us, wondering when the aircraft was going to break into pieces. We were very frightened and I considered getting the lads into their parachutes. Glaring cotton wool all around us, the rain beating like stones on the windows, and the engines pounding away like merry hell! Poor old "Y" – what a beating she took.'

Returning to Furlong's accident, Coggon's search for the wreckage was aided by the Squadron's adjutant, Canadian navigator Flight Lieutenant Gerry Groves. Piloted by Pilot Officer Twiston-Davis in a Harvard, he located the crash site and was able to pass directions. This North American Harvard, a two-seat trainer, was FT102 and was attached for a while for general communications and liaison duties. It was not uncommon for squadrons to acquire light aircraft, and Thirty One is also recorded as having 'owned', whilst at Hathazari, a Beech Expeditor.

Chapter 12

The End Game

The Allies had now built up a tremendous head of steam. Thirty One flew over 1,000 sorties in June 1945, the monsoon not stopping anyone. And, in something of a milestone moment, Rangoon fell to the advance that same month.

Although the capital was now in Allied hands, damage to the docks continued to make air resupply essential, and Thirty One was kept busy there as well as covering almost every other location. After Mingaladon was retaken, a Squadron aircraft was among the first to land.

But the taste of moving onto the offensive obviously went to some people's heads. During an Op *Nickel* raid, one crewmember is reported as having spotted railway trucks and shooting them up with a VGO machine gun. Then, navigator Flying Officer 'Johnny' Brownjohn also got a little carried away:

> 'With the connivance of second pilot John Dunkley, I fired 200 rounds from the VGO gun into some Jap positions which were being 'identified' by Hurri-bomber attacks. The results: (a) an immediate rollicking from the armourer because he had to clean the gun; (b) a delayed rocket from Group HQ, pointing out that a Dakota was not an offensive aircraft; and (c) a disciplinary grounding for a week and a half!'

The monsoon still dominated, as Jack Baines remembers:

> 'A moment indelible in my memory was when we were ready for takeoff with a full cargo of 100 octane to go to the Thunderbolts and Hurricanes at Toungoo. With no warning, a violent thunderstorm struck from the overcast, rattling the metal runway strips like a xylophone. A bolt of lightning hit the gas barrel dump from which we had been loaded, 50ft from our tail. It split one barrel, flames shot up sixty feet and our only impulse was to gun the starter and get ourselves out of there as quick as the old Dak sweetheart would respond. The fire crew smothered the impending explosion before the surrounding barrels got hot, but what a show that could have been!'

Leading Aircraftman Martin 'Scouse' Cullen, a flight mechanic, remembers a similar strike:

> 'It was thundering and lightning, and as I was walking towards the aircraft to run her up, there was a flash which hit an oil drum and also the tailplane. It sent the drum spinning round for minutes; if it hadn't been empty we would have gone for a burton!'

During July the rain was almost continuous for three weeks, with rarely a break of more than an hour. Ground crews worked stripped – shorts and boots soaked – for hours to keep the aircraft serviceable. But, as Stan Walker, one of the Squadron's stalwart men on the ground, recalls, excellent work continued to be done: 'Our crew was the finest propeller-changing squad in the whole RAF. We could change an airscrew on a Dak III from start to finish in eight minutes flat, and there was no lifting gear.'

At the end of each day they went down to the beach at the north end of the strip for a swim before dinner. Dick Ridoutt recalls how rain there was an advantage:

'Bloody pilots! Those props will take a bit of straightening!'

> 'Swimming now became even more enjoyable, enhanced by fresh water showers as the heavens opened up, and we danced in the rain to wash off the salt water. Rain came down in sheets and lasted for five hours at a time.'

There were dangers even on the beach, though, as Walker describes: 'The lovely blue sea was tempting but deadly. After a dip one could come out completely covered in minute, glass-like crustaceans. If you brushed them off your skin they actually cut you enough to make you bleed. A real danger in places like eyes, ears (and other extremities!)'

'That's just about got them straight' Photo from Peter Walker's collection.

Howie Sharpe tells of the sea that 'There was a good beach at the end of the runway and swimming was popular, although there was a six-knot current off-shore, as some lads in makeshift rafts found as they were swept out to sea. Luckily they usually had the navy to rescue them.'

Ron Burton also recalls the swimming area off Ramree, for when invited aboard a navy ship he was asked whether he ever swam in the channel between the island and the mainland. Ron said no because he had seen some jelly-fish. With that the sailors got the cook to throw a line and some meat over the side of the ship and soon several sharks appeared.

Continuing on liaison with the senior service, Flight Lieutenant Harry Clark flew into Toungoo one day in June. Like Ron Burton, he had been invited on board a minesweeper off Ramree and was now fulfilling a promise to give a trip in return:

> 'It was pissing down with rain but we set to and started unloading – barbed wire and mortars. Took off again, still raining, and circled the beacon but we could not get above 8,000ft, so spiralled down again and landed, having to stay the night. I left my WOp/AG and the naval lieutenant to man the two Vickers guns as Dak guards while I and Harold Corey went into a small Nissen hut to sleep. In the middle

of the night all hell let loose as Japs attacked, and we took cover behind trees, nursing our .38 revolvers. The attack went on for half an hour or so. The next day when we flew out, the navy guy said he wouldn't bother again, thank you!'

Among the many hazards of the Far East insects were almost the worst. Termites ate through the main beam of a *basha* so that it collapsed, killing an airman when a jagged piece of bamboo went into his stomach. Anything left on the ground would be attacked. Stan Johnson lost the soles of a pair of boots. Horace Welham had acquired a new leather suitcase, but he put it on the ground; minutes later, the bottom of the case had disappeared. To stop the ants climbing into beds, the legs would be placed in tins full of petrol or water.

In the absence of ground equipment, a spot of improvisation.

Toilets, or latrines, were another 'interesting' experience. Mostly these were merely trenches dug in the ground, 'thunder boxes' being placed above the openings with, perhaps, some hessian screens around. It was a wise move to bang the lid a few times before sitting down in order to clear the swarms of flies! Once a trench became full, petrol would be poured into it and a light thrown in, before it was finally filled in.

This could lead to trouble. One airman, Titch Turner, who was described as 'all bush hat and boots', entered the screen one day not knowing the trench was about to be blown. While he was engrossed, someone lobbed in a light and the thing blew up underneath him. Another airman, entering a latrine, decided to clear the flies not by banging the lid but by throwing a lighted match down the pan. Taking the force of the resultant explosion was said to have been a particularly messy experience.

As the Japanese continued to flee southwards, there were interesting and challenging variations in the DZs. Gene Poulton and Jack Baines (pilot and navigator) recall their part in a July operation. Jack opens:

'Of all the Op *Character* locations, the most difficult was the double ridge at Tawhku, an ancient mountain where a volcanic bowl had filled with sediment to form a fertile inner plateau. We had an urgent drop to make to the unit there, picked up their location, and found their DZ marker beautifully sitting in the deep green bowl right under us. The problem now was to get in – and out again!'

Hilltop DZs brought para-dropping problems which included, not least, swirling winds. Poulton takes up the story from the pilot seat:

'Jack and I called this position the split peak but the first time round it created several problems. The DZ was in a high valley at about 6,500ft, the ridges on each side being 5–600ft higher than the DZ, and they disappeared into the overcast. To the south there was a dip in the west ridge which we called the saddleback which dipped below the overcast. We would approach this from the big valley, make a sharp turn to the north, drop low enough to push out our para-packs, after which we passed a rock projection in the middle of the valley which ended with the two ridges coming together again. We had to climb out on instruments high enough to clear the west ridge before starting the process all over again. Took six passes to get all the cargo kicked out. After several trips to this DZ it became routine, but the first time round was something I'll always remember.'

Even though the Japanese were retreating fast, it still appeared that it would take considerable effort to dislodge them completely. Nevertheless, this is a good time to reflect.

It had been a bitter, arduous, three-and-a-half year campaign. As noted much earlier in the narrative, it simply could not have been conducted without air support, and this was as true at the end as it was at the beginning. Indeed, Troop Carrier Command, within which the Squadron served, was widely recognized in later years as having done just about all the army had asked of it.

Thirty One's efforts during the time it had taken to evict the Japanese from Burma had been utterly stupendous, and to try to summarize them in a line or two is impossible. So we'll simply close this chapter with one reflection on the sheer scale of the logistic support required by the Allied land forces in the campaign. As recorded in *Drop Zone Burma*: 'Each day the Fourteenth Army alone had needed 2,000 tons of rations, and that in an area of mountain, jungle, swamp and dust 1,000 miles long.'

An epic campaign indeed, for which the Squadron was awarded several battle honours. As well as Manipur 1944 already mentioned, there were Burma 1941–1942, North Burma 1943–1944, Arakan 1943–1944 and Burma 1944–1945. Proudly won, all of them – and still proudly flown.

Chapter 13

Zipper, or What?

Now that the back had been broken of the Japanese armies in Burma, the next task for the Allies was to move southwards to clear the Malayan peninsula and retake Singapore. With this in mind, Thirty One was moved out of the front line temporarily – to regroup and to train for the coming operation. This would be named *Zipper*, although nobody seemed certain of the form it would take. Paradropping operations maybe? Glider towing? To the west coast of Malaya? To Singapore itself? All seemed at the time to be possibilities.

To prepare for – anything – the Squadron moved to Tilda in east-central India. Naturally, rumours about the coming task were rife. Benny Watts heard that fitters would be air-dropped with their tool kits. And as one of the pilots, Warrant Officer Dennis Brown, recorded:

> 'We heard that we were to fly back through Burma, via Rangoon and on to Penang Island, trusting that the navy would have taken it by then. We would, so the story went, have refuelled there before going on to Singapore. Most of the planners did not rate our chances of survival very highly, we heard later, so we were lucky it never came to pass.'

Sounds like a one-way mission! But not to worry. The countryside around Tilda was very pleasant, and the brief pause between operations at least allowed the boys time to relax.

But then suddenly, the war was over. Shortly after the atom bombs were dropped on Hiroshima and Nagasaki, the Japanese surrendered.

One would have expected scenes of wild celebration at Tilda, but the reports are somewhat contradictory. Some say the Squadron didn't even have beer available to celebrate the moment – although curiously, the record notes that 'the beer supply at Tilda was magnificent.' Memories clearly differ, and those who recall the survival equipment section producing a selection of celebratory rescue flares for VJ Day, of which 50 per cent failed, might just have been embroidering their subsequent stories. In any case the work still continued because, even though the bulk of the Squadron was in India, there were still detachments at Toungoo, Ramree and Mingaladon. There were still supplies to drop and casualties to bring out, so attention had to remain on the job.

It had been the same with VE Day; indeed the reader might, earlier, have thought odd the complete absence of any mention of it as the narrative moved through May 1945. This was not because the author chose to ignore it, but because of a complete lack of any reference to the event in the available records. Quite apart from official writings there must have been letters from home – news from Europe of what was, after all, a momentous event. And we must suppose that thoughts of going home also began to become more prevalent. But there's nothing to hand.

And so it seems to have been with VJ Day. Even in the marvellously detailed daily diary kept by Mac McLauchlan throughout 1945, it's extraordinary how the end of six years of war is almost casually dealt with. The one and only reference to it comes on 10 August with the entry: 'Rumours of Jap surrender?' Then, quite simply, it gets back to detailing the relentless work.

We may be sure that this doesn't indicate any lack of curiosity on the part of the men of Thirty One. More likely that their focus was very close to their noses: fly the mission; resupply the army; patch the aircraft up on landing; eat; sleep; fly the next mission.

However, Norman Currell describes a new move which, perhaps, sheds some light on the Squadron's low-key VJ Day celebration:

'I was to lead an advance party back to Burma. Initially the destination was to be Mingaladon, near Rangoon. My small detachment was detailed to get the location ready for the Squadron to move into. While there I was instructed to indent for sufficient booze for a victory celebration scheduled for about seven days' time. There were about twenty of us at Rangoon and I thought that there would be about three hundred by the appointed day, so I ordered sufficient for that number. As it turned out, a decision was subsequently made to move the Squadron elsewhere. This left me with about a dozen erected tents plus a mess tent − and loads of booze on the way.

'Various other units were, though, moving through, and I learned that one CO was having a problem housing his crews. I therefore offered our facilities, and he was pleased to accept. By this time the liquor was on hand, although we'd had some difficulty in raising enough money to pay for it (the powers that be were not inclined to simply give us the booze!) So when those transit crews came into our set-up we could offer them not only tents and mess facilities but also a choice of booze – to their great surprise. We were thus able to supply a need and, by the way, not only pay for their drinks but also finance our own. Finally, about two weeks later, we heard that 31 Squadron would be moving through en masse and would pick us up on the way to their new base.'

So they missed their party! Towards the end of August 1945, that new base turned out to be Akyab; the Squadron was going back to the bamboo *bashas* at the station that had been its first Burmese home back in early 1942.

We should note in passing that the Mingaladon team were privileged in one way − they glimpsed at first hand the Japanese commanders as they headed for Rangoon to surrender their armies in Burma.

Wing Commander Altman was at this point relieved by Battle of Britain fighter pilot Wing Commander Brian Macnamara, who actually found his new unit split into four locations: Akyab; Ramree; Tilda; and Mingaladon. Assault training was, of course, off, and a new task was crystallizing. Thousands of Allied prisoners who had been held in jungle camps were being released and needed ferrying out, and this would, increasingly, occupy Thirty One's attention.

With the alteration of the role, the balance of the Dakotas' crews was changing – and it was also necessary to reduce numbers where possible. Several air bombers, flight engineers and so on, who had been employed as dispatchers, were no longer required.

And, with evacuation of casualties assuming primary importance, air medical orderlies (usually known as air medics) had been coming aboard for some time.

The air bombers had played a valuable role, some perhaps retaining more of the 'bomber' heritage than was strictly necessary. Sergeant Laurie Moss recalls: 'Our business there was to bombard Burma with sacks of rice and other goodies, and I can assert with confidence that on my sorties we never missed Burma once.'

And Warrant Officer Cliff Freeman, a pilot, said of a delivery to 5 Squadron at their waterlogged airfield:

'It was a free-drop of sugar and rice – including weevils of course – into what resembled a paddy field. I can see them now, bush hats and groundsheets running with rain, watching three tons of stores landing in twelve inches of water. It must have been the world's biggest rice pudding. I of course reported at the debriefing that the mission was successful and the target had been hit.'

Nigel Piper was one of those now 'unwanted' air bombers:

'With the abrupt ending of the war in August it was decided that the ten or so of us were to be posted off the Squadron. We were flown to Chittagong and then deposited in a transit camp where no one knew what to do with us. Eventually we made our way back to Rangoon via rail from Chittagong to Calcutta and a boat up the Brahmaputra River. Eventually, some three months after leaving the Squadron, we found ourselves in a personnel documentation centre where we were greeted with "Where the hell have you blokes been?" We were given various administrative jobs all over the British area of occupation. I ended up as the adjutant of 49 Staging Post, Palembang, but that's another story. Flight Lieutenant Lloyd Ogden, my great friend, to his huge joy was sent back to Thirty One, by then in Singapore, to be assistant adjutant.'

In fact Ogden's story was interesting in another way. For all that one imagines there must have been huge urgency throughout the war to get people to squadrons, it had taken him a full two and a half years from call-up to front line. What with changes in requirement, sea transits to Canada for training and then to the Far East, and other assorted delays, he had been champing at the bit by the time he had eventually reached Thirty One. Now this latest change meant that his productive time was, in the end, relatively short.

Over the preceding years the crews had done their best to tend to casualties. By contrast, with the arrival of the new medical tradesmen a significant period was beginning. The story of Corporal Bert Edwards, one of Thirty One's most prominent air medics, was told many years later in the *Lincolnshire Free Press*:

'His eyesight wasn't good enough for a pilot. Life is kind, is his feeling about the fact that as soon as he got the bad news about his eyes, he spotted a notice asking for volunteers to "fly with patients", and before he knew it he was on the three-month medical course at Hendon. Strangely, although this was the birth of the RAF air ambulance, the service never had dedicated aeroplanes with red crosses on the side and purpose-built facilities. Because they had a dual use as transport planes it would have broken the Geneva Convention to paint a red cross on the side.

'Bert gained his pioneering experience at the time of D-Day. But by November 1944, with the war against the Japanese in Burma reaching a crescendo, he was sent with some staff to Comilla to use their experience to organize a similar exercise, bringing casualties back between Rangoon and the hospital at Calcutta.

'Bert had this to say about the work: "The Dakotas were by no means ideal for use as an ambulance, as the berths for casualties lying down were along the sides of the plane so there was no access to them from the one side. Medics and doctors in the field would tell us what was wrong with each patient so we'd know where on the plane to put them − a wounded right leg would go on the left, or someone with mental problems through trauma would be put away from the really badly injured people. The RAF doctors were back at base – there was just one medical orderly per plane so we were entirely responsible for casualties in the air. A great many of them were so badly injured that they died on the way home".'

The Squadron was now in Akyab, evacuating casualties and ex-prisoners. But they were not long to remain there, for the focus was moving further south. Soon Thirty One upped sticks again, this time to Kallang airfield in Singapore. From there they began carrying supplies into Malaya and the Dutch East Indies, returning with ex-POWs.

Flight Sergeant John Overton, a WOp/AG, was on the crew of the first Dak to land at Medan, Sumatra. To their consternation, after landing they spotted a Japanese flag flying from the control tower. The pilot, Warrant Officer George Hawkins, reputedly told the second pilot Fred Walker (they were both Australians) to go take a look. Walker delegated that order to the navigator, who in turn deputed John to go. As John climbed down, a car drove up, also flying a Japanese flag, with two Japanese officers and with a soldier at the wheel. In perfect English, one officer asked the crew to come to a local hotel for lunch! There they found a lone British army major, who had parachuted in just after the ceasefire.

Nothing if not versatile and adaptable, a couple of weeks later Thirty One was given in Medan what must have been one of the most unusual cargoes ever carried by an RAF crew. Seventy-two Chinese 'comfort girls' who had been employed by the Japanese were to be brought out. Listed as 'welfare facilities', they were to be flown back to Penang for rehabilitation. Flight Lieutenant Whelpdale was the pilot assigned and was, reportedly, not happy at having to take the girls on his aeroplane. But an order's an order and the mission was accomplished.

For men who had spent years in the jungle, Singapore's nightlife was tempting, and the potential hazards of over-indulgence were a constant concern for the Squadron's hierarchy. But work was the priority; the whole Malayan peninsula, as well as the Dutch East Indies, was rapidly becoming a backdrop for Thirty One's operations, and we can sense the excitement in the following two reports. First, Squadron Leader Spencer Whiting, a South African and, like Macnamara, a former fighter pilot, recalls:

'I joined Thirty One in September 1945 as A Flight commander. Almost immediately we were posted to Singapore and commenced evacuation flights of internees from fields in Sumatra and Java to Singapore. Because of the number of beriberi cases and the effect that altitude had on them, we had to fly low down on all return flights. On 9 October, Norman Currell had the distinction of being the first to land an RAF aeroplane in Borneo since the surrender. This event was written up in newspapers, and some amusement was caused when one reporter awarded Norman the fine title of "Invader" Currell.'

Then, Warrant Officer Ken Brunswick recalls a ferry flight from Akyab to Singapore:

'I was navigating as we carried personnel between the two points. Because of bad weather over the Malayan peninsula, we had to make an emergency landing in Siam [Thailand]. This proved to be quite an adventure, a welcome break after months of operations over Burma. My pilots were Flying Officers Grimwade and Ron Burton, Warrant Officer Benny Bennett was the WOp, and we also had Flight Sergeant McDougal with us, plus fourteen passengers. On approach we saw some people waving flags, but couldn't tell whether they were Siamese or Japanese. We landed, finding a crowd of about 1,000 Siamese, Indo-Chinese and Malayans gathering about us. The reception was overwhelming. They brought out chairs, made us sit down, then handed us glasses of fruit juice. An interpreter took Bob and me to see a local colonel, but this proved an embarrassment for he took us to be envoys of the British government. He gave us tea, assured us of his every co-operation and gave details of local troop dispositions. We explained why we had landed and asked for a guard for our aircraft. This he did, and that evening we were all invited to dinner – and what a dinner. Chicken, fish, rice and several other tasty dishes I can hardly describe. After some speeches we were taken to see a Humphrey Bogart film, being greeted by the cinema manager and a reception committee. We spent the night in two very comfortable bungalows.

'The next morning we had the problem of taking off. The strip had been all right for landing but was very short for take-off. The colonel got the locals to extend it by 300 yards, covering an anti-tank ditch with wood and a layer of sand. It took all day so we had to stay another night with yet another dinner with the colonel. The following morning we got away safely. I should mention that, with no heavy roller equipment, the ditch was made firm by a unit of the Siamese army being ordered to march up and down on the sand for several hours!'

And some trips were even wider-ranging, with navigator Warrant Officer Frank Malone recalling that 'from Singapore we became engaged in taking Australian ex-POWs from the River Kwai region and Bangkok down to Darwin.'

Sadly, during Operation *Mastiff*, the Thai phase of POW evacuation, the Squadron was reported as having lost another aircraft.

Despite the end of hostilities Dakota spares remained in desperately short supply, as illustrated by Taff Evans:

'In late 1945 it was thought worthwhile to send a salvage party into Burma to recover what was worth saving from a recent crash. The party travelled to Rangoon, then onwards to Moulmein. Then up the Salween River in a Japanese vessel, only wooden boats being allowed on the river owing to a number of the RAF's magnetic mines still being there.

'The aircraft had been little damaged by the forced landing, its dilapidated state when the party arrived being due to depredation by local people. All control

Accommodation was either in tents …

… Or in improvised '*bashas*'. Some of these were quite elaborate, featuring home-made furniture – such as the chair that Peter Walker is sitting on in the foreground. *Photo from Peter Walker's collection*

surfaces had been stripped, engine cowlings removed, seats stolen and radios removed. But nevertheless it was a most profitable salvage operation. The party returned with 8,000lb of Dakota spares worth about £12,000. All was returned in the boat and on a raft built of teak logs and bamboo.'

Now that hostilities were over the Commonwealth air forces began to recall their personnel. All the Squadron's Canadians were repatriated at about this time, soon to be followed by the Australians and New Zealanders. In the last year of the conflict about one-third of the crews had been from the Commonwealth, and they'd left a powerful

Doing the dhobi.

There was very little privacy, but needs must.

impression. They were popular people, as fitter Benny Watts told the author of *Drop Zone Burma:*

> 'The crews were more laid back than the Brits. There was one Canadian pilot who wanted to play poker en route with the other three in his crew, so he said "Here you are Benny. Watch the artificial horizon, oil temperature and pressure and give us a call in an hour!"'

Thirty One would never forget them and, in turn, they'd never forget their time with an RAF squadron in the jungles of Burma. Bob Webster, one of the Aussies, recalls the trip home:

> 'One thing that comes most vividly to mind is the final party for the fifteen Australians in Singapore mess on the nights of 7–9 October. It was a bash to end them all and we determined to drink the place dry before departing for Calcutta and home. We had been given a Dakota to fly to Dum Dum – and the CO, being a wise man, said they would pick it up from there later. He wasn't risking an RAF crew to fly with us! The whole fifteen took it in turns at being operating crew as the mood and booze on board took their fancy, and how we got to Dum Dum is one of life's unexplained miracles. On the way, we picked up a few odd Australians who had been on liaison duties in the jungle, mostly army types. They joined in the mêlée and probably prayed hard that we would get them there intact.
>
> 'The finale to this story came about fifteen years later when I met a fellow at a dinner party. He was reminiscing, and told the story of that flight. His final remark was, "If I ever came across one of those bastards who kept me so drunk for days, I'd kill him there and then!" I couldn't keep the secret so admitted my part in the episode, much to the delight of all present!'

In fact another of those Aussies disagrees on a matter of detail with Bob's story. Len Candy says that his 'log book records Warrant Officer Al Baldwin [a Brit] as being the pilot, at least from Akyab, where I joined the aircraft for the flight to Dum Dum. I have always remembered his name as I commenced one of the most pleasant trips of my life, the start of the journey home.'

Perhaps the CO at some point had to dispatch a Brit to rescue the trip, but time has drawn a veil over the details – which is probably just as well. Thankfully, we know for certain that there were no serious casualties!

One thing all the Commonwealth men wouldn't miss was British food. The one item abhorred above all others seemed to be Brussels sprouts. Many had hoped that, once away from rationed UK, things would improve. But RAF jungle fare turned out to be just as bad, especially breakfast. Canadian Allan Coggon commented:

> 'As I recall, it was based upon bread fried in grease, frequently with canned tomatoes on top of powdered eggs. Kippers and sausages were allegedly part sawdust but would receive from the Brits the hearty accolade of being "bang on". I recall some of the names; for example, chopped liver on toast was known as "shit on a raft".'

Certainly, they were adept at supplementing their rations, as reported by Canadian Gerry Groves:

'At Tilda, like most other places, the food was monotonous, so in the evening Otto Altman and I would go out and bag a deer. I remember one evening taking Doc Hallinan with us, and having to restrain him from shooting (at close range) a water buffalo. This was regarded by many as the most ferocious animal – especially when wounded – in the world. Once, after loading a deer in the back of the Jeep, we found ourselves being stared down by a huge hyena. After firing a shot to scare it away it just came closer; I guess it could smell the dead deer. So I had to shoot it, and cut off the tail to take back to the mess as evidence. I always carried a clip of dum-dum rounds, as we were in tiger country and I wouldn't like to rely on a normal .303 round for one of those.'

So the Commonwealth men barely tolerated the food, and to a man they found warm beer not to their taste. Many were said to have taken their beer ration flying, wrapping the bottles in wet jute sacks and strapping them to the outside of the cockpit window in a bid to increase cooling by evaporation. It worked – and they regularly enjoyed a cold beer after landing!

But we shouldn't leave the wrong impression in saying goodbye to the Squadron's 'colonial cousins'. Even if they weren't keen on British jungle rations, those men of the Commonwealth were very much loved and valued, forming life-long friendships with their British comrades. In later years, the Australians and Canadians even formed their own sub-sets of the Squadron Association, joining the parent organization whenever they could make it for reunions. Truly, a fine relationship.

As the Commonwealth men left and long-servers began, gradually, to be repatriated, reinforcements joined. But no posting to the Far East had ever been simple and travelling was often a trial, as Leading Aircraftman Johnny Graham illustrates:

'At Jodhpur, north-west India, I was informed in June 1945 that I had been posted to 31 Squadron. Enquiring as to its whereabouts, I was told it was probably somewhere between Imphal and Rangoon. To cut a long story short, there was a five-day train trip to Calcutta, followed by a sea voyage to Rangoon. Then road transport to Mingaladon, and finally a Dakota ferried me to Akyab. With waiting time included, it took two months.'

New aircrew joining from home found much the same problem. Warrant Officer Norman Cornwell, a WOp, recounts his story:

'On the flight across India, we were informed that Thirty One had left Ramree Island and was probably at Seletar in Singapore, so we were diverted from Calcutta to stage through Rangoon. Things were moving so fast in the Far East that when we looked down on Seletar all we could see on the heavily bombed airfield were Mosquito aircraft. There was no sign of any Dakotas – nor therefore of 31 Squadron. In fact they had been moved to nearby Kallang, an airfield on the outskirts of the city. We soon learned that the sharp end of the Squadron had already moved again – this time to Java. We were to join them in due course but, in the meantime, we were able to explore and experience the local culture. The entire situation in Singapore at the end of the war could only be described as chaotic.'

Returning to Johnny Graham's efforts to join the Squadron, as a reward for embarking on that odyssey from Jodhpur he was awarded the prize of remaining at Akyab on the rear party – and there he remained until Christmas 1945:

'The operation had moved on and there were only a few of us to celebrate the festive season, plus a Yankee radio unit. Between us we had no beer, six bottles of gin – and no mixers. Some didn't fancy neat gin so those who would chance it just pressed on. Imagine, sitting in a bamboo *basha* with a decided lean to port, sweat trickling down our spines and toasting the season with half pints of gin in chipped enamel mugs. Dreaming of a white Christmas was certainly the order of the day. And of the night, for after we'd passed out on the floor we were bitten from head to toe by mozzies, having of course been incapable of climbing under our nets.'

Chapter 14

RAPWI

Thirty One Squadron was not to remain long in Singapore. With the operation's centre of gravity shifting southwards, trips down to the islands of the Dutch East Indies have already featured in this story. Now Thirty One's full attention would be turned to this region. In October the Squadron was ordered to the airfield of Kemajorang (pronounced Kem-eye-rang), just a few miles outside Java's capital city, Batavia.

The narrative alluded earlier to another of the original Japanese objectives, which had been to secure for themselves the oil of the Netherlands East Indies. Java was among the locations attacked in early 1942, and the island had spent over three years under occupation. Many of its former Dutch residents had been imprisoned in camps in the jungle, and Thirty One's mission would now be to provide airlift from the remote interior to Batavia, which was to be the main point for processing these newly released people. From there they would be moved onwards by air or sea – or, if practicable and appropriate, prepared for return to life in Java.

The Dutch themselves were in no position to lead the operation, or indeed to make any significant contribution. Their European homeland had only recently been released from its own years of occupation. And in any case, there was positive antipathy among the peoples of the newly emerging Indonesia towards a return to colonial subjugation, so any immediate Dutch return would have been extremely unwelcome.

The south-west sector of the Pacific theatre of operations had recently been placed under Lord Mountbatten in his enlarged SEAC, so to the British fell the task of dealing with the immediate problem in Java. The mission was known as RAPWI − Repatriation of Allied Prisoners of War and Internees.

They arrived on 24 October, a stream of twenty-two aircraft at fifteen minute intervals. The Squadron at that time was huge, with 600 men who had been, at any one time and for seemingly as long as anybody could remember, spread over several locations and many hundreds of miles. In some ways, therefore, it must have been a relief for the CO to have his team together at last.

Accommodation was at a premium and they set about finding billets. As Macnamara was reputed to have said to the station commander, 'The Dakota does at least have one advantage, which is that, if all else fails, one can sleep in it!'

Continuing operations had not, of course, been the plan for the majority of the

The busy apron at Kemajorang.

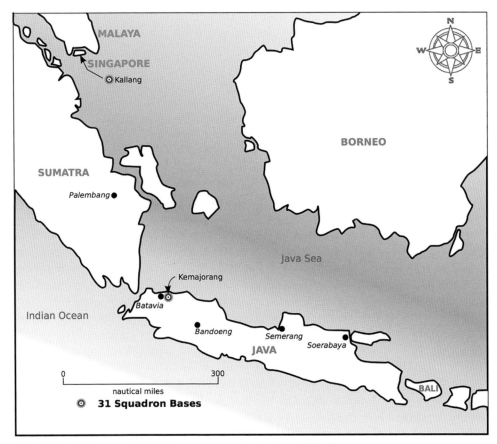

Map 5: No.31 Squadron RAPWI operations in the Far East, 1945–46.

Squadron's people, many of whom had already spent many years overseas. The war was over; they had survived; and they were looking forward to going home and picking up the lives they had left. But the work had gone on with, as already noted, barely a nod in the direction of VJ Day.

Similar conditions had caused trouble in one or two RAF locations where men had found themselves in seemingly forgotten situations. Where there was apparently little meaningful work, conscripts had been left kicking their heels rather than being repatriated and demobilized immediately. At the root of the delays were both the vast numbers of men and the shortage of transport. But that did little to assuage the concerns of those far from home. They knew that swarms of men had already made it back following the earlier end of the war in Europe. They envisaged the jobs, to which they had looked forward to returning, being lost, and feared that their wives and sweethearts would grow tired of waiting for them.

This had led, on a couple of occasions, to well-documented RAF mutinies. None of which had come to very much, but had nevertheless generated potentially poisonous situations for the authorities to deal with.

There was sufficiently demanding work for Thirty One to guarantee that there would be no such problem in Java, but there were also additional complications. The Japanese had encouraged the Indonesians to declare independence as the war ended and to form a local government under Doctor Soekarno. The Dutch didn't recognise this body at the time, but the arrangement nevertheless seemed to be working reasonably well. However, it wasn't moving quickly or decisively enough to satisfy the diverse nationalist factions throughout the islands of the former Dutch colonies. These people held much influence in the countryside outside Batavia and were proving a real thorn in the flesh of the British army units already ashore. Not only did they want the Dutch out, but they didn't want *any* Europeans there. In fact it was possible that some of them actually saw the British and the Dutch as a single entity. And, as in any situation in which isolated renegade groups are operating, there were probably some who were taking advantage of the chaos and disorder to create trouble for its own sake. It might even have suited the nationalist hierarchy to have had renegades taking action on its behalf. And, as we shall soon see, battles around Soerabaya would develop on a scale which suggested that the opposition was far more than just a guerrilla force. It was an extremely dangerous time, exemplified by the murder, soon after Thirty One arrived, of a British army brigadier who was trying to negotiate with a mob.

Little of this was known to the RAF before they commenced their humanitarian mission, and they would soon discover further complexities. As Japanese fortunes had faded, they had introduced Indonesian conscription and trained local troops; possibly to help resist Allied counter-invasion, maybe with an eye to the longer term. But when the Japanese were eventually defeated, many of them handed over their weapons to these newly established Indonesian platoons – or simply abandoned them. The British were not only uncertain how many weapons remained in the wrong hands, but also of how many local troops had 'gone guerrilla'.

Further, there were twenty thousand or so Japanese still in Java. Most were fully resigned to having lost the war and were simply waiting to be repatriated, in the meantime submitting themselves to British command. They were good workers and extremely well disciplined – very useful in fact. But there were some who were suspected of going over to the side of the insurgents, lending their expertise in a bid to stir up trouble. So the British could never have complete confidence in those who were working for them, which meant continually having to keep guard.

Java was a huge country, and the camps were spread far and wide. Japan hadn't complied with the Geneva Convention in publishing names of prisoners and locations of prisons. So the first task was to find the POWs and internees. The independence fighters were strongly suspected of slowing the whole release process down with a view to using some of the unfortunate prisoners as bargaining chips. In many cases the rescuers were having to fight their way in and forcibly free the inmates. The British army just didn't have the resources to do the job, and was relying heavily on the Indian troops they had available. But even that wasn't enough, so on a few occasions Japanese troops had been involved in combat operations – bizarrely fighting on the British side alongside Indians and Gurkhas against Indonesians.

An unholy cocktail, and Norman Cornwell, a keen student of history, enlarges:

'Immediately after hostilities had ceased, reliable evidence estimated that there were something like 123,000 prisoners of war and civilian internees in the area under the jurisdiction of SEAC. Repatriation of the POWs was one problem, but the Dutch internees were a different matter. Tens of thousands were incarcerated on Java and Sumatra, held ransom by insurgent groups of nationalists under the loose control of an Indonesian puppet government determined to hold on to them for political bargaining purposes. Murder, disease and starvation were

The loading party are all Japanese.

endemic. An immediate rescue operation became imperative.

'Both the British Government and HQ SEAC lacked the aid of allies and were extremely wary of being accused of imperialism, particularly by the USA. There was certainly no ambiguity regarding the aims of the intervention. They were clearly defined: the British and Indian armies were responsible for going in and facing a hostile opposition armed to the teeth with Japanese weapons obtained before the end of the war, and forcibly rescuing the civilian internees still held in the interior of the islands before they were either killed or starved to death.

'In view of the paucity of British and Indian troops – the only British regiment involved was the Seaforth Highlanders – Japanese assistance was essential at times, and joint engagements did result in the saving of many British, Indian and Dutch lives. But these were not, naturally, popular with the troops. The situation was certainly an odd one, and there was a general media clampdown. But, although revelations by, for example, the celebrated Laurens van der Post, later came out, it would in general have been an acute embarrassment to the British government to publicize the extent to which we relied on Japanese involvement to complete the campaign. Hence, it was not surprising that the conflict was frequently described as "the war that never was".'

And conflict it would certainly become. For Thirty One, the hugely demanding humanitarian task kept their focus firmly on the job in hand. A few men were repatriated, and others came out to replace them, but getting the Squadron together and settled was the primary task. Spencer Whiting relates:

'Trouble was brewing in Java and I was sent ahead with one aircraft to prepare for moving Thirty One to Batavia. The army didn't particularly take to the RAF coming in – they arrived about the same time – so we had to fend for ourselves in getting lodgings. Eventually we requisitioned the Hotel des Galleries, opposite the Hotel des Indes.'

Those joining the Squadron, not surprisingly, found the situation confusing. Leading Aircraftman Roy Fallows was one of a group of ground electricians who arrived on Thirty One from 146 Squadron, a recently disbanded Thunderbolt unit:

'The airstrip was about a mile from our billet and we had to walk to and fro each day while Jap officers travelled about in staff cars. They would lean forward in their seats and salute us. We the victors and they the vanquished, with them living it up. All Jap troops had been given small arms to protect the Javanese population from Indonesian rebels.'

The airmen arrived by all means of transport. Akyab rear party man Johnny Graham was 'still travelling' well into the new year in an effort to catch up with the Squadron:

'How or why we got a lift on coastal tramp steamer to Chittagong I have no recollection. As we had no money to pay fares, the only bargaining power we had was some vehicles left behind. I don't think His Majesty's government, or the RAF for that matter, would have condoned what we did, but we exchanged a Jeep for our journey. The Captain of the ship *Salama* said that there was no accommodation but that we could make the best of the open decks.

'Anyway we finally left Akyab on 14 January 1946, and it took us three days to get to Chittagong. Then onwards via some place on the Brahmaputra River. Here we boarded a ferry for a nine-hour journey upstream to rejoin the railway to Calcutta. Such was the chaos at the end of the war in the Far East, with servicemen in the most remote and unlikely places, that keeping tabs on everyone must have been impossible. In our case, we left Chittagong with no record of having been there and no notice to Calcutta of our impending arrival. We could have journeyed on up the Brahmaputra and could probably have been with the monks in Tibet to this day!

'In Calcutta, our explanation that we were trying to rejoin 31 Squadron seemed of little importance and, as they were expecting a large influx of personnel, accommodation was at a premium. So once again, after being suitably fed and watered so to speak, we were ushered off on a two-day train trip to Madras. There we were told that we would eventually be sent to Java to join up with the Squadron − when a troopship was available.

'This turned out to be the SS *Esperance Bay*, which conveyed us from Madras to Batavia. It had nothing to recommend it at all. I remember the toilets were down in the bow of this ship and the smell was horrific. And believe it or not, next to those toilets were the detention cells, so as you could imagine everybody walked the straight and narrow. I never heard or saw any more of the ship after disembarking in Batavia. The best thing that could have happened to it was to have been taken out into mid-ocean and scuttled. I think, there, even the fish would have given it a wide berth.'

And, shipping being at a premium, Flying Officer Denys Howard found himself in an even worse vessel when he left Kallang for Batavia with the rear party. They travelled on the collier *SS Bahistan*, which, by all accounts, was barely suitable for carrying coal, let alone human cargo.

Many of the airmen were accommodated in the city of Batavia in requisitioned housing. Quite a novelty after years of jungle *bashas*, even if not in the most salubrious districts. And even if, as in many cases, the houses had previously been occupied by Japanese forces. Benny Watts rejoined the Squadron there and remembers:

'The first shock I received on the journey to the billets from the dock was when I counted many dead bodies floating in the canal. All ranks were armed at all times.

The Seaforth Highlanders were the garrison regiment – hard men fresh from the Burma campaign. Paddy Hamilton and I sat in the Black Cat bar one day with two of them when a shot was fired into the bar by a freedom sympathizer. Paddy and I were about to rush off to the nearest toilet when one of the Seaforths said "Sit still, I'll get him when he surfaces." He had an idea where the gunman was holed up and patiently waited. He fired eventually and went into the building next door to find the dead body. It was said that terrorists used to give grenades to children of about six to ten years of age, who would lob them in an open window of the billets.'

The security situation was certainly confusing. And, as we've already seen, fraught with added complications. Taff Evans wrote a story about a trip to Palembang, Sumatra, but which could equally well have referred to Batavia and perfectly illustrates some of the difficulties:

'After we had gone to bed that night, we were awakened by a loud commotion. There was a lot of shooting and we could hear small-arms fire. We looked out but could not see what was happening, so we acted in the best traditions of the service – we went back to bed.

'The next morning when we went down to breakfast there was a strange RAF officer waiting for us. He was very angry. We were upsetting relations with the Japanese and they had complained that we were not returning the salutes they gave us. Furthermore, the noise we heard in the night was an attack on the hotel by insurgents, and the Japanese had fought them off. It was essential to keep the Japanese sweet, so in future we must return their salutes.

'From then on we took it in turns to stand up in the pick-up truck and solemnly return salutes from the guards as we proceeded to the airfield. I could not refrain from reflecting on the irony of it all. Two months ago the Japanese were fighting to kill us. Now the situation had turned round completely and they were fighting to save our lives from insurgents, and treating us obsequiously.'

Certainly, if any of the men had been under any illusions about how things would be after the war ended in the Far East, it didn't take long for the Squadron's new situation to disabuse them. But nobody back home could possibly have guessed at the situation, as Johnny Graham confirms:

'I can remember, along with others, getting letters from friends and relations saying that the home country was in a state of euphoria following the end of the war, and going on to describe street parties and welcome-home parties for returning servicemen on demob. I, along no doubt with others, did not reply that chaps on our Squadron were still being shot at and killed. Perhaps I should have done!'

The army was bringing equipment ashore at the port of Tandjong Priok near Batavia, as well as at a bridgehead being established at Soerabaya. Number 31 Squadron was joining 904 Wing, which would grow to become a huge, self-contained unit. As well as the Dakotas it would comprise 60 and 81 Squadrons (with forty Thunderbolt fighter-bombers); 84 Squadron (twelve Mosquitoes); two squadrons of the RAF Regiment; and a Spitfire reconnaissance flight. The airfield was extremely crowded.

For the army to effectively conduct their RAPWI work they had to overcome considerable local resistance. By 9 November the situation in Soerabaya warranted the move there of reinforcement Thunderbolts and Mosquitoes. A Dakota dropped leaflets over the town at 12 noon, calling on the Indonesians to give up their arms and disperse. The suggestion was not appreciated and fighting broke out on the tenth, increasing in intensity the following day. Thirty One's aircraft carried urgently needed loads of bombs and ammunition for the fighting aircraft. By the twelfth the Indonesian rebels had brought guns to bear on the airfield at Soerabaya, and Spencer Whiting was fired on in the circuit there. Flight Lieutenant Bowring and crew, flying to Magalang in KN576, came under fire and their Dak was hit in the rear fuselage. The view was that the Indonesian Bofors guns were so accurate that they must have been manned by Japanese – or at least the gunners had been Japanese-trained. Thunderbolts were called in to bomb and strafe these positions. In fact groundfire hits on the low-flying Dakotas caused such concern that, on occasions, Thunderbolts were diverted from primary ground-attack duties to

The tender ministrations of the crews help to minimize the strain on the pitifully emaciated bodies of released POWs.

The chap in the right-hand side of the doorway, wearing glasses, is air medic Bert Edwards, later to be awarded the AFM.

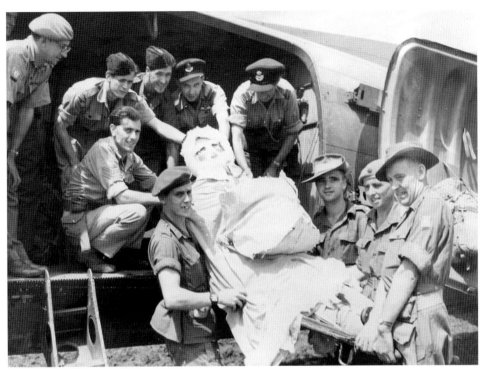

The ungainly and bulky looking stretcher case swaddled in white was not in quite such a bad way as he looks. He was in fact Santa – a part of the Christmas celebrations!

act as 31 Squadron escorts. And a measure of the seriousness of the situation around the bridgeheads was that both Thunderbolts and Mosquitoes were shot down.

Flying Officer Bateson flew General Soekarno, the Indonesian leader, from Batavia to Soerabaya in order that he might broadcast to extremist elements, asking them to lay down their arms and to co-operate with the authorities until an agreeable settlement could be reached. But to no avail. The disturbances continued, and Warrant Officer Sid Condon, a nav, had an even hairier tale to tell:

'On 21 November my logbook tells me that things hotted up. With the help of two dispatchers, we did a free drop to a hospital near Amberawa. This had been cut off by the Indonesians and was being defended by Indian troops who immediately sent soldiers to put out markers. The only approach to the DZ was over the village, then a steep climbing turn to avoid the hills behind the hospital. On the first run-in the Indonesians fired a few wild shots. On the second, third and fourth drops they were more successful. Several small holes, fuel pouring from the port wing tank, my radio transmitter emitting blue smoke, and a nasty little dent in the metal under my seat. Warrant Officer Brown, flying the aircraft, remarked that I'd nearly lost my wedding tackle. I recall that he quickly had both engines running off the damaged tank to empty it, and he looked quite calm about the whole thing – whatever he may have been thinking.'

Readers will be relieved to learn that Sid later went on to become a father! But Flight Sergeant 'Hock' Hockaday, co-pilot, tells a similar tale of a trip to Bali:

'We were sent to pick up some army officers for return to Java. We had been briefed about a mobile anti-aircraft unit which was still being operated by either Japs or Indonesians, and were given what was considered to be a safe height for flying over the battery. To be sure, we added a further 1,000ft. Having taken off from Soerabaya and reaching our safe height we set course. I heard a popping noise which I was not able to locate, and as all instruments were reading OK I asked the skipper if he could hear anything. He asked the navigator to nip up to the astrodome and see if anything was amiss at the tail end. There followed a smart order to "Get weaving, they're shooting at us!" The skipper put the plane into a diving turn to port and when we had sorted ourselves out we observed a neat line of shell bursts that had been creeping up on us behind our tail. The army officers were not too pleased with the violent manoeuvre. At debriefing I told the tale to another pilot. He retorted, "Don't worry old boy, they've been trying to drop mortar bombs on me!" He had been doing a supply drop in the mountains and Indonesians entrenched in the hillsides had obviously thought the Dakota below them had made a tempting target.'

A reporter from *Phoenix*, the journal of SEAC, travelled with the Squadron for a few days in the autumn of 1945, and excerpts from his report, published on 22 December that year, make good reading. He paints a vivid picture, offering also a wry perspective on army and RAF approaches to the problem:

'We reached Batavia three days after leaving Rangoon. The ammunition was being unloaded from the aircraft as we drove through the almost-empty streets of the city the Dutch called the "queen of the east". Farther on in the town almost every third shop was closed and there were scrawled slogans in scarlet and gold on the bare walls of office buildings – "Freedom, the birthright of every nation" and "We don't want to be ruled by the Dutch". In the restaurant *Tiong Hua*, downtown Chinatown, German ex U-Boat and merchant marine officers were dining cheek by jowl with Jap civilians and armed British soldiery. Some of the Japs were cashiers in the nearby bank, retained to clear up accounts.

'I went, with more ammunition, on to Soerabaya – a cargo of 3-inch mortars flown in by C-47s of 31 Squadron. That morning, the great Java naval base was very quiet. It seemed anything but a battle zone. The abiding impression was of silence and sunlight: the residential district an expanse of small, red-brick villas; and the gardens a sea of purple bougainvillea.

'But fighting was still taking place. The Indonesians had some 105mm guns set up across the lake, and they began to shell us while we were eating, the crack and whine coming unpleasantly close. Wispy black columns of smoke were blooming up from a line of houses about 200yds in our rear. "Really," said a brigadier, "This is too much at lunchtime!"

'If it had to be a war, the army favoured dropping the kid-glove policy. So did the RAF. "We could finish them off in a week; why not do it and get it over with?" But of course we weren't at war with them. The job of the British force was to liberate and care for ex-POWs.'

Chapter 15

Darkest Days

The released internees were now coming out in droves. Hundreds – no, thousands – of them. Bert Edwards and his team of medical orderlies were fully justifying their place on the Squadron. As he himself said: 'One of the most heartbreaking aspects was that our patients were utterly emaciated; just skin and bone. The Dakota would normally take twenty-four sitting or eight on stretchers, but the first prisoners were so weak we crammed fifty-six of them in because we had to rescue as many as we could.'

On the face of it, one might have expected those people to have been in a state of euphoria following their release, but such was their weakness that the crews often found them to be extraordinarily quiet and passive. One factor might have been their uncertainty about what the future might hold for them. Families had been split up during the Japanese occupation, and many now faced anxious searches for their loved ones. Most, probably, had no knowledge of the state of their previous homes. With the Japanese surrender, many would have experienced their camps' guarding duties being taken over by Indonesian independence forces, and would not have been reassured by what they'd seen of those people's attitude to the Dutch. So there would certainly have been considerable anxiety amongst the released internees about their long-term future. All in all, it is not overstating the case to suggest that many of the Squadron's passengers at that time were suffering to some degree from shock. Thus not only did the flight teams need their medical expertise, but also their counselling skills and their full reserves of understanding.

Signs of rising tension as the Indonesian independence movement takes hold.

The air medics became renowned for their care and tenderness, with Bert Edwards, who was later to become the chairman of the Squadron Association, receiving a singular honour. Conventionally, the Air Force Medal was awarded only to those who wore an aircrew brevet – and Thirty One's medics weren't officially categorized as aircrew. But in 1946 Bert, for his work on 31 Squadron, became the only corporal in the RAF medical service to receive the AFM.

There had been plenty of opposition to the Squadron's efforts but, up until 23 November 1945, the humanitarian mission had prevailed. That day, however, marked the beginning of the operation's blackest phase, during which it was hard to concentrate on anything other than conflict. Several airmen were returning from the airstrip to their billets in the early evening when shots were fired at their truck, some hitting the woodwork and cab. Everyone ducked, for most were standing up in the back. When they finally reached the billets, all of them jumped down except Leading Aircraftman Gerry Greenstone, who remained standing, quite dead, with two bullet holes in his forehead.

The atmosphere in the city had certainly been deteriorating, but now the reality of the situation was truly upon them. Curfew was imposed and increased security precautions put in place. But, as many forces have subsequently discovered, the 'urban guerrilla' is extraordinarily hard to combat. And the Squadron's worst fears were realized when a similar incident occurred on 21 December. Once again the target was a truckload of airmen, this time the lorry being lifted by an explosion from a grenade or home-made bomb rolled beneath it. Flight Sergeant R. B. Williams (WOp/AG), Corporal W. G. E. Frost (instrument repairer), Leading Aircraftman P. Boyd (safety equipment worker), and Aircraftman First Class G. E. Rowbotham (electrician) were killed, while Sergeant Weeks and Leading Aircraftman Taylor were injured. A nearby Sikh soldier shot and killed several of the attackers.

Terrible as those incidents were, in between them came an event of truly appalling magnitude, something which would shake to the core the British forces in Java. On 23 November, Dakota KG520 'W' took off, piloted by Flying Officer Ray Dight, with his co-pilot Flying Officer Jim Batten, nav Flying Officer 'Ernie' Howe, and Flying Officer Keith Smith (also a pilot, but presumed to be filling another role, perhaps WOp). They were carrying twenty Indian soldiers, while nursing orderly Leading Aircraftman 'Len' Singleton was also with them, probably in anticipation of a return flight with released internees. Soon after departure from Kemajoran they radioed to report that they were returning with engine trouble. Later came another message saying it was impossible to maintain height. A Thunderbolt was vectored to assist, arriving overhead to find 'W' already on the ground in a paddy field, with the five crewmen and several Indian troops standing nearby apparently unharmed.

The crash was close to the airfield and, in view of the short distance, Wing Commander Macnamara set out with a small party from the Squadron and some RAF Regiment men to pick up the downed crew. Bill Ashmore vividly remembers the incident: 'I was off duty at the time the message came through so a few of us jumped into a Jeep with the CO, picking up guns on the way, to try and get to them before any Indonesians did. Alas, though we were out for several hours and saw plenty of hostile locals on the way, we didn't manage to find them.'

Frank Malone, later flying as a passenger in another Dakota, takes up the tale:

'We flew over the crashed aircraft and could see that it was completely burnt out except for the wing tips and tail unit which were quite visible. On landing at base we were informed that all had got out of the aircraft safely.

'It was only later that we learned the awful truth. It appears that after they vacated the aircraft they were taken to the local jail where they were kept all night. In the morning they were taken to a dried-up river bed where, on their knees and one by one, they were hacked to death. Who was first and who was last we will never know.

'What we do know is that in later days as we flew over the spot, we all uttered a silent prayer and thought, surely, "This is a corner of a foreign field that is forever England".'

The details, such as they are, were later pieced together, mainly gleaned from an old woman who was found cowering in the otherwise-deserted village – which was known as Bekasi. Members of the so-called 'Black Buffalo' gang of freedom fighters had apparently invaded the village and chased out the local people. Whether it was pure happenstance that the aircraft had crashed in their vicinity or whether they had arrived after the crash was never established. Nor is there any information as to why and how the armed crew and their soldier passengers – who were also murdered – had been captured.

The woman had led the next morning's search party to the nearby river bed, directing them to a row of shallow, hastily dug graves on the bank. What was clear was that the men had been killed in the most bestial fashion, the majority having finally been decapitated.

The event became known as the 'Bekasi massacre', and naturally caused huge grief, anxiety and anger on the airbase. Not least, there was an overwhelming desire for retribution. But the perpetrators had melted away into the undergrowth, and in any case the army officer in overall command of the Java operation decreed that any punitive action would not be taken in hasty revenge, but after cool consideration. Moreover, it would be conducted not by RAF forces, who were bound to be emotionally affected, but by the army. Almost certainly those were wise decisions.

Particularly hard for the men of the Squadron was that their comrades had been killed while on a humanitarian mission, and the whole month's episodes left a huge impression on those who were there. Bill Ashmore summed up very simply the feeling of shock: 'We seemed to lose more men in Java than we had done in Burma – and the war was supposed to be over. Squadron burials became all too familiar.'

One of the cruelties of war is that so many events have a random aspect. People are simply in the wrong place at the wrong time. Airmen in the lorry with Gerry Greenstone when he was shot reported sensing bullets missing them by fractions of an inch. We shall never know quite why the extra pilot, Keith Smith, was on board the Bekasi aircraft. And, conversely, there were

A headless body is exhumed.

others who had lucky escapes. For example, Frank Malone had originally been planned to be aboard Dight's aircraft as a passenger. As he commented later, fate is indeed a most mysterious thing.

Dedication to their work helped the men to continue their mission. But personnel had already been jumpy about the rebels, and these violent incidents naturally made them doubly so. Leading Aircraftman Harry Jackson, a radar mechanic, vividly remembers taking his turn at airfield guard one night. It was an eerie feeling, he recalled, walking among the tents and *bashas*. He

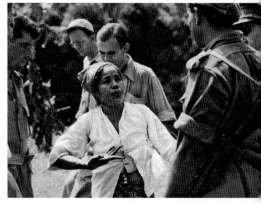

Understood to be a local woman explaining to military personnel where the bodies were buried.

would listen for sounds of a knife slicing through the tent canvas and be glad it was not his throat. The next morning they would invariably find a square or two of canvas missing which indicated thieves had indeed been present. Eventually the canvas would turn up in local markets or bazaars as paintings by local artists. Sometimes a whole tent would go, as Corporal Frank Bowman, a wireless mechanic, recalls: 'On Kemajoran airfield the continuing disappearance of the Flight tents caused concern but, of course, no offenders were ever caught. Rumour had it they used sharp knives on long poles to do the slicing.'

The airfield was defended by RAF Regiment troops but, being such a large area, it was impossible to make it watertight. Bert Edwards remembers approaching to land one day. The crew suddenly noticed that the windsock was missing, then they spotted some locals pulling it along and making good their escape. They radioed air traffic control who sent out a Jeep full of men who recaptured it.

On 13 January 1946, in poor weather, Dakota 'X' flown by Warrant Officer Derek Sharman and Sergeant Ross, with Flight Sergeant Stannard (nav), Warrant Officer Hill (WOp) and air medic Leading Aircraftman J.Reid, clipped the top of a mountain on a return flight, crashed and all were killed. Hill had earlier survived the action in November 1944 when Brian Stanbridge had been shot down.

Coming as it did not long after Bekasi, this accident completed a miserable fifty-two days during which the Squadron lost fifteen men and twenty army passengers. Al Baldwin had particular reason to be sad about this latest accident:

'Derek was my bridge partner, and John Reid, the medical orderly, was normally a member of our crew. Some weeks after the crash, the adjutant approached me and said he had heard from John's father who was upset that none of his son's friends had contacted him. Would I care to write? Not an easy task, but then I thought of the way my own parents had been affected by the death of my eldest brother, aged twenty one, in Singapore when the Japs attacked Tengah Airfield – and that helped a little. Mr. Reid stayed in contact, and some weeks after demob, while in London, I went to see him. He and his wife were still distraught over the loss of their only child, made worse, as with all our Java losses, because the war was supposed to be over.'

The temporary graveyard on the camp at Kemajorang, where many RAF bodies were interred.

Such was the horror of Bekasi that many would not talk about the event afterwards. And this was true for many years, to the extent that some never told even their closest families. Libby van Zyl, the daughter of South African pilot Warrant Officer Dugald (Dougie) Shaw, told the author shortly after her father's death that she 'sensed there was something, but never knew the truth.' But conversely, he had told her some marvellously positive stories about other episodes. Truly, the mind has its own ways of dealing with such things, so let's lighten the atmosphere a little by hearing one of Libby's stories:

'There was a wounded doctor who had been caught by a blast – his eyes had been damaged and they needed a crew to fly him out to Batavia. As dad and his crew were coming in to land they were refused permission as the tower said there was total cloud. Dad maintained it was a miracle because suddenly both he and his crew saw a space in the clouds with a direct path onto the landing strip – the tower could still neither see nor hear them but they made a perfect landing. The guy they had medivac'd out did keep his sight, and dad always thought that that trip was meant to be.'

Chapter 16

Aftermath

A task which was to assume huge significance for the Squadron stemmed from the town of Bandoeng being surrounded by insurgent-held country. Surface resupply had failed, with both trains and vehicle convoys being ambushed, so Bandoeng and back became routine over the ensuing months.

Up to eight machines a day would fly several return trips, taking in food, clothing, medical supplies, petrol and ammunition for the civil and military population. Indeed, the *Batavia Evening News* of 11 February 1946 headlined its report 'The Bandoeng Air Express, as Regular as a London Bus.' It noted that on one particular day 'the Squadron flew in 168 tons of supplies in sixty-four sorties.' The article went on to pay tribute to the massive ground effort required:

> 'These pack-horse patrols are no less an effort for the men on the ground – the fitters and riggers who have earned 31 Squadron one of the best reputations for servicing in South-East Asia. Also for the men of 799 Company, Royal Army Service Corps (Air Dispatch) who load and lash the freight. The Squadron's ground crews are at work by 5.30 in the morning, often squelching through almost knee-deep mud after a night of torrential monsoon rain, getting the aircraft ready for the first sortie. They operate in shifts, the early morning crews going back to their billets for a rest and returning to the airfield in the late afternoon to work up to 6.30pm on the last aircraft to land. The weather at this time of the year is the greatest enemy. Working soaked to the skin is no new discomfort to these Burma veterans – many of them learned this high-speed servicing in similar weather conditions in the rush days of the Arakan campaign – but there are limits to the amount of maintenance that can be achieved in lashing rain. In good weather and bad, the demands on the Dakotas remain the same, and hours lost in a monsoon downpour must be made up some time in the day – usually in the evenings. For the men of air dispatch the bulk of the loading work begins after the 4 o'clock conference every afternoon which decides the following day's programme. They are frequently at the airfield until 8pm to ensure that everything is on board in time for the early morning take-off.'

It's good to see the groundcrew getting their fair share of appreciation. As noted, the weather was often appalling, and Flight Lieutenant Eddy Collyer, who had joined as adjutant as the war ended, had a further, wry observation to make on its effects. His recollection was of seeing rice growing on the cabin floors of the Dakotas. Spilled from damaged sacks, it would drop through the metal floors and start to grow in the dirt and damp below. Indeed there was a story about an aircraft that wouldn't trim out at all. After all the usual engineering investigations, they eventually took up the floor – to discover there a veritable paddy field.

Norman Cornwell tells of Bandoeng from the aircrew viewpoint:

'Bandoeng lies high up, within a ring of treacherous mountains reaching heights of over 1,000 metres. The normal approach to its airfield was to fly between the mountains and volcanoes, on which numerous hostile villages were situated. In the very early days it was not an uncommon experience to come under fire, but these attacks were not sustained and the greatest danger to us was the high ground.

'The town itself has one of the nicest climates on the island but, during the monsoon, after a reasonably clear start to the day, the clouds would rapidly form over the hills, their base levels lowering to cover the volcano summits, producing torrential rain, heavy turbulence and thunderstorms, making access through the gaps extremely hairy. Therefore all the aircrews on the Bandoeng runs tried desperately to get their sorties over as quickly as possible before the gaps between cloud base and mountain passes became too narrow to fly through.'

Flight Lieutenant Morris Averill relates an incident when 37 Brigade was held up:

'We dropped a load of tank spares to an ambushed convoy. It was a precision drop, for we only had a narrow lane 200 yards long to deliver the spares. A signal later received by the CO read as follows: "During the Bandoeng convoy battle one company of my battalion was escorting tanks of the 13th Lancers. On 12 March they were short of ammo and tank spares and asked for them by air. Since their return I have spoken to the company commander and many of the men and they are all loud in their praises of the pin-point accuracy of the drop. The sepoys are absolutely certain that if they get into a tight place the RAF will come and keep them supplied with everything".'

Despite the action, Bandoeng trips could be repetitive, as Al Baldwin observes:

'Nothing could lift the feeling of gloom on remembering, after an early "wakey-wakey", that one was rostered for the four-leg Batavia-Bandoeng shuttle. First there was the gharry ride to the airfield in pitch darkness to be dropped by our respective flight tents, there to shuffle in and read the flying details chalked on the blackboard. On one occasion this familiar routine was disrupted when we discovered that "loose wallahs" had nicked the tent. Only the canvas, mind, they had left the contents untouched so that tables, chairs, carpet and blackboard lay open to the skies.

'Should you feel I exaggerate the unpopularity of the Bandoeng shuttle I can tell you it was used as a punishment on occasions! It was the habit of some of the would-be "train busters" amongst us to beat up the Bandoeng control tower on the first sortie and this came to the notice of the CO. A check was made and the culprits were sentenced to a whole week on the shuttle.

'Just what were they missing? All sorts of good trips: dropping supplies on the governor's palace in Buitenzorg and other isolated garrisons; Batavia to Bali with personnel going on R&R; Batavia to Balikpapan (Borneo) night stop; Batavia to Soerabaya, dropping leaflets en route. And the best of the lot: Batavia–Palembang–Padang–Medan–Singapore – for a night stop, where one could refuel with quantities of Anker Donker (or whatever that beer was called!)'

Most of the Bandoeng work took place in 1946, but to return to the last days of '45 the reader will have noted that Christmas and New Year passed without a mention. Perhaps unsurprising, for with Bekasi *et al* it would have been difficult to feel festive. But servicemen are resilient, and there were certainly attempts to lighten the atmosphere. Although, as Norman Cornwell illustrates, it was difficult to get away from the ever-present threat:

'There were several camps in Batavia that housed the families of ex-internees whose only home was on the island. Their lot was not a happy one as they were forced to live in heavily armed reservations whilst they optimistically awaited the political developments that would enable them to return to their own homes. We used to visit these camps, and liaisons inevitably formed.

'During December 1945, many visits to the camps had to be cancelled due to the hostile activity. However, with Christmas and the new year on

Dutch women and families continue to be grateful to the Squadron.

the horizon it was decided to try to make special arrangements. Special protection arrangements were put into place to ensure our safe journeys and the camps were given perimeter cover by Gurkha troops.

'Christmas Day turned out to be a complete non-starter as the Indonesians, sensing that we would all be full of food and alcohol, concentrated their attention on the British compounds, necessitating our manning defences throughout the whole of the day and night. However, New Year's Eve was quite another story and one that I am unlikely to forget. We had a complete day off from flying, and shortly after lunch the decision was taken to visit one of the camps. With an RAF Regiment escort in armed vehicles, we arrived safely. The refugee camp was widely spread out and, once there, the party split up and dispersed in order to visit our various hosts.

'At first everything seemed perfect as I sat outside in the early, warm evening with my charming hosts, enjoying a very civilized light meal and drinks. Then it all turned sour. As darkness fell one of the Gurkha officers called to inform us that there was a strong probability that our particular area of the camp might come under attack later in the night and extra troops had already been called up and were in position around the camp boundaries. Some time later, when nothing untoward had happened, we were feeling complacent, but this was soon shattered when he turned up again to give us a further briefing. All families were to remain in their houses and lock their windows and doors, whilst all the visiting military guests were to take up a position in the surrounding gardens with their weapons loaded, which for the army personnel were Sten sub-machine guns and, for the aircrew, revolvers. He then explained the defence arrangements. If and when the expected attack started, his own troops would engage them first from their positions on the perimeter, and if there was a risk of a break-through, yellow flares would be fired into the air. In the event of a serious breach in the outer defences, the troops would fall back into the gardens firing red flares, where they would expect to meet up with the military guests, such as ourselves. Once that situation had been reached, we were instructed to fire at everything that moved in the vegetation in front of us. During the early hours of the morning we heard the first sounds of gunfire. Then up went the yellow flares.

'Very soon afterwards the first batch of outnumbered Gurkhas burst into the gardens and the sky was lit up by red flares. For something like twenty minutes, all hell broke loose, with bullets flying in all directions, but in spite of hearing the Indonesians shouting at each other, they seemed content to lay off in the undergrowth and fire from its cover. Above the din, the Gurkha officers and NCOs were barking orders to their men to continue firing and regroup. I had used my Smith and Wesson revolver on a couple of occasions previously when I was caught out illegally breaking the nightly curfew, but this situation was quite different, as both sets of antagonists were on top of each other. With the calibre of the revolver the same as a service rifle, it had a kick like a mule and, in other than professional hands, was not the sort of weapon to inspire confidence. Nevertheless, I certainly put it to use that night. Firing as instructed into the surrounding dense vegetation, I suppose that it could be said that I contributed something to the defence of the camp, even if I suspect it was only to create a noise. A few of the attackers did break cover but were immediately cut down by the Gurkhas who, having reformed, unsheathed their traditional kukri knives and counterattacked. At this, the Indonesians fell back in full retreat, leaving us amateurs to get our breath back once more.

'The Indonesians continued throughout the night to fire off sporadic, long-range pot shots in the general direction of the camp. In the meantime, ambulances arrived to take away the casualties from both sides, and checks were immediately made to establish whether anyone was missing. One such turned out to be a crewmember of ours, who had last been seen disappearing into the undergrowth with his girlfriend late the previous evening, and the situation was serious enough to mount an unsuccessful search party. At dawn however, our somewhat bewildered and dishevelled Romeo appeared from out of the undergrowth, accompanied by his girlfriend. They had been caught in no-man's-land and he had had no alternative but to look after her by taking refuge in the ditch (well, that was his story, anyway!) Whilst lying there they had apparently been alternately leaped over by both Indonesians and Gurkhas. Our man, usually so immaculate, was in a filthy state and his girlfriend had all the appearances of someone who had been dragged through a hedge backwards.

'In spite of all these difficulties, the camp visits still continued and, whilst most of the liaisons were of a temporary nature, serious relationships were established which later resulted in marriage.'

Later in the year an airfield in the interior caused a good deal of excitement. Ken Brunswick remembers:

Nothing was designed better to lift the spirits than having a pretty young Dutch ex-internee serve the tea.

'I remember flying several sorties to Solo in central Java. Owing to the tense situation prevailing between the newly-emergent Indonesian Republicans, the Dutch, and the British forces, RAF flying crews were ordered not to carry firearms there, in contrast with the usual practice. I have a feeling we disobeyed the order, although leaving our revolvers in the aircraft when we deplaned! But we felt naked without them as we mingled with the Indonesians who occupied the airstrip. I recall being transported with the rest of the crew across the airstrip in a lorry. Several fearsome-looking locals sat with us armed to the teeth with swords and guns. At this point the lorry backfired and we prayed that our fellow occupants did not think any of us had been firing on them!

And there was always time for a game of cricket.

'The duty was to pick up Dutch women and children ex-internees which the Indonesians were letting out. A senior RAF officer had to be in attendance at Solo.'

The reason for this last was that the airfield was totally in Indonesian hands, a fact that had the potential to cause difficulties. The most infamous example occurred one day when the CO of 904 Wing was at the helm of one of Thirty One's Dakotas. Several chapters ago, it was mentioned that the red had been removed from RAF roundels to avoid confusion, and now an unexpected consequence was about to manifest itself. Group Captain David Lee, (Air Chief Marshal Sir David by the time he was writing) recounts the story nicely in his book '... *and we thought the war was over*':

'The runway looked all right, about 1600 yards I guessed, but the thing that struck me was that the grass was at least three feet high, more like a field of hay than the borders of an airfield, and I could distinctly see guards lying in the grass with their weapons at the ready. I made a careful approach and a reasonable landing.

'Early Days on the Frontier'. An impression in oils by Ian Wilson-Dick of one of the first flight lines in India.

'Khyber Patrol'. From an oil painting by Gerald Bauer. The original is amongst the Goldstar Collection of aviation art.

'Chitral Relief'. From an oil by Ian Wilson-Dick. Valentias revolutionized the process of garrison changeover on the Frontier.

Dakota Attack, by Gerald Bauer. The Japanese attack Myitkyina, catching Squadron Dakotas unloading. A painting in the Goldstar Collection.

'31 Squadron Departs Mauripur, Pakistan, 1947'. Dakotas over R&I (the Repair and Inspection section), depicted in oils by Ian Wilson-Dick.

'Paveway Tornados', reproduced by permission of ex-31 Squadron Jaguar pilot Mike Rondot. The second aircraft bears the markings of 14 Squadron. Mike has made a successful later career in aviation art and his work may be seen at www.collectair.co.uk.

A Jaguar at low level over the North German Plain.

A Phantom powers off the runway. This particular aircraft bears roundels to match both the dark upper surface and the light underside. Not all aircraft were so cleverly painted

During Tornado times it became fashionable to decorate aircraft to mark anniversaries.

The painters and finishers take a break with CO Wing Commander Steve Parkinson after completing the paint job for the 80th anniversary.

The 90th, as seen in 2004 by cartoonist Corporal Darryl Robinson, at the time an honorary member of the Squadron Association.

The 75th in 1990. The original colour scheme was predominantly yellow, which led to the aircraft being dubbed the 'Flying Banana'. It was not popular, with the see-off team for its first flight said to have registered their disapproval by wearing paper bags over their heads. Subsequently, much of the yellow was toned down with green to give the finish shown here.

The livery which is planned to be displayed to mark the Squadron's centenary.

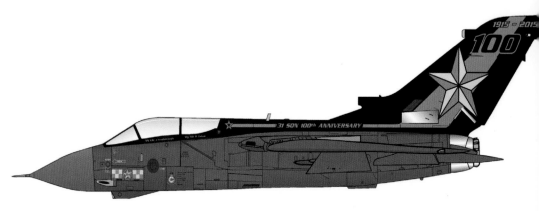

Gulf Conflict nose art

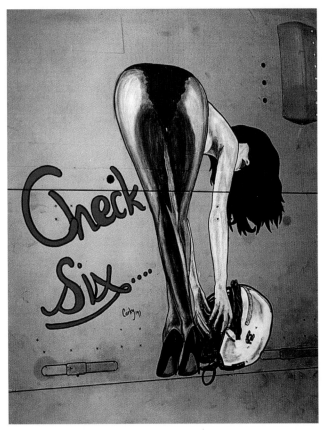

The Squadron's primary artist was Paul 'Corky' Cawthorn. 'Luscious Lizzie' was, incidentally, a Brüggen schoolteacher affiliated to Thirty One – who would later marry Goldstar pilot Keith Taylor.

Amongst the mass of press attention surrounding modern-day operations, the *Daily Star* seemed almost to adopt Thirty One during the Gulf Conflict. Here, they arranged for ex-prime minister Margaret Thatcher to present the boss with the paper's appropriately named 'Gold Star' award. *Daily Star*

The Iraq conflict – or 'Gulf War Two'

The armourers assemble a laser–guided bomb.

A GR4 lands at Ali al Salem with a ruined HAS in the background. It had been acknowledged when HASs had been put up on airfields across Europe and the Middle East that they would offer protection to 'all but direct hits'. What nobody had counted upon was the increasing ability to deliver munitions with such precision. *Photo by Paul Saxby*

NBC kit is no fun to wear at the best of times. In the desert climate it was hell.

The patch which represented the Tornado Combat Air Wing during the Iraq Conflict. It incorporates the badges of II(AC), IX(B), XIII, 31 and 617 Squadrons.

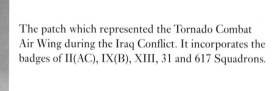

A stunning picture which became well known through exposure in the press. It was taken by Thirty One's Corporal Mark Handford.

With its updated avionics suite the GR4 is virtually a new aircraft. But the external difference between it and the GR1 is, apart from the paint job, limited merely to the addition of the FLIR sensor under the nose. External stores carried are another matter, with a plethora of new equipment appearing during the aircraft's last decade in service.

Left: ALARM. A weapon which has come and gone, withdrawn in December 2013. This early GR4 still sports the black nose inherited from the GR1; later aircraft were all-over grey. With the GR4's arrival the Squadron speedbird marking also disappeared, primarily because the RAF-wide introduction of standard-sized decals made it impractical. Instead, green and gold checked markings, last seen on the Jaguar, were re-introduced.

Right: Brimstone. On deployed ops generally seen on the rear stations, with Paveway laser-guided bombs forward.

Below: A GR4 at low level. The strobe light, an anti-collision measure, catches the camera. *Photo by Ian Sykes*

Right: The flagship GR4, '031'. The store on the fuselage station is Litening III, while on the port outboard is Skyshadow. *Photo by Ian Sykes*

A rare honour for a foreign military unit

The *Fahnenband* awarded by the German state shortly before the Goldstars' final departure from Brüggen.

Given to mark Germany's appreciation of a job well done, Wing Commander Paddy Teakle receives the *Fahnenband* on behalf of 31 Squadron.

'Over to You.' 4 December 2014: Wing Commander Rich Yates hands over ninety-nine years of history to his successor, Wing Commander James Freeborough. Following their flight together, James will lead the Goldstars through their centenary year.

Badges

The original Squadron Badge, awarded in the mid-1930s and believed lost in a fire at Comilla in 1945.

The replacement Badge, with its Queen's crown and lacking the 'Army Co-operation' epithet. The original re-surfaced mysteriously in 1965 and the two now both hang at RAF Marham.

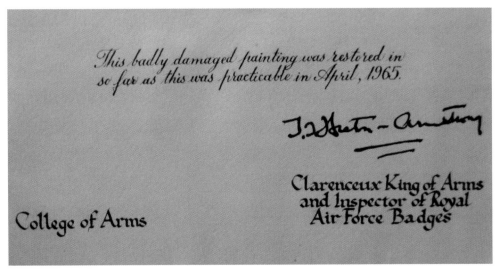

Recorded on the back of the first Badge is the evidence of its restoration by the College of Arms.

Standards

The third Standard is uncased. Air Marshal Greg Bagwell looks on; the standard bearer is Flight Lieutenant Steve Eccles. *Crown copyright*

CO Wing Commander Rich Yates marches his Squadron off after receiving its new Standard. *Crown copyright*

070

31 SQUADRON STANDARD PARADE

29 JANUARY 2014

1915 Farnborough

2014 Marham

The programme for the day. *Crown copyright*

The Squadron's Standards develop over the years

The first Standard, seen here being paraded at the handover from Canberras to Phantoms in 1971, displayed eight battle honours throughout its thirty-year life

The second Standard, however, lived through a period of conflict in which 31 Squadron was very much involved. Although it was presented in 1986 bearing eight battle honours, policy was changed after the Gulf Conflict to permit up to fifteen to be emblazoned. Here we see it wearing its ninth, 'Gulf 1991'.

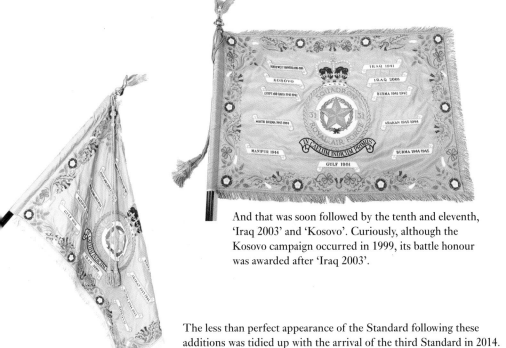

And that was soon followed by the tenth and eleventh, 'Iraq 2003' and 'Kosovo'. Curiously, although the Kosovo campaign occurred in 1999, its battle honour was awarded after 'Iraq 2003'.

The less than perfect appearance of the Standard following these additions was tidied up with the arrival of the third Standard in 2014.
Crown copyright

Stones and monuments

In 2002 the Association presented the Squadron with a stone commemorating its fallen. The stone stands now outside the Squadron's headquarters at RAF Marham.

The Association has placed this fine monument in the gardens of the National Memorial Arboretum at Alrewas. It is already standing, but will be dedicated at a ceremony on the day of the centenary, 15 October 2015. The presiding officer will be the Squadron's senior serving ex-member, Vice Chief of the Defence Staff, Air Chief Marshal Sir Stuart Peach.

'I was not prepared for what happened next as I put on my battered gold-braided hat and climbed out. Sure enough, a small General, whom I at once recognized as Subidio, came marching out to meet me without a smile or any sign of welcome on his face. Before I could even say "Good morning, General," he loosed off a string of Malay, of which I didn't understand a word, but which sounded threatening.

'While I was looking round for some help to interpret this tirade, as that is what it seemed to be, a white woman of about forty with flaming red hair came up behind the General, saying "Can I help?" She had a strong Australian accent and I afterwards learned that this was the famous "Soerabaya Sue" who had broadcast for the Japanese during the war and then for the Indonesians.

'"The General wants to know why you are flying a Dutch aeroplane?" she said. This rocked me back on my heels. I said I was sorry but I didn't understand; the General had been to Kemajoran and knew that I was the commanding officer there. "Why," I asked, "should I want to fly a Dutch aircraft?"

'As she translated this to Subidio, I noticed that he kept pointing to something over my shoulder. I turned and realized it was the red, white and blue RAF roundel on the Dakota fuselage which was exciting him. I very nearly burst out laughing but caught myself in time to avoid what looked like developing into a delicate situation. I explained to our interpreter that these were the normal, peacetime RAF insignia and, although the Dutch used the same colours, their configuration was different.

'Of course it would happen at that moment that the second Dakota taxied in and Subidio at once pointed to its blue and white roundels with the red omitted. At some length I explained that, during the war, all Dakotas in Burma had the red in their roundels painted out to avoid confusion with the "rising sun" emblem of the Japanese who had a transport aircraft very like the Dakota. A long, and to me quite unintelligible, harangue then took place between Sue and Subidio while I waited somewhat impatiently to hear the outcome. "The General knows very well who you are," she said, "but your aeroplane is different to others and, although he believes your explanation, you were very lucky not to have been shot down by his guards when coming in to land".'

Lee's aircraft happened to be the first to have come out of major servicing with the peace-time colours reapplied. Naturally, it was not used on the Solo run again, and even greater care was used at the airfield in the future. On the occasion related above, by the way, the Squadron improvised a Solo-Semerang shuttle with the single, acceptable aircraft, with the rescued internees being trans-shipped at Semerang and the 'rogue' aircraft performing the Semerang-Kemajorang legs. Between them they still managed to evacuate 128 passengers in the day.

Staying with aircraft colour schemes, it was Flight Lieutenant Geoff Hammond and crew who flew the first 'civilianized' Dak, KN399. De-camouflaged, it had been buffed up to a nice silver aluminium finish. They were said to have operated with the first post-war paying passengers in the area, but many years after the event Geoff could not recall who these passengers might have been – or what the operation was about. The record has this to say on the subject: 'During July, scheduled runs were carried out for a month. The aircrews found them a pleasant change, and they speedily adapted themselves to the finer points of airline passenger carrying.'

Geoff's log book shows that he was specially categorized by a pilot from Group HQ, and that they plied a route to Changi in Singapore. He recalls that they flew on civil documentation wearing their best uniforms, and that 'For a while the Squadron became quite adept at the passenger-flying role.' But the full story seems to have been lost in the mists of time.

Transit flights to Singapore, often for in-depth servicing, were relatively relaxing tasks, affording the Java airmen the opportunity to spend a couple of days in relative civilization. Flight crews for these trips were often randomly selected, with passengers a mixture of Squadron aircrew and groundcrew. Norman Cornwell reports on one such flight, on which he flew as WOp in a scratch crew:

'Kemajorang to Kallang is a distance of about 700 miles, but there was a complete absence of radio navigational aids, which meant that all the navigating had to be carried out by astro, map reading or dead reckoning. Needless to say, astro required clear skies above, which on this occasion we certainly didn't have. In cloud, the nav was working on forecast winds and dead reckoning. He gave the pilot two or three important course corrections which, to his horror, were all ignored, as the pilot had decided to fly "by the seat of his pants". It was soon obvious that, to quote a well-known navigational phrase, we were "not lost, but uncertain of our position". The nav decided that shock action was called for, so he systematically folded his maps up, packed them in his navigation bag and handed them over to the captain. With the parting words, "sod it, you don't need me, you are now on your own," he went back to sit with the passengers.

'To counter the problem of a vacated navigational seat, the bemused passengers were handed maps and requested to look out for any viable ground features that might reveal a useful positional fix. In spite of the hilarity that this caused, there were some understandable signs of relief when, after a while, a few breaks in the cloud appeared giving just sufficient time to ascertain the aircraft's position. Once this was achieved, nav duly returned to the flight deck to recommence his duties on a more conventional basis.'

Anything to lighten the routine, but Al Baldwin wouldn't have endeared himself to his fellow crewmembers with japes such as this:

'Not a lot of people knew that placing a fifty tin of Woodbines on that handy little shelf between the windscreens precessed the compass underneath by about 12 degrees. Certainly my nav didn't as I was too chicken to tell him after I made the discovery. Could explain his puzzlement at the 50 knot crosswinds he was encountering!'

There were, of course, trips that required a little more concentration, as navigator Steve Brown relates:

'Preparing for flight to Singapore via Palembang we discover that we have two major generals and the chief of the nursing services on the manifest. "Something is bound to go wrong today," say I. We land at Palembang and off-load one of the two generals. The pilots, Mitch Mitchell and Bill Freitag, discuss with me whether we should fly high or below the weather. Hoping for a smoother flight we opt for

10,000ft. Once at cruising altitude, one engine decides to stop. We head for an island south of Singapore where the map indicates there may be a Jap landing strip. We eventually change our minds and make for Kallang. We are unable to maintain height, and after an hour and three quarters at 90kts we arrive at Kallang at circuit altitude and perform a single-engined landing. The remaining general expresses his gratitude.

'Failures of Twin Wasps were pretty rare at that time. Had we chosen to fly below the weather the Squadron would have been short of one aircraft and one crew, as Sumatra consists of uninterrupted jungle. Indeed, finding Jap landing strips in the Sumatran jungle had always taken a lot of searching, a matter of frustration to us navigators. Later, we got together and solved the problem. The topographical maps we were using were American. Once we had re-plotted the strips in the correct positions we had little further difficulty.'

Flight Lieutenant Len Figg had a similar incident when piloting a Dakota over Sumatra. This time, though, the hazards of the terrain were perceived by one passenger to be lesser than the other health risks:

'As usual, the navigator served tea from old and chipped enamel mugs. Amongst the passengers was a senior nursing sister who, like the others, was served tea. During the flight over the highest part of the mountains, one engine of the old Dakota (which couldn't maintain height on one engine even at 10,000ft) started to splutter. I thought we were all finished, but luckily the engine picked up again in a few seconds. After landing the sister came up to me and said, "Young man, you are asking for trouble serving tea in those chipped enamel mugs." If only she'd known!'

Chapter 17

Job Done

With much of the RAPWI work now complete, and with hostilities also generally subsiding, there were leisure opportunities. Lloyd Ogden recalls Edam Island, known colloquially as Eden, a popular destination:

'I enjoyed seven very restful days on that island, doing nothing but eat, sleep and swim. Taken out there on an RN landing ship, which returned about every two days with supplies, it was the first break I had had since arriving at Bombay in 1943. I have vivid recollections of having camp fires on the coral sand beach with the beers lined up in the water just where the waves broke on the beach. I also managed to get a week's leave in Singers later that year, just before repatriation, managing to get picked up by the provos for being out of uniform!'

And camps full of Dutch women were still a major attraction for the boys although, as Dennis Brown recalls, there were often hurdles to be leaped before goals could be achieved:

'We had noticed on our visits to Bandoeng an oldish American Buick car parked in the hanger. And we also knew that there were several camps around the area where the Japs had held the Dutch women and, separately, the men. We had also heard that these ex-prisoners always welcomed visits from RAF personnel who happened to be in town.

'So we decided to "borrow" the car and go in search of one of the camps during the evening. Having set off through the town, we were near the centre when we all seemed to notice at once a group of men standing around holding something in their hands – which having drawn closer we could see were swords.

'The cry went up "Put your foot down Dennis" (or words to that effect!) and I had no intention of doing otherwise. They certainly wanted us to stop, and as I drove past we heard a crash of swords come down onto the roof of the car. It could have been our heads receiving the blows – they were not a friendly lot.

'So we were through the town and found the camp, and had a very happy evening, but the time had to come when I had to consider getting back to the airport. There was only one way, but I drove back with me thinking "hope they haven't built any barriers along the way." But it appeared to be a ghostly town – nobody on the street at all.'

Not all the female interest came quite up to expectations. On one mission, John Overton remembers that his crew was tasked to fly a Siamese princess from Bandoeng to Batavia. They fully expected a dark-skinned beauty and felt that 'orders of the white elephant (or something)' would be received afterwards. When the lady arrived they estimated she was at least 110 years old, and she was carried on board on a mattress!

It should be said that John did meet and later marry a lovely Dutch former internee, Eve, the story of their meeting owing much to the Squadron's role. A British soldier, Ron Bedford, had been a prisoner in Java at a camp adjacent to one in which Dutch women, including Eve and her mother, had been confined. They had become acquainted when Ron had been on outside working parties and had thrown smuggled goodies to them over the wire. When the time came after the war for Ron to be repatriated he had intended to say a farewell to Eve, but events overtook him. However, he did have time to write a letter, which was later conveyed to Eve by a member of the 31 Squadron crew which was flying Ron to freedom. That crewman turned out to be John Overton and the rest, as they say, is history.

Years later, after much research, John and Eve re-established contact with Ron, who subsequently became a generous and much-loved honorary member of the 31 Squadron Association. And Eve herself retained the connection for many years following John's death.

Nor were the Overtons the only happy couple to come out of Java. Spencer Whiting recalled in 1980 the Hotel des Indes in Batavia as:

'Having been used as a rest camp for a few days at a time for a couple of hundred women from the camps. So our location nearby was a prime spot, as none of us had seen so many lovely girls for a long while. Mine is still with me after thirty five years of marriage – she, her twin sister and mother had been interned in Kramat camp by the Japs for the war years.'

Lloyd Ogden was another, marrying Rose, another Dutch ex-internee who worked with him in the adjutant's office. And there were in all probability more. So the operation may certainly be said to have cemented Anglo-Dutch relations.

Servicemen the world over have wheeled and dealed, and Thirty One's were no exception. One effect of the long far-eastern war was currency anomalies, and for an illustration of how things were in Java – and a spot of deeper thinking, too – we can do no better than to turn again to Taff Evans:

'I had my first lesson in economics and philosophy when I served on 31 Squadron. When we moved to Java we ran into money trouble. As Java was, on paper, a Dutch colony, we could be paid in either pounds sterling or Dutch guilders. But when we went to the shops in Batavia, the traders were reluctant to accept our money as they used Japanese occupation guilders. In theory they were valueless, as they did not have the backing of a national bank, but in practice they were the only currency used for local trade. Our pounds and Dutch guilders were useless, so we were given a small allowance of Japanese guilders for pocket money.

'As we could not use our pounds or Dutch guilders we were allowed to remit them home. We then found that if we took our pounds into the market we could buy Dutch guilders at a very low rate. We could then take them back to camp and change them back into pounds at the official rate, thus making a modest profit.

'I now know that economists call this arbitrage and that thousands of people earn a living by exploiting the differences in exchange rates of currencies. Although we were using a relatively unsophisticated system, it was inevitable that some people would become greedy and try to pass large sums of money through the system. This came to the attention of the authorities and they put a stop to the transfers between sterling and guilders. Our nice little earner came to an end overnight.

'This also gave me a first lesson in philosophy: whenever you are on to a good thing, be sure that some louse will soon come along and spoil it for you!'

Taff's stories are always full of insight, and here's another:

'While on detachment to Palembang, we heard that an officer was coming from Singapore to inspect a hoard of Japanese transmitters and receivers that had been found. He arrived the next day, and when he found that I was a wireless mechanic he insisted that I accompany him. He arranged transport, and a Japanese car rolled up at our hotel. This took us out to the airfield and then on to a hangar on the outskirts.

'A young Japanese officer awaited us and took us inside the hangar. It was piled high with electronic equipment, but when we took it down to inspect it we were completely surprised. The equipment was of poor quality. The coils were crudely wound and had been wired ugly-style. Unlike British and American equipment, the coils had not been secured to the chassis.

'Our officer was rather upset by this. He had clearly been hoping to commandeer this horde of equipment, but it but it was not up to standard. He turned on the Japanese officer, criticizing the poor equipment. The Jap said nothing, but smiled inscrutably. We came away empty-handed.

'As I have now reached my dotage and look at my Japanese television set, I admire the superb quality of the engineering. I sit in amazement at the strides the Japanese have made.'

Eventually it was all over. The internees were pretty well all out and Thirty One was to disband on 30 September 1946. Ironically this would be within a few days of the Squadron's thirty-first birthday.

At least this particular incarnation of the Squadron was to disband. The famous number was destined immediately to reappear in another part of the world, while in even later wanderings Thirty One would serve with 904 Wing again. But for now, none of the present Squadron members would transfer. For them there was to be a well-earned rest and, for many of the conscripts, demobilization at last.

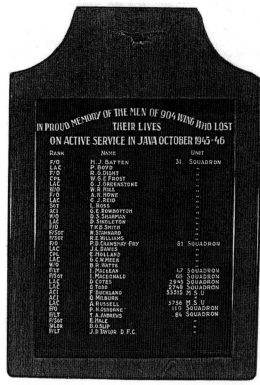

IN PROUD MEMORY OF THE MEN OF 904 WING WHO LOST THEIR LIVES ON ACTIVE SERVICE IN JAVA OCTOBER 1945-46

RANK	NAME	UNIT
F/O	M.J.BATTEN	31 SQUADRON
LAC	P.BOYD	"
F/O	R.G.DIGHT	"
CPL	W.G.E.FROST	"
LAC	G.J.GREENSTONE	"
W/O	W.R.HILL	"
F/O	A.N.HOWE	"
LAC	G.J.REID	"
SGT	L.ROSS	"
ACI	G.E.ROWBOTTOM	"
W/O	D.S.SHARMAN	"
LAC	D.SINGLETON	"
F/O	T.K.B.SMITH	"
F/SGT	N.STANNARD	"
F/SGT	R.E.WILLIAMS	"
F/O	P.D.CRAWSHAY-FRY	81 SQUADRON
LAC	J.L.DAWES	"
CPL	E.HOLLAND	"
LAC	G.C.W.MEEK	"
W/O	B.R.WATTS	"
F/LT	I.MACLEAN	47 SQUADRON
F/SGT	I.MACDONALD	60 SQUADRON
LAC	D.COTES	2943 SQUADRON
LAC	G.TODD	2748 SQUADRON
ACI	F.BUCKLAND	5515 M.S.U
ACI	G.MILBURN	"
LAC	A.RUSSELL	5756 M.S.U
F/O	P.N.OSBORNE	110 SQUADRON
F/LT	T.A.ANDREWS	84 SQUADRON
F/SGT	E.HALE	"
S/LDR	B.G.SLIP	"
F/LT	J.D.TAYLOR D.F.C.	"

The plaque, carved with love and pride by the men of the station workshops at Kemajorang.

Before we leave them, Norman Cornwell sums up this extraordinary RAPWI operation:

'With so little information published from official sources, statistics are hard to come by, but my research has revealed a few. RAF personnel losses during the Java conflict were thirty-two aircrew and ground support airmen, half of whom were from 31 Squadron. These figures do not include the twenty Indian troops who were killed whist flying in a 31 Squadron aircraft.

'The 23rd Indian Division suffered more casualties in the first four months of this campaign than it did in three and a half years fighting in Burma (British army report). There was a higher number of 31 Squadron groundcrew killed in Java than in its whole Burma campaign. The total number of British and Indians killed numbered 622, with 1,440 wounded (British army report). 'Between October 1945 and November 1946, 31 Squadron flew 11,000 sorties and 24,000 flying hours. It carried 129,000 passengers, including 5,000 casualties, and transported 26,000 tons of freight (Squadron records).

'Those statistics do not reflect the label of "the war that never was". We can readily look back with the knowledge that the Squadron lived up to its historic reputation of dedication and high morale throughout those difficult and dangerous times. We certainly did not expect international renown when we left the Dutch East Indies, but at the conclusion of hostilities only three awards were promulgated: Wing Commander Macnamara received the DSO; Sergeant Williams the MM; and our own Bert Edwards the AFM. However, I know there was, and still is, a very strong feeling amongst us who were out there that a battle honour on the Squadron's colours might have been appropriate. That said, as the whole conflict could be described as a somewhat abnormal or even bizarre campaign, I suppose one should only expect an inexplicable reaction.'

Such is life. It's very understandable that those who lived through those darkest days would have appreciated more recognition. But regardless of the true nature of the operation, it wasn't officially defined as 'combat' – so that was that.

There would also be questions over how Thirty One's Java dead would be commemorated, and we shall return later to that aspect. But for the time being, we leave the Java veterans hugely proud of the humanitarian work they had done there, as well as eternally sad at the thought of the bodies of their friends and comrades left in that foreign land.

They could, perhaps, be consoled by Lord Mountbatten's acknowledgement in his writings that 'The Allied [re]occupation of the Netherlands East Indies had been the most complex and hazardous of my whole SEAC Command.'

The permanent Commonwealth War Graves Commission cemetery in Djakarta (formerly Batavia).

The couple of months following the Java Squadron's disbandment were occupied by the pressing business of getting home. For many this would involve a final adventure, as Norman Cornwell resumes:

'After a hilarious farewell Squadron party held in the "Black Cat" bar in Batavia, we were on our way. We were flown to Singapore, from whence this great family was dispersed.

'It would be difficult to imagine a more unexpected and pleasurable scenario to end my 31 Squadron days. At that time, there were dozens of Dakotas lying around the island awaiting disposal. A call was made for aircrew volunteers to fly them back to England and, needless to say, there was no shortage of takers. Our task was unbelievably vague, and laughable to imagine in present-day circumstances. We were to collect our aircraft from the newly opened airfield at Changi, which had been constructed by Allied POWs, and deliver it to RAF Lyneham. When we asked about staging posts and timescales, these pertinent questions were met with a shrug of the shoulders and the well-chosen words: "Just deliver the bloody thing." We looked at each other with undisclosed glee and declared that, as this opportunity was never likely to happen again, we would milk it for all it was worth. Our only fixed plan when we took off from Changi was that we would limit our stops to one night in places we considered uninteresting and spend several days at the more endearing locations.'

Norman's crew were amazed to find that they were free to meander around Thirty One's former operating areas in Burma with no air traffic restrictions whatsoever, and they then set off across the Indian interior to New Delhi. There, they were conscious of passing close to the Squadron's spiritual home – the same area in which, by chance or design, the 'new' Thirty One would soon be operating. Staying with the 'old', though, for a moment more, let's just rejoin the crew as it completed the final leg of its homeward journey.

'Nobody at Lyneham showed the slightest interest in our arrival, and the movements section merely asked us to park the aircraft and hand in the documents. Saying my final farewells to the crew, I was told to go on immediate leave and await my demobilization orders. With that, my operational flying days were finally over; mercifully, I was still in one piece.'

One can almost hear the 'deafening silence' as the engines were closed down for the final time. It must have been an unbelievable feeling. But what stands out is the complete lack of ceremony as service careers came to a close. Inevitable, one supposes; there had, after all, been millions of servicemen to demobilize, and clearly they couldn't all be formally marched out with bands playing. But even so, the final moments – especially of those who had been through so much – couldn't have been other than anti-climactic.

Chapter 18

Back to the Frontier

Some few days after 31 Squadron disbanded in Java it reformed – officially on 1 November 1946 – when Number 77 Squadron was rebadged.

A staff officer somewhere must have had an eye for history, for Seventy Seven's post was custom-made for Thirty One. The Squadron's new mission would return them to Indian skies. There, they would continue their predecessors' work on the North-West Frontier and, just as in Java, a humanitarian task was anticipated.

India was to be given her independence. The British government would announce, in early 1947, that the transition would occur not later than June 1948. But in the face of increasing unrest throughout the early part of '47, the Viceroy, Lord Mountbatten, would advance the date to 15 August that year.

Much of the reason for that change was a consequence of the country's religious makeup, which was making it impossible to agree a structure for the coming home rule. Religious strife, most notably in Punjab and Bengal, would eventually make the only practical solution a partition of the country. In June 1947 it was announced that India would be split, with the Muslim areas forming Pakistan and the larger Hindu and Sikh section forming the new Indian republic.

But no areas were completely of one single religious persuasion. And in some parts, the leaders who made the decision on which side to join were not of the same religion as the majority of their people. Thus many communities – tens of thousands of people – were destined to find themselves effectively trapped on the 'wrong' side of the new borders. There would inevitably be fighting. Thousands would be killed, and there would be countless refugees.

This, then, was to be Thirty One's new theatre of operations. The station was Mauripur, near Karachi.

How, incidentally, did the men of 77 Squadron respond to their peremptory renumbering? This piece by Warrant Officer Cyril Frazer, one of the Squadron's WOps, gives us a hint that their history might already have been a little turbulent:

'My pilot was Flight Lieutenant Tony Smith, who had been with 77 Squadron flying Halifax bombers in Yorkshire. Indeed some half of us were ex-Halifax crews, having discarded our flight engineers, bomb aimers and air gunners to convert to Dakotas in preparation for operations against the Japs. But, like the "other" Thirty One, our preparations had been interrupted by the end of the war. We'd subsequently departed with our ground staff for India and were now based at Mauripur. So some of us saw ourselves as being still on a bomber squadron flying transport aircraft – and we thought this not to be quite correct!

'Now there had been, over a number of months, rumours that we were to return to the UK. And one November 1946 morning the CO, Wing Commander Cooke,

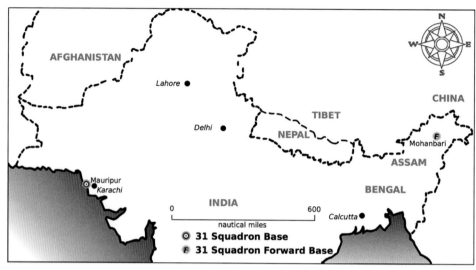

Map 6: No.31 Squadron operations in northern India, 1946–7.

addressed us on parade, an unusual event in those days. "Chaps you may have heard that the Squadron is going home," he said. "Well it's true! No 77 Squadron is returning to the UK. But you're not. From now on you are 31 Squadron!"'

So now Thirty One was in the land that would soon become West Pakistan. The worst of the independence troubles were yet to get underway and, ironically, the Squadron's first task arose 1,200 miles to the east, in Assam. This state lay adjacent to Bengal, part of which was also to be partitioned off to become, first of all, East Pakistan and then, eventually, Bangladesh. But the current problem in Assam wasn't so much to do with independence and religious strife, but rather with India's borders with China, Tibet and Burma. These were subject to incursions and had to be continually guarded. So for the period from November 1946 until February '47, a detachment of the Squadron's Dakotas was dispatched at the request of the Indian administration to operate not so very far from where so many of the earlier Thirty One's epic wartime sorties had taken place. The mission now was Operation *Lohit*, the task being to drop supplies to the 700 men manning the eleven frontier forts of north Assam. The met office had said that only during November and from March to April would weather conditions permit low-level flying among those mountains, so the attempt had to be made at once.

The forts were extremely remote, some being in touch with the outside world only by runner. Ordinarily, the resupply task would have occupied three thousand labourers with mules for months. It was awesome countryside, as Cyril Frazer recalls.

'Some of the DZs were situated in the most inaccessible and desolate regions of the world. In the Dakotas we followed the winding course of the Lohit River and, as the valley narrowed, there was little room to turn. To the west stood mountains 9,000ft high; on the other side snow-topped heights of twice that height.

'All the aircraft we took to Assam had been given a major service and had brand new engines fitted because of the arduous flying conditions. If we came down anywhere we were advised to stay with the aircraft. How we would be recovered I have no idea – no helicopters in those days.

'Airdrops for the day were usually arranged with other aircraft in the same valley or at adjacent DZs in the valley, so that WOps could pass their aircraft's location back via other aircraft in the stream.

'The sixty men of the Assam Rifles who manned each fort had little or no contact with the outside world during their tours of duty and relied on resupply for everything from rice and ghee to kerosene, from cigarettes to medical supplies. Outposts were built complete with watchtowers. They lived inside the stockade – the fence of split logs with pointed tops which surrounded the compound – and were always vulnerable to raids across the disputed borders. It was a grim existence and they were grateful for the Squadron's efforts. The flying was certainly memorable. We would depart in the early hours to get into the valleys and out again by about midday, before the clouds built up to block our exit. These trips demanded extreme pilot skills. For example one dropping zone was Walong, which was situated on a partially dried-up riverbed. We had to quickly drop down very low to the DZ and then climb out fiercely to clear the hills in front, the trees often just missing our underside – and then we'd have to find a crevice in the valley to enable a turn round for the next run.'

Flight Lieutenant Gordon Tricker, a pilot, enlarged:

'The route lay over scenery as magnificent as the Canadian Rockies, across great shoulders of mountain covered with stark, black trees; over the river rushing thousands of feet below in a gorge deeper than the Grand Canyon; and finally through a gap torn out of the hills. In some cases little villages were used as distribution centres, the yellow cross marking the DZ in the middle of a ploughed field scarcely a hundred yards long. All around were trees and rocks, as well as terrified villagers running for the safety of their mud dwellings; clearly they had little

Over the delta of the Brahmaputra River.

confidence in the RAF's accuracy! A diving turn towards the DZ, a sudden clatter of sacks, and a sharp climbing turn away (the fully laden Dakota needed careful handling in a narrow valley 5,000ft above sea level); round and round the tight circuit a dozen times, and then back to base for another load.'

And a report from an observer asserted that:

'Rupa seemed to be the DZ which was the most difficult to get in to. We couldn't get below 400ft and the aircraft was constantly making steep banking turns and abrupt climbs and dives. I didn't know which to admire more – the skill and cool daring of the pilot, or the sheer guts of the dispatchers, staggering about inside the tossing aircraft and yet managing to lift, carry and eject at the proper time 140lb packages.

Some of them had narrow escapes from going out along with their loads, many times being forced to their knees or thrown headlong by some particularly violent manoeuvre.'

The aircraft were based at Mohanbari, a few miles from Dibrugarh on the Bengal-Assam railway. The place had been one of the USAAF fields used during the 'Hump' operations; the NCO aircrew slept in the former American chapel, as apart from the officers' quarters it was the only remaining habitable building. All the huts had thatched roofs. Being situated in a pretty wild area, the base was subject to problems which earlier generations of Thirty Oners would have recognized. Cyril Frazer again:

NCO accommodation at Mohanbari looks tired after the war. (*Photo from Cyril Frazer's collection*)

'We flew in a generator to power the mobile MF radio beacon. It was placed out in the open, but the following morning the severed cable was all that remained. This was surprising, for it normally took four strong men to lift it, but some enterprising locals had had it away. A replacement was flown in and this time it was placed in the quadrangle formed amid various buildings (*bashas*) such as the officers' mess, Squadron office and sleeping quarters. There was constant coming and going, but even so the new generator was lifted and disappeared into the jungle without anybody having seen it go.

'But there were treats. Although the Americans had departed some time before, a US disposal unit remained nearby still trying to clear vast quantities of supplies. We could get for our messes loads of tinned fruit, such as pineapple and pears, the like of which we had never seen before. For smokers, there were 20-carton packs of Lucky Strike and so on.

'The area was among tea plantations, and we joined the ex-pats on evenings at the several clubs nearby. It would always be the same people but would be a different venue on each occasion. One evening over Christmas 1946 I recall the tea planters' wives and families putting on a show for us.'

Many found attractive the grandeur of the area. Leading Aircraftman Alf Tunstall had this to say:

'The operation was the highlight of my five years in "the mob". I was an airframe fitter and was getting a bit "sand happy" after a couple of years in the Karachi area. I loved the jungle in Assam, the monkeys (not the ones on Thirty One's payroll!), the tea gardens, the trips into Dibrugarh etc. I went up and did my stint as a dispatcher – you know, sacks of rice, live goats in crates with chutes etc. I salute those pilots, they were terrific in that incredible terrain.'

The live goats included in the air drops were, reportedly, intended as rations for the local soldiers. In fact some Squadron members commented that much of what was served

An almost idyllic scene at Mohanbari, belying the tough flying on Operation *Lohit*.

up to them throughout the war as 'lamb' had probably been goat, and there seems little reason to doubt this.

Anyway, both the army and the villagers who benefited as a side-effect were pleased with Thirty One's efforts on Op *Lohit*. The supply of those outposts had always been difficult, and porters to manhandle stores through miles of jungle were getting scarcer. The supply position was acute by the time the Indian government sought the RAF's assistance, and Thirty One flew in six months' worth of supplies at a time when it was feared that the garrisons might have to be withdrawn because of transport difficulties. So the interlude could only be rated an outstanding success.

The detachment returned to Mauripur and picked up with the next jobs in hand. Trooping was a major task, as British forces continued to be repatriated. Assistance was given with training up the Indian Air Force, and the refugee problem was beginning to develop as independence grew closer. Corporal Alan Robson served as a radar mechanic: 'We were quartered at Mauripur in tents while the trooping programme was carried out, flying army personnel from Bengal to Karachi in Dakotas. They were then transferred to Stirlings, Liberators and Yorks for the onward flights to Blighty.'

And Cyril enlarges:

'We devoted about six aircraft each day to the task. Mauripur–Delhi for breakfast, and then on to Chaklulia near Calcutta. We always had a full passenger list outward with personnel heading down to Burma and beyond. Each leg was over four hours flying, so the total for the day was around nine hours. It would be out one day and back the next with Burma veterans who were fit enough to fly across India en route for home.'

Cyril also notes that his crew screened the CO designate of the first Indian Air Force transport Squadron, Number 12, in December 1946 in an IAF aircraft. On one of these flights they visited Risalpur, on the Frontier, to bring Thirty One's silver to its new home at Mauripur (it had presumably been stored there since 1941). Cyril later commented that he never actually saw that silver until many years later on an Association visit to the Squadron's German base.

As always on the sub-continent the weather could be exciting. The Squadron did its best, even scheduling its trooping flights accordingly, as indicated in this rather apologetic extract from a passenger information handout: 'You may find that we expect you to leave the ground unnecessarily early in the morning ... this is because ... we aim to avoid operating over high ground when the [monsoon] weather is worst, late in the day.' But it was impossible to avoid all the weather, as Frazer again tells:

'Dakota Rectification' by Des Davies. Des was a corporal on the Squadron, who later pursued a career in aviation technical drawing – including preparing drawings for Concorde. And one can clearly see his talent for the work. He still paints in oils, and for some years was a member of the Guild of Aviation Artists.

'No weather report was available before leaving Risalpur. There was a terrific storm, hailstones rattled on the aircraft, which sounded like being in a tin can being kicked along a gutter. No radio contact with anyone, but we eventually landed at Palam to be informed that all aircraft, including BOAC, had been grounded. All radio stations had been closed down as they thought that no aircraft anywhere in that part of India were airborne.'

The machines were showing signs of age although, given the by now legendary stamina of the Dakota, they usually got the crew home. Warrant Officer Loveridge, in KN637 'B', flew a night cross-country in May, and at the furthest point from Mauripur one engine failed. No other airfields were available so he struggled back to base to make a safe landing after flying for three and three-quarter hours on one engine.

And Corporal Des Davies comments on relations with the expanding IAF:

'I was flying as technical backup on a southbound flight when, over Hyderabad, the port engine began to give trouble. So we decided to drop into the former RAF base at Secunderabad. I checked it over and the port magneto was to blame, so a replacement was ordered. We billeted overnight, the pilots in town and the rest of us on base. The magneto arrived – was fitted, checked, air-tested, and the oil filters checked – and off we went on our task. Picked up our cargo somewhere along the line, and headed off towards Madras and St Thomas's Mount. On our return leg the port engine began to vibrate so the captain said stand by to ditch the cargo. Luckily, we made Poona OK. Dropping the filter, I found a mass of aluminium fragments. I referred this to an IAF engineer who ordered an engine change, and a team was flown from Palam to undertake the job. I assisted, and the IAF treated us very well. We could have English grub or eat what the mess provided – half and half. All ranks ate in the sergeants' mess.'

In May 1947, Squadron Leader David Penman arrived to take over A Flight. He had been a bomber pilot during the war and describes his new appointment:

'At the time I arrived in Mauripur there was a shortage of senior officers and there was some argument as to which squadron I belonged. Thirty One it was, and when Wing Commander Cooke departed for the UK on compassionate grounds in July and did not return I was left in command until Thirty One detached to Palam. Indeed at one time I found myself controlling both 10 and 31 Squadrons.

'Throughout June a great deal of time was spent in both day and night training, the aim being to get pilots categorized in accordance with the newly introduced Transport Command scheme. I was the only person on Thirty One allowed to do the checks, and this continued until July when it ceased abruptly as operational requirements increased.'

While on the subject of categorization we could observe that there's always controversy when the 'trappers' are around. Cyril recounts his story:

'I was first catted in May 1946. They returned in October and I was on the list to be done again. From memory it was two days of written papers and then a screened, scheduled flight. I complained that I was to be done again when there were so many WOps who hadn't been done – only to be told we wanted a good result for the Squadron! This time I got a VIP Cat.'

Penman continues:

'The date for independence had now been radically brought forward, and rumours were rife that we all had to be out of India by 15 August. During July, dependents were ferried to Bombay, and around thirty families with about forty-six children moved into the officers' mess sleeping blocks at Mauripur. At the end of the month personnel were invited to stay in India for one year starting from August. Unsurprisingly there was no rush of volunteers.'

Chapter 19

Independence Days

Friday 15 August 1947 marked both Independence and Partition. Mauripur now found itself in West Pakistan and, as forecast, there would be much grief over many of the new boundaries that had been created. Warrant Officer Maurice Gwin's words describe well the pace of operations around the time:

'In late August we embarked on a major detachment to Palam, India. We had twelve aircraft there, and one day nine aircraft ferried 267 refugees to Rawalpindi, returning with 231 during the afternoon. The next day ten aircraft took 254 to Rawalpindi, returning with 400 the same day. During September we flew supply drops to the 4th Gurkhas in the Punjab – petrol, ammo and rations, and then later that month we went on detachment to Chaklala to evacuate Sikh troops from Kohat. These men had had a rough time with the tribal Muslims and some were wounded. In mid-September we returned to Palam, from where refugee flights continued. But in October we were again detached to Chaklala for Operation *Streamline*, which was Hindu troop evacuations from airstrips at Wana and Bannu in Waziristan.'

Truly, the country of Thirty One's roots. But this time it was terrible. Cyril Frazer again: 'We dropped leaflets on villages telling them to cease killing each other. Outside Rawalpindi airfield we would see groups of men going out, and coming back later with some of them as corpses. We also saw from the air many houses being burnt down and villages completely burnt out and deserted.'

Wing Commander Fothergill, who took command of the Squadron at exactly that point, remembers his initiation:

'It was a very busy and often hectic time shortly after Indian independence, when much of the country – countries now – was in turmoil and communications in disarray. Hordes of refugees were on the wrong side of the new partition and much of our effort was spent in ferrying Hindus from Pakistan to India and Muslims vice-versa. In addition, and as well as transporting mail, we evacuated many British service and civilian personnel from areas of unrest where travel by road or rail was hazardous and lives might have been lost. We also carried out supply-dropping operations to refugees cut off by hostile factions and to areas badly flooded after a heavy summer monsoon.

'So, a variety of tasks and hardly a dull moment, but often long, hard hours, sometimes operating from remote landing grounds with scant facilities. The aircrews were frequently hurried and harassed by would-be passengers and it says much not only for their flying skill but also for their judgment in loading their aircraft without the normal back-up that there was not a single accident. Similar

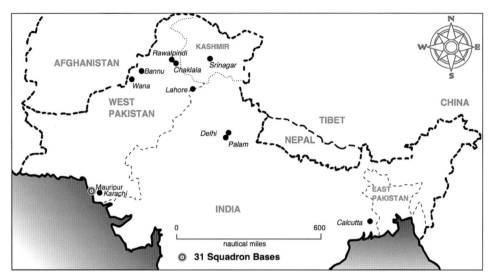

Map 7: No.31 Squadron operations during the Indian Independence/Partition period, 1947. Note: Kashmiri land was subject to claims by both India and Pakistan. For simplicity it is shown separately.

recognition must, of course, be made of the unremitting work of the groundcrews who kept the aircraft serviceable. Although, sensibly, there was no competition between crews in this respect, I believe that the record number of passengers uplifted on one flight was sixty-five local people. When I raised an eyebrow with the aircraft captain afterwards he explained that it was all right because they were all small people!

'Two particular operations stand out. First, the evacuation of 1,859 Hindu soldiers and civilians of the Wana Brigade cut off in the hostile and mountainous Pathan country on the Frontier, by a flight of five aircraft over three days. The brigade commander subsequently presented the Squadron with an engraved silver cup as a "memento of a very great service done the brigade".

'The second operation, destined to be the last carried out by Thirty One in India, was the lift of British civilians, including children and servants, marooned at Srinagar, to Chaklala by eight aircraft over two days. A depressing operation since it involved many who were having to leave their homes, with each restricted to only 200lbs of possessions.'

Srinagar lay in what became – and still is at the time of writing – the area with the greatest problem. Prior to partition it had been anticipated that the Muslim-dominated Kashmir would opt to become part of Pakistan. But at the eleventh hour its Hindu maharajah hesitated, precipitating military action by Pakistani-sponsored guerrilla forces. The maharajah appealed to India for help, with this being offered on condition Kashmir joined India. The UN would later rule that the opinion of the Kashmiri people must be sought before any final solution was reached. To date, India and Pakistan have fought two wars, with this issue high amongst their differences.

The reader might recall the pleasure expressed by earlier Thirty Oners at their interludes in beautiful Srinagar. Sadly, this time, things were different, as David Penman reports:

'In late October while we were still at Chaklala, fighting erupted in Kashmir and we were called to fly into Srinagar to evacuate British residents. The situation was quite serious there, with Muslims advancing on the city and Hindus in defence. Our passengers were allowed a minimal amount of baggage and we really packed them into the Dakotas.

'A typical day was 29 October, when eight aircraft took-off for Srinagar. We flew in petrol in jerry cans as there was none in Kashmir, and a ground party to organize the evacuation. We left Chaklala at 7am and, in perfect weather, flew down a pass between mountains 14,000ft high and covered in snow. We had no oxygen to clear the tops, and at that hour in the morning the mountains were a beautiful sight. In the Kashmir valley smoke and flames were rising from burning villages, and the battle line was only sixteen miles from Srinagar. We had been warned to keep as high as possible until above Srinagar and then to circle down. The airfield was 5,500ft above sea level and without runways, very dusty and very cold. We landed at 8.15am and found the strip swarming with Sikh troops and refugees. We had to wait until 11am for our passengers to be sorted out. Many arrived with large quantities of luggage and furniture and had to be told that only small amounts could be taken. By 11.50 my aircraft was loaded and, with fifteen passengers aboard, I was at Chaklala an hour later. A quick refuel and I was back in Srinagar by 2.25. Six of the other aircraft were still on the ground because of difficulty in parting passengers from their belongings. Eventually all aircraft were loaded and I was last to leave at 5.25pm with nineteen passengers and a newsreel cameraman who took films of the hills and the crew as we made our way back for a night landing, made more hazardous by the appearance of cows on the runway which necessitated an overshoot and a wait until they were cleared!

'The next day we waited while conferences were held to decide what the next move was to be, as an IAF Dakota had been hit by ground fire in the valley. In the end four aircraft were sent off at 10am. This time there was even more difficulty convincing the remaining British civilians that this was their last chance and that "no, we certainly couldn't take a piano!" Some wouldn't leave their belongings and were prepared to take their chances of being chopped up by one side or another – neither could be trusted as both were burning and looting villages. Civilian Daks were rushing troops from Delhi

A village burns as India is partitioned. (*Photo from Cyril Frazer's collection*)

into Kashmir while tribesmen were pouring into the valley at the other end. In the middle the fighting was quite fierce.'

Aside from the terrible events which stained the second half of 1947, many Squadron members made the most of their off-duty hours and had good memories of their time at Mauripur. For example, Air Mechanic Ian Wilson-Dick records that.

'For much of the earlier time Mauripur was a quiet, restful place. My place of work was R&I (repair and inspection) and we weren't too busy. On one occasion Corporal Newman and I were detailed to repair about fifty chairs for the mess! The serious business was done at the model club, where we flew seaplanes and flying boats in an on-base area of shallow, warm water. Early morning was the best time, so that meant weekends. The local wildlife was often employed to launch the gliders. One end of the line was attached to a hook on the aircraft, the other baited with a rissole or the like. Hawks would take the food, dragging the models to altitude.

'We generally worked early in the day to avoid the fierce heat later, so afternoons were usually free for fifteen-minute trips to the beach at Hawkes Bay. There, an R&R centre, complete with cooks, bearers etc, was available for stays of up to a week.'

Alan Robson confirms the pleasures of Hawkes Bay, with its huge surfing waves rolling in from the Arabian Sea, and also mentions the boat trips from Karachi harbour to Sawspit for swimming and overnight stays in beach huts. He has vivid memories of music:

'Whenever I hear the strains of "Summertime", from "Porgy and Bess", I am transported back to the large trooping billets. They began playing requests over the radio entertainments unit channel to which the billets had been wired. It must have gone on a bit, for I can remember a period of silence was once requested by someone! There were two cinemas on the camp, westbound cinema and eastbound cinema, so there was no shortage of entertainment. In addition there was an open-air Indian-run cinema near the camp entrance. In the middle of a tender love scene, a lizard would be seen crossing the screen while stalking a moth. Frequently the picture would go blurred, no doubt due to the projectionist falling asleep. Loud cries of "focus, focus" from the audience and the man would shake himself into action. Then all would be normal again.'

Ray Roberts recalls a trip with Gordon Tricker which took an ENSA troop from Mauripur to an RAF staging post at Jiwani in Baluchistan. They did a show with one of the characters dressing up as a woman which apparently caused an uproar amongst the troops who, not having seen a woman for ages, chased this character all about. On reading the autobiography many years later of Jimmy Perry, the renowned TV sit-com writer, Ray discovered that Perry had been among this troop of entertainers. It's not hard to see where the inspiration came from for the sketches in Perry's renowned 'It Ain't Half Hot Mum'.

And David Penman recalls that: 'We had quite a good life with partners from the British hospital sisters' mess in Karachi. We danced and swam at the Boat Club, had coffee in the YMCA in Elephantine Street, and went to the pictures on camp and in Karachi.'

By November 1947 the worst of the refugee problem seemed to have abated and the whole Squadron had returned to Mauripur. As the year drew to a close, they learned that Thirty One was to end, for the time being at least, its long association with the eastern hemisphere. Once the decision had been made, arrangements proceeded rapidly, with the first aircraft leaving for the UK on 1 December. But although three more departed on the third, operations still continued, as David Penman's journal reveals:

'On 1 December I flew to Bombay to pick up the few remaining RAF personnel in that area. We collected twenty-five passengers including one prisoner under arrest. I believe I made the Squadron's last operational flight in India on the fifteenth, taking off at 7.30 am for Palam with twenty-six refugees. There we uplifted twenty-four small children and took them to Lahore, refuelled, and, with eight passengers on board, headed for Mauripur to land at 8pm having logged nine hours forty-five minutes that day. At Palam we picked up Flight Lieutenant Marshall as second pilot, who turned out to be very good with the children, who were frightened. We had them up front two at a time and they used the headsets to speak to each other.'

Number 31 Squadron was to stand down, the date officially being set as 15 December. Naturally there were many parties to be fitted in, with Penman recalling the official disbandment function as starting on 28 November. About 250 were present, with the party going on well into the following day. He goes on:

'Another "final" farewell party was held on 6 December in the officers' mess, with KP272, "S", flying over in salute. I was flying with Gordon Tricker, with the WOp leader Flight Lieutenant Macdonald transmitting a farewell broadcast. This came through loud and clear in the mess, followed by a further transmission to mark the official opening of the buffet. The pipe band of the Black Watch marched up and down on the lawn and were most impressive.'

The crew landed and joined the party, Tricker recalling that 'Many local dignitaries and senior navy, army and air force officers had been among the guests. By the early hours of the morning, though, when the VIPs and high-ranking guests had left, there were several pairs of trousers going round and round on the punkah fans!'

Maurice Gwin remembers an even later event:

The last 31 Squadron crew to leave India – or Pakistan as it had then become. Squadron Leader David Penman, with his crew Stone, Pegg, Marshall and Cleave. In fairness, it must be stated that Wing Commander Fothergill also claimed to have captained the last aircraft out, while yet another story gives the honour to Flight Lieutenant Tony Smith.

'There was a fair amount of cash in the warrant officers' and sergeants' mess fund, and this was disposed of by a Christmas party which lasted for about two days. One fellow in my billet won a live goose in a raffle. He became so attached to it that he would not have it killed and it continued to live with us until we left for the UK.'

Penman and Gwin in fact ferried an aircraft back to the UK together, variously reported as leaving on either the 20 or 29 December and arriving on 2 January 1948. The remainder of the crew comprised Marshall and Cleave, plus groundcrew Sergeants Stone and Pegg and SAC Moudy. Penman believes this to have been the last 31 Squadron aircraft to leave the sub-continent, although Wing Commander Fothergill also claims that honour: 'I am not sure of the date on which the Squadron was officially disbanded – possibly on leaving Mauripur for the flight home – but I like to

An RAF squadron must have its tea-breaks. Here, somewhere in north-east India, the chap signing the char wallah's tally book is Benny Watts, who was for many years the Association's curator.

think that when I landed my Dak at Lyneham, on 3 January 1948, I brought Thirty One to UK soil for the first time in its long history.'

Whichever the case, Penman recorded memories of his ferry flight:

'After briefing and customs we took off at 7.30am in KP228 "V". In perfect weather we flew at 8,500ft to reach Sharjah at midday, then on to Shaibah, Fayid, Malta and Istres. New Year's Eve in Malta was quite hectic. We eventually reached Lyneham and landed in low cloud and rain on 2 January. We had to deliver the aircraft to a storage unit at Silloth, near Carlisle, but having flown at any time of the day or night at a moment's notice for many years, it was a shock to find out that we couldn't proceed to Silloth until it opened on Monday!'

And that, for the time being, was the end of Thirty One's overseas adventures. During partition the Squadron had worked hard through an extraordinarily significant period in the history of the declining British Empire. Few at the time would have foreseen that the

Differing styles of tea-break at Mohanbari and Mauripur. The date of the Mohanbari picture would have been 1946 - the chalkboard is still headed '77 Squadron'.

early years of the next millennium would take the unit back to a similar area, and a note written later by Gordon Tricker very aptly comments on the significance of Thirty One being in 1947 the 'Last' as well as the 'First' in the Indian Skies. In passing it also records that RAF personnel who had been serving in the area on 15 August were given the option of receiving either the Indian or Pakistan Independence Medal.

Finally, too, after six glorious years, this was also the end of Thirty One's connection with the Douglas Dakota. Given that the greatest part of the Squadron's association with that marvellous aircraft covered the ferocious conflict that raged through Burma for almost four years, in saying an affectionate farewell we can do no better than to borrow again from Roger Annett's *Drop Zone Burma*. He compiled his narrative following many conversations he had had with, among others, ex-Thirty Oners, and the line we would wish to pick out was that the Dakota was:

> 'Not at first intended or designed for combat but, like most Burma veterans, was originally an ordinary citizen.'

Surely, no more appropriate tribute could be imagined.

Chapter 20

Communications Interlude

Thirty One's disbandment was part of a rapid and massive contraction of the services in the immediate post-war years. The gold star was resting after its years of wartime exertion. The Cold War was, however, already in full swing, and in due course the Squadron would re-form as a combat unit, taking its place once again in carrying out Britain's foreign and defence policy.

But even before then Thirty One was not long to lie dormant. An interim mission awaited at Hendon, north-west London, the station known for air pageants held there during the inter-war years. At these events, daring aviators had performed stunts which had startled and astounded the populace. In 1948, it was home to the Metropolitan Communications Squadron.

It was to this unit that the famous Thirty One number plate was passed a mere eight months after the Squadron's disbandment in India. And so ended the brief and only period in this narrative when the gold star was not airborne in the service of the nation. Its new home at Hendon, later to become the location of the RAF Museum, would be Thirty One's first base on British soil since the Squadron's initial formation back in 1915.

Equipped with light communication aircraft, its crews were assigned a miscellany of tasks, as described by its CO, Wing Commander Fane de Salis: 'In March 1948 I was posted to command the Metropolitan Communication Squadron. Our role was VIP transport and to provide flying facilities for general duties officers at the Air Ministry to keep in flying practice. We were equipped mainly with Ansons and Proctors, together with the odd Spitfire. Some time after I arrived at Hendon, and as a result of the drive of the station commander, the numberplate of 31 Squadron was assigned.'

A newspaper article of the time enlarged further on the roles:

'The Squadron maintains a "taxi" Flight of Percival Proctors for the benefit of RAF officers at the Air Ministry and at Transport Command headquarters, who are thus able to make staff visits by air. The Ansons are also available on a "fly-yourself" basis.

'Thirty One also saw the introduction of the de Havilland Devon, and of special-to-type ambulance aircraft. Ansons are generally used for this latter work, and the first air ambulance mission was to land on the sands of Barra, an island of the Outer Hebrides, to take an injured man

A hangar full of Proctors, with a lone Spitfire tucked into the top left corner. National Servicemen at work. *Picture courtesy of Vintage Wings of Canada*

to hospital on the mainland. Stretcher cases may be accommodated, and at least one Anson is always available at Hendon with crew and nursing orderly standing by. Recently an air ambulance was airborne within eleven minutes of receiving a telephone request from RAF Shawbury, Shropshire, to fly a seriously injured airman to hospital. Full details of what was required were radioed to the aircraft as it flew towards Shawbury. Another time, an Anson from Hendon was at RAF Cosford, 113 miles away, within an hour of receiving the call.'

Flight Lieutenant Bryan Toomer, a navigator with the Squadron at the time and later to become a well-respected chairman and vice-president of the Association, recalls that transport crews were, in general, required to be categorized by Transport Command. However, as he says:

'This cat requirement did not, initially, apply to the likes of myself and my three contemporaries, as our job was to fly as crew with officers from the Air Ministry who wouldn't normally be involved with flying which required a valid cat.

'But just before Christmas 1953 came a shock. The CO and nav leader told me that the cat board were visiting in January and that I was to prepare to sit the exam. The board was at Hendon for five days and I waited until the Friday afternoon for the result. To my surprise

'Annie' - an Anson Mk XIX. During its time at Hendon the Squadron used the code VS as well as CB.

I received a C cat. This meant I was qualified to fly with squadron pilots, most of whom were SNCOs and master aircrew, on diverse flights – passenger, freight and so on. Funny old thing, once I'd received the cat I seemed to do standby for ambulance flights every other weekend!'

Thirty One's work was not solely confined to the UK, and newly categorized Bryan soon had an adventure with his crew in an Anson. The story casts an interesting light on the relationship between the 'new' generation and those who'd served during the war:

'We were first to fly to Ternhill in Shropshire to collect spares. Initially we encountered snow cloud and climbed to 5,500ft. The cloud cleared in the vicinity of

Cannock, but the ground was covered in snow and things appeared different. We spotted a railway line after a few minutes and believed it to run close to Ternhill. We let down to 1,500ft but entered fog or low cloud, so climbed again, losing the railway line. The GEE radio navigation equipment was not fully serviceable due to one of the slave stations being off, so I told the pilot I could home to Ternhill

An Anson with air ambulance markings. Its square-cornered windows show it to be a Mark XII.

using the remaining slave signal. He said that he had been to Ternhill on numerous occasions and would call when he saw it.

'We are out of the clag by this time and Master Pilot Jim calls "airfield in sight". I go and sit next to him. By this time he is speaking to Tern and they have answered that they could see us and that we should "Keep a look out for six Provosts joining the circuit." I look down and remark that the airfield doesn't appear to be occupied. Jim says it's because of the snow and that he knows it is the right place. As we fly downwind I see no Provosts, but a single Land Rover on the move. I can't see the runway to any extent, sitting on the starboard side of the aircraft, but we turn finals and Tern gives us clearance to land. About a half mile from touchdown I notice the runway has large stones strewn across it and a haystack on the intersection. But Jim continues his landing, pulling the Anson up well short of the obstruction – and with no burst tyres.

'It turned out that this airfield was Peplow, approx ten miles south of Tern. We backtracked past an astonished farm worker with a horse and cart, past a huge pile of turnips by the side of the runway, and turned at the end to line up for take-off. Brakes on, throttles opened, brakes released, max power and we cleared the haystack with plenty to spare. Called Tern passing 800ft, who said they had sent the crash crew to find us. Landed at Tern, embarrassing trip to the tower, apologies, lame excuse that the runway direction at Tern was 22, the same as at Peplow, and the snow made things appear different. SATCO said he would make a report but not push for it to be forwarded immediately to Hendon. Jim gave a sigh of relief, I wondered if I would be cashiered.

'As soon as the stores were loaded we beat a hasty retreat. Jim, at thirty-three, was an old hand with seventeen years in the RAF. He'd joined as an apprentice, been a pilot since 1941, had done ops on Wellingtons in the Middle East, had been an MU test pilot and had worked in ops at Bomber Command after D-day. Homebound, he pointed out that it would not do either of us any good if this incident leaked out. I agreed, and that was that – or so we thought.

'After lunch we were to head off to Buckeburg, West Germany, and I met Jim and the signaller in the passenger lounge where we were in the habit of scrounging a coffee. As I entered, the sergeant i/c came up and asked me if I would like a DIY kit to get to Buckeburg. Full of indignation I told him not to be cheeky, but it was clear somebody had spilled the beans. I thought Jim had reneged, then remembered we had given an airman a ride to Tern. The sergeant confirmed that our pax had blown the gaff. Ah well, never mind.

'Our first leg to a refuelling stop at Eindhoven was uneventful, and we took off again for Buckeburg at 1615 hrs. Dark of course and few, if any, radio aids available. The GEE was only switched on between 1200–1600 hrs so we were out of luck there. Might get a VHF bearing from Twenthe if they were listening out, but the two aces up front said they would map read for a pinpoint or position line. Sure enough, after about five minutes Jim gave me a position line of a river that, marvel of marvels crossed our track at 90 degrees. But when I plotted it, it showed the groundspeed had apparently increased by about 50kts. Told them I was going to discard the line, but they were insistent they were right – mumblings about having been that way before, up to their necks in blood and bullets. I passed the revised ETA based on their obviously bum position line but decided that I would keep to my calculations and DR our way onward to Buckeburg. Not very difficult, as we had good visibility and little or no cloud at our level (3,000ft). When Minden didn't turn up as they expected, Jim decided to revert to my original ETA. Five minutes later Jim calls Buckeburg and asks if their runway lights could be switched on at full brightness and back to minimum a couple of times. Hey presto, there on the horizon, dead ahead, a pinprick of light brightened and dimmed as commanded. We continued and arrived overhead Buckeberg about ten minutes later. Spot on my ETA. Ah, the pleasures of flying with seasoned veterans!'

Similar differences in experience existed amongst the groundcrew during the period, as John Leggett explains:

'At the time the RAF was in the middle of the Berlin Airlift, during which the Soviets had cut off connections between West Berlin and the rest of the world. Supplies to West Berlin had to be flown in through narrow corridors from West Germany. The Airlift was a massive undertaking, and the RAF's part in it was a huge drain; most of the regular, experienced airmen were concentrated at major airheads, working round the clock, leaving many other stations to be run mainly by national servicemen. That was us, and our qualifications were marginal, but we did have a nucleus of very experienced SNCOs who were brilliant. They knew their business and, to their credit, they got the job done extremely well.

'Chiefy Smith was like a mother hen with chicks and used to get all the Form 700s laid out along a big tray about six or seven feet long. There were all these open tech logs and it was a point of honour with him to get all the aircraft for the next day's flying signed off by 2pm. He was almost obsessive about it and if you'd run on after that time – fixing an oil leak or something – he'd start fussing like an old hen. But he was a lovely man.'

As John says, he was one of those many thousands who were called up during the 1950s for a period of national service. He was a Leading Aircraftman engine fitter, and he subsequently produced a number of entertaining articles for the journal of the Royal Observer Corps. We have their permission to reproduce extracts, so let's first join John as he reflects on a 'fighter' episode:

'Chiefy Smith called me into the office one morning and said "There's a Spitfire coming in today. Now I'm going to put you in charge of it and I want you to make certain that it's looked after and it's never going to let me down."

'Later in the morning this clipped-wing job, TB713, came in and was parked pointing towards the officers' mess. It had come straight out of a maintenance unit down in the West Country where it had been in storage and it was in "battle trim", so an armourer had to come over and check the cannon and guns were clear and then remove them. While waiting. I refuelled the aircraft with 100 octane. So there I was, leaning against the leading edge when the armourer turned up. By rights he should have taken the covers off and made a visual inspection for cartridges and belts. Instead, for reasons best known to himself, he got in, took the tit off, and pressed the button. Now when somebody does that the whole aircraft goes "thud" as all the bolts and firing pins go – that is four machine guns and two cannon. I jumped like a scalded cat from my position leaning beside one of the cannon. If there had been any ammo on board he would have slaughtered the officers' mess, to say nothing of me. I ran round after him and gave him a terrible tongue lashing. And you know what he said? "There's never any ammo in them, you fool!" Silly so-and-so.

'The sergeant than called me in. "We've got some work to do on this kite. Twenty-two modifications are due before it can fly." Now it turned out that it had a Packard Merlin engine, built under licence in America and used in Mustangs and the like. It was a brilliant engine, but the RAF had decreed there were "things wrong with it". To begin with the main oil seals were mounted in alloy in American engines rather than brass. It was quite common to get a leak from the main prop boss seal in American engines, so we had to get a crane over, take off the propeller and replace the alloy seal with a brass one. Then we had to exchange the American magnetos for British "Rotax" mags, and change the plugs. Oh dear, there were innumerable things, and it was quite an education to do the work. I did all the required mods and ran the aircraft up before Wing Commander de Salis took it up for a test flight. He said he was pleased with it, and that was my intro to TB713.

'One day a pilot came down for it and flew it to Oakington, and the next thing we heard was that it had gone u/s there. Chiefy said, "I don't want that damned aircraft lying about – we've got to get it home." I have to say that I hadn't a clue what the hell could be wrong with it because it was running perfectly when it went away.'

It's tempting to comment that engineers always say that! But, not wishing to start a war, we'll get back to John's story:

'I set off in a Proctor with two pilots, one hopefully to bring the Spitfire back. When we eventually found the Spit I went all over it. The only thing I could find wrong was when I undid the petrol cap. Somebody had pushed a long nozzle down into it and had knocked off the filter – which must now be lying in the bottom of the tank. "Sugar", I thought, or words to that effect. "I'll never be able to get that out here. But it's got to get home so I'll take a chance." I put it all back together and, unable to get a trolley-acc, tried a start on the internals. By luck it fired up and, with the two pilots lying on the tailplane, I ran it up. Content that all was OK I signed the travelling 700. The Spit pilot set off for Hendon, while the other pilot and I returned in the Proctor.

'Back home I told Chiefy the tale. "Do you know what?" he said, "I reckon that pilot took the Spit to Oakington just to see some friends. He decided to stay – or perhaps to take a trip to Berlin – so he put the kite u/s. But now it's written up we daren't fly it again until it's sorted." So we trestled up the aircraft in a flying attitude, got one of the Proctor's eighteen-inch long "flag masts", used when an air ranking officer was on board, coated the bottom of it with grease, and probed around in the bottom of the tank for the bits of filter. Having eventually picked up what we were looking for, we fitted a new filter and that was that. A lot of work for somebody's jolly – well, that was my opinion anyway!'

It was quite evident that Thirty One's people were proud of their Spitfires. And the pilots certainly enjoyed flying them. Bryan Toomer recalls one aircraft which came in from RAF White Waltham for a major inspection.

'White in colour, it was the mount of an air-ranking officer. Following servicing it was test flown by a pilot from C Flt – I only recall his name as Sid. Anyway, Sid flew the Spit on several occasions, and eventually White Waltham wanted to know why it had not been returned, seeing as how it had left the hanger two weeks earlier. Sid always had an answer, usually that there was a snag that required another test flight. In the end, White Waltham must have bent the station commander's ear, as OC 31 called for Sid and ordered him to deliver it the next day. The aircraft departed early next morning – after another test flight which involved a low flypast of Hendon control tower!'

Spitfire Mk XVI SL721, the personal aircraft of Air Chief Marshal Sir James Robb, was nominally on Thirty One's complement, although the personalized 'JMR' coding (his full name was James Milne Robb) suggests that it was very much his own aircraft. At the time he was the C-in-C Air Forces, Western Defence Union (a precursor of NATO), and he kept his aircraft finished in 'PR' (high-level reconnaissance) blue. The aircraft has been preserved and is currently a star of the North American air show circuit. The other man is believed to be 31's CO, Wing Commander Fane de Salis. *Photo courtesy of Vintage Wings of Canada*

John Leggett also has a tale which has something to say about the way the post-war RAF was evolving – the relationship between old-fashioned 'bull' and the need, even in peace time, to get the job done. Here, he describes a couple of encounters with RAF Hendon's disciplinary staff:

'One morning as I reported to the section, Chiefy said "Your name's in routine orders. You've got to go up to station headquarters. Tell you what, take my bike and slip up there quickly. Hurry back cos we've got a lot on today."

'At SHQ I parked the bike, walked through, saw the corporal in charge and found out it was a pay query. Having dealt with it I picked up the bike and cycled down the hill back to the Flight. Halfway there I suddenly saw written across the bar of the bike the words "station warrant officer". I stopped in a panic. How the bloody hell did I have the SWO's bike? I looked around and, blow me, there was the man himself standing outside the guardroom staring at me with his hands on his hips. I walked across with his bike. Now the SWO was known as a right sod; there is no other word to describe him. He loved stirring people up. When I got to him he said "You stole my bike." "I didn't, sir. I put mine in the slot at SHQ." "That was my slot," said the SWO. "I'm sorry sir," I mumbled, "I couldn't see your name on it." "Now you're being cheeky," said the SWO, and with that he dressed me up hill and down dale. Plus he had a sergeant "snowdrop" at his side giving him some help. Between them they gave me a right bad time, even remarking on my dress, which was a clean pair of overalls. "Why are you going around the camp in overalls?" In the end he finished with "In future you will not remove my bike from where I place it." "Yes sir." "Yes sir?" "No sir!"

Having escaped I walked back to the rack and found Chiefy's bike which was right on the end. The rack was six slots in a block of concrete and the SWO's slot was "number one." He'd moved my bike over to number six and put his in its place, as a result dropping me in it. That's life, ain't it? So when I got back to the Flight, Chiefy started on: "You've been too long. We've got a lot of work to do." I told him the full story about the SWO playing me up. "He's been sodding you about up at the guardroom while I've got all this work that needs doing? I'll have a go at him about it." I let it go because at the back of my mind I realized they'd all had a good laugh at me.

'About a month later we were coming up to the day of Hendon's AOC's inspection. There was supposed to be no flying that day but, as it happened, we did have a flight. This was for Air Vice-Marshal Pelly in the clipped-wing Spit TB713 and he was going down to Brize Norton to do that station's AOC's inspection. Chiefy had decided that two men would take care of that flight, one of them me. First thing in the morning the two of us pushed the Spit out, put it on the pan and tied it down. I was given a deadline to have the Spit warmed up and ready for the air marshal to fly. He was in the mess and would come out when it was ready for him. I checked my watch and started it up. Coincidentally, the entire complement of RAF Hendon was assembled at the far end of the tarmac. The band was there, but it was all too far away for me to see that our own AOC was coming out and approaching the parade.

'As an aside I'll mention that we had a song for just such an occasion which went: "Stand by your beds, here comes the air vice-marshal. He's got seven rings, but only one ar*****e!" But that's beside the point. Right then, as the band started up to sound the general salute, the temperatures on the Spit were up to what I wanted. So I ran the engine up to flat out and started testing for mag drops. I pulled it back to coarse pitch, which made a hell of a noise, and back to fine again before dropping the revs. By the time I had done, so I'm told, none of the people on parade had heard a jot of the music.

'Having finished, I shut down. But before I could fetch the pilot, the SWO came storming up. "Who gave you permission to ruin my parade?" It seemed that somebody had fallen down on co-coordinating the timing of the various events. But I never had a chance to speak because he didn't stop for air for a full five minutes. He dressed me up and down, questioned my parentage – and my father's parentage. But what he didn't realize was that right behind him was standing Air Marshal Pelly, a small man holding a briefcase, his dress uniform in a bag and his sword. He was wanting to get on his way. But not yet. Old SWO kept rattling on and on. When he eventually stopped for breath a voice from behind him quietly enquired, "Have you finished?" Turning, he saw all the rings on the man's shoulder and gulped. "Yes sir." "Right then, I'd like to get on with my journey if you don't mind." The SWO turned and walked away, his face as red as a beetroot.

'Eventually, the aircraft took off. But it later emerged that Brize Norton's station commander was furious at having had 400 airmen on parade standing around for twenty-five minutes waiting for their AOC to arrive. Two weeks later the SWO was posted off the station.'

A word on the various aircraft operated by the Squadron. The Avro Anson first flew in 1935 as a maritime reconnaissance aircraft and, although it was rapidly outclassed in that guise, it found a niche throughout the war as a trainer, and hundreds of Thirty Oners, both pilots and rear crew, encountered it in that role. Later, it was moved to communications duties. Over 11,000 were built, making it the second most numerous British multi-engine type; it remained in production until 1952.

The de Havilland Devon was a twin piston-engined ten-seat light transport based on the civil Dove. Introduced in 1946, it sold well and, with a typical speed and range of about 150kts and 500nm, it was a useful performer for many years. For lesser tasks the Percival Proctor was a single-engined four-seat communications and radio-trainer aircraft which had entered service in 1939.

It's probably unnecessary to say much about the Spitfire, but there were others. Adding for a time to the variety of the Squadron's types was a Brunswick Söhnkönig II, two of which had been brought back from Germany after the war. This short take-off-and-landing aircraft was lodged with Thirty One whilst its sister aircraft resided at Farnborough. It was later sold.

A Squadron weekend role was giving air experience and navigation training to Air Training Corps cadets, and a number of

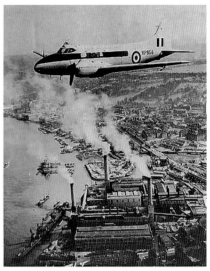

A Devon over Deptford power station on the River Thames. The picture hung for many years in the power station itself. On closure, it was retained by an employee who later permitted it to be copied by the 207 Squadron archivist (207 later flew VP956 in the communications role, but the picture is believed to date from 31 Squadron times). *With acknowledgement to Number 207 Squadron archive, via Raymond Glynne-Owen*

The student climbing out of the front seat of this Chipmunk is the Lord de l'Isle and Dudley, the secretary of state for air – who reputedly wished at the time to remain incognito.

Chipmunk aircraft were brought in to augment the Proctors for this. Jack Pearson, a fitter and SNCO on B Flight, was at Hendon for his second period with the Squadron, having served in India from 1939 until 1941. He recalls the Hendon Chipmunks vividly, as well as an all-white Spitfire; he writes:

'Several leading personages learned to fly with 31 Squadron at Hendon on the Proctors and Chipmunks. For example the then secretary of state for air – Lord de L'Isle and Dudley – was taught to fly in our Chipmunks. I have a particular photograph of him taken by myself. When I showed it to him, he gave me direct orders that under no circumstances were the press to be allowed to get hold of it – or even see it. I remember he used to sign the flight authorization sheets as "Mr. Smith"!'

Another character known to have flown Thirty One's Chipmunks is Wing Commander Ken Wallis, who later became known for building autogyros, including 'Little Nellie' which he flew in James Bond's *Thunderball*. Indeed a grainy picture exists of WG469 in Mill Hill Park, where the wing commander had forced-landed it in 1955 following a Chipmunk engine failure on a trip from Hendon.

And Association member Tony Paxton has a relevant – if slightly unexpected – tale to tell:

'I happen to have been 31 Squadron's first Tornado pilot. That, I realize, is quite a privilege, but it wasn't the only luck that befell me on Thirty One. I also met my wife Helena there, who was the CO's PA and is, therefore, an Association member in her own right. But the real point of this story is that since leaving the service, and now flying Boeings for a living, I also fly small single-piston aeroplanes for fun. For the last few years Helena and I have had a share in a de Havilland of Canada Chipmunk. It is an ex-RAF aeroplane, having served as WG474 and now registered G-BCSL.

Imagine my surprise when I discovered that our aeroplane had once served on Thirty One at Hendon. Along with, according to my book, about ten Chipmunks.'

Communications routine continued but, almost before Thirty One knew it, the year was 1955. The Squadron had been at Hendon for seven years, and the interlude was almost over. Sterner tasks beckoned.

Tony Paxton's ex-31 Squadron Chipmunk WG474 – which was on strength at Hendon from 1953 to '55. Good to see that it's still going strong – and that Helena's flying suit still has a Goldstar Tornado patch on the arm!

Chapter 21

Through the Lens

Ten years after the end of the Second World War, Europe was still full of troops. The 'Iron Curtain', as Sir Winston Churchill termed it, had come down, and Germany had been divided. East Germany, along with the rest of Eastern Europe, was under the sway of the Soviet Union, while the western half of Germany, now known as the Federal Republic, was just becoming part of NATO. The UK had upwards of a dozen combat squadrons based on the continent, together with a full army corps. American units were everywhere, and tensions were high.

Number 31 Squadron was reborn as a photo reconnaissance (PR) unit, flying Canberra jets, on 1 March 1955 at RAF Laarbruch, one of four airfields which had been built close to the Dutch border in the early 1950s. Its new boss, Squadron Leader John Stead, would serve several masters. The unit would be under the command of RAF Germany, while also being assigned to NATO as part of the 2nd Allied Tactical Air Force. The NATO command structure would alter in detail several times over the years but, broadly speaking, 2ATAF, together with its more southerly equivalent 4ATAF, would remain under the umbrella of HQ Allied Air Forces Central Europe. AAFCE's area of responsibility stretched from the Danish border to the Swiss border, from the North Sea to the eastern boundary of the FRG – beyond which stood the massed forces of the Warsaw Pact. At a given point in escalation of hostilities, control of the Squadron would be 'chopped' to NATO.

Among the first to arrive on the embryo unit was Flight Sergeant Eric 'Treff' Treffry, aircraft fitter. This wasn't his first contact with Thirty One. Prior to the Second World War he had been based at the maintenance unit in Karachi and had seen many of the Squadron's engines pass through his section. Now, at Laarbruch, he recalls that 'there were only a few chaps about, three officers and two NCO aircrew, a flight sergeant and a sergeant photographer, two engine sergeants, plus ten to a dozen airmen. For the first few, the main task was to organize the ground installations and to sort out the publications, offices and ground equipment.'

Treff was reputedly dispatched one day to a nearby railway station to collect a crate addressed to '31 Squadron'. It turned out to contain the Squadron's entire stock of accumulated silver – completely unmarked and unguarded.

Aircraft and more aircrew began to arrive in due course, but Treff had just got the first three machines airborne when he was promoted warrant officer and posted. That's RAF life! But he had nevertheless seen Thirty One into the air in Germany.

The new crews coming in were, in part, straight from the operational conversion unit, but were bolstered with a nucleus of experienced crews. Following a working-up syllabus, the Squadron became operational in June, taking its place as part of the NATO forces in north-west Germany.

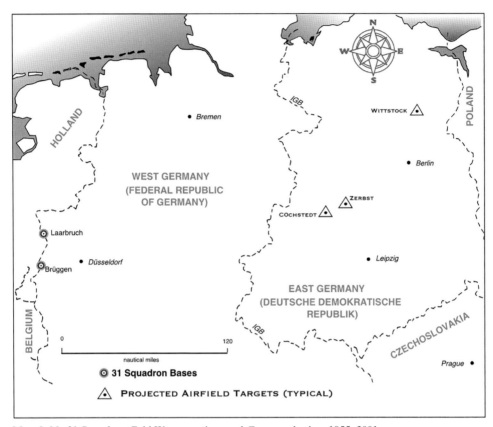

Map 8: No.31 Squadron Cold War operations and Germany basing, 1955–2001.

The Canberra was an English Electric product. A huge industrial conglomerate, the company had not hitherto been known for its aircraft designs. But it had nevertheless built thousands of aircraft under licence for Handley Page and de Havilland, most notably Halifax bombers and Vampire fighters. After the war the company began to produce its own products, first the Canberra and then the renowned Lightning interceptor. But the name of English Electric would not long be associated with its own types, for the air arm of the company would soon be absorbed by the British Aircraft Corporation.

Britain's first jet bomber, the Canberra entered squadron service in 1951. Pre-dating the V-bombers by several years, it was a deceptively simple design. And, as the natural successor to the Mosquito, it had similarly found application as a reconnaissance aircraft as well as a bomber. Remarkably, the last Canberra wouldn't leave RAF service until 2006 – albeit a much later mark of the aircraft fitted with very much modified reconnaissance equipment.

So the initial design must have been excellent. It certainly looked right, and many would describe the Canberra as one of the most elegant aircraft ever. Especially the PR7, which lacked the somewhat ungainly offset canopy of certain other marks. And, even more especially, with Thirty One's Star of India on the fin. This looked particularly fine in the early days when, with high-level PR being the game, the aircraft wore a polished aluminium finish.

Initially, training missions saw the Canberras roaming as far as their fuel would take them – which meant virtually all over Europe. Specific tasks had to be completed of course, but targets could be chosen by the Squadron – often in the form of a challenge. In due course there was even a 'suggestion box' where people would post requests for a particular photo shot. In newspaper parlance, if something of merit occurred or they beat another unit to recording a particularly choice PR target, they would claim a 'scoop'. Flight Sergeant George Thorpe was NCO i/c Thirty One's instrument section for a period and remembers the box:

In its early, high-level livery the Canberra PR7 made a magnificent picture. *The picture is from Brian Ray's collection*

> 'Groundcrew would suggest targets designed to test the skill and ability of the aircrews. For example, we read in the press one day that the royal yacht would be leaving at a particular time, en route with HM the Queen to one of the Dominions. A request appeared in the box for a photograph of the yacht at a certain time and place. A suggestion another day was to photograph Mount Vesuvius from 70,000ft.'

Well! A Canberra – possibly specially lightened and/or modified – did indeed gain the world altitude record at over 70,000ft in 1957, but that was far from a routine occurrence. The crew picking up the Thirty One challenge did, we understand, take the shot of Vesuvius from a more-normal 40,000ft.

Of course it wasn't all training. At one point the Squadron, along with its fellow Laarbruch recce squadrons, Nos.69 and 80, was kept busy with task 1515, photographing the whole of West Germany and those areas of East Germany that could be imaged across the border. Corporal Brian Ray, photo technician, comments that 'the view from 40,000ft with the cameras we had was quite good, so we could see far over the border. We used enormous quantities of F52 film and the aircrews were flying several sorties each day.'

A PR7 shows off the business end. The navigator's nose station, together with camera ports, are visible, as well as the bomb bay which would house a flare crate for night recce. This particular machine belonged to Number 17 Squadron. *Photo by permission of Martin Derry*

George Thorpe recalls 'my time with Thirty One as one of the best of my career in the RAF, for we had a marvellous relationship between officers and men.' The Squadron's complement back then included many national servicemen – conscripts on short engagements. Donald Mosely was one of these and offers his perspective on the working routine, recalling lots of bull and days off:

> 'After training as an air wireless mechanic I arrived at Laarbruch. My first duty was to parade on the Queen's official birthday, and I found myself transported to the runway together with about 4,000 others. We had just formed up when the heavens opened with a tremendous thunderstorm, and immediately the CO yelled at us to dismiss and return to our quarters. There was an almighty scramble to the lorries and we sang all the way back to barracks. Whereupon the skies cleared and we had a beautiful day off!
>
> 'I was then allocated to 31 Squadron. Which, I was told, was about to be presented with colours in honour of active service, and therefore we were to be subjected to a severe bout of square-bashing. Eventually, with much bull and polish, we celebrated the event, complete with white webbing, in front of a very large audience. At the end of the day we had a terrific party in the NAAFI and were all given a long weekend off.'

That colour presentation, on 13 September 1956, was indeed a notable event for 31 Squadron. Units may receive Standards after a minimum of twenty-five years of operational service, so Thirty One's could be said to have been somewhat delayed. But this was understandable, what with all the operational business which had occupied the intervening years, and in fact the timing of the award was very much in line with that of many similar units.

The Standard came emblazoned with eight proud battle honours. At an impressive ceremony, it was presented by distinguished old boy Air Chief Marshal Sir Alec Coryton KCB, KBE, MVO, DFC, RAF, whom we last met as a flight lieutenant on the Frontier in the early 1920s. Present on the day were many former Thirty Oners, including former COs and six members of the '31 Squadron RFC and RAF Old Comrades Association (1915–19)'.

As well as the eight battle honours emblazoned on the Standard, Thirty One had been awarded a further five. Of those, four were categorized as 'not entitled to be emblazoned'. There can be various reasons for non-entitlement. One is that a unit, although involved in a campaign, did not take part in combat. Another, which pertains to Thirty One's particular situation, is that the RAF has followed army custom in not emblazoning honours awarded during the inter-war period. Thus the following 31 Squadron battle honours were not, and never will be, emblazoned on the Standard: Afghanistan 1919–1920; Mahsud 1919–1920; Waziristan 1919–1925; and North-West Frontier 1939.

The fifth of the 'missing' honours is, however, entitled to be emblazoned. It is 'Syria 1941', but missed out because there was, at the time, a limit of eight honours on any Standard. The Squadron's leadership had to decide which of the nine emblazonable honours to omit, and 'Syria' was the unlucky campaign.

Mention of the 'old comrades' makes this an opportune moment to return to the subject of the Squadron Association. Perhaps prompted by the reformation of Thirty One as a front-line unit, an attempt to get the 'Burma boys' together was made in 1955. Just one year later the membership criteria would be extended to cover the entire Second World War period. But the infant organization initially failed to flourish, and would not do so until the Association was re-launched in 1963. This would occur following a Burma reunion at the Royal Albert Hall, and the new Association would thereafter grow in strength with the help of a series of marvellous reunions of its own. It would absorb the remaining 'old comrades' in 1965 and, that same year, membership would be extended to those who had served on Thirty One at any time. Its lively newsletter, *Star News*, would keep members in touch with each other and with the Squadron.

By the late 1950s, opposition defences were becoming more capable, and NATO air forces switched to low-level attack and reconnaissance as tactics began to emphasize getting in 'under the radar'. Thirty One was no exception, and their aircraft now began to reappear in drab grey and green camouflage. The role came to be known as 'tactical reconnaissance' – or colloquially within NATO, 'Tac R'.

The camera fits had to be changed to reflect the new circumstances. Hitherto, a fan of up to six F52 cameras (four in the front hatch and two in the rear) had done the trick, together with one F49 in the rear for vertical survey. Now the main camera was the F95 oblique, of which two would generally be carried in the forward hatch. Occasionally an F22 in the rear would be added, although this was nearing obsolescence by this time. In fact all of these camera types had seen wartime service – although they continued to perform excellently for the RAF and other forces until well into the 1970s. For night work, either two or four F97s were used, synchronized with photo-flash flares released from the flash crate in the bomb bay.

Sqn Ldr Dick Kidney comments on the evolving operation:

'When I first arrived in Germany in 1959, low-flying had been 'anywhere at any time'. For low-level night photo-flashing we went everywhere; often to the UK either for the army kit on offer or because of duff weather on mainland Europe. Much use was made of weather diversions on return. It seemed odd to fly to Castle Martin in Wales to flash some of 'theirs' – Federal German army Leopard tanks – when Germany was full of them! Catterick range was also well-used, but only on a south-to-north direction because of its small size. Even then, any southerly wind above about 20kts meant that photo-flash debris would fall outside the range danger area, occasionally clattering onto the late-night bus from Richmond on its journey up the dale. Apparently the stoic Yorkshire passengers didn't mind being hit by "one of ours!"

'The German citizens were equally tolerant, or so we were told. Once, on Exercise *Royal Flush*, I was tasked to flash the city of Koblenz at 0140hrs local! The Bofors-like noise must have woken a million people. The pictures started at the river, before going up a hillside to a military installation about 600 metres away.'

And Terry O'Halloran, first a corporal and later a sergeant with the Squadron adds:

'The groundcrew's dread was of a flash which failed to release. If an aircraft came back with a possible "hang-up", it was treated with extreme caution. Each flare comprised a magnesium sulphide three-point-five-million candlepower cartridge.

The MFPU was a sizable set-up.

As refuelling was the first job after landing, a dislodged flare could have been nasty.'

An integral element of the Squadron – technically only attached, but very much a part of the family – was Number 3 Mobile Field Photographic Unit. This unit, housed in a series of trailers and caravans, was responsible for processing and interpreting the film and pictures produced by the Canberras. Their finely-honed routine was an essential part of the operational excellence of the Squadron – and shared equally in its exercise and competition successes.

Speed was of the essence in getting the results to whomever had requested the intelligence. As soon as the brakes went on, the navigator, who had spent the important moments of the sortie at the 'sharp end' – lying in the perspex nose – would sprint to the caravan with his verbal and written report. The 'moles' (photographers) would download the film in a trice, and it would be whisked off for processing. The next stage would see the PIs – the photo interpreters – extracting the required information with the aid of 3-D imagers. The Squadron even boasted dispatch riders from time to time to further speed things; Senior Aircraftman Mike Harris was the first, and Brian Ray another. The latter tells their tale:

'One function, apart from photography and having a good time on the bikes, was to take flight plans round to the ATC building on the other side of the airfield. Most of the perimeter road was a one-way system, so this necessitated a complete circuit of the airfield. I seem to recall a best of approximately six minutes, including the stop to drop off the flight plan. This was pretty quick for a distance in excess of five miles, and I recall terminal velocity of 75–80mph being reached for considerable stretches on our Triumph 500 TRWs.'

Innovation was essential to keep ahead of the game. Sergeant Ralph Sutcliffe did two stints as a photographer with the MFPU between 1955 and 1962. His wife Jean wrote in an Association newsletter:

'I well remember the work that went into the training of the 3MFPU lads in preparation for their attempts in 1961 on the Gruenther Trophy. Speed as well as accuracy was essential, and for some jobs I was the guinea pig. Ralph had devised a speedier way of winding the film, so equipment was rigged at home. I had to close my eyes to pretend I was in the dark room, and was timed fitting the film onto the roller and winding. This I went through several times. When the timing got close to what Ralph hoped for, he went back to his lads and squeezed extra effort out of them by saying, "my wife can do it faster than that with her eyes shut!" '

And junior PI Flying Officer Garry Dickenson must take much of the credit for the Squadron's victory in the nighttime '*Royal Flush*' of May 1967. After a lot of trouble

Speed is of the essence when it comes to preparing the recce report, whether the mission is for real, exercise or competition. Aircrew and Photograhic technicians are all part of the relay team. The pictures were taken after the switch to the low-level role, as evidenced by the revised, camouflaged colour scheme. *Brian Ray*

with faulty film production in the cameras, Garry expressed a mistrust of the settings tabulated on the magazines. He returned to first principles and re-calculated the settings. Following a short trial, these were adopted for the final work-up. Exposure failures now became very rare and enabled Thirty One to edge out the USAF. The latter had their new RF-4 Phantoms, and it's true to say that, although the Canberras were now generally facing superior equipment as other nations began to re-equip, RAF training and professionalism often won the day.

In earlier years, the Squadron's groundcrew had had ample opportunity to fly. Indeed they had often been indispensible elements in the airborne effort. With the advent of jets the 'auxiliary crew' element disappeared, leaving opportunities only for what might be described as pleasure trips – which would become increasingly less common with subsequent types. The Canberra offered the last 'easy' opportunity for Goldstar groundcrew to fly, and Brian Ray was especially keen. Indeed his enthusiasm bore fruit in the shape of many of this chapter's photographs. He tells his story:

'The chance to have a ride in a Canberra was not something I had envisaged when joining the RAF in 1955, but I soon realized there were possibilities to fly on the rumble seat when the crew were on "continuation training" sorties. In other words when the navigator didn't require access to the nose to operate the cameras, so a body perched on the folding seat would not be too much of a hindrance. My first take-off was a staggering experience; the engines opened to full throttle, resulting in the distinctive nose-down crouch of power against brakes. Then came a rush as brakes were released, and I was mesmerized as the acceleration just kept going and going. Having reached a height at which to play around I was shown almost everything in the book, with the net result being that I felt a bit queasy – as well as totally impressed! It all seemed to happen so quickly, but a few gulps of 100 per cent oxygen helped calm me down.

'After we landed, Flying Officer Thomas promised he would get me a trip in our T4, WT483, so that I could get my hands on the controls. But before this I flew with another enthusiastic pilot, Flying Officer Taylor, when we did some cloud flying. We swooped in amongst cu-nims whose extraordinarily solid appearance was amazing, and the impression of speed as we clipped some of these, sometimes in a near-vertical bank, was awe-inspiring. The navigator was not too happy in the back with all the banking and rolling about; he remarked that on continuation training flights he usually managed to have a kip!

'Eventually, the T4 flight came up. With Thomas overseeing, this had to be the best three hours I had ever spent as we ranged around the sky. And then a later trip with Flight Lieutenant Tony Ferguson to do the air-to-air pictures was terrific. How beautiful the aircraft looked when flying close together.'

Formating like a fighter. *Brian Ray*

Mention of the Gruenther Trophy and to Exercise *Royal Flush* prompts a word that, over the years that the emphasis switched from pure warfighting to deterring and preparedness, the story told in this narrative inevitably changes from one of operations to one of training. But NATO always needed to know that its forces were ready and capable. The opposition also had to understand this if our posture of deterrence was to be credible. So it was essential from all viewpoints that the operational stance was regularly and rigorously evaluated. One way of ensuring that standards were kept up was by competition, which assumed huge importance in RAF and NATO life.

The RAF's major reconnaissance competition was the Sassoon Trophy, named after a former under-secretary of state for air of the 1920s and 1930s, while NATO's big event was *Royal Flush*, titled in acknowledgement of poker's top hand. The prize for the latter was the Gruenther Trophy, named after a USAF former commander of AAFCE.

With that as background, let's join Flight Lieutenant Tony Burt, who provides a splendid description of what, in 1958, it was like to be in competition:

'Phil Taylor and I from 31 Squadron arrived at Spangdahlen with 80 and 17 Squadron crews from Brüggen and Wildenrath for the 2ATAF versus 4ATAF reconnaissance competition over the period 8–12 September 1958. The Canberras, although by now very much committed to the low-level role, were actually entered for the high-level competition against the USAF RB-66s, the RAF's banner in that year's low-level competition being carried by the Supermarine Swift squadrons.

'The final teams were selected, and the 17 and 31 Squadron crews were to fly for 2ATAF, with 80 Squadron in reserve. The plan was to fly three competition sorties over the three days 8–10 September. The daily competition briefing followed a set pattern. Starting at 5am we had the Europe-wide weather briefing. Then came the navigation brief and a time check administered by the chief umpire. The final act was the hand-out of Form 73 – the all-important target-for-the-day tasking document. Then it was eyes down for business. Where were the selected targets – how many – what maps were needed? A hectic time until we came to the crunch – the navigator handing in his flight plan. This was the tablet of stone – the commitment. If I reckoned the point-to-point elapsed time was 2hrs 55.6mins, then that was it – the die was cast. From wheels up to the time Phil swooped past the Spangdahlen control tower on return we'd have to be exact – any more time used and we were penalized! If we had to descend on track to low level to get the target – and therefore stretch our time – we would have a problem.

'So how did it go? Back to the logbook again where I see that I noted the target locations. On 8 September we flew to Redon (near St Nazaire), to St Jean de Luz (near Biarritz), on to Pau (near Lourdes) and then back to Spangdahlen. The boys whipped off the cameras and sprinted to the MFPU with them for processing, while I handed my traces to PI John Gregory. That was when Phil and I felt best, I guess. The pictures were in the can and the next time we would see them was when they were on the bench under scrutiny by John to extract the information he – and the judges – were looking for. Only when the PI's report was in could we sit back, with fingers crossed.

'And that was the pattern. Day two took us to Corsica (I believe the target was the airfield at Ajaccio), then on to the 4ATAF area, and back to Spangdahlen after a round-robin of France and Germany. Finally came day three, when our route was Avingnon-Toulouse-Angers (on the Loire) and home.

'One of the targets (must have been Redon or Angers) involved a stretch of river and a search for shipping or some such military target. OK on a clear day but we had weather problems. 2,000ft cloudbase, so down from forty thousand we came and I had Phil hauling our aircraft into two tight 270 degree turns so that we could get vertical cover bank to bank of three stretches of water at 90 degrees to each other. I think that was the nearest I ever got to being airsick in a Canberra PR7!

'Three successive days of intensive flying were ended. And the outcome? On 12 September the trophies ware presented in the base theatre by General Gruenther himself, the RAF team captain accepting the award. *The Photogram*, printed weekly at Spangdahlen Air Base, recorded that "The RAF's Canberra team of

Flying Officer P. Taylor and Flight Lieutenant A. Burt won individual honours in the high-level missions." It was a twenty-minute flight back to Laarbruch that day, and Phil and I had the *Royal Flush III* AAFCE high-level reconnaissance trophy safely tucked away in good old WT519! She had done us proud, as had the ground and photographic crews.'

Flight Lieutenant Mike 'Dinger' Bell recalls a similar event:

'We regularly did well in both the Sassoon and *Royal Flush*, and in 1967 we excelled ourselves by winning both. The latter was a night competition where we were pitched against the more advanced RB-66s of the USAF. Alan "Chunky" Harrison and I represented Thirty One at the big prize-giving ceremony at Dutch airbase Twenthe. After meeting Prince Bernhardt we started the serious competition of out-drinking the opposition! I think we won that also, and a vivid recollection is of sitting on a huge cartwheel suspended from the ceiling in the mess watching an unfortunate USAF pilot sprawling on the floor having failed to jump from the side benches to the wheel. Ah, those were the days!'

In 1970 the Squadron's Canberras flew to Deelen, another RNLAF base, for *Royal Flush XV*. That year, each squadron had to select, as one of its three crews, men who had never previously participated, in order to get a good cross-section of experience. Each squadron flew eight sorties, each having three targets. Thirty One's team manager was Dick Kidney, who later wrote:

'Our strength was sixty-one, including the MFPU. It was a mixed bag with an army major as GLO, a naval lieutenant, and a WRAF photo interpreter. She did a great job as PI and was equally effective in keeping everybody's language clean during moments of stress. The officer i/c social arrangements excelled himself. One of the trucks in our convoy rolled through the Dutch customs post carrying 2,000 litres of beer – referred to as "technical stores"!

'The competition was a very close one in the end and we were officially placed fourth. I hesitate to mention individual achievements, but Flight Lieutenant Ed Rouse and crew – Flying Officer Terry Kirkland and Lieutenant Greg Aldred RN – took one target, comprising twelve Leopard tanks, at 390kts. The old Canberra did not handle too easily close to the ground at that speed, but each target had to be overflown at over 350kts and there were timing penalties as well, hence their high speed. Rouse and crew achieved 82 per cent on that target.'

The Canberra was indeed a very speedy aircraft, as Dick later confirmed:

'English Electric built them to stay glued together. The PR7 had a 450kt limitation. When on one occasion a crew surprised themselves by straying into East German airspace through slight navigational error (these things happened, you know!) before you could say "gulag" they were heading west at max chat. The beast was accelerating through 525kts as it crossed back into NATO airspace.'

Returning to *Royal Flush XV*, Dick still considered, even many years later, that:

'We wuz robbed! Why? Well, the Belgian army usually won the trophy for best-camouflaged mobile (deployed) target. During this particular competition they had put out two tough targets. We were one of only three or four squadrons to get coverage of the first. And Thirty One got the only pictures of the second.

'Thus for many of the others the points score in this section was two "nils". There was naturally much whinging about these two targets being too difficult, so the judges found feeble excuses for withdrawing them. They had been high-value targets, about 200 points apiece, and we lost about 260 points. Thus although the final league positions came out with us a mere 78 points behind the winning Canadians, if we'd received our rightful 260 points, we'd have won.

'To add insult to injury, our pictures of the Belgian targets were used later in the VIP display to illustrate the excellence of "their" winning camouflage!'

All aspects of these competitions were taken deadly seriously, as 'mole' Syd Graham describes:

'I was with Thirty One at the time of its great triumph in *Royal Flush 1964*. The MoD attached so much importance to the matter that they flew a technician out from the UK manufacturers to ensure there were no malfunctions. My task was to fit the magazines pre-flight and to ensure that the glass surfaces within the cameras were pristine, as one speck of dirt could ruin the photograph. Especially for the competition I was issued with a dozen brand-new yellow dusters (normally we used rags torn from old bed sheets). After we had won the competition I had to hand the dusters in again! When the victory was announced the entire Squadron was euphoric. As Thirty One had won the high-level and low-level recce competitions in previous years, this win gave us a clean sweep and proved that we were the top photo-recce outfit in AAFCE.'

On the subject of airframe performance, Brian Ray has a little more to add: 'The T4 was lighter than the PR7, not having the large belly fuel tank, and it really could fly rings round most of what the world's air forces were using at the time. In those days our aircraft were the great untouchables – and even when the Hunters came into service they still had a job to out-manoeuvre Canberras at altitude.'

The author, a sometime Hunter pilot himself, can certainly agree with that! But another performance issue which was exercising minds at the time was whether there was much benefit in carrying the ubiquitous tip tanks – the drag in some circumstances perhaps outweighing the benefits of the extra fuel. Brian Ray again:

'Thirty One pioneered the removal of the tanks for fuel consumption trials. One of the crews went for an endurance record and managed to stay airborne for 9hrs 10mins. Reputedly they gave up after this time because of frozen survival packs (the part of the parachute pack on which the crew sat) which was causing their backsides to go numb. They returned only to discover that had they stayed up for a further five minutes the existing record would have been broken! There was still 20–25 minutes fuel remaining, so the trip proved the point for flying without tip tanks.'

Back to the training, and Graham Pitchfork demonstrates what a hard school it was:

'I joined Thirty One in April 1962 as a first-tour pilot officer and was informed by the CO, Wing Commander Charles Dalziel, that it was a Squadron tradition to fly newcomers on their first day. I soon found myself stuffed into a PR7 with Squadron Leader Ramsey Brown and his navigator "Wizzo", so called because of his habit of exclaiming "Wizard!" The weather was poor. Wizzo occupied the rumble seat, I was stuck in the back, couldn't see a thing and hadn't a clue what was going on. It soon became apparent that this state of affairs was also afflicting one other crewmember. I was somewhat confused by the ramblings from the nose as Wizzo thrashed about with his large map. "It should be a road over river bridge – or perhaps it was road over rail. No, it was river over road, that's right." This went on for a while and eventually Ramsay's frustration was beginning to show through his calm demeanour. Thankfully, he decided to abandon the sortie and return to Laarbruch. My log-book shows that we were airborne in WT533 for almost two hours and the remarks column records "low-level nav demo." Undoubtedly a charitable description!

'My initiation to the Squadron was far from complete. The self-appointed senior flying officer and chairman of the bachelors' club was one Tony Lovett. I was programmed to fly with him and we were given the usual five targets in the British zone. Tony added a sixth, which appeared to be a few miles off the coast at Cuxhaven on a low-lying island. Having found the first five, we left the IP on the coast and headed west on a timed run to photograph Tony's target. I looked ahead and saw nothing – panic began to set in. On time there was no sign of the island and it seemed I had missed it. We returned to Laarbruch in silence and I had to admit during the debrief to failure. Later in the evening I heard Tony's voice in the bar explaining that he had just "fixed that new nav" by selecting a sandbank knowing that the tide was in and that it would be under water.

'A few days later I was programmed to fly a check ride with the CO. It comprised another five targets, the last being a "military installation" south of Bremen. We set off for that target but saw nothing remotely military. On landing I noticed that the other crews took an unusual interest in our debrief. I was to learn later that this was the CO's party piece for all new navigators. When the film arrived I could just about make out some old and derelict buildings. I enquired whether that was the target. "Yes my boy," came the reply, "there are the remains of the camp where Herr Hitler incarcerated me for two years after I had been shot down." He then gave me a most important piece of advice for those in the PR business. "Always take a photograph at the elapsed time. The photo interpreter may find what he is looking for even if you haven't seen it." And with that he took me off to the bar.'

Commanding Officers had come and gone but on 3 May, 1965, Wing Commander Bob Price took over. He recalls:

'It had apparently been developing into a Squadron tradition that there was always a baby on the way amongst the aircrew wives. In 1965, there appeared to be a gap in continuity and, after some ribald crew-room discussion, Jones the Welsh (the senior PI, Flight Lieutenant Glyn Jones) turned to me and said, "Well, sir, you are our leader …!" Fortunately, one of the pilots (and his wife) saved me from this problem. We already had five children between two and eight years old – and we were Church of England!'

'Lone Rangers' were still possible in the mid-sixties, including to Aden until final withdrawal of British forces in 1967. They provided welcome variety, but were strictly rationed. They were something of a shopping trip as well as a navigation exercise, and a valuable experience in operations out of theatre. Squadron Leader Geoff Claridge, the nav leader, has a tale or two to tell of one such flight:

'Flight Lieutenant Dennis Turner and myself set off on the first leg to Cyprus on 8 November 1966 in WT 510; this aircraft was a last-minute substitute which had been reported on a number of occasions for excessive fuel consumption, but no fault had ever been found. The flight plan time to Cyprus was five hours; all went well for the first three hours with fuel going exactly according to plan, but suddenly the graph started to dip quite alarmingly. We were past Crete steering due east for Cyprus, and for a while there seemed to be a possibility that we would have to divert to an airfield in Africa. Fortunately the weather was excellent in Cyprus and we eventually landed at Akrotiri with a minimum safe fuel margin. The other legs, Cyprus to Bahrain, onwards to Aden and the return legs to Laarbruch, all showed this marked increase in fuel consumption after some three hours. Faced with the evidence of the fuel graphs, the groundcrew conducted a thorough investigation which eventually located the trouble. It appeared that at a particular stage in the fuel transfer, pump selection activated an electrical fault which caused fuel to be vented out to the atmosphere.

'Our stay in Aden was restricted to five hours on the ground because of the risk to parked aircraft from terrorist activity. Within that time we had to travel into and out of the town and obtain a large quantity of shopping both for ourselves and other members of the Squadron. However, when we got to the guardroom the policeman told us that we were not allowed into town because that particular day was a national holiday and consequently the risk of terrorist acts against servicemen was high. Fearing the wrath of our colleagues more than the terrorists, we assured the policeman that we would not hold him responsible if anything happened to us and took the nearest taxi. Fortunately all went peacefully and we accomplished our mission.'

Geoff also had some views on 'leading from the front':

'During the first part of my tour, the CO was Wing Commander Scott, who led the Squadron with great dash and example in his flying. Towards the end of 1964 he was interviewed at HQ RAF Germany because, some months previously, an inexperienced crew had flown through a prohibited area in East Anglia causing a rather expensive racehorse to injure itself in its stable. The boss returned and gathered the aircrew together in the crew room. He explained what had happened and said that receiving a mild rocket was part of life because, as our commander, he accepted both the brickbats and the bouquets on behalf of the Squadron. However, he went on to say that although he had no wish to dampen the enthusiasm of the aircrew, it would be prudent to take things carefully in the future. If at all in doubt about either the weather or the navigation in low-level exercises, the only solution was to climb and continue at high level.

'The following day six crews were detailed for an exercise in which they were required to take off at ten-minute intervals and photograph the same three targets. Wing Commander Scott and his nav, Graham Pitchfork, set off first with a marginal weather forecast and the rest of us followed at intervals. The first target was in the flat North German Plain and presented no problem, but the second target was in a very hilly area close to the Winterberg ski-jump. As crew numbers two to six approached the second target, picking their way carefully through narrow valleys because of the poor visibility and thick cloud covering the hilltops, they were mindful of the boss's briefing of the previous day. Eventually they all climbed above the cloud and returned to base, only to find that the boss had managed to photograph all three targets!'

There were periods of high tension and alert during Thirty One's time with the Canberra. During the Hungarian uprising of 1956, for example, and while the Prague Spring was being crushed in 1968. There was also the Cuban missile crisis of 1962, which came as close as any other post-war event to precipitating World War Three. Syd Graham recalls that one well: 'Being on standby during the Cuba crisis, not knowing whether "it" was going to happen or not.'

But for all that, it's the exercises rather than the operational events that we hear the most about. Those exercises were sometimes viewed as a threat to the normal, orderly working of the unit, but nevertheless, given the constant need to achieve and demonstrate readiness, they came thick and fast. To the extent that they could almost be seen as the norm, and so much shall we read about them in the coming pages that a word of explanation would be well worthwhile.

'Taceval', the tactical evaluation, was top of the list; an exercise run by the NATO headquarters, it was the external and independent test of a unit's capabilities. 'Maxeval' was next in line, being conducted by an RAF headquarters to ensure that a unit was ready to face Taceval. Being a national event, its results were kept in-house – with the evaluators, who were drawn from the HQ and other RAF bases, being of course 'only there to help.' Try convincing the victims of that, though; as in any dress-rehearsal, the producer could be hard to satisfy, and a Maxeval was invariably tougher than the real thing. A 'Mineval' was the commonest member of the family, and was run routinely by a station as a way of ensuring that its standards were kept up. Lowest in the hierarchy came the 'Microval'. A squadron might lay on one of these for several reasons: to correct deficiencies; to train up new personnel following, perhaps, a rash of postings; or to practise a new role or revised procedures.

Terry O'Halloran expands:

'Taceval was the scourge of the station, with an independent team of umpires who would arrive without notice. They would deploy to the major centres and then watch and observe. HMS Laarbruch would sound – a ship's hooter mounted atop the boiler house. I lived in Holland, nineteen miles from Laarbruch. With the wind in the right direction, we could hear the hooter from there!'

Dead-of-night callouts were usually the worst. But as Terry continues, the unexpected could often be even more difficult to cope with:

'One seemingly minor exercise was called at 5.20pm just as most of the station staff were leaving for home. A long line of cars and coaches leaving the base found the barrier closed, and back to work they went. Mineval rarely lasted more than twenty-four hours, and at 4am next morning this one was terminated. But at 4.20 am a *Quicktrain* exercise was called, this being a 2ATAF generation exercise which necessitated fitting tip tanks, together with night or day cameras and flash crates.

'This latest five-minute tannoy klaxon seemed to last forever. In a daze born of working a full day shift and the subsequent Mineval, Sergeant Robbie Roberts, who was working atop a mainplane with me, listening for the delicate click of an undercarriage up-lock, jumped from the trailing edge of the wing and disappeared, gibbering!'

Station commanders had unenviable jobs, being primarily required to ensure their units' efficiencies. There were various ways of going about it, but it was hard to please everybody. Terry again:

'We had three Minevals on the trot when "Beeno" first arrived as station commander. The first thing he had was a Wing parade on the end of the runway. Next he broadcast to the station: "There will be no (this) ...", "There will be no (that) ...", "and be no (the other) ..." Hence Group Captain Beeno! I never did know his real name.'

Quite so. We wouldn't want airmen getting too much of the other, now would we?!

With no live combat to lend spice, squadron spirit had to find alternative outlets during the Germany years. This, together with the competitive instinct engendered by the exercise and competition régime, led to many japes at the expense of other units. As typified by Terry O'Halloran's report of Number 3 Aerobrigata's visit from Villafranca in 1967:

'We could speak no Italian, their groundcrews could speak no English, so a fantastic three weeks of sign language and good humour would sum it all up. Each trade in the Italian ground staff had a different coloured hat. Needless to say, when they left all their hats were the same RAF colour while many of our number paraded in blue, yellow, red or green head-dress. On the day of departure there was pandemonium in the hangar, for high in the roof girders was the Italian line chief's bicycle. After much excited chatter, with the Italian cargo plane ready to go, it was eventually rescued.'

There was much more of the same. In those days the duty squadron looked after the week's visiting aircraft, and Terry recounts another tale:

'We made our visitors welcome, and at the first opportunity doctored their aircraft with a yellow 31 Squadron star (spray can and stencil) plus "Andy Capp" cut-outs in dayglo material. On one occasion a Dominie visited from RAF Stradishall. Within thirty minutes of landing it was decorated and within an hour I was on the carpet facing Wing Commander Price. "The group captain has just seen the visiting aircraft and says it has been defaced. The markings must be removed immediately. Find the culprit and get the stars removed." I was soon poised with CTC-soaked rag to remove the first star when a voice requested my mission – it was the pilot. I told him, but he said, "You leave them be, I will be away shortly, consider the job done".'

One can certainly see senior officers' viewpoints. What's funny to some can often be severely irritating to others. But 'zapping' nevertheless expanded to epidemic proportions, the game being better when the target was difficult. Terry continues:

'On detachment to USAF Base Hahn, Sergeant Norman Hood was i/c "operation *zap*", and the station flag pole came under attack. Dayglo stickers were appearing near the top by the time the sheriff, the American station security officer, saw two of our lads marching smartly about their business. Drawing alongside in his large station wagon, he wound down the window and enquired when "Y'all were going to stop sticking these little red men awl over the place?" Three had apparently appeared on the inside of his security office window flap! The lads commiserated and assured the sheriff that it was all in good fun, but that they would endeavour to curtail the activity. He drove off, no doubt pleased with himself – but with several more zaps on the side of his car!'

In the end, though, it went too far at Hahn where an enquiry had to be launched. Inside the quick reaction alert pens (high fenced security areas guarded by armed police), two nuclear-armed Phantoms had developed Thirty One fever with stencils and zaps. Even though it later emerged that Norman had bribed one of the QRA inmates to doctor their own aircraft, there was hell to play. One always has to appreciate the line that must not be crossed!

The 'zap' spirit persisted amongst that particular bunch of Thirty Oners even after they had left Laarbruch and the Squadron had relinquished its Canberras. For example in 1975, word reached them that one of Thirty One's old aircraft, WT520, was now a 'gate guardian' at RAF Swinderby. The station commander there, an ex-80 Squadron man (80 having been a PR7 squadron at Laarbruch and Brüggen) had had the aircraft painted up in his old unit's markings. Our intrepid gang prepared a set of the 'correct' markings and, with forged papers showing them to be painters and finishers from RAF Bicester, set to in broad daylight to restore 520 to its former glory. The revision lasted a fortnight before the aircraft was once again displayed in 80 Squadron colours. Not to be deterred, the team returned some months later and this time riveted Thirty One markings to the aircraft. There is no record of how long that lasted!

Whatever the rights and wrongs of 'zapping', it's undeniable that the 31 Squadron of that period had a marvellous spirit. Terry again:

'Our personnel did not departmentalize – we were the Squadron and we worked as one. One day, prior to a grant, we were flying in the morning and getting ready to finish at midday. The duty crew would finish off when the last aircraft was brought in. But a PR7 was in the circuit with a hydraulic warning light flashing, and it finally landed amid the well-disciplined surveillance of the rescue and fire wagons.

A hydraulic pipe had worn through above the starboard jet pipe and dumped the contents of the system into the atmosphere. As a precaution, every aircraft had to be checked before we went on grant, and it was now 10.30am.

'I have never seen so many people armed with screwdrivers at work at one time. "Moles" came out into the daylight; "fairies" (radio/radar), not used to soiled hands, attacked the dirtiest parts of the aircraft; "plumbers" (armourers) forgot their flash crates and joined the mêlée; the "heavies" (engine fitters) and "riggers" (airframes) examined the pipes as the engine nacelles were removed. Several damaged pipes were found and replaced, whilst others were bound to avoid future chafing. All Thirty One's aircraft were fit by 1pm and we went away on grant. It should be mentioned that even the "leckies" (electricians) and "insties" (instrument fitters) gave a hand.'

It would be churlish, of course, to comment that it's amazing how the imminent approach of a long weekend speeds up work!

Sergeant Hood, of Hahn infamy, was invariably to be found at or very near the centre of any madcap schemes that occurred. His memories of the return visit to Villafranca are typical of the times:

'We worked from 7am till 1pm, followed by an Italian meal washed down with a litre of red wine each. Then we'd fall into the coach down to the beach at Lake Garda. I recall Chief Technician Ray Dove, head of the armourers, leading a merry drinking-party one afternoon in a small tavern on the shores of the lake. When the police arrived, Ray showed them how to strip down their machine guns. We all left then, without showing the police how to re-assemble them.'

Then the following year there was a trip to Amsterdam. Norman continues:

'We went to ask Wing Commander Price for a day off to visit Amsterdam. His face lit up at the idea and he spun round in his chair to view the calendar, seconds later dropping his pen on a date to declare a Squadron day out! (It doesn't happen like that anymore!)

'We did the Heineken brewery, and I will always remember the look on the face of the woman checking the bottles at the final stage, when along clattered a few dozen labelled with 31 Squadron zaps. The trip ended with the customary visit to what we used to know as *Kanal Strasse* (sounds more German than Dutch!), where all the young airmen learned something!'

Managing one's finances in Germany wasn't entirely simple, as Dick Kidney, describes:

'There were rather odd currency arrangements at the time. UK cheques were only usable within the wire (usually to pay for lost kit, etc.) and we were not permitted to have German bank

Tea-break, Laarbruch-style; the NAAFI wagon visits during the 1950s. *Brian Ray collection*

accounts. Our pay came in cash and we had to forecast our monthly requirement of deutschmarks, Dutch guilders and "baffs". We'd leave the pay parade with our pockets stuffed with wads of each, so it was just as well that mugging wasn't a part of the scene at the time. Those colloquially-known "baffs" were actually the currency of the BAFVS, the "British armed forces voucher system", which was used in NAAFIs and Malcolm Clubs all over West Germany. I recall there being brown plastic coins as well as the Monopoly-like notes. Those coins came in odd shapes – hexagonal, octagonal and so on, perhaps reflecting the twelve-sided threepenny piece of the day. I should also add that discounted petrol was paid for by coupons, while the exchange rate gave us about twelve DMs to the pound. Marvellous times!'

The expanse of Laarbruch takes on an altogether bleaker aspect during the harsh, continental winter. *Brian Ray*

The original Squadron Badge, signed by King George VI and the Chester Herald and believed to have been lost in the fire at Comilla in 1945, resurfaced in the late 1960s when it was re-presented by the Association to the boss, Bob Price. In the interim a replacement had been commissioned – but the story of the original must be told.

The Canberra's Rolls-Royce Avon engines were started by explosive cartridge, and all who operated the type will remember the characteristic plumes of smoke seen in this picture (and will forever retain in their nostrils the evocative smell). *Brian Ray*

There were all sorts of rumours as to how it had been saved. The then adjutant, Gerry Groves, was later adamant that the Badge was never 'lost' at all: 'It was kept in the Squadron safe. I took this cumbersome safe from Hathazari to Ramree, Tilda, Akyab and on to Kallang. When I left 31 Squadron to take up duties as camp commandant of 232 Group in Rangoon, the Badge was still safely stored in the safe at Kallang.'

But memories do inevitably fade, and the following account by Stan Johnson, an instrument technician from Burma days and later an enthusiastic Association member, seems to ring equally true:

'The fire at Comilla was about to engulf the orderly room *basha* when a "liberator" snatched the Squadron Badge from the wall and removed the frame. He rolled up the parchment and stuffed it inside his shirt for a souvenir ... if he hadn't done so it would have gone up in flames, so let's forgive him. Some years later our hero turned up to an Association committee meeting with it. We debated what was the right thing to do. Certainly not stick it on the cover of the minutes book as suggested by some, or simply have it smartened up to sort out the tears and water stains. No – we should ask the College of Heralds to undertake repairs to it and re-present it to its rightful owners on our next visit to the Squadron.

'I went to the college and saw Sir John Heaton-Armstrong – who had signed the painting in 1937 as Chester Herald. He was now Clarenceaux King of Arms, and he quizzed me deeply about my illegal possession of it. I managed to convince him of our honourable intentions, following which he offered to get his heraldic painters to assess the damage and give the Association a quote for carrying out the repairs. To cut a long story short, all went according to plan and on our next visit to the Squadron we handed it over. On the back of the refurbished painting is a note by Sir John which confirms these facts.'

There was a final twist to the tale. The 'liberator', who saved the Badge from the Comilla fire and brought it to that committee meeting years later, turned out to be Harry Crutch. Avid readers may recall that Harry, also known as Butch, was the chap who was hospitalized after being struck by lightning at Tezpur. Only he, probably, knew exactly where the original Badge had got to all those years ago. But conspiracy theorists will, no doubt, have little difficulty in finding a 'fiery' connection in Harry's various exploits.

Be that as it may, the Badge had returned, and it hangs proudly to this day – albeit in a slightly war-weary state – at Thirty One's current base alongside the replacement. The latter bears a queen's crown and, notably, the 'Army Co-operation' epithet is omitted. Just plain '31 Squadron' which, in view of the changes in role over the years, through 'BT', 'PR' and 'B', is appropriate.

At any rate, Gordon England, together with several other reprobates from the Association, remembers the re-presentation during 'a weekend of epic proportions.' He continues: 'My wife Mavis became lost at one point and missed the station commander's cocktails. Thankfully she was rediscovered stuck in a lay-by with her escorting flight lieutenant – his car having run out of petrol.'

A likely story! Later, at 3am to be precise, the 'old and bold' were challenged by the boss's wife to a sprint around the quarters patch. Having already cooked them 'eggy bakes', Mrs Price went on to win the race easily. She had, reputedly, been an athletic champion in her youth.

By the beginning of the 1970s it was nearing the time when the Squadron would acquire more modern equipment. But many would look back with huge affection on their time at Laarbruch. The proximity of the Dutch border; the chance for many to live within the local community and to make what would become life-long foreign friends; and the opportunity for travel. Yes, generally speaking, the sheer pleasure of being based on the continent was paramount, and this was enhanced by the marvellous spirit on 31 (PR) Squadron. Perhaps there was something, too, in that the period spanned the last days of national servicemen. Whatever it was, it has stood the test of time, for the 'Canberra boys' still return intermittently to Laarbruch – more correctly known nowadays as 'Weeze', or sometimes 'Niederrhein' airport – to re-live their Thirty One days.

Before moving on, let's take just one more trip in a Canberra. Flying Officer Nobby Clark, a navigator with the Squadron in the early seventies, has particular reason to remember the north German weather on that occasion:

'About eight months into my first tour I was flying low-level in the late afternoon of one of those days when there was no cloud but poor visibility. We had completed two of the three targets and were now way off to the north-east of Laarbruch. Turning back homewards, we set up for the last target. Now, flying directly into sun, the visibility had dropped even further. Never mind; I was lying in the glass nose and was navigating by looking directly downwards. I knew exactly where we were and, as the remainder of the route lay over the flat and obstacle-free North German Plain, we pressed on.

'As we approached the initial point for the target the whole of the perspex nose filled with aeroplane. There was a very loud "bump", and I heard the scream of jet engines which weren't ours. My pilot climbed immediately to 2,000ft and we set heading directly for Laarbruch, both shaking like a leaf.

'Fortunately the thump had been only slipstream, and we found out later that the other aircraft had been an RAF Phantom. His estimate of the miss distance was two or three feet; flying down-sun he had seen us just in time to push violently below us. Given that he'd started from 250ft, his recovery from the subsequent dive had apparently been very interesting.'

A hair-raising moment. We shall meet Nobby again, as well as plenty more of that German weather, as Thirty One moves on to adventures new.

Up where she belongs. *Brian Ray*

And down where she belongs. WH792 in later, low-level camouflage hugging terrain typical of North Germany. *Brian Ray*

Chapter 22

Cold War

It was now 1971. The Squadron was to move just thirty miles down the road to another of the 'clutch' stations, RAF Brüggen. They were to fly the McDonnell Douglas F-4M Phantom II, an American aircraft originally designed for the US Navy as a Mach 2 carrier-borne interceptor. But it was one which had subsequently been adopted by the USAF in the attack role, and which had proved itself as a bomber during the Vietnam conflict of the 1960s. During the same period Britain had cancelled its own strike aircraft, the TSR2, then ordered and later cancelled the American F-111. Now the RAF was taking delivery of Phantoms for use first in the strike/attack role – but with a view to moving them later to air defence duties.

The Cold War was at its height – 'Cold War' being a phrase first coined in 1946 by George Orwell to describe the state of military tension and political distrust which existed for forty or so years following the end of the Second World War. NATO, led by the US, and the Warsaw Pact, headed by the USSR, faced each other in a state of uneasy distrust, and the Squadron's new role brought home the reality. Not that the Canberra boys had been unaware, having spent the past sixteen years at high readiness to face whatever mischief the WP might have launched. But somehow, now that Thirty One was to be equipped with the ultimate deterrent, the whole thing became even more meaningful. So let's first spend a moment discussing 'strike' – the nuclear game.

For years, the West had adhered to what was known as the 'massive retaliation' doctrine, commonly known also as 'tripwire response'. Recognising the hugely superior force numbers available to the Warsaw Pact, NATO had let it be known that any attack would immediately be met by nuclear retaliation. The fear of destruction would, it was calculated, deter any aggression. But from the early 1960s – from the time of the Cuba missile crisis, in fact – it began to be recognized that something more graduated was required. And by the time that Thirty One was re-equipping with the Phantom, NATO was in the midst of switching to a doctrine of 'flexible response'. This envisaged a period of conventional conflict following WP aggression, moving on when necessary to deliberate escalation to contain the attack. This would entail selective and then, if necessary, general nuclear response.

The prospect of nuclear conflict was clearly most terrible, with the weapons and process being treated with the utmost respect. So to qualify in the 'strike' role, both air and ground crews needed to be thoroughly trained and evaluated on the procedures relating to what were euphemistically known as 'special weapons'. Security routines; weapon loading and acceptance; route and target study; checklist actions; the syllabus was endless. And all had to be examined before an RAF Phantom squadron could take its place in NATO's front line of deterrence. The 'attack' role, using conventional weapons, was also important, but would take a back seat for the time being while the new unit worked towards strike qualification.

Against this background, let's now hear from the CO of the new squadron, Wing Commander Chris Sprent:

'In June 1971, those of us who had been training on number 9 course at Coningsby made our way to Brüggen to launch 31 Squadron into the Phantom era. At the time the station was gearing up for its first Taceval in its new guise (it already had two Phantom squadrons); quite reasonably, no one really wanted to know about us. I recall spending a good deal of time setting up number four hangar as well as being involved on the periphery of the exercise action. According to my logbook we started flying on 20 July, and after a trip with QFI Geoff Roberts, my nav Tim Boon and I launched Thirty One into Phantom skies.

'A particular challenge was presented by the station's decision to go for centralized servicing. I well recall the frustration of having our broken aircraft towed to a distant hangar for rectification, and we'd be lucky to see them again that day. Then there was the pantomime of having to recover them the next morning. It was infuriating that 14 and 17 Squadrons, living virtually next door to Engineering Wing, could usually beat us into the air. Thankfully, that servicing pattern was reversed once a new station commander came into post.'

The ground had been prepared by the advance party. Navigator Squadron Leader Graham Gibb was OC A Flight and deputy squadron commander designate, and remembers the very earliest days:

'I and my pilot, Flight Lieutenant Dave Pollington, got to Brüggen two months before any other Thirty One people arrived. We took over an empty hangar and started remodelling it into accommodation for the new unit. I remember collecting the silver from the disbanding Canberra squadron – many thousands of pounds worth – in a wheelbarrow! Among other things we built the aircrew coffee bar, the bricks coming from a disused (we hoped!) hut on the airfield which we knocked down.'

It certainly was a period of change for the RAF Germany stations, with squadrons and fleets on the move – Hunters and Canberras giving way to Buccaneers, Harriers and Phantoms. Barely five years later, Jaguars would replace the Phantoms which would in turn displace Lightnings. Indeed such was the rapidity of movement that there was a time when no aircraft's flight simulator was located at the station where the type was based.

A further effect of all this was that, with squadrons of various strengths coming and going, there never seemed to be the right amount of accommodation. So it was unsurprising that OC 31 also faced difficulties on the domestic front:

'Being the third squadron to form at Brüggen we were allocated only very few married quarters for our families, who often had to live many miles from base in unfamiliar housing. Some relished this, but there were also problems. With detachments and round-the-clock working, there were isolated families to care for, many with wives who didn't drive. Both my wife, and others at what might be described as the top of the Squadron tree, had a very real role to play in looking after some of our young families.

'Anyway, we continued with our workup and decided at an early stage on the markings for the new aircraft. These were to include yellow and green checks as befitted the Phantom's fighter heritage. We held our re-formation parade on 7 October 1971, when the C-in-C, Air Chief Marshal Sir Mick Martin, presented us with our Standard. Squadron Leader George Robertson, the pilot flight commander, led a splendid flypast.

'This was also the occasion when we first hosted a visit by members of the Squadron Association, with Bert Edwards as its new chairman. There had been intermittent contact with the Canberra operators but he, with Bill Smart and others, was very keen to develop stronger ties with the current Squadron. We reciprocated that wish, with Flight Lieutenant Hugh Kennedy as our liaison officer, and later Rob Sargent. And so began the close relationship between the Association and the Squadron.'

Soon, a spanner was thrown into the works. When the UK ordered the Phantom it opted to replace its American engines with theoretically more powerful and fuel-economical Rolls-Royce Spey engines – a move which would have the added benefits of bringing work to Derby and improving the balance of payments equation. However, there turned out to be downsides to the deal. Firstly, the Spey demanded more air than the American J-79, so the engine intakes had to be widened – increasing drag and negating performance and economy benefits. Secondly, the Spey was what was known as a 'by-pass' engine – one with a compressor of such a large diameter that some of its air completely bypassed the combustion chamber and turbine, being fed straight into the exhaust – and there was no previous experience of adding reheat to an engine of that type. This latter factor caused endless problems, as pressure surges within the engine caused huge strain to the compressor blades – as well as inducing spectacular 'flash-backs' of flame out of the intakes, right beside the startled cockpit crews. The remedies developed, which included drilling minute labyrinths of air passages in the blades, took much time and expense, and involved limiting flying and suspending training for a period. As Chris Sprent commented: 'Although we were

A Phantom shadow over a parade at 31's new home, RAF Brüggen.

A Phantom flypast on the day the new aircraft took over from its Canberra predecessors.

established for thirty aircrew, we had only twenty-four for the first three years or so. But on the bright side, stopping training meant that the OCU was closed down temporarily, which led to a number of its very experienced instructors being posted to Thirty One. So in the end it could be said that we benefited.'

Nevertheless the exercise routine continued unabated, with seemingly a practice alert every week. In responding to the hooter, personnel never knew until they arrived at work whether it was practice or the real thing, so there was always a degree of tension in the air. This was built on by Brüggen's massive steam siren which, just like Laarbruch's, could wake the dead for miles around. How the locals put up with it – added to the appalling noise of the Speys on take-off – we'll never know. That the station and its personnel brought huge prosperity to the local economy undoubtedly helped. But there surely was also a genuine belief in the part the RAF was playing in maintaining peace in Europe.

Returning to the business of working up in the strike role, the Phantom came equipped with an American nuclear weapon, which brought with it the complications of US 'custodial procedures'. As described by Group Captain Nigel Walpole in *Seek and Strike,* his excellent history of RAF Brüggen, part of the routine was the maintenance of a strict 'no-lone-zone' around any nuclear equipment, within which one was not allowed unescorted. This, together with the 'two-man principle', was at the heart of safety. Certainly, there are many stories of trigger-happy American guards being ready to take a pop at anybody coming anywhere near infringing those procedures – even accidentally. Happily none of these events, to the writer's knowledge, actually resulted in the trigger being pulled.

The Americans were always said to have no sense of humour whatsoever when it came to 'their' weapons, and given the serious consequences of any mistake, one can understand why. But on the positive side the small national team had its own headquarters at Brüggen. 'Little America', complete with BX store and lots of American beer, made them popular people socially.

The weapon release profile involved a pull-up from low level at 500kts, a roll through 120° after weapon release, and a dive back down to low level for the escape. Straightforward enough by day and in clear weather, but more demanding at night or in cloud. And popping up into the airspace layer above the military low-flying areas brought into play the vexed question of the proximity of low-level military airspace to the general aviation area and commercial airspace above. So, during training, much concentration was always required.

Fundamental in planning NATO's nuclear programme was the need to avoid the destruction of its own aircraft by 'friendly' nuclear bursts – if that's not too much of a contradiction in terms. So the whole plan was extremely time-sensitive and needed to be very precisely flown. Aircrew route study was intense and detailed, including radar predictions. The Phantom's excellent AWG-12 radar had a very useful mapping and targeting capability, and the Squadron's aircrew complement had its fair proportion of ex-Sea Vixen and Buccaneer navigators (as well as crews transferred from 14 and 17 Squadrons) who had the experience to exploit it. In time, everybody was utterly proficient and ready to face national and NATO evaluators, with the Taceval requirement including satisfying the USAF capability inspection team.

Thirty One was declared to Supreme Allied Commander Europe (SACEUR) in the strike role on 1 March 1972. Which then brought with it the pleasures of 'standing QRA', in other words holding quick reaction alert, a duty performed for a twenty-four hour period. For aircrew and groundcrew this meant eating and sleeping in 'the shed', almost within touching distance of their Phantom, with its target coordinates already inserted into the navigation system and its weapon already loaded. There would almost invariably be a practice call-out at some time during each shift, with the crew having to bring the aircraft to the point of starting engines. It was a routine that took some getting used to, as George Robertson commented: 'We used to pre-flight the aircraft and the weapon so that we were ready if we were scrambled. It seems bizarre now that we were on a fifteen-minute standby with live nukes. I suppose we should have been anxious at the prospect, but I never was, perhaps because I never really believed it would happen.'

Soon after the Phantom's introduction to Thirty One, a regular feature of the training became armament practice camps (APCs) at the NATO facility in Sardinia. Flight Lieutenant Martin Selves puts some colour onto that particular canvas:

'I always looked forward to annual weapons training at Decimomannu. It was a free holiday in Sardinia, with dinner usually in the Italian officers' club, where the food was superb although in small portions. In the early days my South African nav Mac McDonald took me to breakfast in the USAF mess. The terms "over easy" and "sunny side up" were new to me; the smell of hot, fresh coffee was good, while the early-morning life with those easy-going Yanks was fun.

'After a hard session over Capo Frasca range, forty minutes of constant 4G turns, and a debrief session in the cine room, Coca Cola never tasted colder or better. Then it was lunch at Enrico's "greasy spoon" – his speciality "egg banjos." and other highly indigestible stuff. Delicious! Enrico was eventually honoured by the Queen for his service to the RAF, and his establishment will always bring back fond memories of hot, sweaty flying suits and a welcome rest in the sun.

'Our Italian accommodation block had a bar, or rather a bedroom converted into one. It was known as the "Pig and Tapeworm" and was normally stocked with American beer, piled high in a huge fridge and very cold. As evenings progressed the singing would start, and I remember one occasion when in walked a German pilot with a suitcase. He planted it down with the confidence of a tourist claiming a sun bed and announced "I sink zis is my room." Well, he turned out to be quite a character, and spent some time with us. I can't remember him leaving, and I doubt whether he does either!

'The early morning wave was always best for weapon scores, when the winds were light and the air was smooth. The sun was up but it was still pleasantly cool and the humidity low. The prospect of getting airborne was also high, with a line of serviceable jets and even, possibly, a spare. I was interested in aircraft allocation, as some were more bent than others. Even though the jets were relatively new, many of them already had huge fish-plates riveted over cracks in the wing surfaces. Gun-sight harmonization continued regularly, but even so we all knew that, for example, XV460 fired short and left – or at least we thought it did. Were the authorizers giving themselves the best aircraft? This was important if you had a chance in the weapons competition! The groundcrew all had money in the pot and took a keen interest. Amazingly, the boss had huge amounts wagered on him – and without being disrespectful it was fair to say that he had absolutely no chance of winning!

'In the end, skill and a little nerve showed through, and soon we'd be heading back to Deci after another sweat-soaked session on the range. The Phantom always looked its best over the hills, a big and powerful beast, but all too soon we'd be joining up in close echelon for the flat turn in towards the airfield. Could be a bit ragged, especially if you were number four, but you knew that the whole base – all nationalities – would be watching the spacing in the break. Yes, life was good there, especially with no chance of a steam hooter or a recce test to spoil your day.'

Despite Martin's fond memories, it is worth noting that the Squadron had to change six engines during its first APC, so keeping them airborne was obviously still a problem. Nevertheless, declaration of Thirty One as 'attack combat ready' followed, and now they were ready to play a full part for NATO and RAF Germany.

Before too long, though, another setback occurred. The Phantom certainly originated as a fighter aircraft, but it was unfortunate that the Squadron's first 'kill' should be an own goal. Flight Lieutenants Brown and Boon encountered an RAF Harrier over northern Germany, and 'Min' Brown takes up the story himself:

'The previous week I had happened upon a Harrier and filmed him with cine, sending the pictures to 4 Squadron at Wildenrath to taunt them. On this particular day we were tasked to recce a bridge in the north, and with the photo in the bag we started home. At about the halfway point I spotted another Harrier. Recalling last week's banter, I closed in for the kill, and got it at ludicrously close range. Problem: how to ensure the intended recipients of my proof of skill didn't conclude that the pictures were from last week's sortie. Answer: fly past and make sure he sees me! Sadly, I managed to get far too close and clobbered the underside of his starboard wing pretty firmly.

'Observing a long runway close by, I blurted out a mayday and asked Timmy to hold onto his ejection-seat handle. With full right stick and 'on the doughnuts' (in other words at the angle of attack for approach in that configuration and weight and, therefore, not far off the stall) our speed was 196kts. I will never forget it. Didn't dare lower any flap because there was a long metal pipe swinging from the broken end of my left wing – which I took to be the blown-air supply. No call to the tower, we just stuck it on the ground and then selected hook and flap. Went off the end into the overrun wire doing about 100kts. A wagon soon turned up on my right side. I had landed at Luftwaffe base Hopsten, and a German officer with a clipboard wanted to know the speed I had engaged the wire. When I told him, he asked if I could call it no more than 70kts otherwise he would have to write a report!

'Soon after, a Wessex helicopter arrived and landed close to where the Harrier had parked shortly after us. A large wing commander emerged sporting a 4 Squadron patch on his flying suit. Oh dear! Anyway, after the niceties (?) we were removed back to Brüggen.

'Later, we learned that the Harrier was demonstrating its new photo-recce pod to the whole of NATO. They saw the lot and that's why there were seventeen witnesses for the prosecution and none for the defence. Nobody's fault but my own and nothing at all to do with Timmy — he was playing with his INAS or something!'

Bouncing other aircraft encountered at low level was common practice in those days. As well as being good sport, it ensured that everybody's lookout remained sharp. But the uncontrolled nature of the ensuing mini-dogfights inevitably led the staffs to take a dim view of the practice. Min's plea that 'everybody did it' got him nowhere, and the book was thrown at him.

Even so, the value of practising against low-level opposition was acknowledged and, as George Robertson observed, 'The one positive outcome was the introduction to the syllabus of dissimilar air combat training, and soon afterwards we had a visit from a couple of Chivenor Hunters for a week of fun and games.'

The 'hook' which Min mentioned was a legacy of the Phantom's ship-borne design, being used in RAF service in failure cases when braking or directional control might be a problem. Hook and arrestor cable were almost universally adopted by NATO aircraft and air bases over the following years, not least because there could have been a combat application at times when the full runway length wasn't available for landing.

And he also spoke of 'INAS'. The RAF's F-4 came equipped with this interesting new toy – the 'Inertial Navigation and Attack System'. The idea was that, having warmed the kit up and told it exactly where it was to start with, it would then sense all aircraft motion and know continually where it was throughout the sortie. This was what might be termed a first generation inertial navigation system, similar to that fitted to the Harrier, and Nobby Clark recalls his times with it:

An often-posed picture – Phantoms over one of those famous dams.

'I suspect it was one of the systems which was rescued from the cancelled TSR2, for it really didn't fit the Phantom cockpit very well. It had an analogue interface for the navigator which entailed using a 'joystick' with which you inserted your initial position and any destinations you were brave enough to enter. It took an age to insert any positions that were not within a few miles of you.

'It took up to fifteen minutes for a normal alignment. There were "rapid" align modes available but these were normally used when setting the aircraft up for QRA-type operations.

'Performance was, by and large, poor, and weapon-aiming modes received only limited clearance. But nevertheless the kit gave you drift, track and groundspeed, essential when trying to drop a bomb on time. We used this together with the half-mil and 50-thou maps to achieve really rather remarkable nav accuracy. And what with times over target of +/- 3 seconds, which we regularly achieved, together with bombing errors within 30–40ft using the iron sight, we didn't do badly. So all in all, having flown in the end 2,000hrs on all types of Phantoms, I definitely preferred the ones with IN!'

So inertial navigation was promising – but, as we'll see with Thirty One's next aircraft type, the second generation kit was infinitely better. By the way, the reader might recall that we met Nobby earlier in this narrative – as a very frightened Canberra navigator who had just avoided a head-on collision with a Phantom. Good that the event didn't deter him from making the change to Thirty One's newest type!

We described earlier the turmoil that led the RAF to procure the Phantom. The Royal Navy had undergone similarly huge upheaval, with cancellation of its follow-on aircraft carrier project and the ending, for the time being, of fixed-wing naval aviation. Admirals resigned and pilots left in droves, opening up exchange posts for many RAF crews on the final cruise of the 'last' carrier. But the RN nevertheless retained hopes of a fixed-wing future and, to maintain the necessary expertise, secured posts for some of its people with the RAF. One of those became one of 31 Squadron's very few Royal Navy members. Lieutenant Keith Tatman tells his tale:

'The Sea Harrier was originally envisaged as being a two-seat night fighter, and so several of us observers were plucked from our helicoptering and sent to the RAF to provide a small seam of fixed-wing expertise for the future of the Fleet Air Arm. Postings included Buccaneers, Shackletons and Canberras, and I found myself on the way to 31 Squadron at Brüggen. By that time it was already apparent that the naval Harrier version would never have two seats, so we exchange "lookers" knew that our future would be as aircraft carrier operations officers, and then falling back on our seaman duties. But it didn't stop the exchange programme.

'I loved it. I was one of very few "singlies" on the Squadron, and the officers' mess in general had a small permanent population. I learned to forgive mess-mates the repeated offering of plates of fleshless fish skeletons every time trout was on the menu. But my time off could be spent pretty much as I wanted, and I saw lots of Holland and Germany. I even stationed a caravan on the River Mosel for week-end breaks. However, this was savagely attacked by mice one winter and had to be withdrawn from service! This was just as well because the only simulated attack we were ever able to photograph over the caravan site resulted in an expensive barrel of beer to the engineers to check the over-stressed aircraft!

'All in all it was a wonderful tour. My memories of the RAF, and Thirty One in particular, were of energy, fighting spirit, and camaraderie, along with brilliant weapons instruction and armourers.'

As Keith says there were all sorts of advantages to living at Brüggen. Just as with Laarbruch, the Dutch border was only half a dozen miles away, so families enjoyed the pleasures of both Holland and Germany. It was easy to make weekend trips to the spectacular countryside of the Mosel, the Eifel and the Ardennes. There were annual local festivals such as Karnival and Rhein-in-Flames to enjoy. Skiing was relatively accessible, as were the Christmas markets of the surrounding cities. And the Alps were a day's drive away if one had a slightly longer leave period.

The perks associated with living on the continent included duty-free alcohol, and then there was the advantage of being able to buy a brand-new tax-free car. But, as George Robertson points out, there were hidden drawbacks to the latter: 'When we were all enjoying our bargain autos in the early seventies, house prices were tripling in the UK, so those who stayed at Coningsby and invested in property probably did better financially!'

Learning the language was a skill which, in general, found the Brits somewhat wanting, with many preferring to rely on the simple technique of shouting loudly in English. Attempts met with variable results. George again:

> 'During a squadron exchange, "Dickie Mint" Cave, our social secretary [so-named after one of comedian Ken Dodd's "diddymen"], arranged an outing to a local restaurant. The trouble was, his German was not quite up to it and he booked for *funfzehn* (fifteen) instead of *funfzig* (fifty). So when the whole Squadron plus wives and guests arrived there was some consternation at the restaurant. On the bright side, we had an extra hour's drinking time whilst they rearranged tables to accommodate us!'

Just as the Canberra squadron had been kept busy by recce contests, the new Phantom team became involved with the Salmond competition. The cup had first been presented in 1930 by AVM Sir Geoffrey Salmond, whom Thirty One, in an earlier incarnation, had met when he was the AOC RAF India. The reader will recall that, back then, it had been competed for by the army co-operation squadrons of the sub-continent – and won a couple of times by Thirty One. Now, the competition was run by HQ RAF Germany for all its strike, attack and recce units.

The event tested various elements over the Cold War years, including from time to time call-out reaction, aircraft generation and operational turn-round. But the heart of it was precision navigation and bombing, with 'gates' manned by observers, timed and scored bomb drops, and recce line-searches for minute and heavily camouflaged 'military installations'.

During Thirty One's Phantom era, the contestants included three other F-4 units, as well as two Buccaneer and three Harrier squadrons. So competition was fierce, and the team was thrilled to come third in its first effort in 1972. And even better was to come – with outright victory in 1973. But there were no holds barred between the units, as George Robertson reveals:

> 'We got wind of some skulduggery at one of the other squadrons, so I was dispatched as an umpire to supervise their first wave. The rumour was that they were dropping the 4lb practice bomb at 400kts, whereas the release to service for the real 1,000lb retard specified a minimum release speed of 450kts. During planning they were quite open that they would drop at 400kts. When I asked why, they implicated their boss who confirmed that they had worked up at that speed; it was more accurate, and they weren't going to change at this late stage. I think there was also some earthy language inviting me to go forth and multiply!
>
> 'The other two squadrons cried foul and the errant squadron's first wave bombs were disallowed. They later switched to 450kt deliveries, but Thirty One were by then unstoppable!'

The Squadron also sent teams to the NATO tactical weapons meet in both 1972 and '74. On both occasions the RAF won most of the prizes and thoroughly trounced the

A happy gang of aircrew and groundcrew in July 1971, soon after re-equipping.

Americans. More importantly though, in January 1973 HQ approved the long-promised 'semi-autonomous' engineering pattern, with first and second-line servicing, as well as some scheduled servicing, being delegated to the squadrons. But there were to be no extra men on the establishment, so they had to work hard to make a success of it. And they did, as the boss comments again:

'From then on it was often the weather rather than aircraft serviceability that was our main limitation, and sometimes we had the luxury of six serviceable aircraft. Soon we were matching and often flying more hours than the other squadrons. I can still feel the relief when we became our own masters, as it were.'

The Phantom and its operation made a complex package, with the potential for much to go wrong. As early as March 1973, two of Thirty One's airmen received vigilance awards for spotting a miniscule piece of metal being ejected from the starter door. It turned out to be a part of an anti-icing solenoid valve, and Senior Aircraftmen McDade and Stubbins had potentially averted the serious fire which could have resulted from the hot gas leak.

Something similar happened in 1975 when, following the after-start functional control checks, Senior Aircraftman Baxter noticed what appeared to be a slight misalignment of the outer wing leading-edge flap. Making a closer inspection, he discovered it to be completely detached from its hydraulic jack. The link connecting flap and jack had failed without any abnormal cockpit indication and, had Baxter not noticed the problem, it was likely that a very serious situation could have arisen.

Inevitably, crews weren't always so lucky, as navigator Flight Lieutenant Kevin Toal tells:

'In October 1974 my pilot, Flight Lieutenant Ray Pilley, and myself ejected from XV431 immediately after take-off from Brüggen. The aircraft was pointing almost vertically upwards at the time, and since we ejected at a height of only about fifty feet our survival was probably due to the aircraft having recently been retro-fitted with the new Martin Baker Mk 7 rocket-assisted ejector seats. I received a broken leg and facial burns and we both had back injuries – but at least we were alive.'

In traditional style, fellow aircrew administered suitable medicine, as Keith Tatman describes:

'I was airborne at the time. Because Brüggen was closed we diverted to Wildenrath, learning there that a crew from our Squadron was in hospital. We set off with lemonade and ginger beer bottles – whose contents had been appropriately replaced. The Special Investigation Branch were quizzing the crew, but we nevertheless managed to get some of the necessary "pop" to them. After a short time we were spotted (and heard) by the night superintending sister, who promptly confiscated the illegal hooch and, rightly, threw us – and the SIB – out of the hospital. The end results of all that were that: a) our aircrew recovered; and b) I married the nursing sister.'

That the Phantom had initially been designed to be carrier-borne had, indirectly, contributed to this accident. The aircraft had the facility to have the outer wing sections folded for storage. In this case these sections had not been locked into the 'spread' position and had, consequently, folded on lift off. An expensive 'gotcher'.

The Squadron had earlier tasted tragedy on 25 June 1973 when Flight Lieutenant Hugh Kennedy and Squadron Leader David Hodges crashed into the sea on a warm night near Vliehors range in Holland. David, the nav leader, left Shirley and two children, while Pennie Kennedy was left with Alexis – and young Hugh who arrived just nine months later. Cause unknown, but possibly nothing to do with the Phantom itself. There can be few RAF Germany aircrew who would not attest to the treacherous 'goldfish bowl' conditions which were often to be found around the islands off the northern Dutch coast. Many pilots found the environment taxing, and Chris Sprent certainly felt it keenly: 'It had been a long day on Taceval and I was just ahead of them in the stream. The loss of these two fine men was without a doubt the low point of my tour.'

By the mid-1970s, Thirty One was suffering restrictions on flying hours due to fuel shortage following the second Arab-Israeli war. That event, together with the 1967 conflict during which much of the Egyptian Air Force had been destroyed on the ground before it had even turned a wheel, was now having additional consequences in Europe. Both sides were 'hardening' their airfields, and the Squadron was not slow to react. George Robertson explains:

The sad result of one of the all-too-many accidents which punctuated the Cold War years. The funeral of Hugh Kennedy, lost in 1972 with his navigator, David Hodges, during a Taceval sortie.

'We needed to change our counter-air tactics. Hitherto we were required to attack airfield targets with 1,000lb retard bombs. This would have meant direct overflight of a heavily defended target, with consequently high losses. In addition, the weapons effects were dubious, as the retarded 1,000lb bomb ("retarded" – in other words slowed by a parachute to impact well behind the attacker so that its blast and debris would not affect the release aircraft) would bounce off hardened shelters and would have little effect on runways and taxiways. Our weapons leader, Squadron Leader Trevor Nattrass, developed an alternative tactic involving coordinated attacks using toss deliveries of ballistic 1,000lb bombs. These weapons had sufficient kinetic energy to penetrate concrete, runways and taxiways, and exposure to defences was much reduced. I remember spending many hours studying ingress and egress routes to Cottbus, our pre-planned counter-air target. Trevor's proposals were eventually accepted by their airships at Rheindahlen, and the boss put him forward for a well-deserved AFC.'

At the same time the RAF was embracing the concept of 'survive to operate'. Aircraft were being toned down, with the white being deleted from roundels, leaving only the red and blue (although when white was removed from the roundels on the pale undersides of some aircraft it actually toned them 'up'!) Station buildings were being painted matt dark green, while the south side of Brüggen airfield was being closed off to allow the RAF's own hardened aircraft shelter (HAS) building programme to commence.

A Phantom undergoes a wash down after landing to remove chemical contamination.

The year 1974 saw Chris Sprent leave after a long tour of three years. His replacement was Wing Commander Tom Stonor, who was immediately plunged into the action with a NATO exchange. These events were supposed to enhance both operational proficiency and international understanding but, as Squadron Leader John Nunn recalls, on this particular visit to our Turkish allies social considerations predominated:

'The base was Eskisehir, a hundred miles or so south-east of Istanbul. All went well with the exchange once we had persuaded some of the younger officers to avoid dancing with the Turkish aircrew. We were not convinced that the latter were doing it for fun!

'At the end of the detachment we gave a party for our hosts and their wives. Wing Commander Stonor and I envisaged a "top table" with their senior officers and their wives. All was arranged, with seating plan, flowers, etc. However, when they arrived, their wives were unceremoniously bundled off to a table at the far end of the room – and the top table became "men only". Perhaps the fact that they'd booked a belly dancer for the occasion had something to do with it. Later, we couldn't persuade our own wives that this was a good idea!'

Ah, the essential 'cultural' aspect of NATO squadron exchanges! Many will remember the difficulty of explaining similar adventures to their own wives!

Returning to operations, it could be said
that, to some extent, the RAF used the
Phantom in the attack role rather like a big
Hawker Hunter. Its weapons harked back to
the Second World War, comprising 1,000lb
general purpose iron ('dumb') bombs and
68mm unguided SNEB rockets. Formations
and tactics were, likewise, little changed
from earlier days. However, in some areas,
the new aircraft brought advances.

Firstly, the gun. Unlike earlier fighter-
bombers, the RAF's version of the Phantom
had no in-built cannon, instead using the
SUU-23A podded gun on the centre-line
station when the need for strafing was
envisaged. But what a gun that was – a

At Belgian Air Force Base Florennes a BAF
Mirage V taxies past a Goldstar Phantom. On the
F-4's centreline station is a SUU-23A gun pod.

rotary cannon operating on the Gatling principle. In other words, a six-barrelled, 20mm
unit which, once it was up to speed (which took almost no time) was 'braked' to limit it
to an almost-unbelievable 6,000 rounds per minute. The awesome growl – which came
across as almost a deep-throated hum – will ever be etched in the memory of Phantom
crews. If one got it right, amazing scores were possible. But as always, a gun is only as
good as its aiming system. And if one was a gnat's cock off with the Phantom, a lot of lead
missed the target.

Another area of innovation was in self-defence capability. Up to four AIM-7F Sparrow
missiles could be carried semi-recessed under the fuselage with no penalty to the air-to-
ground weapons load. The Sparrow was a 'semi-active' weapon, meaning that it would
home onto the launch aircraft's radar emissions as they reflected from the target. With
a range of up to about a dozen miles – depending on altitude and fighter/target closing
speed – it could be very useful indeed. Not least because the opposition, knowing that the
formation had such a capability, would be that much more cagey in planning his intercepts.

Occasionally there was a chance to have a go with AAMs on a practice camp at Valley,
firing over Aberporth range in Cardigan Bay. Martin Selves recalls the day in 1972 when
he and Mac McDonald flew photo-chase on another aircraft firing at a target towed by a
Jindivik drone:

'We knew the theory of "English bias", the term used to describe the manoeuvre
which would turn the missile onto a lead-pursuit course immediately after launch,
but we were both taken aback by the weapon's instant and violent turn as it left the
aircraft. Very impressive!'

In combination with the Phantom's pulse-doppler radar, which, unlike conventional
equipments, was well equipped to deal with ground clutter, these missiles offered a
considerable self-defence capability. The radar could be set to 'auto-acquire' targets
coming in from the front hemisphere and the system was, as George Robertson comments,
'Way ahead of its time. Again, though, it was plagued with reliability problems. Its mean
time between failures was just four hours, which meant that any four-ship was more

This aircraft displays a live Sparrow air-to-air missile (rear fuselage station) which could be carried in addition to air-to-ground ordnance. Stores on the other stations include telemetry equipment – almost certainly associated with a trial missile firing.

or less guaranteed to have at least one unserviceable radar.'

But even given this defensive capability, it perhaps wasn't until much later when NATO began to develop the concept of big attack formations, offering self-protection by utilizing the strengths of the various aircraft types in the formation, that F-4s began to be employed imaginatively. By that time RAF Phantoms had moved on to air defence duties, and it was USAF attack F-4s 'riding shotgun' within mixed NATO bomber packages which provided really effective self-defence for the rest of the bombers.

Mention of big attack formations suggests that Brüggen's squadrons ought to have been thinking about working together as a Wing – and indeed in Jaguar days they would fully embrace this concept. Tentative moves in that direction were initiated in Phantom times although, as Keith Tatman tells, not always wholly successfully:

'We lined up one day as number two, a single 31 Squadron aircraft with three others from 14 and 17 Squadrons (who flew together more than us because of their collocation near the main hangars, Thirty One being, mercifully, hidden in the woods some way to the west.) Clearance for take-off given, the lead pilot gave his first nod for military power, his second nod to go to afterburner, and the signal for brakes off was supposed to be the third nod. What we did not know was that the lead pilot needed to put his (undeclared) glasses on at the last minute, lowering his helmeted bonce to shove the glasses inside his bone dome. We interpreted this as the third nod, and let the brakes off in full reheat. Shooting forward, my pilot quickly appreciated the lack of movement from the leader, applied full brakes and cancelled reheat. The lead, having given the fourth (or was it third) nod and released his brakes, shot past us down the runway (smiling, with glasses in place). That left us standing, frantically coaxing our F-4 back into reheat and dribbling after the leader, and being hounded from behind by two other aircraft who knew the drill and were still at full power. It must have looked like the most ragged four-ship take off of all time!'

The Phantom's air-defence origins occasionally brought the chance to venture into areas of the flight envelope hitherto unknown to ground-attack crews. Flight Lieutenant Rob Sargent recalls an air test one day in 1975:

'I was tasked to take a clean aeroplane from the rectification hangar following deep servicing for its air test. The profile would include supersonic acceleration checks and, on departure, Brüggen ATC handed us off to Lippe Radar. The aircraft behaved well and we took vectors for the supersonic leg. We were now just below

Firing in the range over Cardigan Bay during a missile practice camp. The target was a flare towed far behind the Jindivik, but it appears that the drone itself is about to breath its last.

the tropopause and so, on heading and at maximum IAS in dry power, I unloaded to ½G until we had about 30 deg nose-down pitch. Approaching 32,000ft in a fairly rapid descent I selected reheat and eased the aircraft into another climb; we were soon above 36,000ft, just about supersonic and accelerating fast. This kept us legal, as supersonic flight was not permitted in those days in the FRG below 36,000ft. We were close to Mach 2 when we turned back towards base. There were just a few very minor snags to report and so, once the flight test schedule had been completed and F700 signed, we handed the aircraft back to the engineers. Job done – let's head to the bar.

'A month or so later I was summoned to the phone. It turned out that the British claims commission had received a bill for broken windows following a sonic boom. The estimated cost of damages was DM70 and I pleaded guilty. Fortunately it was not a police matter, but I thought I would henceforth stick to practice-bombing missions as they seemed to be safer and far cheaper all round!'

An interesting reflection on how 'foreigners' treated German airspace in those days; at that time it was, of course, absolutely forbidden to fly supersonic over the UK.

So the diverse aspects of the marvellous Phantom continued to impress. But Thirty One's time with the aircraft had been short, and the F-4s were about to be handed over to 19 and 92 air-defence Squadrons as RAF Germany's game of musical squadrons and roles continued.

Chapter 23

Single-Seat

For the first time in the Squadron's history, its aircraft was to be a single seater. Wing Commander Terry Nash was the new CO (designate) and describes the routine:

'I arrived at Brüggen on 12 January 1976. Forming a new RAF squadron at that time was a total joy. My first impression was that there were no aircraft, no pilots, no groundcrew, no tools and no guidance. No baggage to inherit and the opportunity to shape the unit exactly as I wished. Just a pristine hangar and a few boxes of maintenance manuals – and soon there would be a brilliant SEngO to do all the hard work.

'In fact Thirty One's Jaguars were already in position, but were being used by 14 and 17 Squadrons who had re-equipped a little earlier. So my first task was to prise those aircraft loose from the other units, and this I achieved with the help of a small party of groundcrew – a dozen or so – led by the senior engineer on strength, Chief Technician Rogers.

'From these modest beginnings the new outfit grew apace, soon having sufficient groundcrew to mount a full daily flying programme. But although we had a good complement of aircraft, pilots were still in short supply, so that those who were available flew a great deal. To illustrate this point, my own log book for the month of March records a total of forty-five hours, more than twice the usual entitlement, whilst that of one of the junior pilots records in excess of fifty hours. This was over the legal maximum for this type of aircraft, a fact which he unfortunately brought to the notice of higher authority by accidentally flaming out one of the engines as he broke into the circuit with rather greater gusto than was prudent on the last flying day of the month.'

That initial flying rate certainly was extremely intensive, particularly as Thirty One's aircraft were being flown at the time without the usual external fuel tanks. Shorter trips meant extra practice for the groundcrew, speeding their work-up. But the unusual fit did lead to a complaint by the station commander when taxying out one day in one of Thirty One's jets that he 'did not have sufficient fuel to take off.' He was, by the way, the legendary John Walker, the 'father' of the Jaguar force.

The logic, incidentally, of going straight to a full squadron's-worth of daily flying with only five pilots is explained by Terry Nash:

'Having recovered our aircraft and ground-crew from 14 and 17 Squadrons, where they had been learning bad habits, we needed to get them used to a daily flying pattern of four waves of five aircraft. The other squadrons at the time were pursuing a 10-aircraft first wave, nearly all of which were reported u/s on landing,

An early Jaguar, its underside is finished in the original pale grey. Bloodhound missiles of 25 Squadron guard Brüggen's eastern approaches.

thus overwhelming the ground-crew and leading to them spending the rest of the day trying to recover aircraft in order to meet their alert commitments. We, on the other hand, achieved more flying by staggering smaller waves.'

Until the Jaguar new boys could be declared combat-ready, the rump of the F-4 unit remained, and it is illuminating to get a flavour of how the 'Phantom Phlyers' viewed the new type. Gordon Goodman, one of the remaining navs, reflects an attitude not uncommon at the time: 'In the early days, when the Jaguars were cohabiting overnight in the hangar alongside the Phantoms, our groundcrew would put saucers of milk under the noses of the "pussy cats" – to the great disenchantment of the Jaguar airmen who'd find them the next morning.'

Just a bit of friendly rivalry perhaps – although there was more to it than meets the eye. The Jag's gestation occurred during the period when Anglo-French co-operation was high on the list of the two countries' political and industrial aspirations. Jaguar airframes were built by 'SEPECAT', an alliance of BAC and Dassault, while the Adour engines were jointly developed and constructed by Rolls-Royce and Turbomeca. It's hard to believe now, though, that the aircraft was originally specified by the RAF as an advanced trainer to replace the Gnat. Not surprisingly, it quickly became apparent that it was too big, expensive, and unforgiving for that role, and a solution was found which saved the Anglo-French project: Hawk for training; and Jag for ground attack. Not surprisingly, though, the Jaguar was initially regarded by many as a trainer masquerading as an operational aircraft.

Most of the navigators stayed with the Phantom, switching to air defence. But many Phantom pilots converted to the Jaguar, along with a number of air defenders from the Lightning. The latter group became known as 'WIWOLs'; regardless of which squadron they were on, they always seemed to stick together in the bar, beginning every conversation with the words 'When I was on Lightnings.'

Thirty One had its share of those, as well of some of the Phantom types – one of whom was Flight Lieutenant Nigel Day. Approaching the end of his F-4 tour he'd watched as 14 and 17 Squadrons had converted to the 'new-fangled toy with a couple of sewing machines for engines, a black box for a navigator, and instructions in French.' He'd been hoping for a move to Buccaneers but, to his chagrin, had been posted to Jaguars. Worse still, he was to kick his heels for some time before starting a course. During that period his first instincts were reinforced when he was offered a ride in a two-seat Jag with Brüggen's station commander, 'Whisky' Walker. Reputedly he was so unimpressed with the take-off performance that he thought the group captain had forgotten to engage re-heat – but he did change his tune once the jet was airborne. And even more so when he found that he would be lucky enough to convert onto the new aircraft on Thirty One at Brüggen, without having to attend the OCU – a most unusual way of doing things in those days.

In due course Nigel became a Goldstar stalwart, a qualified weapons instructor (QWI), a fours leader and a deputy flight commander. And he, like many others, came to appreciate the Jag's many attributes.

Noted aviation artist and ex-31 Squadron pilot Mike Rondot comments on the machine:

> 'I quickly learned that whatever the other NATO air forces said about the Jag, when there was a big package to lead, the Jaguars were always at the front because they were the only ones who knew where they were all the time, and were not afraid to punch through rainstorms at low level in IMC [instrument meteorological conditions]. The F-104s, G-91s, Mirages and the rest learned to trust the Jaguar pilots and were happy to follow the black smoke in their wake. The name commonly given to marginal weather of this type was 'British VFR' [visual flight rules]. In reality, it was a clue to the prevailing attitude at Brüggen, where preparedness for war was all-consuming. Since the weather en route to our real targets was probably going to be like that most of the time, we had better get used to it and learn to fly in it. The RAF wanted to train as it expected to fight – in dirty weather at low level. After all, you cannot postpone a war until the sky turns blue.'

As for the 'black smoke-trail', there was a sneaky way round this. Reheat killed it and, for reasons various, the Jaguar had the facility to select reheat at less than full military power. So the cunning ones amongst us knew that, when fuel and noise weren't critical, there was a way of remaining a little less visible.

Back to the business in hand, and the Jaguar team were, by mid-1976, approaching 'strike combat ready' declaration and were the sole owners of the Thirty One nameplate. Terry Nash again:

> 'It was busy. Brüggen's runway was closed for refurbishment, so we first detached to Laarbruch. Then to Leuchars to participate in the Strike Command tactical fighter meet and bombing competition – quite an accolade for the new squadron to be selected ahead of the others at Brüggen. Within days of returning to Germany we were again on the road for an APC at Decimomannu.
> 'By the autumn of 1976 we were holding a full QRA commitment despite still being only at half strength for pilots. But by December we were fully declared to SACEUR and had successfully undergone Taceval. It was a breathless pace, perhaps best typified by the fact that the paint on the ops room wall was still wet

when the evaluation started – the decorating having been done by the pilots assisted by wives and families.'

Unlike the Phantom, the Jaguar carried a British 'special weapon', the WE177. But if anybody thought that this change would make procedures easier they were wrong. If anything, things were stricter than ever, with the added complication of tailoring the two-man principle to a single-seat aircraft. And aircraft numbers began to mount up. By 1979, each squadron at Brüggen (and there were now four of them, number 20 having joined 14, 17 and 31 in 1977) had fifteen aircraft and twenty-two pilots. The complicated formula by which NATO matched its nuclear assets to its commitments meant that Brüggen now had to put more aircraft on 'Q' than it had squadrons. And this increased load led to the station's police numbers – which were far more dependent on the need for nuclear security than on preventing petty crime on the station – reaching over three hundred. As *Seek and Strike* records, what with the fifty dogs as well, the security squadron became the biggest unit on the station.

Despite the huge size of the Jaguar Wing, the accommodation problem noted during the Phantom era had been eased with the building of a complex of flats in the nearby village of Elmpt. Luxurious they might not have been, nor particularly well-liked; they were colloquially known as 'Legoland' and the whole complex was eventually razed to the ground in the early years of the twenty-first century. But sociable they certainly were. The flats and messes during the late seventies jumped as the Bee Gees' *Saturday Night Fever* boomed out and the *Schloss Bräu* flowed. The duty-free cars also stood ready to take to the autobahns using concession fuel tokens, and life was good. Although work on the Brüggen Wing was incredibly hard, it was also extremely satisfying; many personnel certainly count their Jaguar times amongst their happiest in the RAF.

The squadrons were fully dispersed for survival, aircraft parked either singly or in pairs in their HASs with small teams of groundcrew ready to turn them round and see them off. Pilots planned in the PBF, the hardened, filtered, reinforced concrete building designed to keep out the worst of the anticipated chemical and nuclear fallout. 'Survive to operate' was in full swing and exercises came thick and fast, each designed to hone the Wing's performance for war – or Taceval.

The dispersed sites had their own catering, but on exercise the rations came from a centralized facility. Ah, those exercise meals! 'Hot' boxes full of lukewarm, greasy, soggy, bacon and egg sandwiches, put

A Jaguar's lair is guarded by barbed wire. Now, the colour scheme is all-over dark green and grey and the aircraft has received its D-prefixed fleet letters (Thirty One being, numerically, the fourth of Brüggen's Jaguar squadrons).

together in some distant kitchen hours earlier. Tin trays with scrambled egg, baked beans and wet tomatoes, all slung in together and swimming about in a reddish-brown gloop. Gulped down while running around topping up the aircraft's hydraulics or planning a mission. Indigestion fodder for sure – but we seemed to think the meals delicious at the time!

That was life in the 'hard'. But there was a 'soft', too. With most squadrons this was a wooden building on the site, built to house crewrooms and day-to-day engineering accommodation. The crewrooms tended to be not much used, even routine life tending to revolve around the 'hard'. But in the case of Thirty One, they still had their own hangar plus its copious accommodation available, so were semi-civilized in their unique 'soft'.

With strike dealt with we turn now to conventional attack. In fact 31 Jaguar Squadron had diverged from the conventional route by training its pilots up to combat-ready standard in attack *before* concentrating on the strike role. Having already demonstrated his innovative thinking by starting his Squadron's work up by flying at an intensive rate with clean aircraft, Terry Nash now explains his thinking on roles: 'Attack involved developing a far greater range of skills, so strike then followed easily. The unusual training pattern also had the benefit that the junior pilots did not stand QRA until combat-ready in both roles.'

The Jaguar had no radar, and of course no trusty directional consultant in the back, but instead came equipped with an extremely accurate inertial navigation and weapon aiming sub-system (NAVWASS). Considering it was only six or seven years newer than the Phantom's INAS, huge strides had been made. Having said that, when the Jag later received upgraded kit in 1983, it made the original NAVWASS look positively stone-age. The pace of development in avionics at the time was truly spectacular.

Even with the early NAVWASS, though, the aircraft began to make its mark in competitions, often trouncing the opposition. And new weapons were also introduced. Unguided rockets had disappeared from the inventory with the Phantom, being replaced by the BL755 CBU (cluster bomb), optimized for attack of armoured formations and designed for delivery from very low level. Each of its 147 bomblets carried a 'shaped' charge which, on impact, would generate a jet of molten liquid which could penetrate several inches of armour. The ground footprint was huge, reflecting to some extent the vast number of armoured targets expected. Perhaps more pertinently, though, the pattern size was an acknowledgement that weapon aiming errors were also, at that time, often substantial.

The general-purpose bombs were much as in Phantom days, although after the Jag had been in service for some time laser-guidance kits began to make an appearance. These, when fitted to the nose and tails of the basic 'dumb' bombs, would permit them to home on to reflected laser energy from the target, which would be designated by a friendly ground-based or airborne laser. This would very much become the normal mode of attack in the future, but was in its infancy during Thirty One's Jaguar days.

The aircraft did, nevertheless, have one item of laser equipment which was useful. The chisel nose housed an 'LRMTS' – a 'laser ranger and marked target seeker.' The 'ranger' aspect speaks for itself, providing accurate distance from the target being attacked and greatly improving weapon-aiming accuracy. The 'marked target seeker' could provide steering in the HUD towards a target which was being 'marked' by a friendly laser, a useful facility. But the problem with both was that laser energy was hazardous to eyesight and, therefore, practice facilities were extremely limited. So pilots were often unable to achieve the full potential of the LRMTS.

Just as in the strike role, there were pre-planned NATO attack missions to be studied. One area of interest was only about 140 miles, or twenty minutes flying, from Brüggen or Laarbruch. This was the inter-German border — sometimes referred to as the inner-German border, or the inner- or inter-German boundary. The first was the correct term but nobody at the time seemed quite sure – so we'll settle for 'IGB'.

The opposition was expected to launch massive armoured attacks across the border into NATO territory. Knowing their initial dispositions and observing the terrain, it was possible to predict likely lines of advance and possible 'choke points' where they might be vulnerable to Allied aircraft dropping CBUs. Of course the operative word was 'likely'. No-one could ever be sure of the course of warfare – as had been amply demonstrated in 1944 when the Germans had made their unexpected armoured advance through the Ardennes. So while NATO stayed alert for the unexpected, it nevertheless pre-planned for the most likely. Squadron pilots, therefore, spent long hours studying routes and probable target areas. And not just on paper, for although it was not generally permitted to fly closer than about ten miles to the IGB, it was possible to make recce visits on the ground and by army helicopter to view the areas of interest. Squadron Leader John White recalls:

'We had a briefing from the resident alert regiment, were picked up by Gazelle helicopters and then flown along our designated attack corridors from the start point to the IGB. We looked at pre-prepared, defensive positions for our own tanks, and had a peep over the other side. We were well up to speed with tank recognition but, even so, we anticipated it being difficult to tell one type from another if ever it came to the heat of battle. Our army escorts told us that we should attack anything with its gun pointing west. For, they assured us, our own tanks would always point their guns east – even when retreating!'

Then there was the offensive counter-air option – pre-planned attacks on enemy airfields, radar and missile sites using bombs and CBUs. Those would have been dangerous missions had it ever come to the crunch, for Warsaw Pact defences were formidable. But still the targets had to be studied and memorized.

During major exercises the whole Wing would brief the real missions, before planning, briefing and launching 'equivalent' simulated attacks on friendly airfields. When the weather was below peace-time limitations, the procedure went ahead as far as the take-off point, followed by an 'elephant walk' of aircraft down the runway. The good thing about those bad-weather episodes was that during the simulated airborne time the pilots were out of the exercise and could relax and have some food or a much-needed wash. Or even a sleep if the mood so suited them!

Talking of getting right up to the IGB, one of Thirty One's commitments for a couple of years was an exercise at the Luftwaffe base at Fassberg. This airfield was located right at the entrance to one of the three Allied corridors which had been set up to permit access over and through DDR territory (East Germany) to Berlin, the city being jointly administered at the time by Britain, France, the US and the Soviet Union.

As a former Harrier flight commander Terry Nash had been associated with the base while this particular commitment had been borne by his previous force. So he was well placed to lead Thirty One there in 1977 for Exercise *Thunderbolt*. Close Air Support was the game, and he recalls:

'Each autumn the tripartite British/French/US exercise was very happily hosted by the Germans, who were grateful for its symbolic significance (Fassberg had been a Berlin Airlift mounting base). The idea was to get the Soviets aware of our presence, but we took care not to be too provocative, and all simulated attacks were pointed away from the border. I have very happy memories of those deployments, not least the eating, drinking and being merry. After all, Hamburg was nearby!'

Wing Commander Richard Howard took over soon after that and remembers the following year's effort:

'Because the French weren't members at the time of NATO's integrated military structure, the tri-national exercise was conducted under agreements specific to Berlin rather than general NATO arrangements. Fassberg airfield was within thirty kilometers of the wire, right in the air defence identification zone, which made approaching to land on the westerly runway more than a little interesting. For example we usually picked up an SA3 'rattlesnake' warning on the radar warner.'

A Cold War curiosity was that it was occasionally possible to take a land trip to Berlin, the rail journey from the IGB leading through that same East German corridor. The city itself was divided into sectors administered by the four powers. Under official auspices it was possible to cross, escorted, into the Soviet sector. John White tells of one such trip:

'Passage was severely restricted. The British, French and US Governments refused formally to recognize the DDR (Deutsche Demokratische Republik), so all dealings were with our 'fellow' power, the Soviet Union. The French and Americans also ran military trains entering Berlin from the west and south-west respectively, but ours ran from Braunschweig in West Germany to Charlottenburg station in West Berlin. It ran daily, except for Christmas Day, to assert our right to passage between the British zone of occupation and the British zone of Berlin. Its whole legal status was based on agreements from the time of Stalin and the Berlin Airlift. Accordingly, the dining car still sold meals and drinks at the prices of the times using long-gone currency.

'We had to apply for papers from the HQ at Rheindahlen well in advance and have accommodation booked – at Edinburgh House in the city. The unit clerk had to check travel documents five or six times to ensure that full stops and capital letters were absolutely correct, otherwise there would be hell to pay when the Russians checked them. Although most Russians, we were told, didn't even know the western alphabet let alone read English or French. The rules and regulations for passenger behaviour were legendary, the threat of court martial hung over anyone who broke them.

'We boarded the train at Braunschweig, going through the border with stops at Helmstedt, where the West German guards were replaced by East Germans, and then on the other side of the border at Marienborn, to change engines for the run to Charlottenburg. At Marienborn the OC, train warrant officer and a military interpreter marched along the platform and halted in front of a Russian officer before going into a small office where all the travel docs were inspected and stamped. I remember that the papers were put through a slot like a letter box to an unseen recipient on the other side. The train was then boarded by a Russian officer with an escort armed with a Kalashnikov, and they both walked from one end to the other. When they got off, all the doors had wooden contraptions placed under them so that they couldn't be opened from the outside.

'En route I remember going past a big tank base at Kirchmöser and being surprised at the bright green colour of the vehicles; all of the countless reconnaissance photographs we had studied (for these tanks were to be our targets) had been in black and white. The old DDR stations still had name signs from Hitler's time, all in gothic script. Very much a time warp, with horses and carts, steam trains, and very tired-looking apartment blocks in Magdeburg. Then there was the ghostliness of Charlottenburg Station – it felt as though it should be busy, but was a rundown shadow of a place.

'We had a long weekend in Berlin, visiting the Brandenburg gate, the Reichstag, Kaiser Wilhelm Memorial Church (the 'lipstick and powder puff'), Charlottenburg Palace and the Soviet tomb of the unknown soldier which, oddly, was in the British sector but guarded by goose-stepping East German soldiers. As British military we were allowed through into East Berlin via Checkpoint Charlie where there was a small museum. For this we wore number one dress uniforms, with our wives dressed accordingly. We spent half a day there visiting such sights as the Russian war memorial. The East certainly did not have the same joyful feel as West Berlin, which had a real buzz to it with numerous clubs, bars and restaurants packed with people having a great time. All in all quite an experience, and there is no doubt that our party was somewhat jaded for the return trip!

'The train really was a symbol of western opulence; as well-maintained and (almost) as lavish as the Orient Express, it was a clash of cultures between socialism and the decadent west.'

Indeed. It has also been said that the food in the dining car was made especially attractive, and eating times arranged, so that East German people on the platform at station stops would, on looking in, see just what they were missing by being in the Soviet bloc! All in all, a somewhat surreal business. The 'long-gone currency' referred to in John's piece, by the way, was the ubiquitous 'baffs', the vouchers described in the Canberra chapter. For reasons probably associated with the terms of the agreement originally set up with the Soviets, they were still used on the British military train, although long extinct elsewhere.

Early Jaguar deployments included flying onto and off the public road system. The first of these events, Exercise *Halt Fair*, took

A Jaguar on final approach to an autobahn.

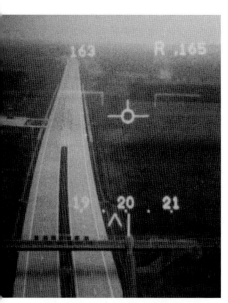

Pilot's eye view through the HUD. Speed in knots is shown top left, radio-altimeter height in feet top right, and heading along the bottom (degrees x 10).

place during September 1977 on an autobahn some twenty miles north of Bremen. Terry Nash made the first touch-down, closely followed by junior pilot and first tourist Flying Officer Gary Rogers, the latter being selected to demonstrate that it was a straightforward operational option available to pilots right across the experience spectrum. The exercise afforded an excellent opportunity to meet and work with members of sister services in an atmosphere of great cordiality. It also proved the tremendous operational potential of the Jaguar operated in this way.

So why would they be doing this? Well, NATO airfields were clearly on the opposition's target list, and staffs were looking at many ways to make attacks more survivable. The Harrier field operation was the ultimate expression of dispersed operations, while the Swedish and Swiss Air Forces were already well advanced with the concept of operating from roads. The idea was well worth exploring for the RAF, while rough field operation was another option. In fact a test pilot came to Brüggen to fly aircraft at various weights off the grass for a few days. Avoiding the sheep, by the way, for a feature of Brüggen airfield was that its grass was kept under control by the local flock.

There can't have been many fighter-bombers of the day which could have tolerated grass ops, but the Jag's big, squashy undercarriage (one could land it like a feather) took it in its stride. In the event, though, neither the grass nor the autobahn option were pursued. Perhaps the logistics of dispersed operations, together with the vulnerability of aircraft in the open and the obviously more complicated command and control aspects, were difficulties that outweighed any possible advantages. So Brüggen battened down in its concrete, its immediate airspace defended by both Rapier and Bloodhound SAMs, and its personnel trained and practised in survival procedures.

Unlike the Phantom, the Jaguar when it was introduced carried no self-defence missiles. For its own protection it relied to a great extent on its relatively small profile. Effective camouflage also made it hard to spot, with the paint scheme now being all-over matt grey and green. Additionally, the aircraft was reasonably easy to fly very low, and its precise nav kit enabled Jaguar formations to fly widely spread – often in what was known as 'card' formation, with no aircraft closer than a couple of miles to its fellows. Each Jag was fitted with an 'RWR' – a radar warning receiver – so the theory was that threats would be picked up early and the formation would route around and away from them. If one aircraft was engaged, the pilot would fend for himself, possibly employing the 'knickers' defence – dropping a single retarded bomb which, it was hoped, would blow up in the face of the pursuing fighter. Meanwhile, the rest of the formation would escape. Many would say that the RWR only gave early warning that one was about to be shot down, or that the warnings it gave were ambiguous. But it was better than nothing and the training routine was realistic — perhaps too much so if the 1982 experience of Flight Lieutenant Steve Griggs was anything to go by. While on recovery to Brüggen he became aware of an RWR warning which indicated that a Phantom was in the vicinity. Practice interceptions were common, and Wildenrath Phantom crews would validate their claims by squeezing the trigger to produce a marker on their film. In this case, for a variety of unfortunate reasons, the pilot actually fired a live Sidewinder missile, which duly shot the Jaguar down.

Steve's accident occurred, by the way, just weeks after his posting from Thirty One to Wing HQ, and preceded his second ejection (a double engine failure), by three months. Clearly, his luck had run out on leaving the Squadron. Although it may also be said that he had a major slice of good luck in the shoot-down incident. Generally a Sidewinder would be expected to proximity fuze close to the cockpit, killing the pilot, whereas in this case the missile had gone straight up the jet pipe, leaving the cockpit undamaged and enabling Steve to eject safely.

This accident story has led us away from describing the Jag's self-defence equipment, so back to the business in hand. Chaff (to decoy enemy radars) and infra-red flares (to lure heat-seeking missiles) were still for the future as far as the Jaguar was concerned. But Brüggen was nothing if not resourceful, and the station commander drove forward a scheme to install a home-built chaff dispenser in the receptacle designed to hold the aircraft's braking parachute – which was generally superfluous, given the Jag's excellent landing performance. The device was designed and built by 431 Maintenance Unit, which lodged on the station, and it worked. Well, mechanically at least; whether it would genuinely have saved many aircraft is open to debate. What wasn't in doubt, though, is that the Taceval team was impressed, the presence of 'active self-defence equipment' enabling them to tick another 'excellent' box on the scoresheet. Later, the Jag would sprout real chaff, flare and jamming equipment inherited from the Buccaneer, and we'll look at that in due course. And the aircraft would also eventually be fitted with Sidewinder missiles – although not in Thirty One's time with the Jaguar.

The year's programme was always busy, and Flight Lieutenant John Goult tells the story of a typical one, 1980:

'During the winter we sent a few pilots to the winter survival school at Bad Kohlgrub in Bavaria. After some fitness skiing, we spent four very cold days and nights with a parachute and rubber dinghy as a home. The nights were made very much more bearable by taking heated river stones to bed with us as makeshift hot-water bottles. There was an escape and evasion exercise where the game was to evade about forty German snow troops – and the unlucky ones who got caught underwent a very unpleasant interrogation until morning. The successful escapees were taken home to a warm bath, a meal and bed. The incentive to evade the captors was obvious.

'In spring the Squadron went to Decimomannu again. Sounds pleasant, but Deci always had some trauma associated with it. This year the fuel ran out and the electricity failed. As the water pumps stopped working, the water was turned off so that the toilets didn't flush. We couldn't even get airborne for an hour to escape the smell.'

Although one or two earlier stories have tended to romanticize Deci, the novelty of the place certainly wore off and there were undoubtedly many problems. Perhaps, though, in the light of the combat conditions many Thirty Oners had had to endure in the past (and would in the future), we should refrain from complaining too much.

The Salmond trophy was still the competition to play for, but NATO contests were assuming increasing importance. The Squadron took part in Tactical Air Meet 80 at Ramstein, where the various NATO air forces were split into halves. Each group consisted of four teams making up a big package for the attacks. John Goult continues:

> 'It was great experience for the first tourists, while Thirty One's four-ship leaders enjoyed their turn to lead the sixteen aircraft with all of the inherent problems of controlling dissimilar types. On one occasion whilst being attacked by fighters, someone shouted "buster" ("select full power, there's a threat around"). The faster F-104s, who had been the last in the stream, soon became the leaders. We also saw a lot of "killing" film from the Rapier missile units that were protecting our targets, and each night the debriefing team assessed our success and attrition rate.
>
> 'The second half of TAM 80 was a team competition for navigation and bombing. Flight Lieutenant Ian "Chunky" Kenvyn and Wing Commander Howard, were members of the international team who won the strafe competition. Chunky also won the individual visual laydown, 5 degree retard and skip bombing competitions. For this he was presented with the Broadhurst trophy.
>
> 'In September 1980 came four days of hell – Maxeval then Taceval readiness phases, to be followed by a full four-day Taceval in mid-October. 31 Squadron achieved an "excellent" grading in all areas, as did the station. This was quickly followed by an exchange with the Canadians. When they left, they kidnapped 'Arris Arietis, our four-foot panda bear mascot. He was officially recorded by the RAF police as missing, and the Squadron soon received a ransom note. They wanted six pilots plus wine, otherwise they threatened to send us one of his ears.'

Returning to the concept of 'British VFR' touched upon earlier, it wasn't really just the RAF who suffered from the often-murky German weather. But it certainly was an ever-present factor, as Flight Lieutenant Ade Cresswell recalls:

> 'A four-ship of ours was visiting 421 Canadian Starfighter Squadron based at CFB Sollingen. The original reason for the trip had been to recapture 'Arris, and the weekend brought many adventures in that respect – perhaps better not revealed! But let's concentrate on the return trip.
>
> 'Monday morning and it's time to go home. The aircraft have been parked outside all weekend and are saturated. Jaguars are just like Mrs C; they get very temperamental when they're wet and cold. All the NAVWASS kits refuse to align, and we taxi out on reversionary systems; we are basically Hawker Hunters. The weather is foul with heavy rain. With hindsight, we should have swallowed our pride and gone straight home at high level under radar control. But in typical Brüggen "can do" fashion we launch off under the overcast.
>
> 'Now, flying at low level over flat northern Germany is one thing, but it's very different in the hilly south, made worse by the shark-infested custard of civil

controlled airspace just above. As we blast along, hanging onto the leader's wing, we flash over a huge airfield on which are parked many aircraft. Our leader surely knows where he is now.

'By way of confirmation, a voice comes through the ether on the emergency frequency: "This is US Base Ramstein. Would the formation which just flew over please contact us?" We can see the leader's thinks bubble; should he own up or pretend he'd never heard the transmission? Another call from Ramstein: "We know you're British because only the Brits would fly in weather like this!" That settles it; the leader makes a quick call, offers profuse apologies and insists we'll never do it again. It seems to keep them happy, and we continue through the soup to Brüggen, where we carry out a visual break to land. Contrary to our expectations we never hear another word about it. Oh, and by the way, the bear was recovered!'

Yes, that's how it was. The author vividly remembers one of his own early Jaguar trips in Germany. On the wing of his flight commander, he flew at low level across the north German plain for an hour and swears to this day that he never caught more than a fleeting glimpse of the ground. The trouble was, there were others blundering around

A Luftwaffe squadron learns a little of RAF party games in the form of 'schooner racing'. Inevitably, more beer ended on the flying suits than went down the throats.

in the murk too, and it's probably just as well that we didn't give too much thought to the possibility of collision.

For some time the Buccaneer force had been making everybody envious by talking about Exercise *Red Flag*, which was held at Nellis Air Force Base, Nevada, just eight miles north-east of Las Vegas. At last, in the early 1980s, the Jags got their chance. A sign at the gate greeted arrivals with 'Welcome to the Home of the Fighter Pilot'. Adjacent training airspace, targets and bombing ranges covered an area almost the size of Switzerland. As well as realistic Soviet-style ground targets, the USAF had set up a specialist squadron of F-5 aircraft known as the 'Aggressors'. These were painted in authentic markings and camouflage and flown, as far as possible,

A Jaguar T-bird bears evidence of having been 'zapped' by the Luftwaffe's 51 'Immelmann' Wing.

according to Soviet procedures and tactics. Better training simply wasn't available – and of course no-one was averse to two weeks in a Las Vegas hotel either.

Thirty One's period there in early 1981 was marred by a fatal Jaguar crash. But nevertheless the team acquitted itself well during the exercise, with the American defenders admitting that the Jags gave them plenty of problems. Perhaps the best comment came from the American squadron commander who said that 'we've flown against the best, and for my money your Jaguar boys are as good as any of 'em and better than most.'

A bonus which always came with *Red Flag* was the training for it. The Nevada ranges permitted flying down to 100ft above ground level, whereas the normal limit in Europe was 250ft. Therefore, before deploying Stateside, the pilots had to work up (down?) to 100ft. This wasn't possible in Germany, but a few remote parts of the UK were allotted for this, with the best being the far north of Scotland. So prior to *Red Flag*, Thirty One would normally head for Lossiemouth for a week or so and race around the area known as 'moon country'. ULL it was called – ultra low-level training; or, as it was subsequently re-named, OLF – operational low flying. Great fun, although extraordinarily hard work. Flying at 100ft and 450kts was demanding enough in itself, but with formation flying, opposition fighters and ground threats added into the equation these were tough sorties.

The Jaguar had by that time begun to receive the Westinghouse AN/ALQ 101-10 jamming pod which was carried on the port outer pylon, the intention being to jam hostile radars which had locked on. Also the Phimat chaff dispenser – to decoy radars – for the starboard outer, as well as the AN/ALE-40 chaff and flare dispenser (the flares being to decoy heat-seeking missiles) 'scabbed' onto the lower rear fuselage. Altogether, effective self-defence equipment, although limiting weapon-carrying options. Pilots were regularly able to practise with this kit on the Spadeadam electronic warfare range in the English/Scottish border country.

A remarkable piece of survival equipment which also began to make an appearance towards the end of Thirty One's time with the Jaguar was the AR5 respirator. Hitherto it had more or less been implicit that once a general nuclear exchange had been commenced there would be little by way of further operations to follow. As the saying went, 'When the nukes start going off, put your head between your legs and kiss your ass goodbye.' But increasingly, post-nuclear ops were being contemplated, therefore more attention had to be paid to survivability. The usual respirator was completely incompatible with flying kit, so what now emerged from the boffins was a combined oxygen mask and respirator. The whole was encased in a full-head, rubber, condom-like arrangement to be worn inside the bone-dome. Naturally it was highly prone to misting up and had the potential both to boil and suffocate the wearer, so it had to be kept continuously ventilated either by the aircraft oxygen system or, on the ground, by a portable device equipped with fans. Readers may imagine for themselves the claustrophobic feel and debilitating effect of such an apparatus, not to mention the potential for it going wrong. Suffice to say that it was not cleared for practice solo use, with training mainly confined to the simulator. The author can claim to have flown in it only once, on a dual instrument rating test 'just for the hell of it.' He passed the test – but perhaps only because he out-ranked the examiner.

We mentioned a couple of paragraphs ago a 1981 accident in Nevada, and that year was turbulent for the Squadron. Three aircraft were lost in accidents, which killed two of the pilots, Flight Lieutenant David Plumbe in Nevada and Squadron Leader Roger Matthews in Northumberland. In fact, in common with most operators of the aircraft, Thirty One lost a fair percentage of their Jaguars. Although none was downed in combat the overall fleet attrition rate was probably on a par with the Luftwaffe's Starfighter – the infamous 'widow maker'.

Some of those accidents could, arguably, be attributed to a particular characteristic of the aircraft. Notwithstanding its fabulous navigation and weapon-aiming performance, the ergonomics of its original avionics controls left a lot to be desired. There can be few Jaguar pilots who would deny having come close to joining the 'unexplained controlled flight into terrain' statistics, for the main NAVWASS control box was positioned deep down behind the control column. Pilots naturally had a tendency to fiddle with 'the kit' while racing along at low level, and some surely paid the ultimate price. Thirty-One's popular New Zealand-born Flying Officer Tim Penn, who flew into flat terrain and lost his life in 1978, could easily have been one such. Cockpit design still had far to go – and when the mid-life upgraded nav kit was fitted some years later the controls were lifted to eye-level. Together with an audio low-height warning, this almost certainly contributed to a reducing crash rate.

By the early eighties, Thirty One's pilot establishment had reduced to eighteen with groundcrew at about 120, although actual aircrew numbers ranged from thirteen to as many as twenty. These variations came about as the RAF's manning people and training organization worked to get the embryo Tornado force built up, and the fluctuations certainly posed challenges to the Brüggen squadrons.

For Thirty One it would soon be 'all change' yet again. But for now, despite the imminent arrival of new aircraft, the Jaguars were very much operationally committed. Indeed in the last years they acquired the additional task of providing regular detachments to

Gibraltar in connection with Operation *Corporate* (the Falklands campaign). Because of the short runway it was usual to operate the Jag clean from Gib, and it was a great pleasure to fly it without the usual encumbrance of heavy external fuel tanks. The primary *raison d'être* of the detachment was naval affiliation, which regularly included strafing a 'splash' target towed by a ship. But the clean fit also offered a golden opportunity to fit in some air combat training. All in all, therefore, Gib detachments provided excellent value. The border with Spain was also, after many years, now open, giving access to the tourist delights and fine golf courses of the Costa del Sol. So everybody was happy.

For Thirty One, 1984 marked the end of the Jaguar story. When the aircraft entered service in 1973 the intention had undoubtedly been that it would have a long innings. For a variety of reasons, not least economies and rationalization across the RAF, many of the jets found themselves being put into storage while still relatively youthful. So although it had probably been planned that Thirty One and its fellow Brüggen squadrons would continue to operate Jaguars for many years, it was not to be. But the Jaguar had done a good job and there was an element of sadness in bidding it goodbye. From its earliest days it had performed wonderfully, winning competition after competition against the best the RAF and NATO could pit against it. So its personnel had had little difficulty in shrugging off those infamous saucers of milk.

And in many ways, although its numbers were drastically reduced, the Jag went from strength to strength once it was withdrawn from Germany. Operating from its remaining enclave at Coltishall in Norfolk and updated with an even more capable navigation and attack system, the aircraft continued its good work for many more years, finding a niche with its economy and easy deployability. Indeed the Jag performed wonders during the Gulf Conflict as we shall see later, not only flying more sorties per aircraft than any other British type but also emerging unscathed. So it was a fond farewell from the Squadron when the time came to trade in for a new model; the aircraft had inspired affection, and the Jag days had been good ones.

Chapter 24

The Fin

In late 1984 Thirty One became the first Brüggen squadron to re-equip with the Tornado GR1. As it did so, the checked nose markings disappeared, to be superseded by a green and gold speedbird, and the opportunity was taken to return the gold star of India to the fins of the Squadron's aircraft. The changeover also heralded the return of the navigator, the first Tornado squadron commander being back-seater Wing Commander (later Air Commodore) Dick Bogg, who had been associated with the new aircraft since its inception in the early 1970s.

The first RAF units to receive Tornado GR1s had been UK-based squadrons which had previously operated the Vulcan strategic bomber. But there could be no direct read-across between the two types. Not least, the Tornado had a fraction of the Vulcan's range and payload. Neither did the Tornado have the range of the Buccaneer, which it was also replacing (discounting air-to-air refuelling which, for both strategic and tactical reasons, was not at the time an option in the central European scenario).

So the RAF was now dealing with a different animal, which needed to be based within reach of its likely targets. Therefore most Tornados would be stationed in Germany, and that would leave no room for the Jaguar with which the Brüggen squadrons had been equipped for, at most, nine years.

Like the Jaguar, the Tornado was a multi-national product, but this time built by British, Italian and West German companies. BAC (later to become BAe) and Rolls-Royce were the major UK participants in the international airframe and engine consortia, known respectively as Panavia and Turbo-Union. The aircraft had had a long gestation, with its origins probably being traceable way back through the Anglo-French Variable Geometry project to the much-mourned TSR2 of the nineteen sixties. In its early days the Tornado had been known as the MRCA, officially the Multi-Role Combat Aircraft but colloquially, and most disrespectfully, 'mother Reilly's cardboard aeroplane' – or alternatively, 'must refurbish Canberra again'. Such disparaging comment reflected the general scepticism which accompanied the MRCA's early development and which plagued the fighter version's difficult entry into service.

But in the strike/attack GR1's case, the ugly duckling became a swan. Not aesthetically, as few could find beautiful the short fuselage with its oversized empennage. For obvious reasons the aircraft become known as 'the fin', but from an operator's viewpoint the machine was a Rolls-Royce. Its range, payload and top speed were greater than the Jaguar's, but the most significant improvement was its immensely sophisticated navigation and attack systems. These enabled it to do all the Jaguar could do – but at night and in all weathers. Its ride was, too, a tremendous advance over earlier types, the swing-wings offering docile landing and take-off characteristics as well as comfort in the turbulence of low-level, high-speed flight. And the cockpit environment was quieter than an airliner's. By the time it came to Brüggen, the aircraft was already more than fulfilling the expectations of the planners, and had memorably shocked the USAF by walking off with trophies on its first entry into Strategic Air Command's bombing competition.

During workup with the new aircraft, Dick came to be known as 'Des' as his 31 (designate) Squadron ran alongside the remaining Jags. And it was also during this period that the Squadron began to be known as the 'Goldstars'. Dick Bogg pays this tribute to his predecessors:

GR1 stands ready. *By the author*

'My own first association with Thirty One had come while I was at Laarbruch in the late 1970s. I served on both XV and 16 Buccaneer Squadrons at the time when there was intense rivalry between the two bases. Maxeval exercises usually involved a very heavy presence of evaluators from the other base. There was no love lost then, and Laarbruch personnel were notoriously hard on Brüggen. But having been a member of the evaluation team for both Maxeval and Taceval, I can honestly say that Brüggen was impressively operational, and I came to the conclusion that XV + 16 Buccaneers did not equal 31 Jaguars.

'As Thirty One reformed with Tornado, one of the earliest opportunities for the new kids on the block to put one over the remaining Jaguar boys was to thrash the other Brüggen Squadrons (14 and 17) at football − simultaneously in the same match! After a suitably liquid lunch it seemed a good idea to have a tri-team match with three sets of goalposts, the other two trying to score goals in either of their target goals. By means fair and foul, we demolished the might of the old-timers in a thrilling game − hardly worthy of *Match of the Day* but which proved that neither was 14 + 17 equal to 31. From that day on, the Tornados continued to show the way.'

The new unit began its flying, albeit with very few aircraft and aircrews, so they were exempted from an early station Mineval which was called. But 'Des' insisted on participating, staggering himself – and the station – by flying the sole available aircraft three times on the first day. Within a year of the first Tornado arriving at Brüggen, three of the Jaguar squadrons had converted to the new aircraft. In the space of twelve months there were three Tacevals at the station; indeed there seemed to be a practice callout every week. With the deployment from the UK a year later of a fourth squadron, there were soon over fifty of the new jets on base.

The groundcrew, under Squadron Leader Martin Davies and Warrant Officer Jeff Field, responded magnificently to the challenge and produced more aircraft each day than anybody had dared to hope. On the aircrew side, there was a mix of experience and youth. About half of the eighteen crews already had Tornado time, with the nucleus having come from IX Squadron at Honington. Around 40 per cent were first-tourists.

The workup reached a crescendo in June 1985 with the Taceval which was to formalize declaration of the Squadron as 'operationally ready' in the strike role. The groundcrew had laboured throughout the preceding weekend to bring the aircraft to the peak of serviceability; almost unbelievably, all thirteen jets allotted to Thirty One were available on the appointed day. Unfortunately, just forty-eight hours before the start of the evaluation, SEngO Martin Davies suffered a suspected heart attack and there was no way he would be fit enough to participate. This was a major setback; however, Squadron Leader Keith Harris, who had seen out Thirty One's Jaguars and who had subsequently moved to join the next Tornado squadron to form, came to the rescue and rejoined for the duration of the exercise. Later, when his own 17 Squadron came to be evaluated, their ground liaison officer fell ill and Thirty One loaned Major Martin Timmis to help out; the debt was repaid.

Training then switched to attack. The aircraft carried the new JP233 airfield attack weapon, which dispensed both heavy-duty runway cratering submunitions and a large number of mines designed to hamper any repair effort. Despite each of these monsters weighing over two tonnes, the Tornado could carry two. Airfield attack became the Squadron's primary role and, since JP233 needed a low-level delivery, most of the training activity concentrated in that area. With the outstanding avionics systems in the Tornado, weapon delivery accuracies were extremely good, particularly automatic attacks using radar which simulated blind conditions. The training progressed through daylight flights over Germany to night, fair-weather formations, principally over Scotland. But it was to be about a year before the procedures could be put to the test in poor weather at night.

Before that would come the Squadron's seventieth birthday, which was celebrated in style at Brüggen. A guest night attended by a number of Association members including the new president, Air Marshal Sir Leslie Mavor, and chairman Bert Edwards (1930s Wapiti pilot and 1946 air medic respectively) kicked off a memorable weekend in October 1985. The Association generously presented magnificent crystal decanters, and the boss promised that they would be put to good use at Squadron guest nights in future. On the Saturday, Jeff Field masterminded a families' day at the Squadron site while, in the evening, an all-ranks dinner was held in a local hostelry. The boss recalls the evening being memorable on several counts:

> 'First, because of a magnificent speech by Sir Leslie, who was received in awe by all who attended. Next, because Horace Welham presented his trophy for the first time to the airman who had contributed most to the overall well-being of the Squadron; Senior Aircraftman Danny Smith was a popular winner and received a standing ovation. And finally the highlight: a cabaret by the airmen, who impersonated the Glenn Miller Band playing the old familiar tunes on wine bottles. It was a night which epitomized 'Squadron spirit' at its best.'

And staying with social events, Flight Lieutenant Stu Peach (later to become Air Chief Marshal Sir Stuart) recalled the traditional Squadron panto, whose performances alternated between aircrew and groundcrew: 'The essential difference between the two? Well the groundcrew would have a set, costumes, a script and funny jokes. The aircrew would have none of those, relying on extemporization on the night. Over the years all the favourites have been (under) performed: Snow White; Cinderella; and Peter Pan – the last-named being the alter ego of aircrew?'

Then it was back to work on the Squadron's night all-weather attack capability. Here are Dick Bogg's memories of Exercise *Western Vortex* at Goose Bay, Labrador:

'This was the ultimate test of man and machine. By the end of the three weeks, all crews had participated in advanced tactical formations, taking off at twenty-second intervals, entering cloud almost immediately, making closely spaced attacks on simulated targets while still in cloud, and not seeing adjacent aircraft until turned onto the final landing approach with about a minute to go before touchdown. A hair-raising experience whether it was a crew's first or its thousandth. The work demanded the highest possible concentration by both pilot and navigator for the full two hours, and an absolute trust in machine and fellow aircrew. Stimulating, yet rewarding.'

This aspect of the Tornado's performance never failed to leave an indelible impression on those new to the aircraft. The author himself recalls vividly a sortie through the Scottish Highlands one dirty winter night, with the terrain-following radar and autopilot pitching the aircraft up and down across mountain and glen as the system followed the contours. Every now and then, as the flight broke out of cloud, there would be reassuring glimpses of the lights of the other three aircraft in the formation, each a couple of miles away on its own track and time, but the whole perfectly coordinated.

Early on, 31 Squadron participated in the NATO tactical fighter meet at Waddington. The exercise provided the first operational outing for the Marconi Radar Homing and Warning Receiver, the aircraft's primary defensive sensor. Flight Lieutenant Bill Read explains:

'In the Tornado, for the first time the RAF had an aircraft that was equipped with a defensive-aids suite that had been custom-designed, as opposed to seemingly random bits of equipment being added as funds allowed, often to the detriment of cockpit ergonomics.

'However, the original radar warning equipment, apart from giving the direction of the threat, had a complex visual display which, together with a raw audio feed, was intended to allow the crew to identify the threat radar. It took much dedication to learn all those various sounds.

'Anyway, this kit was replaced fairly soon with the Marconi equipment. The RHWR was more accurate with threat direction, and it told you in clear language what it thought the threat was. A bonus when the crew was working hard.'

The RHWR proved outstandingly successful, and was complemented by the BOZ 107 combined chaff and flare pod, normally carried on the dedicated starboard outer pylon, with the back-seater able to select how much of each type to dispense and when. The port outer pylon was normally occupied by a Skyshadow ECM pod, designed to jam radar signals emitted by enemy surface-to-air missile systems.

For active self-defence there were twin 27mm Mauser cannon as well as air-to-air missiles in the form of the American AIM-9L Sidewinder. This was the AAM which had made its name with its outstanding successes in the Falklands campaign, and GR1 crews reckoned they would put up a good show with it if jumped by enemy interceptors.

Although air combat was practised frequently in Germany, even better training was afforded by the Air Combat Manoeuvring Instrumentation range in Sardinia, and Thirty One visited Decimomannu several times during the 1980s to exercise this skill. Various NATO fighters would provide opposition, offering a stern test of capabilities and a pleasant variety in training.

Occasionally came a missile practice camp (MPC) at Valley in Anglesey, when live weapons were fired. Unlike their fighter brethren, 'mud movers' rarely got such chances, so the MPC in 1987 came as a welcome opportunity. That all five of the allocated missiles guided successfully – older AIM-9Gs rather than the operational models – was a creditable result. Unluckily, if spectacularly, one fuzed on the Jindivik drone, shooting it down. The crew, Squadron Leader Graham Bowerman and Flight Lieutenant Jerry Cass, were delighted with their confirmed 'kill', but this one had to be disqualified – for the target had actually been the flare which was towed several hundred yards behind the Jindivik. Still, a moral victory – although Graham turned pale at the spoof bill he received for a quarter of a million pounds for the drone that never returned!

In fact a similar 'accident' also happened during a 1989 MPC. This time four Sidewinders were fired – one of which again downed a Jindivik drone. On this occasion Flight Lieutenants Dick Downs and 'AJ' Smith were the culprits.

While on MPCs, it won't do any harm to jump forward for a moment to 1994. This time there were nine Sidewinder AIM-9Gs to fire, and all appeared to go well. There was then an anxious month waiting for the official results – which confirmed that all nine missiles had successfully guided and eight detonated on target. That MPC result was one of the best ever, and the Squadron had high hopes of being awarded the Aberporth Trophy for the year. However, a subsequent rethink in policy ensured that eligibility for the 'Aberporth' would be limited purely to air defence units. Shame!

The first Squadron Standard was presented at Laarbruch in 1956 by Air Chief Marshal Sir Alec Coryton, an ex-31 Squadron Bristol Fighter pilot from the early 1920s. The CO is Squadron Leader Stead.

Sir Alec inspects the Squadron parade.

RAF squadrons are entitled to receive replacement Standards every twenty-five years. So, taking the initial award in 1956 as the starting point, we could say that the next one arrived, in November 1986, five years late. But not to worry; the new Standard, presented by Thirty One frontiersman Air Marshal Sir Leslie Mavor, KCB AFC DL FRAeS RAF, was received at a splendid parade, watched by a mass of families, friends and Association members. Coincidentally, this dovetailed with the handover of command from the now Group Captain Dick Bogg to Wing Commander Pete Dunlop.

The original Standard was laid up in June the following year at the Royal Air Force church, St Clement Dane's in London. As well as, again, a host of Association members, fifteen officers and their ladies attended a moving service. All particularly appreciated an excellent sermon by the Reverend (Wing Commander) Noel James from RAF Brüggen who was promptly offered – and accepted – honorary Squadron membership.

Competitions continued, and the Salmond trophy was still competed for regularly and with great ferocity by all RAF Germany's attack squadrons. In October 1987 the Goldstars came out on top. It was a whole-squadron effort, but certain outstanding contributions must be recorded. The groundcrew team came first by a large margin in the operational turn-round phase. Also, Flight Lieutenant Geoff Rees-Forman and Squadron Leader Pete Goodman won the 'day' category after coming up with the almost unbelievable score for four bombs of three DHs and a five-footer.

In later years, with the increasing frequency of operational commitments, the Salmond became difficult to schedule. But the Goldstars had their own rival in the Startrek trophy. An innovative idea one year was to invite Association members to mark the targets and adjudicate the miss distances, and the boss had several teams on standby in various areas of the country so that all weather eventualities were covered. The targets on the line

The second Standard, presented in 1986 to the Standard Bearer, Flying Officer Greg Bagwell. The CO, Group Captain Dick Bogg, is behind the drums, saluting. Taking the salute is Air Marshal Sir Leslie Mavor, an ex-Goldstar Wapiti and Valentia pilot during the 1930s. *Crown copyright*

The VC10 – the standard tanker for many years, a beautifully stable platform. *Photo by the author*

searches – the nature of which was unknown to the crews – were large gold stars taped to members' cars. On the day, a course was chosen which took in Yorkshire, the Welsh borders, the Wash and Lowestoft, with Leading Aircraftman Tom Haigh (an electrician from Mauripur, 1946–7) and Norman Cornwell (Dakota WOp/AG 1945–6) acting as target markers. They had gathered teams of kindred spirits around them, so each area had ample Goldstar representation – and they all had a good day with plenty of activity passing overhead. The result was as close as it could have been, with Squadron Leader Ed Smith and Flight Lieutenant Jack Calder pipping Flight Lieutenants Mike Humphreys and Steve Day (unkindly, always known as 'Shitty' Day – although he never appeared to mind!) by a mere 0.2 per cent, and the awards were presented the following evening at a good old beer call. The groundcrew, of course, had had their own sweep on the result, with little sympathy for those who'd drawn the no-hopers!

Throughout Thirty One's days as a strike/attack squadron, it had never been policy for the Germany-based units to use their aircrafts' air-to-air refuelling (AAR) capabilities. Attention had been focused on the immediate threat from Warsaw Pact forces just over the nearby border, so there had probably never been a need or the capacity to develop the additional capability. The Phantoms had never deployed far, and when Jaguars had been flown across the Pond for *Red Flag* exercises, UK-based pilots had ferried the aircraft.

But perhaps the Falklands conflict had set the staffs to thinking – for in that case only the single UK-based Harrier squadron had had the immediate capability to deploy to the South Atlantic. Or maybe it was the lessening of tension in Europe – or even some premonition of the coming need to look after the UK's wider interests. But for whatever reason, it was decided in 1988 that the Germany-based Tornado crews would qualify in AAR. Although there never were enough probes to equip all the aircraft, it would nevertheless soon be proved to be a timely decision. Let's hear how one pilot, Flight Lieutenant Frank Neil, described the new science – or should it be called an art?

'The scope for banter is enormous as pilots "joust" with the basket, and the only answer for one who's having an off day is to apply some positive thinking. For the more you miss, the more tense you get, then the worse you fly and, unless you make a positive effort to relax, the less chance you have of making a successful contact.'

The author concurs!

Chapter 25

Back on Ops

Exercises and training continued. But one day in 1990, while the Goldstars were in Goose Bay, Labrador, everything changed. On 2 August the world awoke to hear that Saddam Hussein's forces had occupied Kuwait. The UN was responding and the UK had announced it would deploy Tornados to Bahrain. Naturally, Thirty Oners wanted to be involved in the action – but found themselves twice as far from the Persian Gulf as they would have been had they been at home. To add insult to injury, the massive flow of USAF transport aircraft using Goose Bay as a staging post en route to the Persian Gulf began to interfere with the Squadron's training programme. Worse still, the RAF was having trouble finding transport to bring the team home. Eventually they did get back, but were unsurprised to find that they had missed the first boat.

The UN had passed Resolution 660 demanding that Iraqi forces withdraw, the Arab League was onside, and a coalition was being put together. Numbers 14 and 17 Squadrons had provided the Brüggen contingent to Bahrain – and Operation *Granby*, the UK's contribution to the USA's *Desert Shield*, was well underway. The Goldstars were, though, represented at the scene of the action by four of the groundcrew, who quickly dubbed themselves the '31 Squadron stealth commandos'.

Before moving further, let's briefly summarize what had precipitated these events in the desert. At the time of the Middle Eastern settlement after the Great War, the former Ottoman territories of Iraq and Kuwait had fallen under the British umbrella. Iraq achieved full independence in 1932, followed by Kuwait in 1961. But Iraq always disputed Kuwait's legitimacy. Oil fields, drilling rights and access to the Persian Gulf were all issues. Not least, Iraq maintained that the territory of Kuwait was, rightly, a part of its ancient province of Basrah.

All this had bubbled up from time to time over the years. Indeed some of Thirty One's predecessors at Brüggen had been involved with an earlier skirmish in 1961, 213 Squadron's Canberra B(I)6 aircraft being ordered to RAF Sharjah when Iraqi forces threatened. The Canberras had operated then in the Middle East for three weeks, sufficient for the alert level to subside without a shot being fired.

But tensions continued in the region. From 1980, Iraq became embroiled in an eight-year conflict with Iran, at the end of which she was deeply in debt. And one of her major creditors was Kuwait.

With that background let's rejoin the Goldstars. The aim of *Desert Shield* was to confront Iraq with massive force in the region, thereby encouraging a climb-down. Although at that stage there were no formal plans for Thirty One to move south, there could be a requirement for *roulement* if things dragged on. And if armed diplomacy failed, all options would be on the table. So Wing Commander Jerry Witts, now in command, decided that the Squadron should get as ready as it could – just in case.

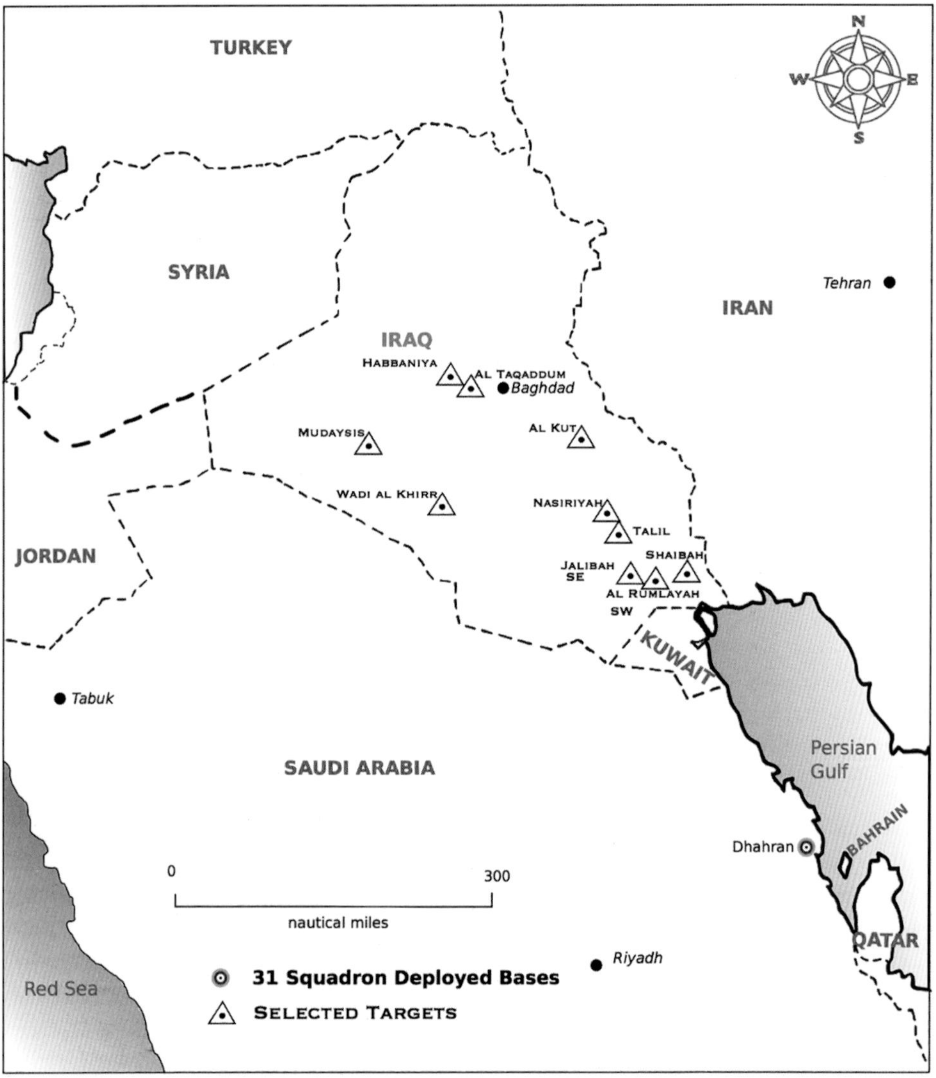

Map 9: No.31 Squadron operations in the Gulf Conflict, 1991.

All the pilots were AAR-qualified by now, and very few tankers would pass by without a Goldstar jet begging to 'prod'. The chance was also taken to fly with weapon types which were usually kept on the shelf – including the four-tonne load of two JP233s. In preparation for engagement by Iraqi fighters there was air combat training with Luftwaffe MiG-29s, automatic terrain following and night formation flying, as well as a remarkable and unusual keenness to fly in full nuclear/chemical protective clothing.

At the same time all the aircraft were brought to the latest modification standard, and enhancements such as secure radios and GPS were fitted. Thirty One coordinated all Brüggen's operational training and servicing, with the remaining aircraft allocated to Engineering Wing for modifications. Unserviceable aircraft were rectified by the remnants of the other squadrons.

All this soon paid off, for in September the Squadron was tasked to provide four crews to Bahrain as a *roulement*. Ably led by Squadron Leaders Steve Randles and John Davies, they departed with a flurry of inoculations, kit issues, and so on. Thirty One was pleased to be represented, although splitting the unit had not been part of the boss's plan. But at any rate, the 'stealth commandos' were delighted at last to have some of their own to look after.

Flight Lieutenant Gordon Niven, one of the deployed navs, was somewhat taken aback by the first words to them on arrival – uttered by a senior RAF officer: 'Gentlemen, you will go to war in this theatre!' For this character, apparently, the diplomatic phase was already over. But Gordon nevertheless enjoyed the operational training, as these words, with acknowledgement to *Out of the Blue Too* where the story first appeared, show clearly:

'Lots of night flying, lots of TFR. There was always something alluring about desert flying. Or, maybe it was just the complete lack of bird sanctuaries, old folks' homes, industrial avoidance sites, towns, etc. It was marvellous. The RAF was operating a three-month rotation and so, in late November, 14 Squadron handed over the detachment to XV Squadron – but we Thirty Oners remained as augmentees. We were cleared to fly down to 50ft which led to some amazing incidents; on one occasion, we were pulling round a turn when I looked over my shoulder to see what must have been the wingtip vortex carving a grove in the sand. We pulled up a wee bit after that! One wag at "shareholders" suggested that we should exceed an operating limit each day and report back, so we could expand the flight envelope prior to the big push! After a pregnant and incredulous pause, the boss thanked the contributor for his suggestion, but reinforced that the normal operating and never-exceed limits were there for a good reason and were quite adequate for the job.

'At about this time, two crews from each Tornado four-ship were on rotation holding QRA in case Saddam should strike first. When on that duty we were equipped with bleepers. It did not matter what time the bleeper went off, nor where you were or what you were doing. Your task was to get to the base, get kitted up and be airborne asap to deliver a retaliatory strike from medium level delivering freefall bombs designed in 1944; that would show him! Well, one night in the very wee small hours our bleeper went off. My trusty front seater didn't stir. For some reason, I thought I would give the number from the pager a ring. Not quite the SOP, but … It turned out that the Jaguar night duty aircrew bloke, being a bit bored, had decided to ring all the pagers on the callout list he had, just to see who was on the other end! I politely informed him of the purpose of the pager he had just rung, thanked him for his interest and suggested he went off and found something else to do! Not a little relieved, I rolled over and went back to sleep.'

Meanwhile, other Squadron members proceeded elsewhere; Squadron Leader Doug Carter, the weapons leader, was dispatched at short notice to give targeting advice at Riyadh, Saudi Arabia – where the HQ of the RAF's Gulf operation had been set up, collocated with the coalition and Saudi HQs.

Later, the boss led a formation ferrying eight replacement Tornados down to Bahrain – non-stop in eight hours – and was able to see firsthand what was going on and how the boys were faring. This enabled the training back home to be refined, as by now it seemed increasingly likely that the remainder of the Squadron would go south at some stage. Several options were open; as well as the Bahrain Tornado detachment, a second had been set up at Tabuk in north-west Saudi Arabia. The former was definitely the preferred location in terms of quality of life. Not only was everyone living in hotels there but, as Arab states went, the country was relatively liberal. Tabuk, on the other hand, would mean primitive living conditions – and no alcohol!

In late October, the Squadron was formally ordered to prepare for deployment as support element to another unit. This arrangement meant that much of Thirty One's 'management' would not be needed, and this was of particular interest to SEngO Squadron Leader Les Hendry, who was about to retire.

As Christmas approached with Saddam Hussein relentlessly pushing the UN towards a conflict, there was no doubt that whoever was in the Gulf in the New Year would be the ones to do the fighting. Early in December, at 5 o'clock one Friday evening (announced in the bar at happy hour!) minds were eventually made up. The Goldstars were off, and there had been a change of plan; they were to head, as the lead squadron, to a completely new location. From 28 December, Dhahran in Saudi Arabia was to be the Squadron's home – and people could expect to be away for at least six months. Most importantly, pretty well all the groundcrew and aircrew would be going as one team rather than being split up as all the other squadrons had been. The date meant Christmas at home and left time, in at least three cases, for weddings.

There was still some reorganizing to be done, though. Les Hendry succeeded in postponing his retirement for the duration. Squadron Warrant Officer Peter Heap had, inconveniently, been sent off to the Falkland Islands for a three-month tour, so Flight Sergeant Ron Fisher stepped up as understudy. The senior flight commanders were already in Bahrain, so Jerry Whittingham moved up to act as the boss's deputy, while senior Flight Lieutenants 'AJ' Smith, 'Stanley' Baldwin and 'Shifty' Young would carry much greater responsibility than usual. Sergeants John Green and Pete Pearston were the mobility officers and did a magnificent job organizing the equipment loads for transport south.

First, though, there was a recce to be done. Les Hendry:

'I was dispatched with Ron Fisher to Dhahran, and we were greeted by the in-theatre Tornado F3 detachment. I had to tell them that the GR1s would need a dedicated area to work from because they used far more ground support equipment than the F3s, including the hovercraft used for loading JP233. Negotiation continued for two days but finally the F3s agreed to move, leaving their line to Thirty One. We also found out there were no aircraft spares available, but were assured that "they" were working on it'.

In fact the spares issue wouldn't be resolved until the end of January, well into the conflict. However, satisfied that preparations could continue in Dhahran, the two men returned to Brüggen to complete the Squadron's preparations.

As news of the deployment was being digested, the 'stealth commandos' returned from their stint in Bahrain looking fit and tanned. On discovering that Thirty One was moving en masse to Dhahran, Corporal Charlie Brown would have none of being left behind and promptly volunteered to go south again; he got his wish.

Flying Officer Rich Cheseldene-Culley (known to his friends as C-squared), newly posted from training, claimed that before he had completed his station arrival procedure he'd qualified in OLF (flying at 100ft), night automatic terrain following, and day and night air-to-air refuelling. He was combat-ready – and therefore ready for *Granby*.

Then it was time for the off, and 0300 hrs on 27 December saw the advance party, led by Squadron Leaders Bertie Newton and Les Hendry, leave on the first of the Hercules transports. Over the next couple of days the rest of the team and equipment departed in the stream of twenty-eight Hercs it took to move the Squadron southwards. Finally, on 2 January, the boss led the first wave of Tornados, now resplendent in 'desert pink' camouflage, on the non-stop flight to Dhahran to join the impressive coalition of American, French, Italian, Canadian and Islamic nations' forces that was assembling in the Gulf region and in countries adjacent to Iraq's northern borders. Eventually, no fewer than thirty-four nations would be represented. As well as the GR1s, the RAF had F3s operating in the air defence role from Dhahran, a Jaguar squadron in Bahrain, and tankers and intelligence-gatherers in theatre.

Dhahran airfield or, more correctly, King Abdul Aziz Airbase, was the size of Heathrow and just about as busy, with a non-stop flow of military and chartered civil aircraft bringing in supplies for the coalition. The weather, though, wasn't quite what most had expected – as Sergeant Andy Wiles comments: 'To everyone's surprise the rain came down heavily just after we got there. We realized we hadn't prepared ourselves properly for this when the armourers' tent nearly floated away.'

As the Tornados landed they were directed to parking slots underneath a row of sunshades and the crews were welcomed by the advance party, who had done a marvellous job setting up accommodation, transport, and the myriad other items needed to get under way.

Ironically, the aircrew team which had been in Bahrain was now on the way home. Gordon Niven again:

> 'It had gradually become clear that Operation *Desert Storm* was going to kick off in mid-January. Our three months were up and, despite now being some of the most experienced crews in place, we were promptly shipped home to be replaced by crews from Laarbruch who had yet to set foot in the desert. So, after three months of training "to go to war in this theatre", off we trotted with the prospect of watching the whole thing on TV and leaving the fighting to someone else!'

On the face of it, better use might have been made of the augmentees, but it's always easy to criticize. Nevertheless, Steve Randles and his team had done invaluable work preparing the ground at Dhahran, and this had helped to enable local flying to start on the first day in theatre.

Certainly, with less than two weeks until the 15 January deadline set by the UN for Saddam Hussein to be out of Kuwait, there was an urgent need to get the aircrew familiarized with the desert environment and to carry out training that had been impossible in Europe. Life was complicated by the temporary shortage of spares, which were coming by sea as were the weapons, but order emerged from chaos. A crew perspective comes from Flight Lieutenant Chris Peace, a navigator:

> 'Like most, I only managed to get two day training sorties and one by night before the conflict began, and we all wondered whether we were well enough prepared. We naturally felt apprehensive about the prospect of live action against well-equipped opposition who had accumulated so much recent combat experience in the eight-year Iran-Iraq War. We felt that Saddam would back down – although we were constantly reminded by media coverage and from intelligence briefings that he might not. The general atmosphere around the Squadron was one of excitement, anticipation and energy, but it was interesting to see changes in individuals as tides of tension ebbed and flowed. Those you would have expected to laugh it off seemed, at times, to be the most affected by the uncertainty – and there were definitely some who had difficulty accepting the reality of it all.'

On the day after arrival, the boss was called to a meeting at the UK Air HQ in Riyadh, where he learned that the Squadron would be supplemented by six recce Tornados and eight crews from II and XIII Squadrons. Added to the elements of IX, 14 and 17 Squadrons already attached, this would bring under command personnel from a total of six units. Remarkably, the detachment included three other wing commanders: OC II Squadron (Al Threadgould); OC IX Squadron (Ivor Evans); and OC XIII Squadron (Glenn Torpy – who, incidentally, would later become chief of the air staff). All in all, a distinguished team under OC 31 Squadron.

Having had a tip-off prior to the meeting about the recce element, Jerry Witts had asked Les Hendry how many more groundcrew he would need to support it. The answer was twenty-two, a figure Jerry took to the meeting. By contrast, Air Vice-Marshal Bill Wratten, the RAF air commander in the Gulf, had been told by the engineers at Air HQ that 120 additional groundcrew would be required. Asked which was the correct figure, Jerry stated he never doubted his SEngO's opinion, and the air marshal simply smiled. History shows twenty-two to have been correct! When the recce aircraft eventually came aboard (not, in fact, until the eve of hostilities), the detachment was up to twenty-one GR1/1a aircraft – the largest of the Tornado detachments.

Throughout the build-up the Squadron received a steady stream of visitors. Fortunately, there was no time for spit and polish, and those who came saw things as they really were. John Major, the newly installed prime minister, met many of the personnel on 8 January. The chief of the air staff, who had visited before the arrival of the main party, had been received by the CO of the advance party. Bertie Newton reports:

> 'Being the senior GR1 man on the spot, I was delegated to show him our side of the house. Part of the presentation was to revolve around the hot-weather trial of the charcoal-lined protective suit – modelled by myself. Unfortunately the zip of my flying suit burst shortly before the chief's arrival, but he didn't comment on my dishevelled, sweating, charcoal-streaked appearance.'

In fact Bertie had history in the sartorial area, for on another occasion he had been the victim of one of the classic practical jokes of recent years. Part of the routine of arriving on a new unit was to have one's 'mug shot' taken for distribution around the various offices, and when Bertie reported to Brüggen's photo section he was dressed, as usual, in his flying suit. No problem; only a head and shoulders picture was required, so drop the top half of the flying suit, slip on a shirt, tie and best jacket, and all would be well. Normal procedure. But the photographer was in mischievous mood that day and, as well as taking the official shots, he was struck by the news-worthiness of a full-length picture. This fell mysteriously into the wrong hands, and thus it was that the next edition of the station magazine contained a dreadful shot of Bertie in all his glory – number one jacket, long johns, and flying suit round his ankles. Mindful of the magazine's large circulation, the station commander took a very dim view of this, and the perpetrators of the crime suffered a very one-sided interview.

Back to Dhahran. By now, the boss and two other nominated officers had been briefed on the overall plan and on the detachment's specific targets if combat started. The Tornados' initial task was to be offensive counter-air (OCA), with the aim of neutralizing the Iraqi air forces so that the anticipated interdiction campaign and air support of advancing land forces could be conducted in conditions of air supremacy. The aircraft's speciality was runway busting with JP233, and attacks would also be conducted against other OCA targets such as AAA and SAM sites, HAS areas, and aircraft in the open – using general-purpose bombs, sometimes tossed in from a distance.

The busy line at Dhahran, Saudi Arabia. *Photo by Les Hendry*

As the UN deadline ticked past at 0800 hours local time on 16 January, training flying ceased, the aircraft were loaded, and crews stood at readiness. Tension grew, but the deadline passed quietly, and by 1730 hours it seemed that nothing was going to happen. In the early evening, however, Squadron Leader Pete Rycroft (ex-Thirty One executive officer and now back to run the ops desk) called the boss and told him to go to work immediately. Jerry Witts remembers:

'Group Captain Cliff Spink, the RAF commander at Dhahran, met me with a top secret signal which, in very few words, told us to go to war. A quick check of the

Armourers labour hard to load a JP233. The front half of one of the two weapons is about to be mated to the pylon. *Les Hendry*

plan showed that we would have to take off at about 0130 hours local to reach our target shortly after 0300, the official "off" time for Operation *Desert Storm*. This gave us three or four hours to get everything buttoned up and ready to go. By now the rest of my formation had arrived, and after I had given them the outline we busied ourselves with our preparations. We were, of course, apprehensive but there was no time to brood about it. We filled the time by briefing ourselves to death: R/T procedures; tanking procedures; route and target details; enemy defences; friendly forces; escape and evasion in the event of going down; and so on ad infinitum. It was a strange atmosphere because many of those around us weren't aware of what we were about to go and do. Hence questions such as "if they're going night flying, do they want the weapons taken off the aircraft?"'

Then it was time to go. Predictably, they walked to their aircraft far too early and sat there in strained silence waiting for take-off time. Once airborne, things were a lot better; they were busy and there was less time to worry. A crew-member's thoughts: 'The sky was full of aeroplanes, the AWACS radio channels jammed with mission after mission checking in. This was history in the making and there we were, right in the middle of it. It was all very exciting. Then, sooner than seemed possible, it was down to low level, lights off, across the border and …'

And being 'over the border' was a new and sobering experience for all of them. Chris Peace again:

'I personally found that my best mental defence mechanism was to treat the missions as "just another sortie" – and for the most part they were. But each trip had moments when you really couldn't fail to notice that things were much more serious. At 0415 hours on my first mission, inbound to Jalibah at 200ft, my most vivid memory was the intense blackness of the night. But for the occasional Bedouin camp fire, you couldn't have told which way was up. We were number eight in the stream and, as we approached the target area, we could watch the attack developing ahead of us. My particular aircraft performed as advertised throughout the attack, only giving us one moment of anxiety when the radio altimeter refused to lock on. The heart rate reduced as we ran safely homewards, and only then did we get a chance to ponder the large explosion we'd felt somewhere close below the aircraft during the attack. But after landing we saw the evidence – when Charlie Brown pointed out a neat 23mm hole through the rudder from anti-aircraft fire.'

The Tornado proved itself a resilient warhorse. AAA damage is shown here around the aft end. *Les Hendry*

A massive media presence had built up over the preceding few weeks, and air and ground crews had been in demand for interviews by the media. Renowned reporters such as Kate Adie and Peter Snow had called in; conventional wisdom had it that the intrepid Kate's appearance was a sure sign that things were getting really serious. Now that the conflict had started, reporters in the Gulf were brigaded into media response teams. Competition to get into one of these had been extremely fierce, and the Dhahran group included Chris Morris from Sky TV, Ramsey Smith from the Mirror Group, Nick Constable from the *Daily Star* and Tom Carver of BBC Radio. They lived with the Squadron on a daily basis, and a good rapport was established.

From the time the boss's formation landed from their first mission, the MRT were in attendance and hungry for interviews. Flight Lieutenants Ian 'Ob' Long and Jerry Gegg became instant celebrities, with lurid accounts of their exploits; but notwithstanding all the bravado, there was also honesty – such as that found in these recollections from young C-squared:

> 'Of course, I was frightened and apprehensive at the impending task. I am deeply superstitious and found myself constantly touching any pieces of wood I could find. After the boss's formation went in on the first night, I just wanted my team to do its bit and get our first mission over. I didn't want to let Thirty One down, having only just arrived on the Squadron, but more importantly I wanted to get home alive to Caron and six-month old Louise. After the first few trips it got a bit easier, except for the nagging dread in the back of my mind after seeing the two Johns on Iraqi TV looking very much the worse for wear.'

This last was an indication of the downside of media coverage, being a reference to XV Squadron POWs John Peters and John Nichol who had been paraded on Iraqi TV in a grotesque propaganda performance. Thankfully, they were returned unscathed at the end of the conflict. Post-conflict, JP was to join Thirty One, where he kept the boys endlessly amused with the antics surrounding the publication of the book *Tornado Down*, which told the story of his and John Nichol's experiences. After tracking JP through the book launch, the personal appearances, the visits from the literati, the filming of the TV programme, and then the genesis of the sequel to the book, the crewroom felt very much that it deserved a collective beer for its forbearance!

Given that opposition defences were proving fearsomely strong, commanders decided early on that standing off from the target and tossing the bombs in would be a better option. So Thirty One only used JP233 on the very early days of operations, after which the aircraft were each loaded with eight 1,000lb 'dumb' bombs. This caused issues for the engineers, as twin-store carriers originally designed for use by Harriers had to be used. During one very rapid turnround, a carrier could not be removed from its pylon. Time was tight and SEngO made the decision to make the aircraft armament system live on the ground and explosively eject the carrier from the aircraft. Horsehair matting and anything else that would break the fall was placed under the aircraft. As Les Hendry says: 'The aircraft survived the incident, the carrier did not!'

There were several other examples where engineering ingenuity was required. Les again:

> 'The CO and I had devised a system for having spare aircraft available for each wave. If eight were planned there would be another four in the same fit manned by standby crews. If a primary team crewed-out they would rush over to the nearest spare, which was all fired up (one engine) and ready to go. This worked well in the early days of the war when spares were frequently used. We had hard rules as to which

unserviceabilities would still leave the aircraft as "war goers" and which would not. In particular, the ECM system and IFF had to be fully functional before taxi. On one particularly tricky night we had used up all four spares when we were informed there was to be another crew-out due to a BOZ pod failure. There was no choice; I quickly decided to ask the crew to sit tight while we replaced the pod. Armament electrical systems may, conventionally, only be worked on when there has been a "no volts" test carried out. Clearly, with engines already running and electrical power fully on, this couldn't happen in this situation, and the face of the SNCO armourer who was tasked with changing the pod was a picture! I stood right by the armourers as they replaced the pod, providing "top cover". I was fully aware that had anything gone wrong I would probably be on a Herc straight back to Germany – but this was war! In the event nothing did go wrong, and the eight-ship departed on time.'

Then there were the drop tanks. Because of the range to the targets it was decided to replace the normal 1,500 litre underwing tanks with 2,250 litre tanks usually carried by the F3s. Frantic calculations followed to see whether the all-up weight of weapons, large tanks and the self-protection package would be within limits. In the event it was within 'war' limits, with the critical element being the heat generated in the tyres while taxiing to the end of the runway. The tyres did survive during the Gulf Conflict, although overheating would prove a problem in subsequent operations during high summer – one which could only be solved by factoring in lengthy cooling-off periods prior to take off.

From day one it was all-out effort as the air war progressed, with some of the targets being places familiar to earlier generations of Thirty Oners: Habbaniya; and Shaibah. During the first seven days, four Tornados were lost; thankfully, none was from Dhahran, although sad news came of the death of popular ex-Jaguar Goldstar Nigel Elsdon, at the time of the conflict the CO of 27 Tornado Squadron. It was not an easy time for anybody, but the phase brought air and groundcrew very close together. Many later remarked that they never expected again to experience the kind of relationships that formed between Squadron members during that memorable period.

As the offensive continued it became clear that the Tornados and other aircraft involved in OCA had done their job and that the Iraqi air force was not going to fight. Even the SAMs were silenced, and this permitted a change of tactics, with aircraft making medium-level attacks above the murderous AAA that surrounded the Iraqi airfields. Ironically, this change coincided with the Dhahran detachment's first combat loss, when Flying Officer Budgie Burgess and Squadron Leader Bob Ankerson of 17 Squadron went down near Jalibah in ZA403. Fortunately, they ejected safely, being returned after the conflict.

This switch to medium level did not, incidentally, apply to Dhahran's recce element, which continued its singleton, night, low-level effort throughout. Nicknamed 'Scud hunters' following their successful detection of several of the elusive missiles, the majority of their work was, nevertheless, concerned with identifying Iraqi troop dispositions.

Following ZA403's loss, an aircraft being ferried from Laarbruch to Tabuk was diverted to Dhahran as a replacement, and the crew was instructed to stay with Thirty One for the duration. It turned out that they were from 27 Squadron, bringing representatives from yet another unit under command.

In the midst of all this, Warrant Officer Heap turned up after his Falklands sojourn. Flight Sergeant Fisher had been an outstanding understudy, but it was good to have the full engineering team back in harness.

Jerry Witts and his team at Dhahran in 1991.

By early February things were still going well, especially after Buccaneer aircraft were rushed to Bahrain to act as designators for the Tornados' laser-guided bombs. The emphasis switched to daylight raids, dropping LGBs with great accuracy on Iraqi targets.

Throughout the whole period, though, the opposition continued to make life uncomfortable for the detachment operation at Dhahran. Charlie Brown reports:

'It was mid-January, just a night or so after our Tornados had begun to strike deep into Iraq. The groundcrew who had been on the day shift had just returned to the Al Nimran hotel in downtown Al Khobar, just a few minutes away from the airbase at Dhahran. We were relaxing in our rooms watching Sky TV. As the Squadron had been in the news from time to time, any of the boys who had starred on the TV would have to buy a crate of beer on return to Brüggen. I was already on the list – so nobody else was going to get away with it!

'I suddenly became aware that the hotel's fire bells were ringing. Sergeant Bob Petrie, my roommate, and I stared at each other in horror; this was the air attack warning! We quickly donned our gas masks, grabbed our NBC [nuclear, biological and chemical] gear and headed for the next room to get away from the large plate-glass windows in ours. We were immediately confronted by a highland version of Quasimodo, who was shrieking "The bells, the bells!" at the pair of us – it was a very agitated 'Klunk' Charlton. The three of us rapidly got into our full NBC kit and, as the hotel had no proper shelters, settled down on the floor to see it out.

'None of us knew what to expect next, but we were soon to find out. In the distance came an unnerving "thump – thump – thump". Not very loud, but we all felt the hotel walls shake. The three of us exchanged worried glances. Then it came again; "thump – thump – thump." It was definitely getting closer.

'We sat there awaiting the advance of the exploding bombs. Please miss us. Then, all of a sudden, a crash as our door almost burst off its hinges. And there was Pete Pearston standing there screaming "Get out – I think there's an air raid on!" So our approaching wave of Iraqi bombing turned out to be a heavy-handed rigger sergeant who was attempting to beat down every door in the corridor in his efforts to make sure everybody was awake! Slightly ashamed, but certainly relieved, the three of us sat out our first – but definitely not our last – false alarm.'

In fact not all Scud warnings were false alarms, for many Iraqi missiles *were* launched in the general direction of Dhahran. Most were either spectacularly intercepted by the American Patriot air-defence missiles based nearby, or landed harmlessly in open areas – but a number of American troops were, sad to relate, killed late on in the conflict when a barracks in Al Khobar suffered a direct hit.

We should also comment on the mention of 'NBC kit'. The Iraqis were suspected of possessing the capability to fit chemical warheads to their Scud missiles; as a precaution, anthrax vaccinations were administered to detachment personnel. In the event, the threat did not materialize, but the part those vaccinations may have played in a variety of unpleasant symptoms later experienced by veterans of the conflict – known generically as 'Gulf War Syndrome' – is still being debated.

During all this time the boys received marvellous support from the Association, who at Horace Welham's (a Burma campaign fitter) instigation, had been sending 'Red Cross' parcels full of boiled sweets, toiletries, and other extremely welcome gifts. And in mentioning welfare we shouldn't neglect the vital work done by the rear party. Families back at Brüggen were, naturally, extremely concerned, and Chief Technician 'Pip' Shepard received endless praise for the care and dedication he brought to his job of liaising with distressed families.

At Dhahran there were also literally hundreds of air mail lettergrams – 'bluies' as they were affectionately known – to read and answer. But what the boys wanted most, of course, was a drink or two. The only place to get this was Bahrain, so Squadron Leader Vince Mee, the detachment's senior intelligence officer, promptly set up 'liaison' briefings with the Buccaneer detachment over the causeway. In this way, all the aircrew were able to get a spot of R&R at least once during the fighting. The groundcrew were not so fortunate but didn't resent at the aircrews' perk, understanding that it was well-deserved after several weeks of non-stop aerial action.

The performance of the aircraft in combat began to inspire considerable affection, reflected in the application of pet names and various examples of 'nose art'. 'DA' was the first to be christened, as 'Dhahran Annie', and this was followed by the boss's aircraft, 'DB', which became 'Luscious Lizzie'. Every time an aircraft flew an operational sortie, a palm tree was added to the proud tally below the cockpit. Even 'Arris, the Squadron mascot, got in on the act and was taken on a bombing raid as well as having his photograph in the papers.

Operations continued at a high rate throughout February, but by the end of the month it was obvious that the enemy was beaten. On the twenty-eighth a halt was called to hostilities. The Iraqis had quit Kuwait and the objective had been achieved. There was enormous pleasure at this and relief that the Squadron had come through unscathed. Even better, the news came within a few days that the POWs were alive and well and about to be released. Quite naturally, attentions turned towards home.

On 16 March 1991, the boss and his navigator 'AJ' Smith led the Goldstars back to Brüggen, non-stop as they had deployed. What a welcome accompanied their arrival; the RAF Germany band was there, and pretty well all the station's personnel turned out. After an official greeting from RAF Germany's deputy commander, the crews were whisked with their families to the crewroom for a well-deserved beer – or three.

With the aircraft gone there was time in Dhahran for relaxation, shopping for gold in soukhs, and a little sightseeing. A curiosity of the deployment had been that, despite the turmoil in the Middle East and the hitherto closed nature of Saudi society, the Squadron's men had always felt welcomed by the local people. This short, reflective piece by Sergeant Andy Wiles captures the mood and atmosphere of the after-conflict period:

'Arris Arietis, the bear. He's had his own logbook and has flown in a Tornado over Iraq – and maybe in other types. His first name stems from the distinguished Goldstar CO, Sir Arthur Harris. 'Arietis' may refer to a star in the Aries constellation – but he's generally just known as 'Arris. The main problem has been his vulnerability to capture by other squadrons, to the extent that there is no certainty that the current bear is in fact the original. Over the years ransom notes have been received from, inter alia, the Las Vegas mafia ('… bits of 'Arris are already in our freezer …') and a Canadian Starfighter squadron from the Black Forest (predictably demanding much booze as the price of the bear's return.) But by far the best capture must have been …

> 'The site was now devoid of Tornados. Equipment and spares were being boxed up, and pax lists for those still remaining were complete. I'd run out of things to do so, as I had a truck, I and another chap went off for a ride. We first headed into Al Khobar and then drove along the coast road, skirting the vast Dhahran airbase and heading for Half Moon Bay. The area there was desolate but stunningly picturesque; there were tyre tracks leading off the road towards the pinkish sand dunes, so I thought to follow. We got about twenty yards before becoming stuck! Our truck was for on-road use only, with pathetic tyres – and was being handled by a decidedly on-road-only driver.
>
> 'We tried putting car mats under the drive wheels but these were spat out to the other side as the vehicle sank deeper; the back axle was now buried in sand. By this time the sun was sinking and dusk falling. The road remained empty and desolate; I had a sense of helplessness, feeling responsible. Then, to our relief, a police car appeared. I caught the crew's attention with gestures and we fell upon their mercy. They were friendly, and expert at encouraging the truck from the sand. With really clever clutch use and us pushing, we were free in no time.'

The main body of the groundcrew returned to Brüggen over the next few days by VC10 to memorable welcomes, and everyone received a richly-deserved month's leave before work started on restoring the Squadron to its peacetime footing. In the midst of this, ten of the air and groundcrew were flown to London, all expenses paid, to attend a *Daily Star* lunch at which the boss received the newspaper's 'gold star' award on the Squadron's behalf. This was presented by ex-PM Margaret Thatcher who was most complimentary about Thirty One's contribution to the Gulf Conflict, and indeed about the RAF in general.

By the end of April personnel had returned to duty, but aircraft were in short supply because of the need to restore them after the rigours of desert operations. This, as well as catching up on scheduled servicing, involved the removal of the desert camouflage and with it, sadly, the beloved nose art. It was also time to say goodbye to close friends as the posting system got back into gear.

… that by the nurses at Wegburg hospital, who would accept nothing less than dinner served, without trousers, by Goldstar aircrew.

During this period there was yet another example of the support offered by the Association, with the chairman's note in *Star News* suggesting that members might like to show tangible appreciation of the boys' efforts in the Gulf. He mentioned that the Association itself had already resolved to donate a sum of money towards a post-Gulf 'bash', and went on to wonder whether individuals might also like to 'buy the boys a pint.' An extremely thoughtful gesture, and an example of the warmth that exists between Thirty One's former and present members. As Flight Lieutenant Jerry Gegg commented at the time when writing the Squadron's regular piece in the Association's newsletter, 'The Goldstars (current) would like to thank you all for the messages of support and gifts that were received in Dhahran.'

In fact re-reading Jerry's summer 1991 article triggers another couple of post-Gulf memories. He wrote: 'Having got everyone back safely in mid-March, we then bade a temporary farewell to three crews who had to wing their way down to Bahrain to sit on standby for two and a half months just in case the Iraqis decided to do something stupid.'

These were people who had not taken part in the conflict, either because they had returned home on the first *roulement* before the start of hostilities or because they had not been combat-ready in time for the action, and the continuing Bahrain detachment was formed by a composite Brüggen squadron, nominally Number 17. Jerry's article went on:

'Thankfully for all concerned, their only problems were a lack of money and too much beer and sun! At the end of May they returned and, for the first time in about eight months, we were all back as a whole again. For three of our number, Ian Long and JEngOs Nick Watson and Steve Wilkinson, it was an ideal time to get to know their new wives – Maria, Lisa and Linda – as they had been married just before leaving Brüggen for the Gulf.'

Chapter 26

Policing the New World Order

So that was it, wasn't it? Iraq done with? Well, the pursuit of Iraqi forces fleeing towards Baghdad had ended as they'd crossed the border from Kuwait. Even at the time it was well recognized that it would have been better to have dealt more comprehensively with Iraq's army and leadership. But the stated political objective had been to liberate Kuwait. And in reality, world opinion at the time had no appetite for watching further treatment being meted out to a beaten and retreating Iraqi army – and especially so after the media broadcast the comments of an American pilot operating over straggling enemy columns to the effect that 'This was a turkey shoot.' Little did we suspect then, however, that failing to complete the job would lead to the Tornado force's further involvement in Iraq lasting, on and off, for over twenty years.

For now though, the summer of 1991 was largely a period of readjustment and there could have been a tendency towards anticlimax. However, the Squadron took advantage of training opportunities as they became available and decamped in June to Decimomannu for a weapons detachment. While they were there, the Gulf honours list was announced. This included the award of the DSO to the boss, Wing Commander Jerry Witts, an MBE for SEngO Les Hendry, and Mentions in Dispatches for Bertie Newton and Flight Lieutenants Chris Drewery and Kevin Baldwin. Everyone who served in the Gulf would receive a campaign medal, as well as Saudi and Kuwaiti medals.

Subsequently it was announced that 31 Squadron would be awarded the battle honour 'Gulf 1991'. And it was pleasing to note at the same time a significant change to policy regarding the emblazoning of battle honours on Squadron Standards. Up until that point there had been a limit of eight honours displayed. Now, the limit was raised to fifteen, and 'Gulf 1991' became the ninth honour to be emblazoned on Thirty One's Standard. Although no-one could have foreseen it at the time, it was as well that the policy was changed. For over the coming years the Goldstars' Standard would have to return to the embroidery shop several more times for further additions.

A word of explanation, by the way, of why the previously missing honour 'Syria 1941' did not reappear at this point. Although it had only been omitted because it was over the then limit of eight – and that limit had now been raised – it turned out that the official view now being held on the matter was that 'the original limit of eight was interpreted as being the limit for the world wars.' So it seems that, unless there's a further policy change, the Squadron's entitled battle honour 'Syria 1941' will forever remain unemblazoned.

Now that time has permitted sober reflection and analysis, what are we to deduce from the efforts of Thirty One and its fellow GR1 units in the Gulf Conflict?

That air power alone could never win a war? Still true, perhaps – but the ground operation after the six weeks of air strikes was minimal, only requiring one hundred hours to complete.

The losses during the low-level airfield attacks of the first week inevitably precipitated press comment, which mostly leapt to the hasty conclusion that the RAF was doing it wrong. But OCA is a dangerous role; nobody ever thought that it would be otherwise. The RAF and most similar forces had had no reason to believe that they would ever have been able to conduct such a campaign at anything other than very low level, underneath the radars. But the Tornado force did prove that it had the capability to switch to medium level once it became clear that the option was available.

All in all, the Gulf campaign confirmed the need for flexibility perceived by the RAF as far back as 1988 – when the Germany-based Tornado force started to broaden its horizons by training in AAR.

Jerry Witts' eventful stint in the chair came to a close in February 1992 when he was replaced by Wing Commander Ian Hall. The new CO was delighted to come aboard and recalls:

> 'Here was I, a brand-new Tornado pilot, parachuting into a crewroom knee-deep in Gulf heroes. An interesting experience in itself. When I joined, the Goldstars were operating from the former QRA area on the far side of the airfield, this temporary home being the Squadron's third on the trot. In fact they hadn't been in their own site for fifteen months. First there had been the Gulf, then a "bolthole" to Wildenrath while Brüggen's runway was resurfaced; and latterly the Squadron's own area was being refurbished. It was certainly time to come home.'

The reader will have noted the reference to the 'former' QRA site, and now would be a good time to take stock of recent changes.

The political situation in Europe had been evolving, and Brüggen's posture in response had been modified accordingly. In October 1986, nuclear readiness had been relaxed from fifteen minutes to twelve hours, so QRA as it had existed for so many years had effectively ended. It was said that, the previous Christmas, crews on QRA had called up their oppos in East Germany and exchanged the season's greetings. Not the first such story, it must be admitted, but it's a nice thought, reflecting signs of tensions easing.

In November 1989 the Berlin Wall was breached, followed in 1990 by German reunification. Both the Soviet Union and the Warsaw Pact (WP) were dissolved in 1991. Later, in 1999, the first of the former WP members would join NATO. So the map of Europe was in the process of being re-drawn. Brüggen would finally lose the strike role in 1998, with the 'special weapons' being ferried away in the night. In general, people were glad to see the back of them. QRA had never been the most popular of duties, and that crews would no longer have to satisfy the intense scrutiny of the WST – the Weapons Standardization Team – could only have been described as a relief.

The end of the nuclear role was a significant milestone – although of course the nation retained its nuclear deterrent in other forms. But the Cold War situation of two heavily-armed blocs facing each other, poised to react, had been an extraordinary period of world history. The concept of mutually-assured destruction seems in retrospect a terrible one, and it certainly attracted its fair share of critics at the time. But what is indisputable is that, during the era of nuclear deterrence, Europe remained relatively free from conflict. Which is certainly more than could have been said for the preceding thirty-five years, which had seen two world wars. The Goldstars, at their West German bases, had been a part of the reason for peace in Europe during the latter period. Number 31 Squadron's job had been to be ready – to train and to watch – and they had done it well.

Following the easing of tension, the world might have hoped for a more peaceful period. Certainly the politicians, mindful of huge expenditure during the Cold War, were optimistically planning to reap a 'peace dividend'. But even throughout that period of deterrence and readiness Britain had been involved in several small-scale operations, so it isn't altogether surprising that our story continues by recording more active service for Thirty One in the era following the Cold War.

Returning to 1992, a post-Gulf list was compiled of lessons learned and recommendations. Many were too difficult or expensive to implement in the short term: buy more aircraft, procure better weapons, and so on. But others were immediately achievable, and one such was the recommendation that all aircrew deploying to an operational area should first undergo a combat survival course, including training in 'resistance to interrogation'. Such a course was available but had hitherto been reserved for masochists destined to become Squadron escape-and-evasion specialists; now it was to be for all. Thus it was that the author found himself, at the age of forty-four, spending a decidedly chilly, painful and unpleasant week on Dartmoor in December. Very … er … character building!

So much for survival training, but the face of flying training, too, was being changed by the necessity now to do a lot of it overseas. The Germans had reduced their forces as had the British following the end of the Cold War, in some ways going further. The newly reunited Germany had other matters with which to concern itself and defence was a low priority – to the extent that the RAF was now barely permitted to low-fly in Germany at all. This meant that the Squadron had to look elsewhere, and now, on most days, Thirty One's Tornados could be found turning round at British bases after using the UK low-flying system.

And neither was low flying now the be-all and end-all. Although the Goldstars still had to be ready to employ traditional tactics, they now needed to broaden their expertise. So on most days the Squadron would also refine skills learned during the Gulf Conflict: AAR; medium-level bombing; and night formation flying. While aircrew were being asked to stay current at an enormous variety of skills, they were also facing economies – which inevitably meant continued reductions in flying hours. Flight simulator fidelity was increasing and some training could be transferred. But in a situation of decreased flying hours, simulation never seemed to compensate fully.

The travelling continued, with Oman, Alaska, Labrador and Nevada featuring on the itinerary as the Goldstars trained. All were to provide invaluable training for, as forecast, there would soon be further operational business.

In July 1992, Iraqi operations against its own minority peoples came to world attention. Thirty One was at once involved, as Ian Hall recalls:

'We were at Goose Bay, coming to the end of a three-week *Western Vortex* exercise. It had been an intensive period; the aircraft had been difficult to keep up to scratch and the groundcrew had worked long hours. On the last but one morning I told them how much I had appreciated their efforts and announced that there would be three days off upon our return to Brüggen. Great rejoicing! But at six o'clock the following morning I was awoken by a phone call from the station commander back at home. We were immediately on our return to prepare for deployment to the Middle East. End of promised stand-down, and of course the news went down like the proverbial lead balloon. But, as usual, the lads buckled to.'

The sense of *déjà vu* for those who had been with the Goldstars in 1990 was uncanny. Almost two years to the day after they had heard of Iraq's invasion of Kuwait – and they had been in Goose Bay then, too – Saddam Hussein was at it again. In the event, this time none of the Germany-based squadrons were required to move south, but Thirty One held readiness until November.

It was just as well the call didn't come, for although the boys were ready to do the necessary, they really thought they shouldn't deploy until they'd got the medals from their last adventure! Eventually, the RAF system ground its way into action, and on 6 October – nineteen months after the end of the conflict – the station commander was able to present the Gulf campaign medal to fifty-two men and eleven officers. A fine occasion and a proud moment. The small numbers pointed up how rapid the turnover had been, especially amongst the aircrew; by the end of 1992 there were only five remaining on Thirty One who had fought with the Squadron in the Gulf.

The time to return to the desert, though, was not to be long delayed. Tornados from Marham had been deployed to Dhahran since September, and in December 1992 it was Brüggen's turn. Number 14 Squadron took the first stint, with the boss leading Thirty One's takeover just after Christmas. The groundcrew were drawn mainly from 14 and 17 Squadrons, who formed themselves into an amalgam they named 147 Squadron; to ensure standards were maintained, there was a sole Goldstar technician, Sergeant Paul Meehan, whose name had come out of the hat when Thirty One was asked to provide one man. Paul had been on leave at the time the draw was made – but of course it had been done scrupulously fairly …!?

The task this time was Operation *Jural*, the UK's contribution to Operation *Southern Watch*, a coalition effort to police Iraqi airspace south of the thirty-second parallel.

'Air policing' – a term not used in this narrative since the 'Frontier' chapters. But there's nothing new under the sun, and now a coalition of nations had declared a 'no-fly zone' in southern Iraq in support of UN Security Council Resolution 688, which forbade the Iraqi régime from oppressing its minority peoples. Several nations were contributing forces to police the zone, and it was towards this end that Thirty One was directed.

The routine was mainly medium-level reconnaissance, a role to which the crews were quite unaccustomed. The Tornados were now equipped with the new TIALD pod (Thermal Imaging and Airborne Laser Designator). Two prototype versions had seen successful service in the Gulf Conflict, and the RAF now possessed two production models and a handful of aircraft modified to carry them. Although primarily intended for target designation, they made excellent reconnaissance devices, and the Tornados reconnoitred ground activity while USAF, USN and French aircraft provided fighter sweep and escort, electronic support and 'Wild Weasels' to suppress ground fire. The whole was monitored by US AWACS aircraft and refuelled by tankers, including RAF Victors and VC10s based in Bahrain.

As the Goldstars were getting to grips with this new role, relations with Saddam began to deteriorate further. Iraq deployed additional SAM units in the no-fly zone, while her fighters made incursions and provocative flights. On 27 December an Iraqi MiG-25 was shot down by an American F-16; a *démarche* was issued by the coalition and, from then on, it was only a matter of time before more serious action would have to be taken.

All depended on political approval, and on 12 January 1993 the go-ahead was given for a large-scale raid on Iraqi air defence and command and control systems. The squadron changeover was still underway and 14 Squadron crews still remained in theatre; by this time, too, the detachment had been reinforced by two 617 Squadron crews from Marham.

The four-ship chosen the next day by the detachment commander (OC 31) was mixed, Goldstar representation comprising the lead navigator, Flying Officer Chris Platt, with Flying Officer Simon 'Gilbert' Hulme and the ubiquitous C-squared as number five and spare. The spare didn't, in the event, need to cross the border as the raid went off in text-book fashion during the evening. The Tornados scored DHs with LGBs on two air defence installations at Al Amarah in eastern Iraq, with the targets being designated by TIALD pods.

Five days later a similar mission was flown against another bunker at An Najaf, again with Platty out in front. This time Flight Lieutenants John Stockings and Jack Calder flew as number three, while Gus Cullen and Torben Harris flew the spare – which again didn't need to enter Iraq. Result – another hit. The bulk of the Squadron back at Brüggen were mortified that Stockings, who was a popular but extremely garrulous first-tourist, should have got in on the action. Opinion was that there would now be no reining him in, and that it was only a matter of time before his grinning face would be on the front of the tabloids telling 'how I done it!'

The press had, in fact, been briefed on the missions, but there had been a partial news blackout during the build-up period and there was no press presence on the airbase or admission that coalition forces were operating from any particular country. This stemmed from the hosts' request for discretion, and one could see their point; Middle Eastern politics are complex, and although some nations in the area held broadly anti-Iraq positions – for many and varied reasons – several of them had to share a border with Iraq and they all had to sustain their own diplomatic positions within the Arab community. Thus, officially, at the time the Tornados were 'somewhere in the Middle East.'

However, it was impossible to disguise the fact that hundreds of missions were being flown from one particular airbase, and the papers had no difficulty in putting two and two together. *The Daily Star* revived its Gulf Conflict 'gold star' connection, and even *The Guardian* mentioned Thirty One by name. The stories prompted a lovely letter from Bert Edwards, the chairman, who expressed the Association's good wishes to the boss and all who took part in the action. He went on: 'Though no official mention has been made about which squadrons did what, we are led to believe it was you and Thirty One who carried out the operation.'

There were no coalition losses on either of these raids, which seemed at the time to have the desired effect; the Iraqis withdrew their SAMs and ceased their fighter incursions. The RAF's perfect score was a great tribute to the efforts of air and groundcrews of all the squadrons involved. Most importantly, no damage had been caused to the civilian areas and sacred sites that lay adjacent to some of the targets. Which was an important point, for the operation was conducted on a knife edge of international support.

The TriStar – it looks huge when close up. *By the author*

For coalition operations it was essential to be able to refuel from allied aircraft. Here, a KC-10 of the USAF. *Photo by the author*

Perhaps the greatest challenge of them all – the short 'donkey dick' hose on the end of the boom of an American – or perhaps French – KC-135. Great fun! *Photo by the author*

This relatively short episode has warranted detailed coverage because it embraces all the ingredients which would mark many of the operations in which RAF Tornados would subsequently be involved around the world: international political considerations, including aspects relating to the UN; intense press scrutiny; avoidance of collateral damage; and world public opinion.

The Squadron returned home soon afterwards, with the exception of Ian Hall who remained at the helm of the first and only 'non-formed unit' in theatre – an amalgam of individually detached crews which replaced Thirty One. The trial was not judged a success, and detachments reverted thereafter to formed squadrons. But in that short time he can claim the novelty of having flown with navigators from all the RAF's GR1 squadrons. Naturally, none was as good as a Goldstar nav!

Following the easing of tension in Europe between East and West, a number of opportunities arose for friendship.

The first occurred during July 1993, when Thirty One was tasked to escort four Hungarian fighters to the International Air Tattoo at Fairford. On the day of the outbound sortie, the brief would be by telephone through an interpreter before launching the GR1s and MiG-21 Fishbeds from, respectively, Brüggen and Hungary. The rendezvous was to be in German airspace down by the Czech border, and the Goldstars were to lead the Hungarians to Brüggen for lunch and refuelling before taking them on to Gloucestershire. These would be the first former WP fighters to land in the former FRG, so it was important that there were no hitches. Moreover, the MiGs were very tight on fuel and the pilots didn't speak English – so the weather needed to be fine and the brief had to cover every eventuality. All went well until Ian Hall led his pair airborne – only to see extensive mist and low cloud rolling towards Brüggen. Too late to stop the MiGs, which had already taken off, so on with the RV and hope for the best. But luck wasn't airborne that day, and by the time the mixed formation arrived back in the Brüggen area a thunderstorm was raging over the field. There was no option but to divert to the Luftwaffe base at Nörvenich, where they all landed – the MiGs with five minutes fuel remaining.

The Germans barely blinked at this mixed British and Hungarian formation landing for lunch at no notice, and they even produced MiG-qualified engineers who had formerly served in the DDR. The onward trip to England went beautifully, as did the return three days later. And word had it that the HQ 2 Group met man, being ultimately responsible for one of the least accurate weather forecasts of all time, had the mother and father of a dressing down from the Senior Air Staff Officer.

Another perspective on the former 'East' comes from Squadron Leader John Scholtens, whose last flight as Thirty One's exec in January 1995 included a little of the newly-available sightseeing. Leading a pair of GR1s, he and his pilot, Squadron Leader Ed Smith, enjoyed a grandstand view from 1,000ft (much higher than they or any RAF crew had ever anticipated they'd fly if the worst had come to the worst) of the ground they had learned by heart in the Cold War. Scholtens takes up the story (first told in *Seek and Strike*):

'As we crossed the deconfliction zone on a misty winter's day, nervous tension and an eerie silence took hold; there were no radio calls, no tell-tale signals on our RHWR, and little evidence of former WP equipment on the ground, yet we flew on in silence with bated breath for a full five minutes into that once-forbidden land. It was as though a spring had snapped on the mighty Soviet war machine. We flew over the now-disused Zerbst and Wittstock airfields, passed close to Brandenburg, Neuruppin and Altengrabow airfields, and within thirty miles of Berlin. The once proud base of Zerbst, which had concentrated NATO minds for so many years, now lay abandoned, a sad sight with HAS doors wide open and no sign of life. A feeling of great elation engulfed us as we realized the enormity of what had gone before – with this first-hand evidence that it was truly over.'

Air policing over Iraq continued throughout the decade, initially based in Dhahran. But terrorist activity there, which killed a number of Americans in the domestic accommodation, led to a change of venue. Flight Lieutenant Pete Foster wrote in *Star News* in 1996:

'In my previous article I commented that things can only get better. Well they didn't! It was decided by some bright spark that we would be safer moving somewhere a little more remote. And that turned out to be Al Kharj, a Saudi base in the middle of the desert. To sit in our impromptu mess under the camouflage netting and listen to the team waxing lyrical about the lost delights of Dhahran was quite something. One moment we'd been in individual rooms with showers, a small but well-equipped kitchen between five of us; the next we were seven to a tent with field catering and toilets without doors! But the Goldstars rose to the occasion. In no time people were producing multi-piece bedroom suites made out of the packaging in which the drinking water had been delivered.'

By contrast, during 1997, there was also a deployment to the massive and well-found Turkish base at Incirlik to police Iraqi no-fly zones from the other end. Operation *Northern Watch* was, as its name suggests, the equivalent of the Saudi-based *Southern Watch*. While one had the aim of preventing harassment of the marsh Arabs of southern Iraq, the other was largely directed towards protecting the Kurdish people north of the thirty-sixth parallel from Saddam Hussein's forces. RAF representation was normally Jaguars or Harriers, with the Goldstars filling in just twice.

Before covering the next operation, it's necessary to say a few words about ALARM (Air Launched Anti-Radiation Missile), another weapon which was specifically designed for employment by Tornados. It didn't come into service quite as early as JP233, but

Another mascot of the mid-1990s was Wally the goat, presented by a number of departing aircrew. During his lifetime he was lodged with the shepherd who looked after the herd of sheep which grazed RAF Brüggen's green acres – having been operated upon to prevent unwanted sheep-goats. He was brought out for ceremonial occasions, here participating in the handover between departing boss Ian Hall and the incoming Steve Parkinson.

employed a particularly innovative concept. Designed to home onto the radar emissions of SAM and AAA systems, its primary mode was direct attack. But because the enemy is smart too, it would be possible for him to switch off his radars as the missile homed, thereby denying guidance to the ALARM. Therefore, a secondary mode was provided which would involve firing a salvo of missiles into the overhead of the area of interest. These would then deploy parachutes and drift downwards looking for targets. Radars would switch off to avoid attack by ALARMs, leaving the area defenceless as the bomber package pressed home its attack against adjacent targets. If, knowing bombers were inbound, the SAM operators switched their radars back on to engage, then zap! – the ALARMs would slip their parachutes and home in. Clever stuff. GR1s could carry nine of the missiles although, with external fuel tanks and self-defence pods aboard, three was a more realistic load.

Clearly SEAD (suppression of enemy air defences) was a specialist role, and initially it was confined to one squadron at Brüggen – Number IX. Later, though, the Goldstars had also picked up the capability.

With that as background we move, in 1999, to Kosovo, with its complex and confusing political background. Troubles had rumbled in the Balkans since time immemorial. If

Tito's socialist régime, which ran from post–Second World War through to the end of the 1980s, had done nothing else, it had largely suppressed nationalist differences. But in the run-up to its final disintegration in the early nineties, historical troubles had resurfaced. Most recently, a NATO (UN) peacekeeping mission had been set up (to which British aircraft, but not Tornados, had contributed), and this had run on into the Bosnian War of 1992–5.

Later, the vexed question of Kosovo came to the fore, with Serbians and ethnic Albanians vying for supremacy. Particularly nasty forms of civil warfare broke out, with the international community struggling to prevent humanitarian disaster. United Nations Security Council Resolution 1199 demanded a ceasefire, with NATO coming to the brink of air strikes in 1998 before the situation cooled temporarily. But the cauldron erupted again the following year, leading to NATO's Operation *Allied Force* from 24 March until 11 June – with Thirty One participating.

Flight Lieutenant 'Snakey' Snaith enlarged in his dispatch to the Association newsletter at the time:

> 'Serbians and Kosovars had been fighting each other for centuries. However, the break-up of the Former Republic of Yugoslavia (comprising Serbia and Montenegro) was the catalyst for renewed conflict between the two peoples. Increasing evidence of human suffering called for tougher action against 'ethnic cleansing'. In a bid to stop Serbian aggression, NATO commenced an air campaign.'

Operation *Engadine* was initiated by the RAF over Easter 1999, with Tornados in the forefront. It was an eerie atmosphere, with wives at Brüggen seeing their husbands off to plan and brief in the evening before themselves returning to routine business.

Take-offs were at around 2300hrs, with landings back in the early hours. The weather was poor, with thundery buildups hindering en route AAR. LGBs were released from 20,000ft, but crews were still engaged by AAA even at that altitude. Long, tough missions, and to ease the transit burden some of the RAF's effort was soon deployed forward. Flight Lieutenant Phil Bayman tells of the move:

> 'Our move to a French air force base in Corsica was sudden. The Goldstars sent six flying crews and eight ground personnel down to Solenzara to support the contribution of IX Squadron. We were greeted by former Goldstar boss Group Captain Jerry Witts, our detachment commander. During our four-week stay, the Goldstars flew all the RAF operational sorties launched from our Mediterranean paradise, with the humble IX Squadron limiting their Corsican role to training flights around the island. We couldn't help but feel that this may have had something to do with our erstwhile DetCo. In fact poor weather forced many of the planned operational sorties to be cancelled, but this was not without its consolations as it enabled much time to be spent on the nearby beach using the French Air Force's sailing equipment. It was hell!
>
> 'The operation saw the new Paveway III LGB being dropped for the first time in anger. Similar in its employment to Paveway II which was used in the Gulf Conflict, it's approximately twice as big and is effective against targets such as underground storage facilities and bunkers. Also, 31 Squadron successfully fired ALARM against surface-to-air missile sites, the first time that this weapon had been fired in anger since the Gulf.'

The CO, Wing Commander Robbie Low, recalls the campaign from his perspective:

'Initial sorties from Brüggen were up to six and a half hours in duration, routing through France to Nice, before refuelling as we crossed the water towards Italy. Then over Florence, before taking up one of up to about ten refuelling tracks over the Adriatic. After topping up we'd hold over Sarajevo usually, then push on according to the time plan. Targets started off in the Pristina "bowl" and moved north, including Kralijevo (a factory), Novi Sad (oil refinery/storage) and even Belgrade itself (that was a militia HQ which turned out to be within 500m of the HQ of the Serbian air defence system – we weren't aware at the time of its location).

'We got blitzed early on by numerous SA3 launches and AAA. "Gilbert" Hulme (by now a flight lieutenant and the pilot QWI) and his nav, Squadron Leader Adrian Frost, were mentioned in dispatches for their leadership on one particularly hairy night. Return routes were the reverse, although first you had to find your own tanker – they never seemed to be where planned. Later, after we received clearance to route through the Czech Republic, Slovakia and Hungary, two hours were cut from the flight time. German ATC was fantastic, giving us direct tracks home and diverting civil traffic around us. The Hungarians had some funny moments, their best call being to a snooty "Speedbird" captain – who was told to "get out of the airway, as I have an undisclosed number of allied aircraft on a very important mission – your passengers will just have to wait their turn!" Once we moved to Solenzara, flight times reduced to under three and a half hours.

'The weather throughout was awful, we brought back bombs as often as we dropped because of total cloud cover and targets in freezing fog with no thermal signature. LGB seeker heads rely on perfect optical qualities and are designed for one trip only – but our bombs did so many trips we worried that they would degrade. TIALD pods were operating outside the cleared temperature limits and we broke a few. We had to re-route for weather all the time, and the aircraft engines got hammered with the icing and high-level heavyweight tanking.

'The main breakthrough was the use of ALARM. We definitely took out one SA3 (thought to be the one that had earlier shot down an F-117 stealth fighter); its radar was confirmed by two sources as radiating before our attack and it stopped at calculated impact time. By the final mission we were allowed to coordinate mixed SEAD/bombing missions, including an airfield attack. We used Paveway III against HAS and weapons storage areas, and ALARM against the SA6 defences. We didn't see the missile impacts because of the terrain on our side. But the package commander (a USAF F-16 pilot) was on the other side of the MEZ and called out "good job" exactly at the planned impact time. The only downside was that there is now, I understand, a complete ALARM in the Belgrade air museum; there was swampy terrain around so it's possible that one missile in "loiter" mode just floated down in its chute without going bang. All in all, I don't think ALARM got the credit it deserved; it made a huge difference and allowed the HARM shooters [HARM – an American anti-radiation missile] to fire reactively as they wanted.

'It was on the way back to the tanker on that final coordinated mission that AWACS announced it was all over – as the controller put it, "the Serbs have surrendered".

'I'll always remember the operation for the AAA; it scared me more than anything, and the Serbian air defences were very proficient. When it was over we had a bit of R&R in Corsica, although "rest" might be the wrong word. For example Phil Bayman, who was driving our van on a social trip to downtown Bonifacie, unknowingly dropped his wallet getting in. Moving off, he clobbered a bollard on the edge of the harbour. Doing a runner, he then contravened so many traffic laws that we thought the vehicle chasing us must be the police. But it turned out to be a very kind lady who was trying to return the wallet she had seen him drop!

'All in all the operation was a surreal experience. In the early phase, most of the folk who lived on base at Brüggen would turn out each night to watch the six-ship and up to three tankers get airborne – hundreds lined up along the front of the ops block. And the whole campaign was, of course, very political. Despite it being a NATO operation both the Americans and the French appeared to us to have, to some extent, their own agendas. And, as always, the military's ideas of what would or would not be achievable didn't always accord with the politicians' expectations.

'The German connection was particularly interesting, given that these were the first offensive missions launched from German soil since the Second World War. Generally, the peace campaigners at Brüggen's gates got short shrift from the riot police, who brought water cannons and huge dogs! And even the most ardent local anti-RAF campaigners would phone the station to pass on their thanks and good wishes to the crews taking part, and would then line the fence for the evening take-offs. I should also mention that the German press were pushing the case throughout for Germany to develop an effective AAR capability (as they subsequently have done) using the RAF's as a model.

'The Squadron worked its socks off from the start of April (Easter weekend) until early June. The whole of Brüggen's effort was centralized and I got hugely frustrated by other units taking credit for Thirty One's efforts. And it seemed it was only after I pointed out to CAS a newspaper article about army police dogs getting medals that he went in to bat and got medals for the aircrew who flew the missions!'

It all brings home what an extraordinary business it was to have been conducting live combat in European airspace – with civil air traffic to contend with, not to mention neutral countries. Robbie Low later recalled being routed by AWACS one dark and dirty night through Albanian airspace, as well as refuelling over Rome on another occasion – normally it was absolutely forbidden to refuel over populated areas because of the obvious possibility of bits dropping off. Perhaps this cryptic radio exchange is a good one with which to round off:

AWACS Controller: 'Sir, you appear to be infringing Bulgarian airspace. Why is that?'

Goldstar Nav Flight Lieutenant Ross Marwood: 'Because they're not shooting at us there!'

There were no British aircraft losses throughout the short campaign, which was a great testament to the training and professionalism of all involved. Afterwards, the chief of the air staff, Air Chief Marshal Sir Richard Johns, commented that:

'The air campaign had been a decisive element in the operation to bring peace to Kosovo. When such joint operations are considered, air power – while no panacea

Map 10: No.31 Squadron operations in the Balkans, 1999.

– would usually be the primary instrument of initial reaction because it could be deployed and withdrawn quickly, demanding less human and material commitment to achieve political objectives while involving fewer political risks.'

A further sally in the age-old argument that victory cannot be achieved without 'boots on the ground'? Perhaps, although we might reserve judgment until the day when lasting peace comes to the Balkans.

It was announced in January 2003 that 'The squadrons which took part in the allied air campaign over the Republic of Yugoslavia are to be awarded the battle honour 'Kosovo' following approval by Her Majesty the Queen. Four of those, who took part in the air strikes in 1999, will be permitted to emblazon the honour on their Standards. Those awarded that right are Number 1 (Harrier) Squadron and Numbers IX, 14 and 31 (Tornado) Squadrons.'

Chapter 27

Coming Home

The millennium was fast approaching and the Goldstars were to spend it in the Kuwaiti desert. Ali al Salem was yet another new base for middle-eastern operations and, as Phil Bayman commented, 'This will be the second Christmas away on ops in three years for most of us. Ah well, never mind. First in the Indian Skies, and now First in the Millennium Skies.' And his prediction came true, Robbie Low reporting later that 'Thirty One launched the first RAF sortie of the new millennium – at 0500hrs (0000hrs GMT) – on an operational mission from Kuwait.'

Readers may recall the speculation which preceded the century changeover regarding possible chaos with date-enabled electronic systems, and the Squadron was not immune from worry. Phil continued: 'We might be working really hard on 1 January combating the millennium bug. My alarm clock and CD player, as well as the block TV, will probably have the answer. But I can't wait to see what happens to SEMA (the RAF's computer network)'

In the event there seemed to be no problem, although not all the systems were working entirely satisfactorily. Association president Dick Bogg attempted to phone through the old boys' New Year greetings to the current team but was unable to get a line.

Although countless missions were flown across the border at the time, as befits the season all of them went off peacefully. Corporal Ady Tarrant put the groundcrew perspective on detachment festivities:

'Many trips were organized to see the sights of ye olde Kuwait City, and very nice it was too – with not a sandcastle in sight. On Christmas Day, Santa, usually known as Warrant Officer Wark, visited at 0800hrs with presents for all the linies. Then it was off to the Holiday Inn for a day by the pool sunbathing. The Squadron has left its mark on Ali al Salem (affectionately [?] known as Ali al Slum) by painting a massive gold star on the side of one of the partly destroyed hardened aircraft shelters left behind after the liberation of Kuwait – impressive work by the lads. New Year's Eve was spent at a BBQ and bonfire. Not ideal, but what else could we do?'

If readers were to look back now to the Jaguar pages of this book, they might be shocked at the number of reports of accidents during what was, after all, entirely training flying. Thankfully, the Tornado era (thus far) has seen far fewer. Perhaps the new aircraft was better, the nature of the operation different, or the training smarter. Probably all three.

But the Squadron has nevertheless lost several Tornados, starting as far back as 1987 when Squadron Leader Ivor Walker and Flight Lieutenant Steve Lloyd ejected from ZD738, 'DD', following a double hydraulic failure. This was one emergency which, in theory, should never occur in the Tornado, and the post-accident investigation uncovered

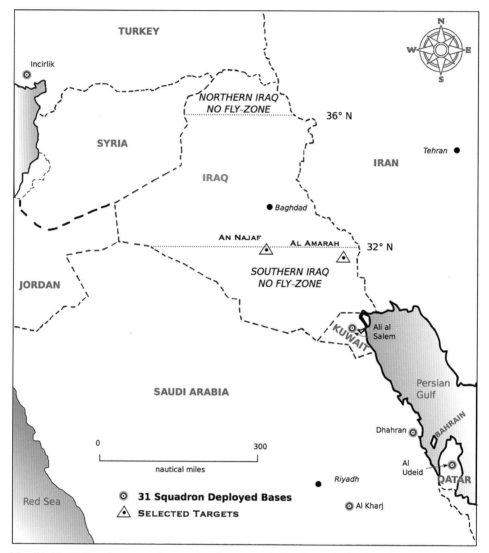

Map 11: No.31 Squadron operations during the post–Gulf Conflict period and the Iraq Conflict, 1992–2003.

a previously unrecognized design flaw which needed to be fixed. The aircraft crashed near the summer show at Kirkbymoorside in Yorkshire, a spectacular arrival not only for the spectators but also for Steve – whose first trip on the Squadron it was.

Later, in 1999, Flight Lieutenant 'Dicky' Wright was killed while on the weapons instructor course at Lossiemouth. A most popular character, his obituary recorded that 'he had always been prominent in Squadron activities. He was particularly well liked by the groundcrew, an accolade which few aircrew can honestly claim. It was a great achievement for a first tourist to be selected for the demanding QWI course, and it was tragic that it ended in that way.'

And in 2006 a GR4 (belonging to another squadron) crashed on Holbeach range in the Wash. Both 31 Squadron crewmembers escaped; given that the aircraft suffered a massive bird strike and lost both engines, they had little option but to step over the side.

The event of summer 2000 was the Tornado reaching the furthest south-eastwards in its history – with the Goldstars heading for Darwin, Australia. It was the Squadron's first visit there since the end of the Second World War. Flight Lieutenant Rich Yates reports:

'Although I'm not the best person to comment on all the details, having at the time been at RAAF base Edinburgh to fire an ALARM missile on the range there, I've been informed by all those who visited Darwin that it was the best detachment ever! Exercise *Pitch Black* included day and night missions in large multi-aircraft packages over a wide, unrestricted area of the outback. In addition, the Squadron made the most of the opportunity to see the sights and wildlife of Northern Territory. The boss and flight commanders even went to the RAAF Tindall summer ball, a magnificent event.

'The one big regret of the detachment was that we were unable to meet up with the Australian section of the Association. I, and others, had only five days in the country – but thanks nevertheless to Dick Ridoutt (Dakota pilot from 1944–46 and leader of the Australian old boys) for his understanding and perseverance.'

Rich would go on to have a remarkable four Goldstar tours. On completion of his third, as a squadron leader, he wrote to the newsletter to say not farewell, but *au revoir* – to which the editor replied that there was only one way he could return. And so it would happen in 2012 when the, by then, Wing Commander Yates would take over as boss. We shall undoubtedly hear more from him as this story unfolds.

In a similar timescale, longevity of a related type was displayed by Chief Technician Mark Stevens, who retired in 2009 after a remarkable 21 years, 21 days and 88 detachments – also in four ranks – on Thirty One. An incredible record.

We now return to JP233 with the news that, in April 2000, the last of the runway-attack weapons was shipped out of Brüggen to be withdrawn from service. Once the great hope, it had had its operational baptism in the Gulf Conflict. But it had received mixed reviews, its very-low-level delivery requiring a steady, level flight profile for what proved to be an uncomfortably long time, enabling anti-aircraft guns and missile radars to draw an all-too-accurate bead on the aircraft.

It was disappointing that things turned out so. The Tornado/JP233 combination had been a genuine effort to procure an integrated aircraft/weapon system, the complaint having previously always been that new aircraft had entered service with old munitions. So it was ironic that JP233 should not last long in service.

There were other reasons apart from the aircraft's vulnerability during the attack run. The objective of OCA is to prevent enemy aircraft flying effectively, and there are various methods of achieving this aim. One can shoot them down; one can destroy them on the ground; one can destroy their radar direction units; and one can damage their runways, preventing them from taking off. The last was the means aimed for with JP233 but, during and after the Gulf Conflict, it had become apparent that destroying aircraft on the ground was now becoming more feasible. Medium rather than low-level attacks could, in many scenarios, be conducted because of improvements in enabling assets such as defence suppression aircraft and weapons; and this, together with improved weapon delivery accuracies, now meant that HASs could be attacked with a high chance of success.

Ostensibly the ultimate grounds for JP233's withdrawal were international anti-mine protocols to which the government had signed up. In reality, though, few in the RAF's Tornado force were sorry to see it go.

It would not long be missed, though, for other enhancements were on the horizon. Most important was the upgrade of the aircraft to GR4 standard, with the new variant beginning to appear at about the turn of the century. The airframe and engines were unaltered, but the GR4 included many avionic and computer enhancements. Most notably, its built-in sensors were supplemented by forward-looking infra-red, FLIR; this, together with night vision goggle (NVG) compatibility, permitted crews to fly 'passively' at night and low level. In other words without recourse to TFR, thereby denying the opposition the chance to detect its radar emissions. Neither FLIR nor NVGs function in cloud, but nevertheless represent a considerable increase in capability.

Other upgrades included GPS navigation and an upgrade of the Skyshadow jamming pod to Mark 2 standard, together with avionic redesign which permitted the integration of new weapons such as Storm Shadow, Brimstone and Paveway IV, as well as sensors including RAPTOR and Litening III.

31 Squadron has accumulated a mass of silverware over the years. Most is displayed in cabinets in the current crewroom, and is brought out to the tables on formal mess dinner nights. Ranging from an inter-flight tug-of-war trophy to Exercise *Royal Flush* winners cups, the artefacts cover all eras.

We'll come to many of these equipments in due course, but for now let's just consider how it must be to fly with FLIR and NVGs. Perhaps the first thing to bear in mind is that NVGs, mounted on the bone dome, are heavy and bulky. So there's the physical aspect, and with the mental fatigue from concentration added it's no wonder that Snakey Snaith's comment after his early trips was that 'I don't think I've ever worked so hard in my life.'

Bill Read puts a little more flesh on the bones:

'I often find myself glancing out of the corners of my eyes around the "goggs" at the inky blackness outside the cockpit and asking myself "What the hell am I doing?" before starting to giggle to myself at the awesomeness, yet simplicity, of the technology that is allowing me to fly at low level as if it was daylight. I often wonder what people think when driving past home base at night when we are practising landing with all the airfield lights turned off − they see an aircraft (with

The sugar shaker is one of a pair presented in 1934 by the CO, Squadron Leader C. J. S. Dearlove, and Flight Lieutenant A.J. Holmes.

its nav lights on, purely as a safety measure) descending into a blacked-out field. The world is just shades of green and black and you probably wouldn't pass the reading-the-numberplate part of your driving test wearing NVGs, but until you have done it you really cannot believe it. On a reasonably clear night you wouldn't believe the number of aircraft that are flying over the UK at night – from over Scotland you can see the aircraft in their holding patterns waiting for their turn to land at Heathrow! And if you're into astronomy – well!'

In March 2001, Thirty One was the first squadron to take the GR4 to Exercise *Red Flag*, which offered a fine opportunity to stretch its new legs. Operating with the TIALD pod and LGBs, the GR4s were the only aircraft on the 'friendly' force not to be targeted successfully by the defending SAMs.

Also with the introduction of the GR4 came a change of camouflage scheme to reflect the general move up from low-level operations to medium level. The aircraft were now finished in all-over grey, with adhesive decals replacing painted markings – the change incidentally leading to the demise of the 'painter and finisher' trade. The opportunity was taken by the Goldstars to revert to green and gold checked markings similar to those carried during the Jaguar and Phantom eras – partly, perhaps, because the speedbird wouldn't fit the new, standardized size of decal.

Defence cuts and contractions began to bite, and the RAF was moving out of Germany. Brüggen would be the last station to close, and, not long before it did so, the Association old boys made a last trip to visit their Squadron abroad. After the usual heroic bid to keep up with the social pace of the youngsters, Johnny Wheeler (a WOp/AG dating back to Java in 1945/6) reflected that they'd needed a brief lie down after the activities of a rather chilly lunchtime and afternoon. But, he reported, 'By evening we were raring to go again, and it was off to the Hotel zur Poste in Elmpt for dinner – planned to be in the garden. Thank heaven they were able to accommodate us all inside, or it might have finished us off!'

The collection includes a number of intricately constructed and detailed silver aircraft. The plinth for this BE2c bears the inscription 'Presented to 31 Squadron RAF by the Officers, 1921–1924'.

As RAF Brüggen finally closed, the author reported in *Star News*:

'An era is nearly over. Hard to believe it's coming to an end. The Goldstars are leaving Brüggen, and the RAF's leaving Germany. The last one out will, no doubt, turn off the lights. The job's been well done for half a century, and there will certainly be much written about it in due course.

'I did two tours there, and they were as different as chalk from cheese. Not because of the aircraft, for the switch from Jaguars to Tornados was, after all, just a change to another strike/attack jet. But more because of the way the change in role and world politics affected life. Friday nights in the bar just weren't the same the second time; whilst all four Jaguar squadrons had been almost permanently in residence and happy hours had always been riotous, more often than not at least two of the Tornado squadrons were on the road. And, being away so much, their people tended to look more for family time than for happy hour when they were at home.

'Low flying in Germany was completely finished – partly, and inevitably, because of the cumulative nuisance caused over the years to German villages by our aircraft. Not to mention the Starfighters and F-16s of the Dutch and Belgians.'

The end formally came on the weekend 15–16 June 2001. President of the Association and former CO Air Commodore Dick Bogg was present and sent this dispatch:

'The highlight of the weekend was the formal parade held on the Friday afternoon when the remaining squadrons marched onto the apron to the music of the RAF Central Band. After the inspection, normal drill ceremonial took an unusual turn with the presentation of *Fahnenbänden* to Brüggen's squadrons. In rather a similar way that we add battle honours to our Standards, German units are awarded a ribbon *(Fahnenband)* to theirs, and for the first time ever the German government decided to honour RAF squadrons with *Fahnenbänden*. The local German Luftwaffe general presented these on behalf of his government, and Wing Commander Paddy Teakle, the current CO, proudly collected the 31 Squadron award.

'Thereafter, the remaining Standards were paraded in front of Brüggen's personnel for the last time. As the parade headed into the afternoon sun there was a final flypast and, officially, the RAF presence in Germany was at an end. What a moving ceremony, particularly for the eleven former station commanders who had witnessed "the end".'

On 21 August the boss led a six-ship of 31 Squadron aircraft from Brüggen to their new home at RAF Marham, Norfolk. Barring the station commander's machine, which would follow later, they were the last RAF aircraft to leave the base. For the second time in its existence the Squadron would be stationed back in the UK. This last overseas stint had lasted forty-six unbroken years. 'First in the Indian Skies' – and now Thirty One had been 'Last in the German Skies'.

A strange hush must have fallen over Elmpt village. Although the British army was to take over the station, the residents would certainly miss the RAF, who had been there for the best part of fifty years. Perhaps they'd enjoy the silence, for as mentioned before the sound of jet noise must have got them down at times. Especially from the Tornado because, unusually for a tactical aircraft, it uses reverse thrust to shorten the landing roll. So not only are its take-offs deafening but also its landings.

Chapter 28

War on Terror

Not long after the Squadron's homecoming came a date which, for all who lived through it, would become impossible to forget. Tuesday, 11 September 2001 – the infamous Nine Eleven – the terrorist attack on the twin towers in New York. Events of the day had no immediate effect on Thirty One, but major repercussions would become apparent downstream. The USA had earlier declared a 'war on terror' directed against a variety of rogue organizations and states worldwide. Iraq was one of those, and further Gulf business would soon arise.

More immediately, though, a perhaps unique occasion took place in 2002 when the Association presented the current Squadron with a fine memorial stone.

Nominally to mark 31 Squadron's eighty-fifth anniversary, the stone memorial's unveiling had been delayed because of the move from Brüggen. Now that the team was settled at its new home at Marham, the time was right, and *Star News* described the event:

> 'We stood in the sunshine, the brisk April breeze rippling across manes of white hair and balding pates alike. The wind – that same wind that brushes airfields the world over – plucked at the Standard, borne proudly by the Squadron party. The Reverend (Wing Commander) Lance Clark conducted the short service of dedication, during which young and old bowed heads to remember departed comrades. They had left us in many distant theatres of conflict, and we thought particularly of those who had no known grave or other memorial. In the sunshine we sang *Jerusalem* and *I Vow to Thee My Country*; the Standard was marched off, and the formalities ended. The stone, our eighty-fifth anniversary gift, stood – a tall and everlasting memorial – outside the Squadron's new HQ at RAF Marham.'

Upwards of sixty members and families, together with a sizeable Squadron contingent, attended that fine and moving ceremony. There can be few, if any, other squadrons with such strong and enduring bonds with their former members, and the Association president took this as the theme for his opening words:

> 'The stone is, we believe, unique among RAF squadrons. I pay tribute to chairman Bryan's part in the whole project. [Retired Flight Lieutenant Bryan Toomer, who had navigated the Squadron's Ansons during its Hendon days]. His energy and persistence shone through every aspect of the gift: initiating and organizing the appeal; visiting quarries to specify and select the piece; consulting on the style and content of the plaque bearing the inscription; and pushing through the collection and transport arrangements (it weighs, literally, a ton). The committee and the Squadron also made invaluable contributions, and of course members' generosity

made it all possible. But without Bryan's leadership I really don't think it would
have got done.'

This was the first time the Association had visited the Squadron since the boys had moved
home from Brüggen, and their hosts, with their wives and their families, had gone to a
lot of trouble to make the day worthwhile. The 'old and bold' were delighted to hear the
news that boss Paddy and his Goldstar formation would have the honour of leading the
Tornado element of the RAF flypast which would be mounted in June 2002 to celebrate
the Queen's Golden Jubilee.

Returning to operations, tensions had been continuing to rise in Iraq throughout the
first years of the new century. They were to come to a head in spring 2003 in the brief
campaign known as the 'Iraq War' – or, colloquially, 'Gulf War Two'. Before getting to
that point, we'll look at events en route.

The end of 'Gulf War One' had left unfinished business. The Squadron's continued
participation on Operation *Southern Watch* and its sequels bears witness to that, but one
of the issues not mentioned thus far is Iraq's alleged possession of weapons of mass
destruction – nuclear, biological and chemical – or at least the capability and will to
construct and store such weapons. Iraq had certainly used chemical weapons during
the Iran-Iraq war, and the régime's statements on future intentions had been evasive
and ambiguous. The UN had imposed a routine of weapons inspections, and whilst it
seemed that no confirmed signs of actual WMD, or even their storage or construction,
had been found, neither was it clear that the inspectors had been given access to every
site or facility.

The evidence was inconclusive. UN resolution 1441 gave Iraq a 'Final opportunity
to comply with its disarmament obligations or face serious consequences.' But the more
cautious pointed out that this resolution, crucially, did not authorize the use of force
against Iraq. Numerous 'peace' protests worldwide reflected this belief, while the US
faced accusations that it was merely looking for an excuse to attack. Indeed, the fact that
the Americans had unilaterally listed 'Iraqi régime change' as an objective as long ago as
1998 was taken by many to be unacceptable.

Nevertheless, the US moved forward during early 2003 with attack planning, while
simultaneously attempting to shift the UN towards a position of unanimity. Enormous
diplomatic effort was expended, too, on establishing the legal basis for an attack.

It proved impossible to reach consensus and, by the time the new campaign began on
19 March, only the UK, Poland and Australia stood alongside the US. At this point, we'll
leave the politics and return to operations.

The Squadron deployed on 2 January 2003 to Ali al Salem (AAS) airbase in Kuwait on
Operation *Resinate South*, on-going policing of the southern Iraq no-fly zone. From the
outset it was clear to Paddy Teakle – as it was to most at home – that bigger things were
in the offing. AAS was already being prepared for expanded ops, and Paddy was lucky
enough to be party to the base commander's planning.

At this stage, he reports, the wider strategy still envisaged a two-pronged attack on
Iraq, with forces based in Turkey and the Gulf. Strike Command was planning for the
Marham squadrons to man Incirlik, in the north, with the Lossiemouth Wing deploying

to AAS. Indeed, ships were at that moment bound for Turkey with Marham's weapon stocks on board. Thus, Paddy was left with the dilemma of how to conduct his planned *roulement* at the end of January – and indeed with the nagging worry that Thirty One might actually be homeward bound at the very moment things got interesting. In the end, he gambled by bringing his reinforcements to theatre as well as retaining the originals, so from early February onwards he had a full complement of eight aircraft and twelve aircrews. His instinct proved correct, for Turkey never came on board and most of the GR4 effort was eventually mounted from Kuwait.

By the time the fighting started (the British side of the operation now being named Operation *Telic*), there were eighteen Tornados, thirty-six crews and over three hundred engineers at AAS, with elements from numbers II(AC), IX(B), XIII and 617 Squadrons supplementing the Goldstars. This bore echoes of the situation in which Thirty One had entered the Gulf Conflict but, until a worryingly late stage, the command structure this time was still unspecified. Then, just days before the start of offensive operations, the AOC paid a visit and told the Wing that there would be no overall commander declared – but that OC 31 was to be *primus inter pares* – in other words the lead squadron commander. How this was to be made to function was to be left entirely up to Paddy!

This might appear a fudged basis on which to plan, but Paddy did indeed manage the mixture. He decreed that they would work entirely as a Wing, and to this end designed the 'Tornado Combat Air Wing' badge which all instantly adopted. There would be no such thing as squadron shifts amongst either air or ground crew; the whole would work as one. Naturally, there were differences of opinion on this *modus operandi*, but no serious discord throughout.

On the eve of battle the Association newsletter felt moved to comment on the situation:

'The world stands poised for … we know not what. On paper, it should be possible for the UN to bring Saddam to heel. If not the UN, then the committed allies ought to be able to do the job. But there's still great unpredictability about the outcome. At this point we still hope that "armed diplomacy" will have the desired effect of solving the immediate problem without resort to conflict. We have just heard that the Squadron's tour of duty in the Gulf has been extended to six months. Our thoughts have been, and continue to be, with them and their loved ones back home. May they all be safely back together before too long.'

Almost simultaneously, just before the outbreak of hostilities proper and during what might be termed the preparation phase, Paddy and his pilot, first tourist Flying Officer Pete Bielby, were called on to drop two LGBs on an Iraqi air defence target which was threatening coalition aircraft. The *Eastern Daily Press* (Mark Nicholls, writing in Norfolk's local newspaper), latched onto the youth of the pilot in their story about the incident in its 17 March edition:

'It was a true baptism of fire for the young pilot on his first mission over Iraq. Bielby explained: "We were going on a mission to patrol southern Iraq and my aircraft was late getting airborne. It then emerged that someone else in our formation had been shot at, so we were told to bomb a selected target." Within ten minutes of crossing the Iraqi border on his first mission over hostile territory, the young pilot bombed an Iraqi air defence target at An Nasiryah. He knew that some pilots have flown eighty missions in such conditions and not attacked a target. "Before I went on that mission, I was nervous," he said: "It was so different to what I had been used to. I was quite relieved to get back".'

The crewing arrangement had ramifications, in that Pete's inexperience precluded the crew taking a leading role in the air. However, Paddy had no qualms about this, for not only was the Wing well provided with experienced airborne leaders, but the situation also permitted him to concentrate his energies on coordination of the overall effort – a task which, at times, and with several other squadron commanders in the

Paddy Teakle, with his young pilot Pete Bielby at Ali al Salem in 2003.

picture, required concentration, diplomacy and nimble footwork.

So they were all set. The synchronized land and air assaults were planned to be staged in traditional style – with the air forces first taking out the opposition's air defences. Thirty One's specialized roles were first, interdiction, and second, suppression of enemy air defences. But now the immediate requirement was for close support of ground forces. Additionally, although there were elements of dedicated recce squadrons in theatre, Thirty One's experience of the new 'RAPTOR' recce pod (they had been working with it during the preceding two months of Operation *Resinate*) meant that the Goldstars were in demand for that role, too. And air raid warnings were occurring every couple of hours for the first few days of ops, causing everybody (including the press corps) to 'mask-up' in full protective equipment for long and uncomfortable periods. So 'Scud-hunting', too, became a major priority.

In addition to the RAPTOR pod, the Wing was also introducing two other major new systems to service – the Storm Shadow stand-off missile and the Mark 2 version of the ALARM anti-radiation missile. Five roles – demanding all of Paddy's considerable powers of coordination and all of the detachment's versatility and concentration.

Ali al Salem was a small base which the RAF had set up to support recce operations. Now, as well as the Tornado Wing, a US Marine Corps force and the RAF's support helicopters were quartered there. A potential recipe for chaos. But they managed; the campaign was fought and won.

There was little Iraqi opposition – indeed intelligence had shown the Iraqi air force had gone so far as to bury a number of its aircraft. Regardless, though, the Squadron played its part in the military operation with distinction. The Wing dropped 250 precision-guided bombs including, somewhat counter-intuitively, four inert weapons. Those 'concrete' bombs were employed in areas where extreme accuracy was required in combination with minimal collateral damage – demonstrating the lengths to which the coalition went to apply exactly proportionate force.

Amongst the highs and lows, it was easy to identify the nadir. All of the Wing's personnel had been prepared for possible combat losses – but the shooting down of a IX

The big ones. Storm Shadow stand-off missiles.

And the new recce pod, RAPTOR, is also a monster.

Squadron aircraft by 'friendly' fire – a US Patriot missile – was very hard to take. It was utterly avoidable, leaving disbelief and anger amongst the Wing's emotions.

The Association did its bit again throughout by dispatching boxes of sweets and goodies to the boys in the Gulf – but were disappointed to learn that BFPO had failed to deliver them until the day before the return. Similarly with ex-Squadron Warrant Officer Peter Gipson's parcels of books and magazines, this consignment also being overtaken by events. 'Quite simply,' Peter said, 'the war was won too quickly for us!'

Association members also waited anxiously for news, and Flight Lieutenant Ben Morrell told it this way for them as he wrote for *Star News*:

'During our original flying on Operation *Resinate South* we encountered a fairly aggressive response from the Iraqi air defences. I was on the receiving end of a number of firings, including AAA and SAMs. But by flying reconnaissance with the RAPTOR pod, we were able to take pictures while over thirty miles from a target, staying out of harm's way. There then followed a period of uncertainty as diplomatic efforts continued. But on 18 March the boss called everyone together to tell us that we were going to war in two days' time.

'I could almost write a book on my experiences during Operation *Telic* (now there's an idea!) but I'll keep it short. We flew a large number of RAPTOR reconnaissance missions, locating many SAM systems and doing battle damage assessment of targets hit by the coalition. We flew many missions in support of ground troops; these were the most demanding sorties because of the targets' close proximity to friendly troops and civilians. LGBs (either Paveway II or III) were our primary weapons, while ALARMs were fired at targets in the Baghdad area.

'By the end of hostilities (twenty days later), the Squadron had flown over 600 hours. Our "freedom bird" homewards was an RAF TriStar that picked us up from Kuwait International Airport. Ten minutes into the flight one of the windows cracked, but the captain continued to Cyprus where we all had the opportunity to experience our first beer in four months while the aircraft was fixed. In the morning, with very sore heads, we re-boarded and touched down at Marham four hours later to be met by our families and loved ones. We then dispersed to the four winds for a spot of well-deserved leave.'

The following extracts from coverage in 30 April's *Eastern Daily Press* summarize the homecoming nicely:

'The broad smiles, the hugs and warm embraces – and a few tears – said just one thing; it's great to be home. For air and ground crews from 31 Squadron, it signalled the end of four long months away from families and loved ones, many of whom were at RAF Marham yesterday to meet them as they returned. This was no ordinary homecoming; this was a return from war. And that feeling underlined the strength, the warmth and the relief in the embraces. Wives and girlfriends greeted husbands and partners, and children ran out excitedly to meet fathers. It was a magical moment.

'Wing Commander Paddy Teakle spoke of his pride in the efforts of the air and ground crews who had participated in the "liberation of Iraq." "I have lived," he said, "with Iraq as part of my life for fourteen years but never set foot there. I hope one day to go there as a tourist and stay in the Baghdad Hilton." For airmen, of course, that was the euphemistic name given to where downed crews were held by Saddam Hussein's forces. For Sonia Teakle, his wife of twenty-one years, the time had been worrying. "We just get used to the situation," she said, "But when the aircraft from IX Squadron was lost it was horrendous, it was awful. There was a mix of emotions; relief that it wasn't anyone from 31 Squadron and at the same time guilt because other families were suffering".'

As with all recent campaigns, the issue of media coverage became a major one, and it must have been difficult for those commanding and fighting to have to bear the spotlight's full glare. Of course the press carried its usual quota of silly stories – 'squaddie has to buy his own desert boots' and the like – but it was good to see that the Tornado element appeared to be reported this time as having its equipment and tactics perfectly tailored to the job in hand. Audiences at home were transfixed by the pictures that unfolded on TV, and none who saw it will ever forget the BBC's John Simpson broadcasting minutes after he had been wounded and his translator killed in an attack by a friendly aircraft. Many commanders, though, undoubtedly found unfortunate the broadcast American intention to 'shock and awe' – which certainly had the potential to become a hostage to fortune.

Indeed the phrase seemed to haunt all the subsequent discussion – by politicians and press – of the campaign, its basis and its aftermath. Not least, of course, there had been no political unanimity on the use of force at this particular juncture. And, arguably, there had been inadequate planning for the post-attack situation in Iraq. But, once again we'll steer clear from those higher matters and confine ourselves to congratulating the Goldstars on an exemplary air campaign.

Both Squadron and Association were delighted by November's honours list, which saw the newly promoted Group Captain Paddy Teakle being awarded the Distinguished Service Order in recognition of his outstanding leadership of the Tornado Wing. Three other Goldstars were also decorated for their contributions. Squadron Leaders Paul Smith and Richard Hammond were mentioned in dispatches, while Squadron Leader Simon Hadley received the Queen's Commendation for Valuable Service. Later, it was announced that the Squadron would add to its record the battle honour 'Iraq 2003'.

Again we might have hoped that the job was done. Especially following democratic Iraqi elections, Saddam Hussein's capture, and his subsequent trial and execution. But the gloomiest predictions of some of the campaign's detractors were fulfilled. Factional conflict, unrest amongst the population, shortage of commodities and broken infrastructure plagued the land. It would take several years to bring stability to the country (or what was hoped, at the time, would be stability). Throughout much of that time the British army would remain in theatre, with RAF Tornados and helicopters supporting them. To those who argued that foreign forces should not be 'occupying' Iraq, it must be clarified that, by this stage, the coalition was there at the request of the new Iraqi government.

As a part of the continuing effort, the Squadron completed two Gulf deployments during 2004. The base was now Al Udaid in Qatar, which had the advantage of offering American infrastructure and security. But on the other hand Qatar was that much further from the action, and operational flights were now as long as eight hours. Indeed some aircrew flew 200 hours in three months. Missions were a mixture of border reconnaissance and 'cab-rank' type airborne standby to assist ground forces, and it was on one of the latter that the new boss, Wing Commander Al Byford, had what he described as an epiphany moment:

'Orbiting over Mosul at 2am one morning, it occurred to me that Goldstar crews seventy years earlier must have been doing something very closely related and not that far away. Now, as then, there's an element of deterrence in the work, for it seems that the bad guys have learned to associate aircraft noise with swift retribution – and the air presence is helping to keep heads down.'

Having mentioned the introduction of the RAPTOR pod (the acronym standing for Reconnaissance Airborne Pod for TORnado), it's opportune to discuss the development of air recce in recent times.

For many years there had been specialist reconnaissance squadrons. Indeed Thirty One itself, in its Canberra days, had been one such. During the Tornado's early operations, recce had been limited to specialized variants of the aircraft (Mark GR1a) operated by II(AC) and XIII Squadrons. The mid-life update correspondingly produced a recce GR4a, but the introduction of podded equipment and the plethora of regular, small operational detachments in various theatres meant that, in time, all crews had to turn their hand to the role. Bill Read clarifies the evolving situation:

'The VICON pod, about the size of a one hundred gallon drop tank, was used a great deal to monitor Iraqi forces between the two Gulf conflicts. It was succeeded by the DJRP – the digital joint reconnaissance pod – which, as its name suggests, employed video collection instead of the earlier wet film.

'In December 2001, II(AC) Squadron was tasked with bringing RAPTOR into RAF service, but such were its reliability problems that it was still an immature system when it was sent to Ali al Salem for 31 Squadron crews to fly with during Op *Telic*. Indeed a Goodrich technician was deployed in an attempt to keep the pods flying.

'The system has the capability to send imagery via a data link to a ground unit to speed up the analysis of important tasks. One RAPTOR pod could image most of the UK in one sortie, such is the capacity of the system. The problem then is how to sift all that information. There are probably not sufficient imagery analysts in the world to fully exploit the sheer amount of information that one download could generate. During *Telic*, one sortie in particular stands out in the memory. Imagery was obtained quite by chance of a very large collection of mobile Iraqi SAM systems, apparently all lined up in rows as if for a stock check. It was assumed that the equipment was being handed over between units, and a suitable "removal system" was called into action to nullify the stock check!'

Staying with sensor evolution, advances in technology over the years also produced major improvements to targeting pods. In 2010, the Tornado GR4 received the Litening III pod to replace the TIALD, which had originated during Gulf War One. Essentially, improvements to optical resolution meant that much more detail could now be seen by the crew. The pod picture may be viewed on the pilot's multi-function display as well as the back seater's, and in common with RAPTOR, its pictures may be data-linked to ground forces.

All in all, then, although the Goldstars were not nominated, in their Tornado incarnation, as a recce unit, they maintained much expertise in the role.

Back at Marham, life continued to evolve. And in spring 2006 Flight Lieutenant Ian Abson reported on a development affecting the Squadron's autonomy:

'In March we moved home. Not far in terms of distance, but it has given rise to a fundamental change in our day-to-day operation. 31 Squadron's new home is across the airfield on the north-east HAS site and is part of the move towards RAF Marham's "Tornado Wing" concept. The Goldstars have moved into new quarters, engineers on the ground floor and aircrew upstairs. Using the collective removal and DIY skills of the whole Squadron, the building now has an acceptable level of green and gold and is suitably decked out in memorabilia depicting our proud heritage. The memorial stone also had to be moved, and was rededicated in its new position at a service presided over by the station padré, in the presence of a number of members of the Association.

'The operational side is now shared with II(AC) Squadron, the two units using the same planning, briefing and debriefing facilities. The Goldstars would like to thank all the personnel of the other lot for their hard work before and during the move, allowing a smooth transition from one site to the other. A great deal of credit must also go to our own engineers, who have managed a seamless transition from line to HAS operations.

'So we're semi-joint, and it's now quite likely that a 31 Squadron pilot will fly with a II Squadron nav, be tasked by a 31 Squadron QWI and then get airborne in a II Squadron jet supported by 31 Squadron engineers. The combined effort of both aircrew and engineers has considerably improved aircraft availability.'

Simultaneously, groundcrew were awarded the newly-introduced 'combat-ready' patches which, in line with the aircrew equivalent, mark the completion of an individual's work-up. A novel recognition of what we've known all along; that a squadron is nothing without its groundcrew. And Thirty One's have always been amongst the finest.

In terms of engineering excellence, the Squadron has continually striven to improve, with ever-increasing demands for economy providing an additional incentive. An example came in 2007 when Wing Commander Dean Andrew was able to announce in his speech to the Association's annual reunion that 'We've increased engineering output by 40 per cent while reducing establishment from 135 to 115.' In response to the collective gasp from all the long-suffering ex-techies in the audience, the new boss continued: 'but the engineers don't work harder – they just work smarter!'

At times, though, management banter seemed to descend into gobbledegook. Flight Lieutenant Phil Todhunter attempted to explain to *Star News* readers a little more about the joint engineering effort mentioned above – as briefed to him by his flight commander: 'The engineers provide three aircraft for two waves when their team is flying and two aircraft for two waves when the other lot are flying. When the flow of aircraft is drawn on a white board, it resembles a hamburger. The pattern's known, of course, as the burger system.' At that point, Tod had thought it more likely that the man was describing his likely future employment when he was asked to leave the RAF, also noting that the briefing had failed to mention the gherkins.

The *Star News* editor couldn't resist commenting that he hoped readers weren't being told a whopper. He also mentioned that 'He'd need to grill Tod a little more when next we meat.'

And to prove that mumbo-jumbo remained alive and well in 2009, Wing Commander Ian 'Windy' Gale, the following boss, told Association members that he'd 'spent a full day with the Harrier force, spreading some of our LEAN love and good practice.' LEAN is, apparently, an acronym for some kind of engineering philosophy. But in view of the cuts which would befall the Harrier force just two years later, perhaps spreading LEAN wasn't such a good idea after all!

The diversification of training mentioned earlier continued through the next few years. Todhunter now tells in 2007 of a Squadron deployment to the Czech Republic:

'We set off for Exercise *Flying Rhino* to Namest Airbase. The first weekend left the Czechs wondering if they had done the right thing in letting us land! The British army ran the exercise, the first part involving us flying close air support sorties to train NATO forward air controllers.

'Squadron members were all staying in a hotel in the town of Trebic near the airbase. The town seemed to cope very well with the RAF and army detachments filling their hotels and restaurants. The middle weekend of the exercise saw most of us driving to Krakow. After an evening sampling the local brew, we had a very sobering and sombre visit to Auschwitz. Although probably not on everyone's list of tourist destinations, every person who went was glad they'd taken the opportunity to do so.'

Workup training which preceded on-going operational commitments, mainly in the context of preparation for flying operations, has been mentioned before in this volume. But the nature of the business meant that, as time went on, the Squadron also needed to be well up to speed in ground operations. Prior to the 2006 deployment, Tod described some of the Goldstars' pre-deployment training:

'Some might call Exercise *Golden Charcoal* practice bleeding, although others, such as our survival, evasion, resistance and extraction officer, Flight Lieutenant Chris Wright, would call it essential. The exercise had several aims: to allow aircrew to revise actions on ejection over enemy territory, including escape, evasion and combat search and rescue (CSAR); to best prepare groundcrew for recovery of a diverted Tornado GR4 from within Iraq; and to develop initiative and leadership at all levels.

'Following individual reinforcement training at Marham, the Squadron deployed to the local training area, some in two Merlin helicopters of the joint personnel recovery flight of 28(AC) Squadron from RAF Benson. The afternoon saw the aircrew undergoing training with Chris Wright, the emphasis being on the use of the GPS radio and on evasion and extraction techniques. This was enhanced by a capability brief by a crew from the 352nd Special Operations Group, RAF Mildenhall, whose MH-53 Pave Low helicopters specialize in CSAR.

'Meanwhile, groundcrew training continued in preparation for a situation when an aircraft has diverted in emergency to an airfield within Iraq and a forward aircraft recovery team (FART) must be deployed. Combat medics who had recently returned from a tour at the British military hospital Shaibah offered training in battlefield casualty drills. A Fuchs NBC recce vehicle demonstrated operations in chemical, biological, radiological and nuclear environments, while an EOD team conducted mine awareness training to further mitigate the significant threat still posed by mines on current operations.

'Finally, our ground liaison officer, Capt Rupert Davis, LI, carried out fighting withdrawals with sections of groundcrew armed with rifles, smoke grenades and copious amounts of cam cream sported in true RAF style. This would all prove effective as the evening part of the exercise commenced, with personnel taking part in an overnight escape and evasion exercise.

'The mission for the "downed" aircrew was to be extracted to safety as soon as possible; however they would face a formidably well-motivated hunter force – their own groundcrew! Throughout the night the aircrew endeavoured to make good their escape through a variety of methods available to them including local "agents", AWACS, and a rebel Lynx helicopter. The amount of ordnance put down by the hunter force proved too much for some aircrew who found themselves on the wrong side of engineer and ops staff weapons and one-way questions. However, most made it through the night to the final extraction by the returning Merlins.'

It's hard to avoid concluding that Tod is having us on with his acronym for the 'forward aircraft recovery team!' But not to worry, and, to confirm the incredible realism of recent training, we'll jump forward to Wing Commander Jim Mulholland's story from 'war week' in 2011.

'The team dealt with everything that was thrown at them, which included the arms and legs of 'amputees in action', a group of ex-soldiers who have lost limbs in combat. These guys use a great deal of fake blood, "losing" the limb again to test the first-aid skills of both the engineers and the aircrew.'

Tod's description of the real thing in 2006 shows just how useful pre-deployment training can turn out to be:

'The Tornado detachment at Al Udeid is well established. August was a particularly difficult time for the British army, whose operations were moving south as they handed over the provinces individually to Iraqi security forces. This meant many large, vulnerable convoys, and any offer from us of assistance was gratefully received. Although not formally tasked, any spare time airborne was used to call up British forward air controllers, who were often able to vector us toward any ongoing operations or IED incidents.'

'During the detachment an aircraft diverted into an Iraqi airfield with an engine problem. A rescue mission had to be undertaken by engineers led by the JEngO. This was the moment the Goldstars' GLO had been waiting for. Hoping for a re-enactment of his "liberation of Iraq" days during the main land war, he strapped knives, pistols and rifles to his person. After ensuring his "section" of ground crew (it couldn't be a "flight"!) was similarly attired, he set in motion the rusty wheels of the RAF transport section to get his troops onto a C-130 for the four-hour flight. On arrival, they cast rifles aside and took spanners in hand to remove the damaged engine and replace it with a shiny new one. Although the GLO was disappointed not to have been immediately mortared as he stepped off the C-130, he contented himself with becoming a mobile airfield defence back up – ably supported by the 20,000 US marines who were based there. Much to his disgust, the greatest danger he faced whilst on the ground was the sight of the stranded navigator's four-day-old underpants.'

Mention of workup exercises for operations reminds us that 'Taceval', the fearsome beast which had seemingly dominated almost every waking moment (and almost every page of this story) during the Cold War, had all but disappeared. With so many live ops occupying the RAF during later years there was very little time available for those formal evaluations. The forces were continually proving their capabilities for real, and in any case the threat against the static home base had, at least for the time being, receded.

But higher command still needed to measure the performance of its units, albeit now in deployed scenarios and in concert with allies, and exercises would have to evolve to reflect the new situation. The earliest days of this change dated back to 1994, and what gradually emerged for the Tornado force was a series of deployed Tacevals, usually mounted at now-disused RAF bases such as St Mawgan. They were very different from the original, and Robbie Low describes one such exercise:

'The forward operating base on this occasion was RAF Fairford, and the deployment comprised not just the Tornado force but also all the associated "non-formed unit" personnel who were added – ground defence, catering, ops, supply and so on. These people came from all sorts of bases and joined by bus, being "trooped in", en route exercising the real mounting station at South Cerney. These were joint operations, and we were joined for the duration by Swedish air force Gripens.

'We concentrated on day and night close air support tasking; indeed we mounted ground CAS alert for twelve hours a day. Home was a tent city constructed on a corner of the airfield – although the Swedes, probably wisely, opted to live in downtown hotels. Catering was a field kitchen – great food for such a huge deployment but short opening hours, so one had to be sharp or go hungry.

'Flying weather was poor but the exercise staff kept us busy with IED exercises and mortar alerts twenty-four hours a day. The Taceval team outnumbered the aircrew, and every day seemingly also saw some senior officer or politician, complete with entourage, requiring entertaining.

'The middle Saturday brought ground training, and on the Sunday everyone was shipped to Swindon for R&R. Not quite Las Vegas, so the older element decided that we'd rather walk the few miles into the local village for a nice pub lunch and an afternoon of beer drinking. We were arrested by the MoD plods as we walked back around the peri-track on the way home. They were completely cool about it and gave us a lift back to the accommodation!

'There were some rumours about goings-on in the shower blocks, but it turned out to be more or less legitimate – two couples in separate events, one pair married and the other two engaged to each other.

'All in all the exercise was quite unlike any Taceval I'd known before – with many signs of how times were changing. The non-formed unit personnel got a taste of military camping and the incessant alerts and alarms – but it was the old school who had experienced real Tacevals who seemed to react best to all the injects and to cope most satisfactorily. I have a feeling, though, that it was the evaluation team who learned the most.'

At last the current phase of the Iraq business seemed to be reaching a conclusion. In November 2008 the Squadron completed its last detachment to Al Udeid, and the final British combat forces were withdrawn by the following May. American forces pulled out by the end of 2011, and the earnest hope was that the troubled country could progress from there. By 2014, of course, it would become clear that those hopes had been in vain.

But that was for the future, and in autumn 2009 the Association newsletter reported that:

'Operation *Telic* is over. The Tornado GR4s are home from the Middle East for the last time, their mission supporting allied troops in Iraq complete. They first deployed in 1990 and now the job is done. We wish our Squadron well on completion of its task. But of course there's always Afghanistan ...'

Indeed there would "always be Afghanistan" – as we shall soon see. But before leaving Iraq for this particular time let's summarize the Squadron's efforts there. Starting with the build-up to the Gulf Conflict, there had been seventeen operational detachments to the Middle East in as many years, each for an average of three months. First of course there had been Operations *Desert Shield* and *Desert Storm*. Then Operation *Jural*, policing the southern no-fly zone from Dhahran as part of the coalition's Operation *Southern Watch*, had continued unchanged until, in 1997, the mounting base had moved to Al Kharj, Saudi Arabia. In 1998 the task had metamorphosed into Operation *Bolton* and moved to Ali al Salem in Kuwait. Another re-naming to Operation *Resinate (South)*, until the Iraq War, which had prompted a further redesignation as Operation *Telic*. And this, with a further move to Al Udeid, Qatar, is how it had remained until the end of the work to restore stability and infrastructure to Iraq.

Interspersed had been Kosovo, as well as a couple of detachments during 1997 and '98 to Incirlik in Turkey for Operation *Warden* – the UK's contribution to policing the northern Iraq no-fly zone. The coalition effort there was originally known as Operation *Provide Comfort*, but later Operation *Northern Watch*.

All in all a massive commitment, not just for Thirty One but for the whole Tornado force, and surely not one which could have been envisaged when the aircraft was procured during the Cold War.

Throughout these operations, defence reviews and cuts kept coming, with military-minded members of the population hoping that each would be the last. 1992 brought 'options for change', then 2005 another round.

And there was to be no respite from cuts, as 2010 brought a change of government and another defence review. Tornado and Harrier squadrons were in the sights, and it would not be overstating the case to say that the announcement of the complete demise of the Harrier force came as a shock to most. Naturally, the Tornado people were relieved, but would still suffer reductions.

Back in the 1980s the Tornado forces were huge. But since those heady days, all the F3s (the air defence variant) had been withdrawn. Already, eleven squadrons of GR1s plus an OCU at four bases had been reduced to seven plus the OCU at two stations. Numbers 16, 17, 20, 27 and 45 Squadrons had disappeared. Some of those disbandments had been announced at the most inopportune and insensitive of moments; for example, while squadrons were still in the Middle East having performed heroically in Gulf War One. Now in 2010 we were to expect a reduction of a further two. Naturally the Goldstars were worried – and so was the Association. The boss, Wing Commander Jim Mulholland, with as much behind-the-scenes assistance as could discreetly be mustered, pulled out all the stops to make our case, and was ultimately pleased to report to the Association that 'We've escaped the axe. Thirty One is the third most senior Tornado squadron in the RAF, and we are continuing your proud heritage.'

This time it was XIII and 14 Squadrons which were to disappear from the Tornado inventory, and it was stated that, by 2015, the remaining GR4 force was planned to comprise only two squadrons and an OCU. Naturally, further reviews can never be discounted, so we will not be resting on our laurels.

But nor should the nation underestimate the burden on the ever-decreasing armed forces, as articulated by boss Jim. His next words came in spring 2011, but the message reflects the general trend of the post-Cold War years:

'The Tornado GR4 is now the only capable and credible UK air-to-ground platform that can deliver the effect required on the ground. Every Tornado front-line squadron will spend eight months away on operations in the next twelve, in addition to their exercise and workup programmes; the effect on families and morale should not be underestimated. When you add the uncertainty of recently-announced redundancy into the context above, the stress which my men and women are coping with is unhealthily increasing. There is little certainty about their future, other than that it is uncertain, and many are talking openly about their concerns. This gives me a difficult management challenge because I am asking them to do more and work harder without being able to assuage their future concerns. The initial trawl for voluntary redundancy did not get the numbers required, so we are now entering a period where compulsory redundancy boards are sitting; we are asking a lot of our people at the moment.'

Amidst all this talk of reductions, a note of celebration. It came as a surprise to many to find, in 2007, that the Tornado had achieved a major milestone. Dick Bogg, Thirty One's first Tornado CO, could hardly believe it:

'The Tornado has been in RAF service for twenty-five years now, and is still going strong. BAE Systems, hitherto British Aerospace (and even earlier, British Aircraft Corporation) hosted a bash at Marham, inviting all contactable former Tornado squadron commanders. Thirty One was well represented by Bogg, Witts, Hall, Parkinson, Teakle, Low and Byford at what proved to be the "dinner of a lifetime". It was preceded by a flypast of two Tornados in close formation, without lights, in the dark, engaging reheat over the mess and climbing vertically. What a way to announce "dinner is served!" The chief of the air staff, himself a former Tornado squadron commander, presided, and a splendid evening was enjoyed by all. So now for the next twenty-five years!'

Chapter 29

Family Business

Throughout this narrative the reader may have noted that families have received no more than a passing mention. Which in a sense is right; the story has been of the Squadron, its people and its exploits. But equally, it's wrong, for nothing the serving people have accomplished has left their families untouched. And certainly nothing they have achieved could have been done without the support of their families.

The nature of family life within the military has changed enormously over Thirty One's century. In the early chapters of this story young servicemen weren't expected to have wives to worry about. George Eccles, in his memoirs, described the situation succinctly:

> 'No airman was "officially" married until he was twenty-six years of age, at which time he could receive marriage allowance. Officers were not regarded as being married until they were thirty years of age or had reached the rank of squadron leader, whichever came first.'

Certainly, no family accommodation was available at the time for those not qualified. Moreover, for an officer, early marriage could have been a decided black mark on the individual's career record.

During the Second World War everybody was unaccompanied. Families endured the blitz back home and coped as best they could while their men served thousands of miles distant in India or the Far East. Babies were born – mostly, we like to think, less than nine months after the men went abroad! Many of those offspring didn't meet their fathers until they were almost of school age.

Post-war it became the custom to marry younger, and by the 1970s there was for the first time both accommodation and full allowances for all marrieds. For most of the Germany years the Squadron's personnel led very much the family life.

But once deployed operations became the pattern in the 1990s, things began to change again. Detachments became longer and more frequent. Not by the standards of the frontiersmen, who set off by troopship for five years overseas service. And certainly not compared with those Second World War conscripts who were dispatched eastwards for unknown durations, many not to return for four years. We acknowledge, too, that these days there are mobile phones, e-mail and Skype. But nevertheless, today's detachments do bring their own pressures on the family.

The nature of the service family has itself evolved with time, with significant changes occurring in the years around the millennium. Many wives now have their own careers, which might or might not coincide with their husband's postings – and might indeed in some cases be the primary consideration. House ownership and renting off-base has become more popular, with married quarter occupancy correspondingly reducing and mess life altering. Marriage is no longer the norm, with less formal arrangements becoming common.

We have noted that the Squadron couldn't have achieved all it has without the support of the wives. But we must balance this by acknowledging that, in some circumstances, wives back home have themselves needed welfare support. Some, for example those left behind in Germany – far from family and friends while their menfolk were deployed on operations and exercise – found it difficult to cope, and an unhappy lady at home inevitably saps a serviceman's efficiency. Normally, the hugely resilient family of military wives has itself rallied around to offer the required support, and squadron commanders and warrant officers in particular have always appreciated the unseen and unpaid work put in by their own wives.

So all these factors have combined to make for an evolving pattern of squadron life over the years. But now we must modify our thinking to take into account one further social change. Because, with the increasing numbers of women serving on active units, an entirely new dynamic is afoot. At the very least, we must now adapt our phraseology to say that a squadron can't achieve all it is asked to do without the support of its 'spouses and partners'. There must also be children to consider when the women deploy, and it's true that extended families play a large part in that respect. But could it be that, nowadays, there are also 'unaccompanied husbands' to worry about when a squadron goes away on operations? An intriguing thought!

So much for the immediate relatives. But Thirty One has itself developed characteristics greater than merely those of a group of people. As Sergeant (becoming Flying Officer) Frank Johnson, an English pilot from 1944–6 who later emigrated to Australia, said:

> 'For me the Squadron was a family, such as my school, my university and my own family. It was a body of persons with common objectives and faults, and I cherish my sojourn there.'

And in due course the Squadron spawned another 'family', too. This narrative has been scattered throughout with references to 'the Association', and the tale can most certainly not consider itself complete without a little more on that august body.

To recap, the old boys who were on the Frontier during the First World War formed an 'old comrades' association. Then, post-Second World War, the Burma veterans formed their own group. By the mid-1960s the 'Thirty One Squadron Association Royal Air Force' had reached more or less its mature form, welcoming all ex-Squadron members regardless of period served.

And a flourishing body it is. The author well remembers his first contact with the Association while on the Tornado OCU course at RAF Honington as CO designate. Like other squadron commanders before him and since, he received a mysterious note inviting him to 'meet the chairman', and so it was that, in a pub in deepest Norfolk one November evening, he first met Bert Edwards.

Bert was one of the air ambulance stalwarts from Java, and over a couple of beers he enthusiastically told the story of the Association's gestation and of its good relationship with the Squadron. Naturally, he acknowledged, the ebb and flow of personalities had led relations to wax and wane with time. But throughout, the ethos of the relationship had continued and now it was at a high point.

Who could resist such an honest and impassioned approach?

Certainly, over the years many examples have arisen of the warm relationship between Squadron and former Squadron. Through the Association's annual reunions and newsletter we may illustrate the enduring comradeship and family feeling generated by service on Thirty One. But Gordon England (Dakota observer) tells of receiving a phone call which must, initially at least, have come as something of a shock:

'Among the Stanbridge crew shot down over the Kabaw Valley in 1944 was Bob Armstrong, who died some six weeks later of his wounds. His daughter Margaret was born just before the accident and rang me in 1987 having eventually found out, via the Red Cross, "who she was" (is!). The papers from the Red Cross had included a plan of a *basha* showing me occupying the bed next to her father's − and her first words on establishing contact forty-three years later were "Hello Dad!" She reckoned I qualified as the nearest thing she now has to a father.'

Some distant operational events produce feedback years afterwards. For example the following paragraph appeared in the original Thirty One history, *First in the Indian Skies:*

'In early August 1943 there occurred an unusual operation. Flying Officer Akers in FD791 was flying from Chittagong to Dum Dum when one of his passengers spotted what he took to be a dinghy and alerted the crew. Akers turned and began to search in poor visibility, locating a dinghy ten minutes later. The WOp reported the position and the aircraft circled the spot until relieved by another 31 Squadron aircraft. Captained by Warrant Officer Rutherford, this aircraft arrived and dropped supply containers to the men in the dinghy who, it had now been established, were a downed RAF Wellington bomber crew.'

And that, apparently, was that. Lucky Wellington crew. But many years later one Les Baldry, late of 215 Squadron, who now worked for the company which printed the logo on the envelopes in which the 31 Association's newsletters were distributed, got talking to ex-WOp John Overton. The subject came up of the event and they compared log books. It turned out that they had more in common than they'd guessed. Les puts a little more flesh on the bones:

'The Wellington ditched on 29 July, just short of its target − Akyab. The five crewmembers boarded the dinghy and drifted away, out of sight of the Japanese-occupied shore. After drifting for several days, early on the morning of 4 August a low-flying Spitfire came out of black storm clouds and the pilot spotted us, then departed as another monsoon storm erupted. A lone Dakota later overflew the dinghy and reported its position, resulting in another Dakota dropping containers later in the afternoon, giving us food and drink. It was a very emotional experience seeing those great white parachutes billowing down with great accuracy. Next morning the dinghy bumped ashore on an island in the Bay of Bengal.'

Having made the contact, Les Baldry presented the Association in 1992 – forty-nine years on – with a memento in the form of a painting of a 215 Squadron Wellington. Of passing interest, too, is that the bomber crew's target, Akyab, had been a 31 Squadron base the previous year and would be again in 1945.

Given the magnitude of the events many of the Squadron's people lived through, it is small wonder that some memories have a darker tinge. Johnny Graham spoke in 2007 about his pent-up feelings about Thirty One's time in Java:

'Down the years we have got the impression that it had to be hushed up and that we had done something wrong. I was there with Thirty One from January til September 1946, but we got no recognition at all. Whenever, after the war, I mentioned the trouble, I received sceptical looks. I remember one woman saying she thought Java was an island in the West Indies. At that point, you give up!'

In referring earlier to Dugald Shaw's sense that 'someone up there' was directing his flying, we also alluded to the uneasy feelings he occasionally, had about the Bekasi massacre. His daughter wrote:

'Something else I will mention, and this he only spoke of once and I know he regretted telling me and maintained it was never spoken of by either the Squadron members or any RAF people after that. It had come up, strangely enough, at a RAFA meeting in Johannesburg when someone had asked him if he was in Java at that time and Dad had nodded and walked away, obviously not wanting any further recognition given to the event. Later he spoke about a 31 Squadron Dakota going down while he was over there and the crew being butchered by the villagers. Dad had actually flown over the village and seen some of the crew alive so he knew they had survived the crash. However, when they reached the village, they were all dead. My mum had never heard him speak of it before, but she knew he was haunted by an incident. I don't know if there are any references to the incident in the records you have. Maybe I should not have mentioned it. You can delete this if you want.'

We didn't, of course, delete it. Dugald surely wasn't alone in having held his feelings pent-up for so long. And now that he was ready to talk and write about them, it helped to have comrades who would understand.

The Association itself was able to assist its veterans with related Java matters. One concern was the official commemoration of those lost in the campaign. The location of some graves was known, but not others. The events happened well after the end of the war, so for a start there was uncertainty as to who would be looking after the dead men's graves and monuments.

It was after the millennium when this question came to the Association, and research revealed the following:

'For the purposes of memorials and the upkeep of graveyards, the Second World War is deemed to have ended on 31 December 1947. The National Memorial Arboretum in Staffordshire commemorates those who died after that date, while earlier deaths fall under the aegis of the Commonwealth War Graves Commission. The only exception to that rule is that the post-war Palestine troubles, whose dates spanned the switchover, were deemed to fall into the "Second World War" category.'

So Thirty One's Java dead were looked after by the CWGC. The locations of most of the names were known. A few were commemorated by engravings on a column in Kranji

Cemetery, Singapore. Others were buried in a beautifully peaceful military cemetery in Jakarta (the current name of the city which Squadron members knew as Batavia).

But still, as late as 2005, some were unaccounted for, and this continued to cause grief to the, by then quite elderly, survivors. And indeed to the dead men's families.

One of the primary references the veterans had been using was a magnificent wooden plaque which had been carved in the somewhat primitive surroundings of the station workshops at Kemajorang some time after the worst of the unrest in Java had subsided – with, we imagine, a great deal of love and respect. It commemorated those members of 904 Wing who had died during the operation, by far the majority of whom were 31 Squadron personnel. Following the disbandment of the Wing at the end of 1946 the plaque was moved to the chapel at RAF Tengah in Singapore, where it hung until, as far as could be discovered, the RAF withdrew in 1972. Thereafter there is no further record of its whereabouts. The Association has pursued all relevant lines of enquiry: RAF maintenance units where such items are commonly stored; the RAF chaplaincy service; the British high commission in Singapore; and so on. But there's no trace. So there remained only a photograph to go on.

It eventually turned out that errors in some of the names, perhaps owing to the rather basic workshop facilities or by imperfection in the surviving photograph, were causing the difficulty. One of the 'missing' Thirty Oners seemed to be recorded on the memorial plaque as being G. J. Greenstone, but searches for records of his grave under that name had always been fruitless. Given that he had always been known to his friends as 'Gerry', there had never been any reason to search differently. But eventually detective work revealed the carved 'G' to be incorrect. It should have been a 'C', Greenstone's given names actually being Cecil Jeremiah. And there we were; with the correct information, his grave was located.

The discovery of Jerry Greenstone's grave left only one unaccounted for, but the name of the remaining missing man, Phil Boyd, defeated all searches. One day though, long after the original enquiries to the CWGC, an e-mail came with a surprising explanation. The name 'Boyd' had in fact been an alias. Although the man enlisted as such, his real name was apparently Kupinsky. And sure enough, under a headstone bearing that name in Jakarta war cemetery, he lies in peace.

Why would he have altered his name? Might there have been some German – or east-European – connection in his ancestry that he preferred the authorities not to know about? We cannot tell, but the CWGC's information provided a further element of closure to his colleagues who served in Java.

On the lighter side, in 2005 Stan Johnson enjoyed a splendidly nostalgic event at a 'We'll Meet Again' weekend:

'Dame Vera Lynn was the guest of honour, and she had earlier produced the famous photograph of herself with the Thirty

The grave which eluded detection for so long – owing to the Squadron member's change of name.

One gang in the jungle sixty-one years previously. So the organizers thought it would be a wonderful thing to invite some ex-Thirty Oners, and consequently, Johnny Ashby, Les Sumption, Cyril Frazer and our respective families found ourselves there being treated as VIPs. It certainly was marvellous, and on stage we four old-timers held hands with Dame Vera and sang *We'll Meet Again*. It was an unforgettable day. Who could have imagined, all those years ago in Agartala, that we'd be singing with Vera Lynn in Sussex sixty years later?'

Some flashbacks from the past are totally unexpected. Fred Cunnell, a navigator who served on the Squadron in 1945−6, received an interesting package through the post in the year 2000. Not only did it contain a medal, but also his royal warrant. Both well-deserved and very welcome, no doubt. The curious thing, though, was that Fred had been promoted to warrant officer in 1945! He had left the regular RAF thereafter and continued in the reserve until 1953, at which point he had been awarded the medal. This delay could all have been down to the Post Office, although the RAF's administrative organization might possibly shoulder some of the blame. It's hard to know whether to laugh or cry. Cry perhaps, for there was no back pay due. But on the other hand laughing can be the only answer – for the gong turned out to be the Air Efficiency Medal!

So what is it that singles out the 31 Squadron Asssociation from the others? Well firstly, unlike organizations such as the Burma Star Association which commemorate moments in time and which will inevitably die as those who lived those events pass on, Thirty One's Association is lucky enough to stand by the side of a live organization − the Squadron itself − which continues to provide new members. And indeed offers a continually evolving focus of interest. There's a mutual benefit: Association members are proud of what their current-day equivalents are doing; while Squadron members know they have the active support of their predecessors.

Secondly, the Association exists for all ranks and all trades. Many parallel organizations are, for example, aircrew only. And, while it is all too common for units to pay no more than lip service for the oft-quoted phrase 'our people are our most valuable asset', there can be no doubt that the mutual respect often talked about in the services is truly embodied in the 31 Squadron Association.

From early and informal reunions based around Blackpool boarding houses, through annual remembrance ceremonies by country war memorials, to formal dinners, the Association has flourished. Blessed with generous and energetic committee members who have worked in the fields of fundraising, welfare, publicity, social and memorabilia, it continues to do so.

The relationship between the Squadron and the Association has manifested itself in many ways: the much-appreciated parading of the Squadron standard at the Association's annual reunions; in the Association's provision of field targets for the Squadron's navigation competition; in the presentation by the Association of the memorial stone; and many more.

For much of this chronicle we have been indebted to those who kept the records and wrote the histories at the time. It can't have been easy on the Frontier and in the jungle. Nor can it have been simple to keep track of the Squadron's official business while wars proceeded and moves occurred – witness the incidents we've recorded earlier of the loss and then mysterious reappearance of the official Badge, and of the discovery in 1945 that all the records from 1938 had been mislaid. But that events were recorded at all was down to individuals. Often pressed men, no doubt, but from time to time a more willing volunteer would emerge. Here's a story by one such, told many years later by Bob Gillin, a Canadian navigator from Ontario. It was entitled 'making history'.

'Late in 1944 I was authorized in DROs to put up my second ring. That same morning Flight Lieutenant Fairweather, our adjutant, called me into his office. "As of today, Gillin, you are the Squadron historian." I was delighted. I might have got some jo-job like mess secretary. I knew nothing about being a historian, but I was given a highly competent and very agreeable corporal who taught me what I needed to know. He had office space, two wide-carriage typewriters (I could type a bit) and a pad of forms on which to record the Squadron's daily activities. Someone apparently wanted to know how many pounds of rice, how many rounds of 25-pounder shells, how many mules, etc the Squadron transported each day – and we recorded that information.

'Two pleasant memories of this assignment remain with me to this day. The first is that, in the eight months or so that I did it, I didn't have to record the death of a single Squadron member or the loss of a single aircraft.

'The second is that I learned something that was applicable to me personally. In the month-end summary, there was a space headed: "commanding officer's estimate of morale" – or something like that. I took the sheet to Wing Commander Altman, who looked at it for a moment and said: "Gillin, you've been here a lot longer than I have. You write it and I'll sign it." I've always been grateful for that order. It made me think about what makes an intricate organization like a squadron function at peak efficiency. Prior to joining Thirty One in July 1943, my pilot John Aldrich and I had been under-employed at another unit – which had been an unhappy time. What a contrast with Thirty One. We were flying to airstrips code-named "Aberdeen", "White City" and so on in the Arakan, two sorties a day, two days out of three. Nobody had time to complain. So I learned that high morale is a by-product of being busy in a worthwhile job.

'Anyway, on days when I wasn't flying I helped my corporal type up the records, and began to discover snippets of Squadron history. I probably bored the fellows in the mess to the point where someone suggested "Why not put together those bits of history? Some of us would be interested." I did, and also typed up a copy of an old Squadron song. It comprises twenty-five verses, of which this is typical:

"At the crack of dawn we stifle a yawn and leap to our latest assignment;
Risking our lives – taking other men's wives to a suitable place of confinement!
So we're off like a flash on a desperate dash to save some poor girl's consternation;
Of producing a child – in surroundings as wild – as a godforsaken hill station".'

Gillin was a schoolteacher both before and after serving with the RCAF, and was with the Squadron until May 1945. There's something in the way he recounts his story that demonstrates a rather special understanding of humanity. And, incidentally, the CO's reported words show wisdom and insight, too. Certainly, with people like these serving

The Canberra generation restore one of their own at Newark Air Museum, just beside the A1 in Nottinghamshire. The initial state of this ex-81 Squadron PR7, WH791 was daunting for the team of volunteer enthusiasts Steve Innes, Dave Brackley, Paul Figes and Dave Morgan.

A final and most satisfying touch – Terry O'Halloran unveils the Gold Star. Terry is the vice-chairman of the Squadron Association, and the driving force behind the restoration.

on Thirty One, it is small wonder that not only were the deeds special but so was the ethos.

To round off this gallop around peripheral aspects of 31 Squadron's life, here are a couple of stories to illustrate links with former members.

Curiously, 31 Squadron's first Canberra PR7, WT509, was still in service after the millennium. Fellow Marham Squadron, 39, which operated primarily the PR9 variant, had 509 towards the end of its life, serving as a 'Christmas tree' by providing spares for the Squadron's T4 aircraft. One or two of the Goldstars' ex-Canberra men were very keen to see 509 preserved, and indeed for a while it seemed that it would become a gate guardian either for the station or for 31 Squadron. But in the end the plan proved impracticable; such had been the volume of spares robbed that too little of the aircraft remained.

But that didn't deter our Canberra men. A hulk at Newark Air Museum required some TLC and, in return for some project management and a lot of elbow grease, Terry O'Halloran acquired the right to repaint it and renumber it as WH792. Restored by a dedicated team it now proudly masquerades at the museum in full 31 Squadron markings.

Secondly, and in a neat link with the past, a twenty-first century Goldstar GR4

And now the aircraft is proudly displayed as 31 Squadron's WH792. The team celebrates a good job done.

navigator (or more correctly these days, a WSO – a weapons system officer) delighted the old-timers by finding himself a most appropriate secondary duty as regular crew on the Battle of Britain Memorial Flight's Dakota. Flight Lieutenant Jim Furness tells of 2012's flypast in honour of HM's Diamond Jubilee.

'Strong headwinds, low cloud and rain showers threatened to call a halt to the proceedings. The planned groundspeed for the fly-past was 150kts, but the poor old Dak tends to top out at around 152kts airspeed! So any headwind over 2kts would mean that we would be off groundspeed. The only option was to leave the hold early and don't get late. All well and good, but when leading in a big formation there is only so slow/early you can go. 'Doglegs,' I hear you cry. Yes, all well and good, but you can't bumble around Wapping and Hampstead Heath losing time, especially whilst dragging a formation around. So you take stock of the wind and leave the hold and get busy with the mental gymnastics.

'Our DC-3 leaks like a sieve and, when forced to fly through rain, water pours in just below the windscreen, soaking one's legs. I barely noticed this as I struggled to pick out our lead-in features. We punched through the squall with four minutes to go to find London laid out before us, pretty much bang on track. It sounds blasé, but finding the Mall is a piece of cake when you know what to look for. You might think that Tower Bridge, Parliament and Big Ben must be obvious, but from above they're really not that prominent. Before you say it, what about the Shard and the Gherkin? Yes, they are pretty noticeable, but way off track, so for the purposes of today's trip they weren't much use apart from signalling that it was indeed London we were looking at. The big feature is the river Thames; even from the relatively low altitude of 1500ft it clearly bends away to the south showing the north side of Victoria Embankment. Hungerford and Waterloo bridges point out the Strand and from there you just follow straight ahead to the Mall and Buckingham Palace.

'The crowd was incredible. I could have sworn you could hear them over the noise of the engines. As we turned north I looked back to see the Red Arrows painting the city red white and blue, in stark contrast with the grey overcast. The old Dak had given it all she had and got the job done – as she always had. It was one of the proudest moments of my career to date.'

Flight Lieutenant Jim Furness, a Goldstar Tornado navigator, moonlights with the Battle of Britain Memorial Flight, flying the Dakota. Here, he seems happy that he's got his massive formation 'on track and on time' for HM the Queen's 2012 Diamond Jubilee flypast down the Mall and over Buckingham Palace.

To close this chapter, and without wishing to descend too far into sentimentality, a couple of final anecdotes. First, a very touching tribute paid by Horace Welham several years ago to a departed friend:

'Sadly, *Star News* has reported Corporal Jack Webster's departure to number one hangar. I was lucky enough to have known him both during and after the war. He was always known on the Squadron as "Old Jack", even though he was probably no older than the rest of us. It was his walk and his deportment; he appeared to be flat-footed, moving with shoulders and head slumped forward as though he was guiding a plough. He was a Brighton lad, as was our Squadron warrant officer, Dusty Moore – who did his best not to allow Jack anywhere near any respectable parade he was taking. But Jack never altered. Always a cheeky grin as he slouched along. A kind, generous and lovely gentleman.

'Oddly, we all thought, Jack married a professional dancer. In fact Vi was a dance teacher and Jack would be roped in as her assistant in teaching ballroom and sequence dancing. He would say nothing, but as her partner he would demonstrate the steps as well as putting on records for the music. My wife Marjorie and I were among their many pupils, and we had many pleasant times at their classes and Saturday dances.

'The note in *Star News* brings my dancing days flashing back and I can see old Jack putting on the music while Vi waits, perfectly poised, arms and head correctly aligned. Then Jack shuffles, flat-footed, to the centre of the dance floor with that permanent smile on his face. We all loved him. But then he was a Thirty Oner.'

And finally, the ethos is summed up by these brief, informal and heartfelt words spoken at the reunion dinner in 2010 by Ken (Taff) Evans, a Dakota WOp/AG:

'We're old and weary. But I'd like the Squadron youngsters here to know that when we wake up on reunion weekend and look in the mirror, we see again that eighteen-year-old we used to know.'

Taff's words that evening were, quite rightly, greeted with warm and supportive applause.

Chapter 30

In Caelum Indicum Ultimus

As this story moved through the conclusion of the Iraq operations in 2008, we made the comment that another task loomed on the horizon. And almost immediately, Tornados began to relieve Harriers in Afghanistan (those same Harriers which, barely a year later, were to disappear from the inventory following defence cuts).

This chapter's title could be accused of being misleading in the sense that Afghanistan is clearly not India. But there are nevertheless justifications. First, by some definitions, Afghanistan lies within the Indian sub-continent. Second, operations in connection with the so-called 'war on terror' spill over the Pakistan border. Not, as far as we know, UK operations – but there's nevertheless no doubt that the current-day Squadron is very conscious that its former bases and operational areas in the old North-West Frontier lie barely a stone's throw distant. And finally, the original BE2, Armstrong Whitworth and Brisfit aircraft operating from their Frontier stations did, on many occasions, conduct missions into Afghanistan. So there is much in common and, as we shall shortly see, even the natures of the operations have uncanny similarities.

A word of background to this twenty-first century commitment. Afghanistan has, seemingly, always been in conflict. Long before the three British wars of the nineteenth and early twentieth centuries, tribal factions had struggled for armed supremacy. Early Thirty Oners became familiar with the scenario, with periodic skirmishing continuing up until the time the Squadron left the Frontier in 1941.

During the Cold War, Soviet–US rivalry manifested itself in competition to build Afghan infrastructure. Indeed it is said that the Americans constructed Kandahar's airfield, while the Soviets built Kabul's. The Soviet Union's interest was driven by its desire for access to the oilfields of the Persian Gulf, and in support of this aim the USSR fought a ten-year conflict in Afghanistan starting in 1979. The US responded by arming and financing Mujahideen fighters. During that period the Soviet air force operated from Kandahar airfield, which was severely damaged.

Following the Soviet withdrawal there was relative quiet. In 1994, though, the Taliban challenged Afghanistan's Islamic government by taking Kandahar. Kabul followed in 1996.

When introducing the USA's 'war on terror' earlier, we mentioned a variety of rogue organizations and states worldwide. One such was the Islamic group Al-Qaeda, which had also set up a base in Afghanistan in 1996. The US believed that Al-Qaeda's leadership, including Osama bin Laden, bore responsibility for Nine-Eleven, and they demanded then that Afghanistan's Taliban government hand them over.

This did not happen and US forces invaded Afghanistan in October 2001; by November the Taliban had been chased from Kabul. Further American action continued through

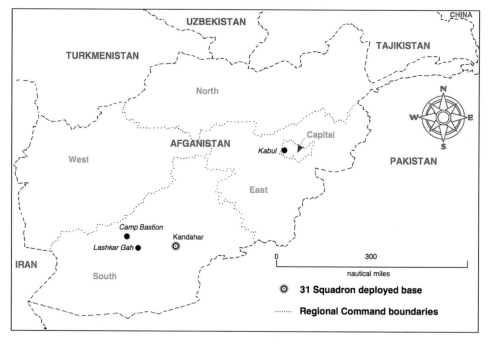

Map 12: No.31 Squadron operations in Afghanistan, 2009–2014.

the turn of the year in the mountains of the Tora Bora before, it was believed, Osama bin Laden crossed the border into Pakistan.

From 2001 onwards, with Hamid Karzai's new government backed by the International Security Assistance Force (ISAF), which had in turn been established by the UN, the task has been to attempt once more to bring stability to the country. The hope was that a stable and democratic Afghanistan would no longer provide a haven for terrorism. In this endeavour NATO soon took the lead, training a new national police force as well as a standing Afghan army. British forces operated mainly in the south of the country, with Harriers in theatre from 2004 as well as a large force of support helicopters and other aircraft. British army units have borne more than their fair share of the burden since, suffering numerous losses and terrible casualties.

Even before Thirty One was deployed to its new theatre, the Squadron had a 'mole' in the ISAF HQ in the shape of former boss Air Commodore Paddy Teakle, who, in early 2009, gave Association members an idea of ops from the main base:

'The scale is breathtaking, and Kandahar has become the busiest single-runway airfield in the world, with nearly 5,000 movements a week. When you also consider the complexity of mixing heavy transport aircraft with fighters, helicopters and unmanned air vehicles you can appreciate the challenge. Not exactly Gatwick standards; not least, I don't suppose they have many instances of goat strikes at Gatwick!'

Thirty One was the second GR4 squadron to pick up the new commitment in the Goldstars' historic theatre. Flight Lieutenant Mark Thompson provided *Star News*, in 2010, with its first report from Operation *Herrick*:

'Helmets and body armour are the order of the day during the approach to land in the TriStar, which reminds us we will be living close to the action. Having been used to the orderliness of Al Udeid, the ramshackle nature of Kandahar airfield is something of a surprise. Very few of the base roads are metalled so, when it rains, the fine dust that pervades the place turns to sludge. Fortunately, for the first two-thirds of our time the skies were clear, though this made for some chilly nights.

'The fine conditions have been a blessing for flying; with the highest ground reaching over 22,000ft it's comforting to see the mountains we're flying level with. The scenery is stunning, but with barely any vegetation it's an unforgiving environment down there. As soon as we launch, we are aware of how busy the airspace is. The lower levels are full of rotary and unmanned aircraft, there are transport aircraft all over the place, and multiple fast jets all trying to find a usable bit of space to support the troops. The fast-air types include B-1s, A-10s, F-15s, Belgian and US F-16s, and French Mirages. Add the myriad tankers required to support this amount of air power and we get some pretty crowded skies.

'The Tornados have been supporting everyone, from Canadians, through Italians to the Polish. The early days were pretty quiet; however, a few shows of force kept people on their toes and some confirmed IED finds kept everyone's spirits up. The imagery from the RAPTOR pod is much requested, so these missions provide some of the best support available to ground forces.

'While similar procedurally to the last years of Iraq ops, Afghanistan has featured much more activity on the ground. We're likely to be pulled off planned tasking while airborne in support of a developing troops-in-contact situation. This really gets the heart pumping as we have to quickly assess a rapidly-changing situation, with friendly forces asking for protection. What with working out what's happening on the ground with the help of a sometimes-agitated JTAC, organizing often-congested airspace, reorganizing air refuelling plans, weapon-to-target matching, and evaluating whether you are cleared to strike within the rules of engagement, and if so under which one, we're pretty glad to have two in the jet and four brains in the formation.'

The newspapers, including the serious press, gave the Squadron's efforts considerable coverage. But instead of concentrating on the operation they homed in on an aspect which picked up on something new for the Goldstars. Women in the cockpit!

This development had been coming for some time of course, but the press loved the angle that Thirty One's team in theatre boasted an all-girl crew in nav Squadron Leader Nikki Thomas and her pilot Flight Lieutenant Jules Fleming. The *RAF News* reported that 'The RAF's only female Tornado pilot in Afghanistan is just one of the boys.' Nikki reportedly told them that 'when we are air-to-air refuelling, the tanker crews are a lot chattier with us than with the guys.' So much for communications security, then!

Anyway, the *Sunday Times* had the two ladies' story on the front of its last News Review of 2009, reporting that 'Nikki gossips on the phone to her sister about boys, shoes and bombs.' The article told how she had the role of Squadron warlord, and mentioned that she is the only female Tornado-qualified weapons instructor. The reporter, unsurprisingly, probed whether the job required aggression and macho behaviour, and Nikki's reply was thoughtful: 'Aggression is certainly not a character trait I would look for in a pilot or a navigator. I think being competitive – mostly with yourself – and always aiming high is important, but so is being level-headed.'

Wise words indeed, amongst the journalistic froth.

The nature of the flying in Afghanistan is also thought-provoking. Many years ago the Goldstars were known as an 'army co-operation' squadron, as evidenced by their first official Badge. Although a number of other squadrons so-named have retained the 'AC' in their titles, Thirty One's went when the original badge disappeared in the fire at Comilla, India. When the replacement badge was issued it lacked the 'AC' endorsement, presumably reflecting that the Squadron had, in the interim, changed role – through bomber and transport to recce. But even though not formally named now, there is no doubt that much of Thirty One's post-Iraq work has been pure 'army co-operation'. Whoever could have envisaged the Tornado being employed in that role when it was first designed and introduced as a Cold War strike aircraft?

Strafing with the 27mm cannon in 'shows of force'? That must have been a long-odds bet, too. Incidentally, the insurgents learned quickly; often a very fast, very low pass would be sufficient to deter and disperse them.

Nowhere are the parallels better illustrated than in the 1930s writings earlier in this story by Bertie Mann, as exemplified by one the reader might recall:

> 'Operations mostly concerned the maintenance of safe transit by road of troops and supplies, but frequent patrols were mounted to discover and chase hostile tribal incursions, and to investigate or quell any local uprising. [ ] The recce pilot would also check all bridges and culverts were intact, for the tribesmen regularly brought them down. A favourite trick of the rebels was to fill an empty 50 cigarette tin (discarded by the British in large numbers from "issue cigarettes") with wet picric acid explosive and bury it in the sand where troops would pass. The explosive dried in the hot sun and the makeshift mine was ready to blow a soldier's foot off.'

How sad it is that IEDs continued to kill and maim British troops eighty years later. But how wonderful that the Goldstars' amazing new recce capabilities have enabled the detection of so many threats and the prevention of further loss of life.

It's on operations that the engineers show their full worth. Here's an extract from a citation awarded to Thirty One's team by AOC 83 EAG following that first Squadron Afghan deployment:

> 'The 31 Squadron engineering team, commanded by Squadron Leader Kiley Pescott and supported by Warrant Officer Ady Betts, with a management team known as the 'diamond 9', have served on the Tornado detachment since 13 October 2009. They have ensured a flawless 100 per cent delivery of aircraft to meet both the flying programme and ground alert serials for two and a half months. This amounts to more than 310 sorties flown without a break and the number is still rising. A variety of uncontrollable factors conspired to deflect them from their goal. They were subjected

to rocket attacks, no-notice requirements to launch outside ground alert hours, day and night scrambles and the vagaries of the Afghan weather.

'This flawless delivery was no mere statistical achievement; every sortie was classified as a "duty carried out". Additionally, sorties curtailed for weather or other factors, or aircraft forced to return early because of technical issues, were consistently replaced with a spare in the correct role fit and in good time to fly a replacement mission so that ground forces received the air support they required This outstanding effort undoubtedly saved lives and was an effort not lost on many soldiers and marines, who have been unstinting in their praise for the Squadron's contribution.

'The focus and leadership of the engineering management team at all levels, combined with their genuine care for those under them, was matched by a highly skilled and motivated team across both shifts who demonstrated a total commitment to success. [ ] This motivation and collective desire to deliver air power in support of the Afghan campaign is what marks this achievement out as a true team effort, with personnel at all levels genuinely responsible for an outstanding period of success.'

A marvellous tribute to a great bunch of airmen. 'EAG', by the way, stands for 'Expeditionary Air Group'. The RAF has, in view of the many overseas operations underway in recent years, reincarnated a few of its old formation numbers, 83 EAG among them. It's also of note that the Kandahar unit is known as 904 Wing – the very same Wing of which Thirty One was a component in Java during the 1945–6 RAPWI operation.

During the first decade of the twenty-first century the GR4 was equipped with an updated suite of weapons which made a perfect match for its brilliant new avionics: Storm Shadow, Brimstone and Paveway IV. Taken together these offered a step change in precision capability against a range of static, mobile, soft and hard targets.

The first, Storm Shadow, we have already met in Iraq during the 2003 conflict. Brought into service by 617 Squadron as CASOM (Conventionally Armed Stand-Off Missile), by the middle of the decade it was in widespread service across all the Tornado squadrons.

The second new weapon, Brimstone, began life as an advanced anti-armour weapon – a cluster bomb replacement. The Brimstone weapon system centres on radar-guided anti-armour missiles with warheads optimized to defeat the most modern battle tanks. Number 31 Squadron was the lead squadron for this new capability, tasked with developing front-line employment procedures. Two of the central figures in this work were the Squadron's weapons flight commander, Squadron Leader Jim Mulholland, and the Air Warfare Centre's SO2 Weapons, Squadron Leader Rich Yates. We have also, of course, already met the two of them: Jim, as a wing commander, commanded the Goldstars during its 2009/10 Afghan deployment; Rich, on his fourth tour on Thirty One, would be at the helm for the 2013 deployment. Here, he tells more of Brimstone:

'The first version of the weapon entered service in 2005 after highly successful test firings in the USA. Highlights of the trials programme included weapons released by 31 Squadron crews as part of the operational evaluation. In 2007 a second version of the weapon was introduced: the "Dual Mode Seeker" (or DMS) Brimstone. This combined the selectivity of laser guidance with the terminal accuracy of an active radar seeker. In Iraq, Afghanistan and Libya its precision made it very useful in the contemporary operating environment.'

As we've already seen, in this new world of warfare being conducted in the media spotlight and with world opinion deciding whether campaigns might be continued or not, avoidance of collateral damage is in many cases of paramount importance. So it's unsurprising that the last of the three new smart weapons is the Paveway IV, a small, 500lb class laser-guided bomb. It entered service on Tornado GR4 in 2009, bringing capabilities unseen in previous generations of bombs, such as airborne fuze delay selection and trajectory definition. With a GPS guidance option as well, the weapon overcomes one of the disadvantages of pure laser guidance, the need for clear weather. All this allows crews to tailor the weapons effect to a given target and to limit collateral damage. These characteristics have been key to the success of operations in Afghanistan.

Given the advent of RPAS (often known as UAVs or drones, but more recently 'remotely piloted air systems'), any discussion of whether two-seat aircraft are more effective than single-seaters may now be almost superfluous. But it's still worth recalling that the Tornado replaced the single-seat Harrier in Afghanistan. Here, we record the views of Goldstar pilot Flight Lieutenant Nick Cogley, who has flown both single and two-seaters who commented on the question when writing in the book *Jaguar Boys*:

'The Tornado has rightly been the platform of choice for the crucial roles that have characterized the needs of the Afghanistan conflict and the unexpected requirement for intervention in Libya. There is no doubt that operating as a part of a crew in both of these operations has renewed my belief in the power of effective teamwork. The pilot is able to concentrate on flying the aircraft, while the WSO can concentrate fully on the battlefield sensor picture, which is becoming ever more complex. Indeed, the complexities of modern rules of engagement mean that it may often require more than one mind to make the correct decision when it comes to weapon delivery. Once that often-critical decision to release a weapon from the aircraft is taken, the dynamics of a moving target mean that while the pilot focusses on manoeuvring the aircraft quickly into the weapon release basket, the WSO is able to track that target without distraction from before launch to after impact.

'Having said all that, the Tornado's replacement is to be a single-seater, so we can only hope that the promised further avionic advances prove operationally effective.'

In passing we've mentioned Libya. Encouraged by recent experience of armed interventions in areas of the world where trouble was threatening Western interests, NATO nations in 2011 resolved to act against Colonel Gaddafi's régime. The UK committed GR4s and Typhoons to fly a series of missions, with GR4s flying a number of extraordinary round trips from Marham to North Africa. Later, the joint force was based forward at Gioia del Colle, near the heel of Italy. Because of Operation *Herrick* commitments, 31 Squadron was not heavily involved in these operations. However, the Squadron did provide crews and engineering support to RAF Marham, which conducted Storm Shadow raids during the conflict. As Rich Yates explains, this was concurrent with 31 Squadron operations over Afghanistan:

'One vignette shows the flexibility of the modern Tornado crew. Flight Lieutenant Dave King conducted a Storm Shadow raid against Libya in August 2012 from

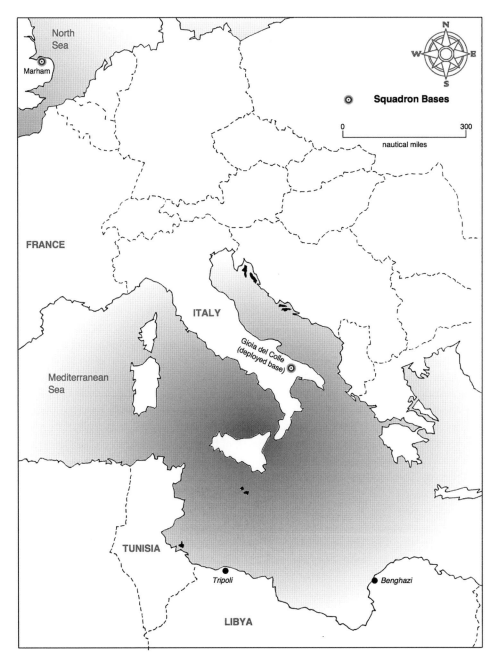

Map 13: Tornado operations against Libya, 2012. This was not a 31 Squadron operation, although 31 Squadron personnel and aircraft augmented other units. It is instructive to contrast the distances involved with those envisaged (map 8) for Tornado missions in the aircraft's early days.

RAF Marham, before returning home via a refuelling stop in Italy. Thirteen days later he was conducting a low-level show of force with us to deter insurgents in Helmand Province in Afghanistan.'

From a military viewpoint the short Libyan campaign was outstandingly successful, not least in seeing Storm Shadow and Brimstone coming to maturity. The régime was toppled, but we must leave the long-term political outcomes for others to gauge.

Anniversaries and ceremonial occasions continued. In 2011 came the twentieth anniversary gathering of those who had fought 'Gulf War One' from Dhahran. The following year saw a 'Tornado thirtieth' dinner. And in 2014, 31 Squadron was presented at RAF Marham with its third Standard. The reviewing officer, Air Marshal Greg Bagwell CB CBE MSc RAF, was most appropriately chosen; as Flying Officer Bagwell, he had been the Standard bearer in 1986 at the presentation of the new Standard's predecessor. That's the way to 'keep it in the family'!

It could either have been a supreme coincidence or a piece of smart organization by those who have an interest in the symmetry of history. Did the staffs have tidy minds – or was it pure chance? Whichever was the case, 31 Squadron found itself rostered, in September 2014, for Afghanistan on what would be the RAF's final fast-jet deployment there, covering the withdrawal of British troops from theatre. 'First in the Indian Skies' – and now 'Last in Afghan Skies'; army co-operation work – now, as then. A neat ending to the story.

By this time insurgent activity in the country was at a relatively low level. Whether as a result of successful operations by the coalition and the Afghan forces which had been trained and organized to replace them, or whether the Taliban were simply content to bide their time until they had the field to themselves again, we cannot say. At any rate it came as little surprise to the Goldstars that their spell in theatre this time was quiet. Only one live weapon had to be expended, and much of their effort was devoted to clearing up after what had been a long and arduous detachment for the British forces in general, and for the RAF Tornados in particular.

This is not the place to discuss the political merits and demerits of dispatching British forces to Afghanistan in the twenty-first century. Nor to enter the vexed discussion of whether or not our ground forces were adequately equipped for what turned out to be a colossal and sustained anti-guerilla operation. Suffice it to say that, for now, Afghanistan is a safer place for its population and also one less able to harbour anti-western terrorist organizations. And also to note that the Tornado force has, to all appearances, conducted itself immaculately. Once again, the air task given to the Goldstars – and to the RAF in general – has been well done.

Camp Bastion, the major ground base, closed down at the beginning of November, and Thirty One's final days at Kandahar included a moving Remembrance Day ceremony attended by HRH Prince Harry. Then, once again, they were the last to leave the sub-continent, turning off the lights before they flew their six GR4s, via Akrotiri, to Marham – arriving on 15 November. Yet another chapter in Goldstar history had been written. The media made much of it, and it was good to see that they picked up on Thirty One's connection with an event almost a century earlier, the Third Anglo-Afghan War.

The Tornado force returned to a contingent posture, one that had been held in parallel to Operation *Herrick*. As well as operations during those last years, the Squadron had conducted a number of exercises, including one at a location euphemistically referred to as 'somewhere in the Middle East'. Indeed the aircraft were ferried back from Kandahar via, as well as Akrotiri, this mysterious location. The political sensitivities of the various nations in the area, and indeed of those with interests in the area, must be respected, for it is a region which continues to seethe beneath the surface. And evidence of that had already been emerging in a further eruption.

Let's just remind ourselves that, in autumn 2009, the Association newsletter reported thus:

> 'Operation *Telic* is over. The Tornado GR4s are home from the Middle East for the last time, their mission supporting allied troops in Iraq complete. They first deployed in 1990 and now the job is done. We wish our Squadron well on completion of its task. But of course there's always Afghanistan …'

Words which tempted fate, perhaps, and sure enough, in late 2014, we had cause to re-issue the modified piece. All that was required was the transposition of a couple of words, and the new paragraph read as follows:

> 'Operation *Herrick* is over. The Tornado GR4s are home from Afghanistan for the last time, their mission supporting allied troops in Afghanistan complete. They first deployed in 2009 and now the job is done. We wish our Squadron well on completion of its task. But of course there's always Iraq …'

Yes, it was Iraq again. In summer 2014 an organization whose name translates variously as IS (Islamic State), ISIL (Islamic State of Iraq and the Levant), or ISIS (Islamic State of Iraq and Syria) made rapid advances into large stretches of Iraq. The target was chiefly the Kurdish areas of the north, although the Baghdad government in general looked vulnerable; indeed the newly reconstituted Iraqi army proved incapable of resisting IS forces. Apparently well-funded and organized, IS was also active in adjacent Syria, where insurgents had for some years been attempting to unseat the régime. The overall aim now appeared to be to create a 'Caliphate', a cross-border Islamic state, and the fighters employed brutal practices, particularly against non-Muslims who got in their way.

While the western attitude to the Iraqi government was broadly supportive, the position on Syria was less clear; certain western governments had themselves been supporting anti-régime forces, some of which now appeared to be IS-aligned. NATO member Turkey, abutting both Iraq and Syria, anxiously watched trouble brewing just across its southern border, an additional complication being that its own Kurdish population regarded itself as one with the Iraqi Kurds who had been among victims of the fighting. Overall, an incipient conflict with massive potential for overspill; and in the first instance a situation from which thousands had fled, creating an immediate refugee problem.

A substantial international coalition began to form, with the UK's initial commitment being Tornados. These would be used in the reconnaissance role over Iraq to identify both insurgents and refugees. In August, when the call came, OC 31 Squadron was acting station commander at RAF Marham, so he was right at the heart of the planning. Six Goldstar aircraft deployed on Operation *Shader* to RAF Akrotiri, in Cyprus, together with a Voyager tanker/transport aircraft. They set up the initial routine and carried out the first week's operational flying, before handing over to another squadron. This permitted Thirty One to return to Marham to complete preparations for their planned, final Afghan deployment.

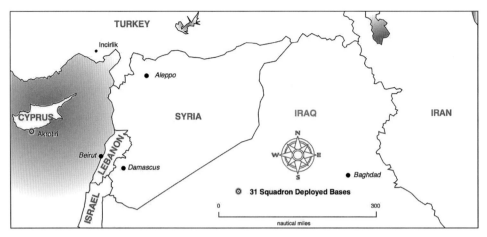

Map 14: Tornado operations in response to Islamic State activity, 2014–15.

As the politics of the coalition developed, UK forces later began to be involved in offensive missions over Iraq using both GR4s and RPAS. At the time of writing, other members of the coalition are already conducting air missions over Syria, so we wait to see how things develop. At any rate the signs are that this could again become a long mission, and 31 Squadron's next Operation *Shader* deployment ran from February 2015. While Akrotiri continues to be the deployed base, it lies far from the operating area, and one could imagine a closer location being sought. Incirlik, in Turkey, last used by the Goldstars during Operation *Northern Watch* in 1997/8, could be an option, although the current Turkish political position may preclude its use this time.

Alongside all the operational work, the centenary approaches, with preparations continuing. Rich Yates, having completed his tour in command, handed over in December 2014 to Wing Commander James Freeborough, and it is James who will lead the Goldstars through their one hundredth year.

A number of celebratory events are planned, including the opening of an ambitious museum of the Squadron's history to house much of its accumulated memorabilia. But chief amongst the milestones will be 15 October 2015's unveiling and dedication, on the day of the one hundredth birthday, of a monument. Presented to the Squadron by the Association, this is sited at the National Memorial Arboretum at Alrewas, Staffordshire, and the guest of honour at its dedication will be the Squadron's senior living member, Air Marshal Sir Stuart Peach, KCB CBE ADC BA MPhil DTech DLitt FRAeS RAF. Sir Stuart, who served with the Goldstars as a young navigator back in the Tornado's early days and subsequently commanded another Tornado squadron, currently holds the post of Vice Chief of the Defence Staff. Given that his career has seen the Tornado move from infancy to old age, it is most fitting that he should preside at an event which will occur during Thirty One's thirty-first year with this fine aircraft.

The monument's dedication is planned to be marked by a flypast, not only of Tornados but by those other Squadron icons, the BE2c and the Dakota. Altogether a treat for Goldstars old and young, and we confidently predict that more than a few eyes will be, at the very least, moist.

We've come a long way in a century, from BE2c to Tornado.

And the crews have changed a lot too. Flight Lieutenant Sasha Sheard, who opened our story, walks out for an operational mission over Afghanistan in 2013. *Crown copyright*

Chapter 31

Crystal Ball

T his volume simply must conclude with a chapter 31. But what should it contain? The story we've told is of 31 Squadron's history, and there's normally no place in a history for speculation on the future. The road ahead is simply too unpredictable. But let's, nevertheless, have a go.

In general we like to think that, as civilization advances, dialogue and diplomacy will tend to reduce the need for armed forces. But the end of the Second World War didn't bring the expected calm to Europe. Nor did the cessation of the Cold War yield the hoped-for peace dividend. Harmony in the Middle East seems as far away as ever, with the rise of militant Islam seeming to be leading us towards more, rather than less, conflict. So there is absolutely no reason at present to believe that the nation needs fewer defence forces – and thus we should feel confident in wishing our Squadron continuing good fortune for the future.

The plan, as it stood in mid-2014, was for 31 Squadron, along with IX(B) and XV(R) Squadrons, to be the last three RAF Tornado units, with the aircraft's final out-of-service date scheduled for 2019. By that time the multi-role Typhoon force will be at full strength and the Lightning II squadrons will be building up.

By the end of its projected life the Tornado will have been in service for thirty-seven years, a remarkable stretch for a strike/attack aircraft. And if the Goldstars do turn out to be the 'last in the Tornado skies', they will have operated the Tornado for one third of their, by then, 104 years of service.

At that point the Tornado bomber force, which in the mid-1980s comprised eleven operational squadrons, will have been succeeded by a couple of squadrons of RPAS plus some forty single-seat F-35 Lightning IIs. Of course these new types are expected to be extremely effective, but nevertheless this will be an extraordinarily small force. The few F-35s will be joint RN/RAF assets, so one cannot imagine that the RAF's share of the squadron nameplates will amount to more than a couple.

It's said that the reason for having a plan, though, is to give us something to change. Thus it was, therefore, that with the upsurge of IS in Iraq and Syria in late 2014, it was announced that a third operational GR4 squadron would be run on for another year to help the Marham Wing respond to this new development. So 12 Squadron was re-activated, and the current force assumption could continue to evolve to reflect changes to the threat and to national commitments.

It is hard to believe that, in this troubled world, there will not be further calls on a substantial British military force. Whether or not 31 Squadron Royal Air Force will be involved we can only surmise. Certainly, many squadrons with lower numbers have already disappeared. But the fact that Thirty One has been dormant for only eight months of its first century puts it surprisingly high up the RAF's seniority list. So we can only hope that a place in the order of battle will continue to be found for a unit with such a splendid spirit and history of distinguished service.

We have no doubt whatsoever, that, should future Goldstars be called to serve their country, they will do so with a professionalism and expertise which will reflect the glorious deeds of their forbears.

Appendix A

31 Squadron Commanding Officers

Captain C. Y. McDonald	October 1915
Major C. R. S. Bradley	March 1916
Major S. Hutcheson	May 1917
Major R. G. H. Murray MC	July 1917
Major E. L. Millar MBE	December 1918
Flight Lieutenant D. H. M. Carberry MC DFC	August 1919
Squadron Leader A. L. Neale MC	January 1920
Squadron Leader A. T. Harris AFC	January 1921
Squadron Leader A. C. Maund CBE DSO	May 1922
Squadron Leader A. A. Walser MC DFC	May 1924
Squadron Leader H. S. Powell MC	June 1924
Squadron Leader J. O. Archer CBE	November 1925
Squadron Leader J. F. Gordon DFC	April 1926
Squadron Leader B. Ankers DCM	March 1931
Squadron Leader C. J. S. Dearlove	February 1934
Squadron Leader R. M. C. MacFarlane	November 1934
Squadron Leader J. L. Airey DFC	October 1935
Squadron Leader A. V. Hammond	October 1936
Squadron Leader F. F. Wicks DFC	October 1938
Wing Commander G. J. L. Read AFC	April 1939
Wing Commander W. T. H. Nicholls	December 1940
Wing Commander S. E. Ubee AFC	June 1941
Wing Commander H. P. Jenkins DFC	September 1941
Wing Commander W. H. Burbury AFC	June 1942
Wing Commander H. A. Olivier	May 1943
Wing Commander W. H. Burbury DFC AFC	January 1944
Wing Commander R. O. Altman DSO DFC	February 1945
Wing Commander B. R. Macnamara DSO	September 1945
Squadron Leader D. W. S. Evans	September 1946
Wing Commander B. G. F. Drinkwater	September 1946
Wing Commander J. M. Cooke DSO DFC	November 1946
Wing Commander C. Fothergill	September 1947
Wing Commander A. R. Fane de Salis	July 1948
Wing Commander R. E. Ridgway DSO	March 1950
Squadron Leader C. G. St D. Jeffries DFC	April 1952
Squadron Leader N. Williamson DFC	November 1952
Squadron Leader R. F. V. Ellis	November 1954
Squadron Leader J. C. Stead DFC	March 1955
Squadron Leader F. H. P. Cattle AFC	July 1957
Squadron Leader L. A. Ferguson	January 1958
Wing Commander P. A. Kennedy DSO DFC AFC	February 1958
Wing Commander C. T. Dalziel	June 1960

Wing Commander P. H. L. Scott AFC	December 1962
Wing Commander R. G. Price	May 1965
Wing Commander R. L. Bennett	May 1967
Wing Commander R. J. Offord	October 1969
Wing Commander J. C. Sprent	July 1971
Wing Commander T. H. Stonor	August 1974
Wing Commander T. J. Nash AFC	July 1976
Wing Commander R. J. Howard AFC	July 1978
Wing Commander P. Edwards	December 1980
Wing Commander J. W. A. Bolton	May 1983
Wing Commander R. Bogg	November 1984
Wing Commander P. Dunlop AFC	November 1986
Wing Commander J. J. Witts	August 1989
Wing Commander I. S. Hall	February 1992
Wing Commander S. L. Parkinson	August 1994
Wing Commander S. Randles	February 1997
Wing Commander R. Low	February 1998
Wing Commander I. D. Teakle OBE	September 2000
Wing Commander A. J. Byford	May 2003
Wing Commander D. Andrew	January 2006
Wing Commander I. D. Gale MBE	May 2008
Wing Commander J. P. Mulholland	October 2010
Wing Commander R. Yates MBE	October 2012
Wing Commander J. A. Freeborough	December 2014

Appendix B

31 Squadron Locations

Farnborough (A Flight)	England	October 1915
Gosport (B Flight)	England	January 1916
(C Flight)	England	May 1916
Nowshera (Pir-Pai)	India	December 1915
Risalpur	India	March 1916
Mhow	India	April 1920
Cawnpore	India	November 1920
Peshawar	India	October 1921
Dardoni / Miranshah	India	April 1923
Ambala	India	March 1924
Quetta	India	December 1926
Drigh Road (Karachi)	India	August 1935
Detachment at Fort Sandeman (India)		
Lahore	India	October 1938
Peshawar	India	April 1940
Karachi	India	March 1941
Detachments at Shaibah and Habbaniya (Iraq)		
Lahore	India	September 1941
Detachments at Bilbeis, Shandur (Egypt)		
Akyab	Burma	February 1942
Dum Dum (Calcutta)	India	February 1942
Detachment at Dinjan (India)		
Lahore	India	June 1942
Detachments at Dinjan and Tezpur (India)		
Palam	India	February 1943
Detachments at Agartala, Dhubalia (India)		
Agartala	India	February 1943
Kharagpur	India	June 1943
Agartala	India	October 1943
Basal	India	June 1944
Agartala	India	November 1944
Comilla	India	January 1945
Hathazari	India	February 1945
Ramree Island	Burma	May 1945
Detachment at Toungoo (Burma)		
Tilda	India	August 1945
Akyab	Burma	August 1945
Detachments at Ramree, Mingaladon and Toungoo (Burma), Tilda (India)		
Kallang	Singapore	October 1945
Kemajorang	Java	November 1945
Mauripur	India	November 1946
	(Pakistan from August 1947)	
Detachments at Mohanbari and Palam (India), Chaklala (India, then Pakistan)		

Hendon	England	July 1948
Laarbruch	West Germany	March 1955
Brüggen	West Germany	October 1971
	(Germany from 1990)	

Detachments at Dhahran and Al Kharj (Saudi Arabia), Incirlik (Turkey), Solenzara (Corsica), Ali al Salem (Kuwait)

Marham	England	August 2001

Detachments at Ali al Salem (Kuwait), Al Udeid (Qatar), Kandahar (Afghanistan), Akrotiri (Cyprus)

Appendix C

31 Squadron Aircraft

The author makes no claims as to the completeness of this list, and readers are advised to treat it as a representative sample. Following the serial numbers, many aircraft show an additional identifier 'x'. This is the local fleet number, which various aircraft may have carried from time to time.

BE2c / BE2e

4131	crashed		4143	
4157			4164	
4308			4310	crashed
4355			4356	
4403			4408	
4432			4434	
4452	'First in the Indian Skies'			
4464			4465	
4484	BE2d		4549	
4554			4584	
4689			A2930	
A3073			A3098	
A3101	crashed		B4472	BE2e, crashed

Armstrong Whitworth F.K.8

C3588

FE2b and Farman F27

There are no recorded details of serial numbers

Bristol F.2B Fighter

D7807	'A'		D7813	
D8097			E2257	'E' or 'F'
E2501			F4315	
F4320	'D'		F4390	'R'
F4463			F4485	
F4495			F4555	
F4594			F4604	
F4643			F4658	
F4664			F4665	
F4683			F4689	'B' (crashed)
F4707	'A'		F4746	
F4758			F4839	'F'
F4915	'J' (damaged Sep 27)			
F4942	'H'		F4951	'J' (crashed Jun 25)

F4958	'L'	H1428	'L'
H1457	'E'	H1461	'F'
H1497		H1510	'H'
H1686		J6621	
J6623		J6625	
J6634		J6640	'K' (crashed 1 Aug 26)
J6641	'E'	J6647	'K' (damaged in crash 1922)
J6649		J6650	
J6651	'B' (crashed)	J6652	'A'
J6654	'O'	J6657	'P' (crashed)
J6675		J6689	
J6732		J6750	
J6754		J6757	
J6758		J6771	
J6782	'O'	J6796	
J7683	'L'		

Westland Wapiti MkIIA

J9388		J9389	
J9400	'D'	J9481	'G' (damaged in crash 1936)
J9499		J9502	
J9504	'E' (damaged in crash 1936)		
J9505		J9506	
J9507	'K' (damaged in crash 1934)		
J9510	'F'	J9720	
J9724	'E'	J9725	
J9730		J9731	'C'
J9735		J9737	
J9740		J9744	
J9745	'G'	J9746	
J9759		K1126	
K1271		K1273	(damaged in crash 1934)
K1277	'H'	K1283	
K1291	'B'	K1292	
K1296		K1302	
K1307	'N' (crashed 1934)	K1309	

Note: serials J9725-59 are sometimes reported as Mk V aircraft, with a longer fuselage and fitted with a message pick-up hook.

Vickers Valentia

JR8063	(ex Victoria)	JR8231	(ex Victoria)
JR8232	(ex Victoria)	K1312 *	(crashed in Iran)
K2340 †	'A' 'City of Delhi'	K2342	'D' or 'V'
K2807		K2808	
K3168		K3169	
K3600		K3609	(destroyed K3, Iraq, 6 May 41)
K3611	'Z' (crashed in Iran)	K3613	
K4634	'B' 'City of Lahore'		
K4635	'C' 'City of Calcutta' (crashed Risalpur)		

One Valentia was named 'Sirmur', in recognition of funding provided by the Rajah of Sirmur; its serial is unknown.

* This aircraft also reported as KR1312
† This aircraft also reported as KR2340

Douglas DC-2

AX755	(written off 13 Apr 42)	AX767	
AX768	(crashed 24 Jul 42)	AX769	(damaged 27 Sep 42)
DG468		DG469	
DG470	'R'	DG471	'S' (crashed 23 Oct 41)
DG473	(struck off after forced landing 14 Jun 42)		
DG474	(destroyed Jan 42)	DG475	(shot down Egypt 8 Dec 41)
DG476	'Y'	DG477	'Z' (the unit's first DC.2: SOC 8 Nov 43)
DG478	(damaged Feb 42)	DG479	'B'
HK820	(damaged Aug 41)	HK821	
HK837		HK847	

Douglas DC-3

LR230 *	'D' (damaged in air raid 6 May 42)		
LR231	'E' (destroyed in air raid 6 May 42)		
LR232	'S'	LR233	'H' (first DC-3)
LR234 *	'K'	LR235	'J' (crash landed 12 Jan 43)
MA925		MA928 *	(crashed Agartala 25 Mar 43)
MA929 *	(missing 27 Jan 43)	MA943	

* Aircraft marked thus are reported by some sources as being C-53s (in USAAF parlance the 'Skytrooper', the C-47 being known as the 'Skytrain'). Whilst the C-53 was also a military development of the DC-3, it lacked the C-47's reinforced cargo floor and had a narrower cargo door.

Douglas C-47

FD775		FD783	
FD787		FD788	'O'
FD791	'W'	FD792	'S'
FD793	(shot down by fighter 28 Oct 43)	FD799	'Y'
FD800	'U'	FD801	'K'
FD802	'Q'	FD803	
FD809		FD810	'H'
FD811	'V' (crashed Jan 44)	FD813	'G'
FD820	'E'	FD823	
FD834	'R'	FD835	
FD875	(damaged 29 Jan 45)	FD886	
FD899	'N'	FD916	
FD919		FD932	
FD943		FD948	
FD949	'V' (shot down by fighter 8 Nov 44)		
FD953		FL512	
FL516	(shot down by fighter 8 Nov 44)	FL533	
FL535		FL537	

FL540		FL543	
FL544		FL555	
FL556		FL571	
FL573		FL574	'E'
FL575		FL576	
FL577		FL594	'Z' (missing 22 May 45)
FL611		FL642	'H'
FZ571		FZ585	
FZ597		FZ 612	
FZ648	(burnt out 9 Jan 45)	FZ676	
KG481		KG520	'W' (lost 23 Nov 45)
KG541		KG542	
KG548		KG554	
KG560		KG698	
KG720		KG725	
KG758		KJ844	
KJ846		KJ860	
KJ884		KJ915	
KJ951		KJ956	
KK164		KK166	
KK167	'X' (crashed 8 Jun 45)	KK168	
KK173		KK174	
KK214		KK215	
KN206		KN212	
KN226	'C'	KN305	
KN339		KN348	
KN368		KN384	
KN399	(silver – '31 airline')	KN421	
KN426		KN503	
KN535		KN536	
KN545		KN546	
KN554		KN560	
KN561		KN563	
KN569		KN576	
KN581		KN618	
KN623		KN679	
KN699			

C-47

(No.77 Squadron at Mauripur, re-badged on 1 November 46 as 31 Squadron)

KJ863		KJ934	
KK150		KN637	'B'
KN639	'H'	KN667	
KN668	'Z'	KN672	
KN677	'M'	KN690	'D'
KN693	'W'	KN697	'L'
KP225	'AW'	KP228	'V' (last in Pakistan)
KP229	'P'	KP232	'K'
KP234	'C'	KP242	'X'
KP250	'G'	KP272	'S'
KP275	'U'		

Avro Anson C XIX

PH559 *	(Mk XII)	PH757 *	
PH759 *	(Mk XII)	PH814 *	
PH816*	(air ambulance)	PH817 *	(air ambulance)
PH841*		PH845 *	
TX155		TX160	
TX165		TX170	
TX185		TX195	
TX203		TX217	
TX222		TX239	
VM317		VM327	
VM362		VM378	
VM382		VM390	
VP510		VP519	

* These aircraft were Mk C XII

Percival Proctor MkIV

HM342	(MkIII)	LZ622	(MkIII)
LZ627	(MkIII, crashed Apr 49)	LZ700	(MkIII)
NP156		NP244	
NP290		NP302	
NP361		NP396	

Supermarine Spitfire

PM659	(Mk XIV)	SL721	(Mk LF XVI)
TB713	(Mk IX)		

de Havilland Devon C1/C2

VP956	VP975

de Havilland Chipmunk T10

WG469	WG474
WZ853	WZ873
WZ874	WZ875
WZ876	

English Electric Canberra PR7

WH773	WH775	
WH779	WH792	
WH800	WH816	
WJ816	WT483	(T4)
WT507	WT509	
WT510	WT511	
WT512	WT513	
WT515	WT516	
WT518	WT519	
WT520	WT521	
WT522	WT532	
WT533		

McDonnell-Douglas Phantom FGR2

XT906*	XT909*	
XV397	XV402	
XV404	XV409	
XV422	XV426	
XV427	XV431	(crashed 11 Oct 74)
XV433	XV440	(crashed 25 Jun 73)
XV460	XV465	
XV469	XV476	
XV480	XV483	
XV489	XV491	

* Trainer variants – rear cockpits equipped with throttles and additional flight instruments, as well as facility for a removable control column. Fully combat-capable.

Sepecat Jaguar GR1

XX150 *	'DZ'	XX747	'DG' later 'DJ'	
XX818	'DE'	XX844 *	'DZ'	
XX847 *	'DY'	XX956	'DK'	
XX968	'DB'	XX975	'DJ'	
XX971	'DE' crashed 21 Mar 78	XX976	'DK'	
XX977	'DL'	XZ377	'DF'	
XZ378	'DG'	XZ384	'DG'	
XZ386	'DB'	XZ389	'DM'	
XZ390	'DM'	XZ391	'DF' later 'DP'	
XZ392	'DE'			

* T2 aircraft

Panavia Tornado GR1

ZA455	'DP'	ZA461	'DK'	
ZA492	'DJ'	ZA554	'DM'	
ZA589	'DC'	ZD707	'DB'	
ZD710	'DC'	ZD711 *	'DY'	
ZD713*	'DX'	ZD715	'DB'	
ZD719	'DD'	ZD720	'DF'	
ZD739	'DE'	ZD740	'DA'	
ZD741*	'DZ'	ZD746	'DJ'	
ZD747	'DK'	ZD748	'DG'	
ZD790	'DL'			
ZD811*	'DY'	ZD812 *	'DX'	
ZD843	'DH'	ZD844	'DE'	
ZD873	'DD' (crashed 1987)	ZE116	'DG'	(GR1a)
ZG771*	'DW'			

* Trainer variants - rear cockpits equipped with control column, throttles and additional flight instruments. Fully combat-capable, although lacking some of the usual navigation displays.

The GR1a, ZE116, was an aircraft modified for the recce role with space for internal infra-red cameras in place of its guns. On an attack squadron such as 31, its recce bays were empty but unusable. The absence of guns was, of course, an operational limitation. A peacetime drawback of this model was the lack of the gun ammunition bays – which were normally available for baggage on landaway sorties.

Panavia Tornado GR4

All GR4s are ex-GR1. Initially they continued to bear 'Dx' squadron identifiers on the fin. Latterly, however, the aircraft have worn 3-digit pooled force numbers.

ZA393	'008'	ZA395	'009'
ZA398	'010'	ZA447	'DE'
ZA452	'021'	ZA458	'024'
ZA472	'031'	ZA492	'DJ'
ZA542	'035'	ZA550	'DD'
ZA553	'DI', '045'	ZA554	'DM', '046'
ZA564	'053' 90th livery	ZA591	'058'
ZA608	'070'	ZD709	'078'
ZD712 *	'080'	ZD713*	'DX'
ZD745	'093'	ZD747	'DK'
ZD748	'DG'	ZD788	'098'
ZD811*	'DF'	ZD843	'DH'

* Trainer variants

Abbreviations and Glossary

Note: the RAF in India incorporated local words (of various languages / dialects) into its own vocabulary, modifying many of them. Here, we use 'Ind' to indicate such a word, or a corruption of such a word, without making any claim of accuracy.

AA	anti-aircraft, ack-ack
AAA	anti-aircraft artillery
AAFCE	Allied Air Forces Central Europe (command)
AAM	air-to-air missile
AFB	air force base (US)
AFC	Air Force Cross (medal)
AFM	Air Force Medal
almirah	(Ind) wardrobe
AOC	Air Officer Commanding (of a Group)
AOC-in-C	Air Officer Commanding-in-Chief (of a Command)
ATC	air traffic control
AWACS	Airborne Warning and Control System – the command and control point in the sky
babu	(Ind) clerk
BAC	British Aircraft Corporation
BAe	British Aerospace
basha	(Ind) hut made of palm leaves and bamboo
BFPO	British Forces Post Office
bhisti	(Ind) water carrier
Blighty	(slang) Britain
BOAC	British Overseas Airways Corporation
bolthole	deployment to another base during re-construction
burra	(Ind) great, important
burra sahibs	(Ind) British officers
CAS	close air support
CAS	Chief of the Air Staff
chaplis	(Ind) sandals, slippers
chai	(Ind) tea (usually translated in the RAF as 'char')
charpoy	(Ind) wood-framed bed with straw mattress
chelo	(Ind) get a move on
chota	(Ind) small
chota hazri	(Ind) breakfast, banana and tea
chupatti	(Ind, other spellings also), flat cake, coarse bread
CO	Commanding Officer
CNAC	China National Aviation Corporation
CWGC	Commonwealth War Graves Commission

DDR	Deutche Demokratische Republik (East Germany)
DFC	Distinguished Flying Cross (medal)
DH	dead hit, bull's-eye
dherzi	(Ind, also derzi or dharzi) tailor
dhobi	(Ind) laundry
dhurri	(Ind) rough cotton rug
DROs	daily routine orders
dumba	(Ind) type of sheep
durbar	(Ind) tribal chiefs' gathering, conference
D/R	(also DR) dead reckoning (navigation without external fixes)
DSO	Distinguished Service Order (medal)
DZ	drop zone (of parachutes)
EAG	Expeditionary Air Group
ECM	electronic counter measures
ENSA	Entertainments National Service Association
erk	(slang) the lowest rank of airman
ETA	estimated time of arrival
ex-pat	ex-patriot (Briton living and working abroad)
F	degrees Fahrenheit, temperature measurement system then in use
faqir	(Ind) holy man
four by two	strip of cloth used for cleaning rifle barrels
FRG	Federal Republic of Germany (West Germany)
GEE	type of radio navigation aid
gewjaws	(Ind) showy trinkets, cheap jewelry
GLO	Ground Liaison Officer – army officer attached to an RAF squadron
GPS	global positioning system
GOC	General Officer Commanding
gharry	(Ind, various spellings) horse-drawn cab. (RAF slang) any vehicle
gulli gulli man	(Ind) street juggler
HT	high tension (electricity)
HUD	head-up display
i/c	in charge
IED	improvised explosive device
IFF	identification friend or foe (electronic equipment)
IMC	instrument meteorological conditions (unable to fly visually)
JEngO	Junior Engineering Officer (of a squadron)
jihad	(Ind) religious war, holy struggle
jirga	(Ind) assembly of elders
JTAC	Joint Terminal Air Controller
khel	(Ind) small tribal division
konna	(Ind) food
khassidar	(Ind) locally enlisted militia
khitmagar	(Ind) bearer
Kuki Khel	(Ind) small tribal group, clan
kukri	(Ind) Gurkha weapon, machete-like

lb	pound (imperial weight)
LGB	laser-guided bomb
linies	airmen working on the (line of) aircraft
LT	low tension (electricity)
Madda Khel	small tribal group
me'msahibs	(Ind) wives, ladies
MF	medium (radio) frequency
MM	Military Medal
MO	medical officer
Mohmands	(Ind) a tribe
moochi	(Ind) shoemaker
MEZ	missile engagement zone
MPC	missile practice camp
mullah	(Ind) religious preacher
malik	(Ind) priest, tribal headman
MT	motor transport
MU	maintenance unit
Naga	People/tribe of north-west Burma
NBC	nuclear, biological and chemical
NCO	non-commissioned officer
Nips	(slang) the Japanese
nullah	(Ind) valley, watercourse
OC	Officer Commanding
OCA	offensive counter-air
OCU	operational conversion unit
ORs	other ranks
OTU	operational training unit
pajama	(Ind, pyjama also) trousers
Pathan	(Ind) a tribe
PI	photographic interpreter
POW	prisoner of war
pugaree	(Ind) turban
punkah	(Ind) fan
QFI	qualified flying instructor
queen mary	articulated low-loading lorry
QRA	quick reaction alert
QWI	qualified weapons instructor
R&R	rest and recuperation
RPAS	remotely piloted air system
r/t	radio telephony
SAM	surface-to-air missile
SA3	Soviet (supplied) SAM system
SA6	Soviet (supplied) SAM system
SACEUR	Supreme Allied Commander Europe

SATCO	Senior Air Traffic Control Officer
Scud	Soviet (supplied) surface-to-surface missile
SEAC	South East Asia Command
SEAD	suppression of enemy air defences
SEngO	(Squadron) Senior Engineering Officer
shikara	(Ind) pleasure boat, up to 10-seater
SHQ	station headquarters
Sirkar	(Ind) the government
SNCO	senior non-commissioned officer
snowdrop	RAF policeman (derived from white-topped cap)
SOC	struck off charge
SWO	Station or Squadron Warrant Officer
TFR	terrain-following radar
thunderbox	primitive lavatory (not WC)
tiffin	(Ind) a light meal, generally applied to 'tea'
tonga	(Ind) two-wheeled pony or donkey trap, taxi
u/s	unserviceable
Verey	(light) – type of pistol-fired red flare
VFR	visual flight rules
wallah	(Ind) an employee on a specific duty, as in 'char wallah'
WEM	Wireless Mechanic
WOp	Wireless Operator
WOp/AG	Wireless Operator / Air Gunner
WMD	weapons of mass destruction
WSO	Weapons System Officer
yd	Yard- imperial measurement

RAF ranks. Note: abbreviations have changed over the years. For those ranks still in existence, the current official abbreviations are shown

AC2	Aircraftman, Second Class
AC1	Aircraftman, First Class
AM2	Air Mechanic, Second Class
AM1	Air Mechanic First Class
LAC	Leading Aircraftman
SAC	Senior Aircraftman
Jnr Tech	Junior Technician
Sgt	Sergeant
Chf Tech	Chief Technician (C/T also in common use)
FS	Flight Sergeant
WO	Warrant Officer
Plt Off	Pilot Officer
Fg Off	Flying Officer
Flt Lt	Flight Lieutenant
Sqn Ldr	Squadron Leader
Wg Cdr	Wing Commander

Gp Capt	Group Captain
Air Cdre	Air Commodore
AVM	Air Vice-Marshal
Air Mshl	Air Marshal (AM also in common use)
Air Chf Mshl	Air Chief Marshal (ACM also in common use)
MRAF	Marshal of the Royal Air Force

Modern aircraft equipment:

Jaguar:

AN/ALE-40	Scabbed to the lower rear fuselage, the equipment may dispense chaff to break the lock of hostile radars or flares to decoy heat-seeking missiles
LRMTS	Laser Ranger and Marked Target Seeker. Fitted in the nose, the equipment provides ranging information used to calculate weapon release point, as well as giving steering information to a target being marked by a friendly laser designator
Phimat	Pylon-mounted chaff dispenser designed to break the lock of hostile radars
AN/ALQ 101-10	Pod-mounted repeater (deception) radar jammer

Tornado:

BOZ 107	Pylon-mounted chaff and flare dispenser designed to dispense chaff to break the lock of hostile radars or flares to decoy heat-seeking missiles
Brimstone	Missile for use against smaller (but heavily armoured) ground targets, it comes in two versions. The basic missile scans targets with a millimetric-wave seeker, identifying them by comparison with its built-in database. The DMS (dual mode seeker) version adds a laser guidance capability
FLIR	Forward Looking Infra-Red. Pod-mounted under the GR4 nose, this equipment, together with night vision goggles, permits crews to operate 'passively' in clear weather at night
Litening III	Laser designator pod; succeeded TIALD. Also provides digital, down-linkable recce capability
LRMTS	As Jaguar
Paveway II	1,000lb laser-guided bomb
Paveway III	2,000lb laser-guided bomb. Incorporates refined flight trajectory capability
Paveway IV	500lb laser-guided bomb equipped also for GPS guidance. Its advanced electronics offer increased accuracy and trajectory shaping, offering enhanced weapons effects with a relatively small warhead
RAPTOR	Reconnaissance Airborne Pod Tornado; provides digital, long-range oblique imagery
RHWR	Homing Receiver and Radar Warning. Furnishes the crew with information on radars illuminating their aircraft
Skyshadow	Programmable, pylon-mounted response jammer designed to break the lock of hostile radars
Storm Shadow	Long-range, conventional stand-off missile, which navigates by means of GPS and terrain matching. Carries a penetrating warhead
TIALD	(GR1) Thermal Imaging and Laser Designation pod. Used both for recce and to designate targets being attacked by laser-guided weapons

Bibliography

Annett, Roger, *Drop Zone Burma*, Pen and Sword, 2008
The Army in India and its Evolution, published in Calcutta, 1924
Barthorp, Michael, *Afghan Wars and the NW Frontier, 1839–1947'*, Watson Little Ltd
Article in *Batavia Evening News*, 11 February 1946
Article 'Bravo Juliette', *RAF News*, 15 January 2010
Cowie, Ian and Jones, David, *Out of the Blue Too*, Halldale Media Group, 2014
Dudgeon, Air Vice-Marshal Tony, *Hidden Victory*, The History Press, 2001
Article in the *Eastern Daily Press*, 30 April 2003
Franks, Norman, *First in the Indian Skies*, Life Publications, 1981
Hall, Ian, *Jaguar Boys*, Grub Street, 2014
Lee, Air Chief Marshal Sir David, *… and we thought the war was over*, Thomas Harmsworth, 1991. By kind permission of Thomas Harmsworth Publishing
Liddell Hart, Basil, *History of the Second World War*, Orion Publishing Group London, 1971
Nicholls, Mark, article in the *Eastern Daily Press*, 17 March 2003
Pearcy, Arthur, *Dakota at War*, Ian Allan Publishing, 1982
Article in *Pheonix*, the journal of SEAC, 1945
Shores, Christopher, *History of the Mediterranean Air War, 1940–45, Vol 1*, Grub Street, 2012
Shores, Christopher, *Dust Clouds in the Middle East*, Grub Street, 1996
Soldinski, Zygmund, *Wings Over Asia Volume 2*, by permission of CNAC Association, www.cnac.org
Thomas, Janine, article in the *Sunday Times News Review*, 29 December 2009, by permission of The Sunday Times / NI Syndication
Tomkins, Mark, article in *Air Mail*, RAFATRAD Ltd, April 2000
Walpole, Group Captain Nigel, *Seek and Strike*, Astonbridge Publishing, 2001
Williams, Julie, article in *Lincolnshire Free Press*, 6 January 2004

Index

General Index

AAFCE 196
AAR 252, 268, 275
Aberdeen, landing strip 108, 305
Aberporth range 228, 250
Aberporth trophy 250
Abu Dhabi 62
Admin Box 104, 108
Adour 232
Adriatic Sea 276
Afghan Wars 316, 318, 319, 320, 323
Afghanistan x, 13, 16, 66, 199, 297, 309, 311, 314, 316
Afridi, tribe 11, 16, 20
AFVG 246
Agartala, airbase 90, 98, 100, 101, 115, 117, 121
Al Udaid, airbase 295, 297
AIM-7F, Sparrow missile 228, 229
Air Bombers 138, 139
Air Efficiency Medal 304
Air Landing School 74, 77
Air mail service 36
Air Medical Orderlies 139, 155, 156
Air policing 3, 32, 270, 273
Akrotiri, RAF 208, 316, 317, 318
Akyab, airbase 77, 79, 80, 84, 97, 138, 140
Al Amarah 271
Al Kharj, airbase 273, 297
Al Khobar 263, 264, 265
Al Nimran Hotel 263
ALARM, missile 274, 275, 276, 281, 288, 290
ALE-40 243, 337
Ali al Salem, airbase ii, 279, 286
Allied Force, Operation 275, 292, 297
ALQ 101–10 pod 243, 337
Al-Qaeda 309
Al Udeid, airbase 295, 297
Altengrabow, airfield 273
Ambala, air station 32, 38, 43
Amberawa 153
Ambulance aircraft 139, 140, 187, 188, 330

Amritsar 13, 18, 19
An Najaf 271
Anthrax 264
AR5 respirator 244
Arakan Hills 79, 89, 90, 102, 104, 108, 305
Arakan, Battle 117, 130, 136
Arboretum, NMA 318
Armistice 18, 23, 67, 73
Armstron-Whitworth Atalanta 70
Armstrong-Whitworth F.K.8 20, 309
Army co-operation x, 7, 47, 55, 214, 224, 312, 316
Army estimates 28
Arrestor hook 222
'Arris Arietis 241, 264, 265
Assam 79, 82, 85, 91, 108, 111, 174, 176
Assam Rifles 175
Association, 31 Sqn vii, x, 42, 47, 96, 117, 124, 144, 156, 178, 199, 213, 218, 248, 251, 264, 271, 281, 284, 285, 290, 298, 300, 302, 304, 318
Atom bombs 81, 137
Attock Bridge 8
Australians 142, 143, 144, 281
Autobahn ops 238, 239
Avro Anson 187, 188, 189, 194, 285
Avro Vulcan 246
Avro, le Rhone 27
AWACS ix, 260, 270, 276, 277
AWG–12 radar 219

Bad Kohlgrub 240
Badge, 31 Sqn 55, 122, 213, 312, plate 13
BAFVS 213
Baghdad 67, 267, 290, 317
Bahistan, SS 150
Bahrain 62, 72, 208, 253, 256, 257, 264, 270
Bali 154, 161
Baluchistan 11, 44, 62, 183
Bandoeng 160, 168

Bangladesh 174
Bangkok 141
Bannu 13, 180
Barra 187
Basal, airbase 112, 117
Basrah, RAF 71, 72
Batavia 146, 149, 150, 151, 303
Battle honours 136, 199, 266, 267, 176
Bazar Valley 11, 25
BE2c x, 1, 3, 5, 7, 14, 87, 283, 318, 319
BE2d 14
BE2e 14
Bekasi 157, 158, 159, 162, 302
Benala, SS 5
Bengal 79, 84, 173, 174, 176, 301
Bangladesh 174
Berlin 190, 191, 236, 237, 238, 268, 273
BFPO 290
Bicester, RAF 211
Bilbeis, airbase 76
BL755 235
Black Buffalo gang 157
Black Cat bar 151, 172
Black Watch 184
Blackburn Buccaneer 217, 224, 240, 246, 263
Blackpool, landing strip 91
Bloodhound SAM 232, 239
BOAC 178
Boeing 247 71
Bofors gun 152
Bolton, Operation 297
Bombay 1, 179, 184
Bomber Transport 58, 70, 74
Borneo 141, 161
Bosnian War 275
BOZ 107 249, 262
Brahmaputra, River 139, 150, 175
Brandenburg, airfield 273
Brewster Buffalo 80
Brimstone missile ix, 282, 313, 316
Bristol Blenheim 61, 69, 73
Bristol F.2 Fighter, Brisfit 25, 27, 35, 37, 46, 250

Bristol Pegasus 58, 59
Broadhurst trophy 241
Broadway, landing strip 107
Brüggen, RAF 204, numerous
    216–284
Brunswick Söhnkönig II 194
BT Flight 58, 59, 60, 61
Buckeburg, airbase 189
Buffer States 16, 21
Burma Road 79, 86
Burma Star Association 111, 304

C-46 83, 103
C-47, Douglas Skytrain 88
C-53, Douglas Skytrooper 88
Calcutta 88, 101, 109, 111, 120,
    143, 150, 177
Cambodia 79
Cameras, F22, F49, F52, F97 198,
    200
Canadians 89, 142, 144
Canberra B(I)6 253
Canberra PR7 numerous 196–216
Capo Frasca range 220
Cascade, landing strip 80
Castle Martin range 200
Catterick range 200
Cawnpore, air station 27, 29, 31,
    32
Chaff 240, 243, 249
Chaklala, airbase 95, 112, 120,
    180, 182
Chaklulia , airbase 177
Changi, RAF 166, 172
Char wallah 41, 113, 185
Character, Operation 135
Chin Hills 95, 98, 118
China 78, 79, 86, 103, 117, 174
Chindits 79, 91, 92, 108
Chindwin River 79, 93, 105, 108,
    117
Chitral 54, 64, 65
Chittagong 80, 124, 139, 150, 301
Clarenceaux King of Arms 214
Clutch stations 216
CNAC 80, 88, 103
Cold war 187, 216, 237, 268
College of Heralds 214
Comfort girls 140
Comilla, airbase 122, 125, 140,
    213, 312
Coningsby, RAF 217
Corporate, Operation 245
Cosford, RAF 188
Cottbus, airbase 227
Crusader, Operation 75
Cuban missile crisis 209

CWGC 171, 302
Cyprus 73, 208, 317
Czech Republic 273, 276, 294

D-Day 123, 140
Daily Star 261, 266, 271, plate 8
Dakota numerous 70–186, 301, 307
Dardoni (Miranshah) 13, 30, 43,
    65
Darwin 141, 281
de Havilland Chipmunk 194, 195
de Havilland Devon 187, 194
de Havilland Mosquito 151, 152,
    153, 197
de Havilland Sea Vixen 219
de Havilland Tiger Moth 118
Decimomannu, air base 220, 233,
    240, 250, 267
Deelen, airbase 205
Deir ez-Zor 73
Delhi 74, 82, 111, 120, 172, 177,
    182
'Desert pink' camouflage 257
Desert Shield, Operation 253, 297
Desert Storm, Operation 253, 297
Dhahran, airbase numerous
    256–273, 297, 316
Dhar 13
Dhubalia, airbase 90
Dimapur 110
Dinjan, airbase 82, 83, 86, 87, 98,
    114, 115, 116
DJRP 292
Dorsetshire, HMT 35
Dohazari 105
Douglas DC-2 70, numerous
    71–89
Douglas DC-3 numerous 71–89
Douglas Sleeper Transport,
    DST 81, 83
Drigh Road, RAF 50, 58, 62, 71
Drosh 45, 55
Dum Dum, RAF 86, 88, 100, 143,
    301
Dutch East Indies 79, 140, 146,
    171

Edam Island 168
Edinburgh, airbase 281
Egypt 58, 62, 74, 75, 76
Eindhoven, airbase 189
Elmpt 234, 283, 284
Elysia, SS 1
Engadine, Operation 275
ENSA 115, 183
Eskisehir, air base 227
Esperance Bay, SS 150

Expeditor, Beech 132
Exporter, Operation 73

F-5, Aggressors 243
F-16 271, 276, 311
F-18 Hornet ix
F-104 Starfighter 241, 244, 265,
    284
F-111 216
F-117 276
Fahnenband 284, plate 12
Fairford, RAF 272, 296
Farman 9
Farman F27 14, 16
Farnborough 1
Fassberg, airbase 236
FE2b 14
Flexible response doctrine 216
FLIR 282
Flying pig 58
Flying Rhino, Exercise 294
Fort Hertz, airbase 86, 92, 98
Fort Sandeman, airbase 39, 51, 53
French Indo China 79

Gangaw 121
Ganges River 98
Geneva Convention 128, 139
Germany, East (DDR) 236, 237,
    238
Germany, Federal Republic
    (FRG) 196, 230, 273
Gibraltar, RAF 245
Gilgit 64
Gioia del Colle, airbase 314
Glider ops 107, 112, 118
Gloster Gladiator 72
Goats 176, 274
Golden Charcoal, Exercise 294
Goolie chit 11, 12, 90
Goose Bay, airbase 249, 253, 270
Gosport 5
Gosport tube 36
GPS 254, 282, 294, 314
Granby, Operation 253, 257
Gripen, Saab 296
Gruenther Trophy 201, 203, 204
Guilders, Dutch 169, 213
Guilders, Japanese 169
Gujranwala 19
Gulf War syndrome 264
Gurkhas 14, 23, 43, 82, 95, 96,
    119, 126, 148, 162

Habbaniya 62, 68, 71, 262
Haditha 69
Haft Kel 74

Hahn, airbase 211
Halt Fair, Exercise 238
Halton, RAF 51
Handley Page Halifax 173
Handley Page O/400 22
Handley Page V/1500 22
HARM missile 276
Harvard, North American 132
Hassetche 73
Hathazari , airbase 124, 132, 213
Hawker Harrier 217, 221, 223, 239
Hawker Hunter 206, 217, 222
Hawker Hurricane, Hurri-
    bomber 73, 100, 104, 117, 133
Hawkes Bay 183
Heinkel 111 71
Hendon, RAF numerous 187–195,
    285
Hercules, C-130 257, 262
Herrick, Operation ix, 311, 314,
    316, 317
Highland Queen, landing strip 80
Himalayas 40, 64, 79
Hindu 173, 180, 181, 182
Hiroshima 137
Hkalak Ga 86
Hmuntha 110
Holbeach range 281
Honiang 117
Honington, RAF 247, 300
Hopsten, airbase 221
Hotel des Galleries 149
Hotel des Indes 149
Hotel zur Poste 283
HUD 235, 239
Hump 79, 86, 102, 103, 176
Hungarian uprising 209

IED 53, 312
IFF 262
IGB 236
Imphal 79, 105, 108, 110
INAS 222
Incirlik, airbase 274, 286, 297, 318
Indian Flying Corps 2
Indian Air Force 8, 65, 75, 80, 177
Indian National Army (Party) 96
Indonesia numerous, 146–164
Internees numerous, 140–169
Iran 73, 74
Iran-Iraq War 258, 286
Iraq 61, numerous 67–76 and
    253–297, 317
Iron Curtain 196
Irrawaddy, River 93, 105, 110, 130
ISAF 310
ISIS (ISIL, IS) 317

Jagdalak Pass 22
Jaguar GR1, SEPECAT numerous
    231–246
Jakarta 171, 303
Jalalabad 20, 22, 25
Jalibah 260, 262
Jandola 21, 53
Java 79, 116, numerous 146–172
Jhelum 32, 41
Jindivik drone 228, 230, 250
Jiwani 62, 183
Jodhpur 144, 145
John Haig, landing strip 80
JP233 248, 254, 259, 261, 281
Jural, Operation 270, 279

Kabaw Valley 117, 301
Kabul 3, 10, 22, 309
Kahan 12
Kallang, RAF 140, 144, 150, 166,
    213
Kandahar 10, 309, 310, 311, 313,
    316, 317
Kangla 123
Kangrim 15
Karachi 22, 36, 44, 49, 51, 67, 71,
    75, 173, 176, 183
Kashmir 40, 41, 95, 112, 181, 182
Kemajorang, airbase 146, 159, 165,
    170, 303
Kharagpur, airbase 95, 101, 113, 116
Khartoum 75
Khyber Pass 9, 20, 22, 23, 26, 32,
    33, 39
Kickers 105, 106
King Abdul Aziz Airbase 257
Kirkbymoorside 280
Kohat, air station 9, 21, 27, 63, 180
Kohima 79, 108, 109, 110, 111
Kohima Epitaph 111
Kosovo 274, 275, 277, 278
Kranji cemetry 302
Kuki Khel Mohmands 9
Kunming 86, 87, 103
Kurdish people 274, 317
Kuwait 253, 257, 263, 267, 270,
    279, 286
Kwai River 141

Laarbruch, RAF 47, numerous
    196–215, 233, 236, 247, 250,
    262
Lahore, airbase 7, 11, 19, 27, 58,
    62, 75, 83, 89, 90, 107, 121, 184
Landi Kotal 10, 26, 39
Laos 79
Las Vegas 243, 265

Lashkar (tribe) 26, 34
Legoland 234
Lewis gun 9, 15, 34, 54, 72, 75
LG138, landing strip 76
LGB 263, 271, 275, 283, 290
Libya 76, 314, 315, 316
Liddel Hart, Basil, author 79
Lightning, English Electric 197,
    217, 232
Lightning II F-35 320
Litening III pod 282, 292
Lockheed 12A 85
Lockheed Hudson 85, 89, 93
Loe Dakka (Dakka) 20, 23
Lohit, Operation, River 174, 177
Longcloth, Operation 91
Lossiemouth, RAF 243, 280, 286
Lower Topa 40
LRMTS 235, 236
Luang Chaun 131
Lucknow 34
Lushia Brigade 121
Lyneham, RAF 172, 185
Lysander, Westland 80

Ma'aten Bagush 76
Madras 150, 179
Magalang 152
Magwe 80
Mahsud, tribe 14, 15, 16, 21, 28,
    43, 66
Makvan 44
Malaria 118
Malaya, Malayan Peninsula 77, 79,
    137, 140, 141
Malik 20, 26
Manchuria 78
Mandalay 81, 86, 124, 127
Manipur, River, State 99, 111, 136
Manzai 53, 54
Marobi 15
Marham, RAF 270, 284, 285, 286,
    290, 293
Marsh arabs 298, 306, 314, 316
Massive retaliation doctrine 216
Mastiff, Operation 141
Mauripur, airbase numerous,
    173–186
Maxeval 209, 241, 247
Medan 140, 161
Media response teams 261
Meiktila 125, 126, 127
Memorial stone 285, 293, plate 16
Mersa Mutrah 75
Messerschmidt Bf.110 76
Metropolitan Comms Sqn 187
MEZ 276

Mhow, air station 27
Microval 209
MiG-21, Hungarian ii, 273
MiG-25 270
MiG-29 254
Millennium 279
Mineval 209, 210, 247
Mingaladon 77, 80, 133, 137, 138, 144
Miranshah (Dardoni), air station 13, 30, 43, 65
Mohanbari, air station 176, 185
Mohawk 82, 83, 84, 92
Monument 318, plate 16
Mosul 71, 292
MPC 250
MRCA 246
Mules 30, 65, 99, 106, 107, 174, 305
Mullah 13, 20
Murree Hills 40, 48, 120
Museum, RAF 187
Muslim 173, 180, 181, 182, 317
Myinmu 125
Myitkyina, airbase 82, 83, 84, 85, 86, 103, 117

NAAFI 199, 212, 213
Nagas, people 109
Nagasaki 137
Nagin Bagh 41, 42
Namest, airbase 294
National Service 187, 190, 214
NAVWASS 235, 241, 244
NBC kit 263, 295
Nellis, airbase 243
Neuruppin, airbase 273
New Zealand 142
Ngazum 125
Nickel, Operation 120, 133
Niederrhein Airport 214
Nine Eleven 285, 309
No-fly zone 270, 274, 286, 297
Northern Watch, Operation 274, 297, 318
Nörvenich, airbase 273
Nose art 264, 266, plates7,8
Nowshera 1, 8, 33
Nuclear weapons 216, 219, 234, 244, 268, 286
NVGs 282

Oakington, RAF 191
Oman 62, 269
Old Carthusian 22
OLF 243
Oscar 84
Ottoman Empire 3, 19, 253

Padang 161
Pakistan 173, 174, 180, 181, 184, 309
Palal 87, 95
Palam, air station 90, 178, 179, 180, 184
Palembang 139, 151, 161, 166, 170
Panavia 246
Pashto 5, 11
Pathan (tribe) 26, 54, 56, 181
Patriot SAM 264, 290
Paveway II LGB 275, 296
Paveway III LGB 275, 276, 290
Paveway IV LGB ix, 282, 313, 314
PBF 234
Pearl Harbor 77, 78, 79, 88
Pegu 131
Peplow, RAF 189
Percival Proctor 191, 194, 195
Peshawar, air station 23, 32, 38, 43, 60, 64, 112
Phantom FGR2 (F-4M) numerous, 216–231
Phantom RF-4 202
Phimat pod 243
Phoney war 63
Photo-flash flares 200
Phylis, Operation 102
Pigeons 16, 26, 37
Pir-Pai, air station 1, 4
Pitch Black, Exercise 281
Poona 44, 122, 179
Popham panel 33
Prague spring 209
Pratt and Whitney Twin Wasp 131, 167
Prickly heat 41, 94, 116
Provide Comfort, Operation 297
Punjab 23, 34, 43, 44, 173, 180

QRA 211, 220, 222, 233, 255, 268
Qatar 291, 297
Quetta 44, 48
Quetta earthquake 48, 49, 51
Quicktrain, Exercise 210
QWI 233, 276, 280

RAF Regiment 126, 151, 156, 162
Ramree Island, airbase 79, 95, 123, 128, 129, 134, 137, 138, 213
Ramu 104
Rangoon 65, 77, 80, 117, 133, 138, 140, 213
Rapier SAM 239, 241
RAPTOR 282, 288, 290, 292, 311
RAPWI 146, 151, 168, 171
Royal Army Service Corps 100, 160

Rawalpindi 2, 7, 40, 112, 180
Razmak 45, 46, 60
RB-66 204
Red Flag, Exercise 243, 252, 283
Resinate, Operation 286, 288, 290, 297
Rheindahlen 227, 237
RHWR 249, 273
Risalpur, air station 5, 7, 9, 10, 22, 23
Riyadh 255, 258, 261, 264, 265, 178
RNAS 3, 14
Rolls Royce Avon 213
Rolls Royce Spey 218, 219
Roundels 97, 111, 164, 165, 178
Royal British Legion 111
Royal Flush, Exercise 200, 203, 205, 282
Rupa, DZ 175
Russia 3, 44, 64, 74, 87, 237
Ru-Ywa 124
RWR 239, 240

SACEUR 220, 233
Salmond competition 224, 241, 251
Sarajevo 276
Sassoon Trophy 203, 205
Sawspit 183
Scud missile 262, 264, 288
SEAC 97, 106, 149, 154, 171
SEAD 274, 276
Seaforth Highlanders 149, 151
Secure radios 254
Seletar, air station 144
Semerang 165
Semi-autonomous servicing 225
Serbia, Serbs 275, 276, 277
Shabkhadar 9
Shader, Operation 317, 318
Shaibah, RAF 62, 67, 70, 72, 74, 185, 262
Shandur, airbase 75, 76
Sharjah, RAF 62, 185, 253
Shawbury, RAF 188
Shinwar tribe 24
Shock and awe 291
Shwebo 81
Sidewinder, AIM-9 240, 249, 250
Sikh 19, 23, 55, 173, 180, 182
Silloth, RAF 185
Silver, 31 Sqn 178, 196, 217, 282, 283
Simla 40, 50
Singabil 101
Singu 124

Sinzweya 104
Skyshadow pod 249, 282
SNEB rocket 228
Soerabaya 148, 151, 153, 154, 161
Solenzara, airbase 275, 276
Sollingen, airbase 241
Solo 164, 165
Somerset Regiment 20, 23, 24
South Africans 95, 130, 140, 159
South Cerney 296
Southern Watch, Operation 270, 274, 286, 297
Soviet Union 73, 74, 111, 190, 196, 236, 237, 243, 268, 273, 309
Spadeadam range 243
Spangdahlen, airbase 204
Special weapons 216, 234, 268
Squadron Standard 250, 267, 199, 251, plates 14, 15
Squadrons and units, RAF:
  1 Sqn 278
  II(AC) Sqn 258, 287, 292, 293
  4 Sqn 221
  5(AC) Sqn 37, 82, 83, 139,
  IX(B) Sqn 247, 258, 275, 278, 287, 291, 320
  10 Sqn 179
  12 Sqn 320
  XIII Sqn 258, 287, 292, 298
  14 Sqn 217, 219, 229, 231, 247, 248, 253, 262, 255, 258, 270, 298
  XV Sqn 247, 255, 320
  16 Sqn 247, 298
  17 Sqn 198, 204, 217, 219, 229, 231, 247, 248, 253, 258, 262, 270, 298
  19 Sqn 230
  20(AC) Sqn 37, 234, 298
  25 Sqn 232
  27(B) Sqn 37, 65, 79, 262, 298
  28(AC) Sqn 37, 63, 67, 294
  36 Sqn 95
  39 Sqn 306
  45 Sqn 298
  52 Sqn 103, 112
  60(B) Sqn 37, 65, 79, 151
  69 Sqn 198
  77 Sqn 173, 174, 185
  80 Sqn 198, 204, 211
  81 Sqn 151, 306
  84 Sqn 151
  92 Sqn 230
  114 Sqn 7
  117 Sqn 75
  146 Sqn 149

194 Sqn 85
203 Sqn 69
207 Sqn 194
213 Sqn 253
215 Sqn 301
216 Sqn 58, 59
271 Sqn 123
353 Sqn 103, 112
617 Sqn 271, 287, 313
3 MFPU 201
4 FTS 67
83 EAG 312
151 OTU 113
431 MU 240
904 Wg 151, 164, 303, 313
Squadrons and units, other forces:
  2nd Div 130
  2 ATAF 196, 204, 210
  4 ATAF 196, 204
  3 Aerobrigata IAF 210
  5th Indian Div 105, 108
  12 Sqn, IAF 178
  13th Lancers 161
  Fourteenth Army 117, 127, 128, 136
  20th Indian Div 125
  23rd Indian Div 171
  XXXIII Corps 121
  37 Brgd 161
  81st West African Div 102
  421 Sqn RCAF 241
  799 Coy RASC 160
Srinagar 41, 181, 182
St Clement Dane's church 251
St Mawgan, RAF 296
Startrek trophy 251
Storm Shadow missile 282, 288, 289, 313, 314, 316
Streamline, Operation 180
Sumatra 140, 149, 151, 167
Supermarine Spitfire 151, 187, 191, 192
Supermarine Swift 204
Survive to operate 227, 234
SUU-23A gun 228
Swinderby, RAF 211
Sylhet 105, 108, 109, 110, 119
Syria 67, 73, 76, 199, 267, 317, 318, 320

Tabual 104
Tabuk, airbase 256, 262
Taceval 209, 217, 219, 226, 233, 240, 247, 296
Tactical Air Meet 241
Tactical Fighter Meet 233
Tactical Weapons Meet 224

Taliban 309, 316
Tandjong Priok 151
Tank, air station 14, 21, 33, 36
Tehran 74
Telic, Operation 287, 290, 297, 317
Tengah, RAF 158, 303
Ternhill, RAF 188
Tezpur, airbase 83, 85, 87, 98, 114, 214
TF, TFR 249, 254, 255, 282
Thailand 79, 128
Thal 21
Thetkegyin 121
Thuderbolt, Exercise 237
Thunderbolt, aircraft 128, 133, 146, 151, 152, 153, 156
Thursday, Operation 104
TIALD pod 270, 271, 276, 283, 292
Tibet 174
Tiddim 87, 99, 117
Tilda, airbase 137, 144, 213
Tornado Combat Air Wing 287, plate 10
Tornado F3 256, 257, 262, 297
Tornado GR1/GR4 ii, ix, 195, 244, numerous 246–298 and 309–321
Toungoo 80, 96, 125, 128, 129, 131, 137
Tour length 119
Transport Command 123, 179, 188
Tribal areas 16, 46
Tripwire response doctrine 216
TriStar 272, 290, 311
Troop Carrier Command 97, 136
Tullyhall, landing strip 105
Turbomeca 232
Turbo-Union 246
Typhoon 314, 320
Twenthe, airbase 189, 205
Two-man principle 219, 234

ULL − ultra low level 243
UNSCR 660 253
UNSCR 688 270
UNSCR 1199 275
UNSCR 1441 286
Urdu 5, 11, 45, 55, 63
USMC 288
USAAF 86, 88, 103, 106, 118, 176
USAF 202, 216, 220, 229, 247, 270, 272, 276

Valley, RAF 250
VC10 ix, 252, 266

VGO, Vickers guns 99, 118, 133
Viceroy 13, 37, 39, 50, 173
Vichy French 67, 73
Vickers Valentia numerous, 58–77
Vickers Victoria 37, 59
Vickers Vimy 58, 59
VICON pod 292
Victor tanker 270
Vietnam 79
Villafranca, airbase 210
Vliehors range 226
Voyager (A330) 317
Vulcan, Avro 246

Walong, DZ 175
Wana 21, 34, 35, 53, 54, 180, 181
War on terror 285
War week 295
Warsaw Pact 196, 216, 236, 252,
   268
Waziristan 14, 15, 21, 25, 26, 28,
   43, 53, 64, 66, 180
Wazirs, tribe 11, 15, 16
WE177 234
Weeze Airport 214
Wellington, Vickers 185, 301
Western Vortex, Exercise 249, 269
Westland Wapiti 37, numerous
   46–77
White City, landing strip 305
White Waltham, RAF 192
Wild Weasel 270
Wildenrath, RAF 204, 221, 226,
   240, 268
Wittstock, airfield 273
WIWOLs 232
WMD 286
WST 268

'Y', Operation 74
Yazagyo 118
Yunnanyi 103

Zaps 211, 212
Zerbst, airfield 273
Zero 83, 84, 103, 104, 107
Zipper, Operation 137

Personnel Index
Abson, Flt Lt Ian 'Abbo' 291
Adie, Kate (reporter) 260
Airey, Sqn Ldr J.L. 322
Akers, Fg Off 301
Aldred, Lt Greg, RN 205
Aldrich, John 305
Altman, Wg Cdr R.O. 'Otto' 144,
   305, 322

Andrew, Wg Cdr Dean 293, 323
Ankers, Sqn Ldr B. 322
Ankerson, Sqn Ldr Bob 262
Annett, Roger, author 111, 186,
   338
Archer, Sqn Ldr J.O 322
Armstrong, FS R.K. 118
Arthur, LAC J. 51
Ashby, LAC Johnny 304
Ashmore, Fg Off
   W.H.'Bill' 129, 156, 157
Aubrey, FS A.W. 131
Averill, Flt Lt Morris 161
Ayres, Len 95

Bagwell, Fg Off Greg, later
   AM 251, 316, plate 14
Bailey, AC1 F. 51
Baines, Fg Off Jack 133, 135
Baldry, Les 301
Baldwin, Flt Lt Kevin
   'Stanley' 256, 267
Baldwin, WO Al 143, 158, 161,
   166
Ball, LAC Arthur 'Arty' 115, 125
Baptie, Fg Off T.W. 104
Barker, Lt G.C 11
Barthorp, Michael (author) 23
Bateson, Fg Off 153
Batten, Fg Off Jim 156
Baugh, Flt Lt 88
Baxter, SAC 225
Bauer, Gerald, artist plates 1,2
Bayman, Flt Lt Phil 275, 277, 279
Bedford, Ron 169
Bell, Flt Lt Mike 'Dinger' 205
Bell, Sgt D.F.B. 110
Bengree, Flt Lt 77
Bennett, FS R.S. 131
Bennett, Wg Cdr R.L. 323
Bennett, WO Benny 141
Bentley, Ivor 'Chota' 106
Beswick, Fg Off G.E. 101
Betts, WO Ady 312
Bielby, Fg Off Pete 287, 288
Birdwood, Gen 31
Bishop, Flt Lt 71
Boardman, LAC Johnny 107, 108
Bogg, Wg Cdr Dick (later Air
   Cdre) 246, 247, 249, 251, 279,
   284, 298, 323
Bolton, Wg Cdr J.W.A 323
Bond, LAC M. 51
Boon, Flt Lt Tim 217, 221
Bowerman, Sqn Ldr Graham 250
Bowers, Cpl Norman 94
Bowman, Cpl Frank 158

Bowring, Flt Lt 152
Boyd, LAC Phil 156, 303
Boyd, Lt L.C. 14, 15
Bradley, Cpl 68, 70
Bradley, Maj C.R. 7, 322
Bray, Sqn Ldr Peter 91, 100, 107,
   110, 123
Brockbank, Flt Lt 100
Broughton, LAC Jimmy 124
Brown, Cpl Charlie 257, 260, 263
Brown, Fg Off Eric 83
Brown, Flt Lt 'Min' 221
Brown, Flt Lt Steve 130, 166
Brown, LAC George 37, 38, 39, 45
Brown, Sgt T.B. 117
Brown, Sqn Ldr Ramsey 207
Brown, WO Dennis 137, 153, 168
Brownjohn, Fg Off
   E.A.'Johnny' 133
Brunswick, WO Ken 141, 164
Buckland, Fg Off G. W.
   'Ginger' 13
Burbury, Sqn Ldr Bill, later Wg
   Cdr 77, 80, 83, 84, 85, 91,
   108, 111, 113, 123, 322
Burgess, Fg Off 'Budgie' 262
Burgess, LAC 'Butch' 75
Burnside, Sqn Ldr Dudley, later
   Wg Cdr 59, 60, 67, 68, 70, 74,
   77,
Burt, Flt Lt Tony 204, 205
Burton, FS Rowland 'Ron' 126,
   134, 141
Bush, FS George 72
Butler, Capt W.J. 23
Butley, WO M.W. 117
Byford, Wg Cdr Al 292, 298, 323

Calder, Flt Lt Jack 252, 271
Cameron, AM2 16
Candy, WO Len 143
Carberry, Capt D.H.M. 20, 322
Carden, Sgt 112
Carr, LAC Ken 88
Carter, Sqn Ldr Doug 255
Carver, Tom (reporter) 261
Cass, Flt Lt Jerry 250
Cattle, Sqn Ldr F.H.P. 322
Cave, Flt Lt Richard 'Dickie
   Mint' 224
Cawthorn, Cpl 'Corky' plate 8
Chadwick-Brown, Fg Off E. 34
Chalk, Sgt 70
Chapple, Flt Lt James 62, 66, 68
Charlton, Sgt 'Klunk' 263
Cheseldene-Culley, Fg Off Rich
   'C-squared' 257, 261, 271

Churchill, Rt Hon Winston 19, 67, 196
Claridge, Sqn Ldr Geoff 208
Clark, Fg Off Nobby (later Flt Lt) 214, 222
Clark, Flt Lt Harry 134
Clark, Rev (Wg Cdr) Lance 285
Clarke, Sgt Norman 44, 51, 53
Clayton, AC1 J. 51
Cleave, Signaller 184, 185
Coggon, Flt Lt Allan 96, 125, 126, 131, 132, 143
Cogley, Flt Lt Nick 314
Collard, FS 103
Collyer, Flt Lt Eddie 160
Colville, Fg Off 129
Combe, Plt Off Gerald 33
Condon, WO Sid 131, 153
Connaught, Duke of 34
Constable, Nick (reporter) 261
Cook, FS 85
Cooke, Wg Cdr J.M. 173, 179, 323
Cooper, Captain Colin 4, 5, 8, 9
Corey, Fg Off Harold 134
Cornwell, WO Norman 144, 148, 161, 162, 166, 171, 172, 252
Coryton, Flt Lt (later ACM Sir Alec) 30, 32, 34, 35, 199, 250
Coughlan, Plt Off 84
Cox, Lt A.S. 13
Cresswell, Flt Lt Ade 241
Cronk, LAC A. 51
Cronyn, Lt V.P. 6
Crutch, LAC Harry 'Butch' 98, 214
Cullen, Flt Lt Gus 271
Cullen, LAC Martin 'Scouse' 133
Cullingworth, Cpl Austin 'Jeep' 82, 83, 87, 88, 101
Cumming, FS R.W. 131
Cunnell, WO Fred 304
Currell, Flt Lt Norman 129, 138, 140, 141
Curry, Lt R.A. 21
Curtis, AC1 R. 51

Dalziel, Wg Cdr Charles 207, 322
Dark, LAC Wyndham 60, 65, 71, 97
Davies, Cpl Des 178
Davies, Fg Off S.H. 105
Davies, Sqn Ldr John 255
Davies, Sqn Ldr Martin 247, 248
Davis, Capt Rupert 295
Day, Flt Lt Nigel 232
Day, Flt Lt Steve 252
de Gaulle, Gen 73

Dearlove, Sqn Ldr C.J.S. 283, 322
Delaney, Flt Lt Arthur 100, 104, 108, 110, 112, 119,
Devonshire, Lt F.V. 26
Dhar, Maharajah of 13
Dickenson, Fg Off Garry 201
Dight, Fg Off Ray 156, 158
Douglas, WO C.K. 'Dougie' 117
Dove, Ch Tech Ray 212
Downs, Flt Lt Dick 250
Drewery, Flt Lt Chris 267
Drinkwater, Wg Cdr B.G.F. 322
Dudgeon, AVM Tony 67
Dunkley, Plt Off John 133
Dunlop, Wg Cdr Pete 251, 322
Dwyer, Fg Off Michael 44
Dymond, Peter 113

Eastley, Lt Charles 8, 9, 10
Easton, Cpl G. 51
Easton, Jock 115
Eccles, LAC George 1, 35, 41, 45, 63, 66, 299
Eccles, Flt Lt Steve plate 14
Edwards, Cpl Bert 139, 152, 155, 156, 158, 171, 248, 271, 300
Edwards, Wg Cdr P. 323
Eisenhower, Gen 81
Ekers, Sgt Len 'Hawk' 118, 119
Ellis, Sqn Ldr R.F.V. 322
Elsdon, Wg Cdr Nigel 262
England, WO Gordon 125, 214, 301
Evans, Sqn Ldr D.W.S. 322
Evans, LAC S. 51
Evans, Sgt Ken 'Taff' 122, 128, 130, 141, 151, 169, 308
Evans, Wg Cdr Ivor 258
Evenett, AC1 Tony 52
Eyre, Lt 5

Fairweather, Flt Lt 305
Fallows, LAC Roy 149
Fane de Salis, Wg Cdr A.R. 187, 191, 192, 322
Faqir of Ipi 51, 52, 60, 64
Farr, Sgt Tommy 70, 74
Ferguson, Sqn Ldr L.A. 322
Ferguson, Flt Lt Tony 203
Field, WO Jeff 247, 248
Figg, Flt Lt Len 167
Finberg, Bobby 95
Fincham, Sgt D. 51
Findlay, Fg Off 38
Fisher, FS Ron 256, 262
Fleming, Flt Lt Jules 311
Fletcher, Lt H.E. later Capt 4, 15, 16

Foot, FS 85
Foster 11
Foster, Flt Lt Pete 273
Fothergill, Wg Cdr C. 322
Frazer, WO Cyril 173, 174, 176, 178, 180, 182, 304
Freeborough, Wg Cdr J.A 318, 323, plate 12
Freeman, WO Cliff 139
Freitag, Plt Off Bill 166
Frost, Cpl W.G.E. 156
Frost, Sqn Ldr Adrian 176
Furlong, Sgt E. 'Jack' 131, 132

Gaddafi, Col 314
Gale, Wg Cdr Ian 'Windy' 294, 323
Gandhi, Mahatma 19, 34
Gay, Plt Off 38
Gegg, Flt Lt Jerry 261, 266
Gibb, Sqn Ldr Graham 217
Gibbs, FS A.C. 110
Gillin, Flt Lt Bob 305
Gipson, WO Peter 290
Goodman, Flt Lt Gordon 232
Goodman, Sqn Ldr Pete 251
Gordon, Dougie 114
Gordon, Sqn Ldr J.F. 322
Gordon-Dean, Lt 12
Gould, Fg Off Nat 104, 112
Goult, Flt Lt John 240, 241
Graham, Cpl Syd 206, 209
Graham, LAC Johnny 144, 145, 150, 151, 302
Grant, Sgt H. 51
Green, Sgt John 256
Green, Morris 87
Greenstone, LAC C.J. 'Gerry' 121, 156, 157, 303
Gregory, John 204
Griggs, Flt Lt Steve 240
Grimwade, Fg Off Robert 141
Groves, Flt Lt Gerry 132, 143, 213
Gwin, WO Maurice 180, 184, 185

Hadley, Sqn Ldr Simon 291
Hadnett, Sister Harriet 119
Haigh, LAC Tom 252
Hall, Wg Cdr Ian (later Gp Capt) ii, 268, 269, 272, 274, 323
Halley, Capt R. 'Jock' 22
Hallinan, Flt Lt Francis 110, 115, 144
Hamid Karzai, President 310
Hamilton, Paddy 115, 151
Hammond, Flt Lt Geoff 165

Hammond, Sqn Ldr A.V. 322
Hammond, Sqn Ldr Richard 291
Handford, Cpl Mark ii, plate 10
Hanscombe, Cpl Ron 95
Hanson, George nav 86
Hardman, Fg Off Donald 11,
    28, 43
Harris, Flt Lt Torben 271
Harris, SAC Mike 201
Harris, Sqn Ldr A.T. (later ACM
    Sir Arthur) 28, 29, 30, 33,
    34, 35, 265, 322
Harris, Sqn Ldr Keith 248
Harrison, Fg Off Alan
    'Chunky' 205
Hawkins, WO George 140
Haynes, AM1 George 19, 23, 24
Heap, WO Pete 256, 262
Heaton-Armstrong, Sir John 214
Hendry, Sqn Ldr Les 256, 257,
    258, 260, 261, 267
Herring, Cpl H. 51
Hill, FS R.W. 111
Hill, FS W.H. (later WO) 118, 158
Hoare, Lt L.T. 11
Holmes, Lt A.J. 283
Hockaday, FS 'Hock' 154
Hodges, Sqn Ldr Dave 226
Honeyman, LAC Eric 89, 115
Honeyman, Sqn Ldr R.G. 100,
    112
Hood, Sgt Norman 211
Hopkins, Fg Off A. 100
Howard, Fg Off Denys 150
Howard, Wg Cdr Richard 237,
    241, 323
Howe, Fg Off Ernie 156
Howell, Flt Lt 'Tiny' 71, 75, 76,
    77, 84, 85
Howser, Sgt 84
Hulme, Fg Off Simon 'Gilbert',
    (later Flt Lt) 271, 276
Humphreys, Flt Lt Mike 252
Hunting, Capt G.L. 7
Hussein, President Saddam 253,
    256, 270, 274, 287, 291
Hutcheson, Maj S. 8, 322

Irwin, Lord 39

Jackson, Fg Off John 'Jacko' 95,
    96, 101, 102, 104
Jackson, Fg Off 32, 34
Jackson, FS, RNZAF 104
Jackson, LAC Harry 158
James, Rev (Wg Cdr) Noel 251
Jamieson, FS R. 106, 111

Jeffries, Sqn Ldr C.G.StD. 322
Jenkins, Wg Cdr H.P. 74, 75, 76,
    80, 81, 84, 85, 322
Johns, ACM Sir Richard 277
Johnson, Cpl Stan 113, 122, 135,
    213, 303
Johnson, FS (later Fg Off)
    Frank 300
Jones, Flt Lt Glyn 207

Keeping, Lt E.G. 113
Kelly, Plt Off Bill 'Flash' 74
Kennedy, Flt Lt Hugh 218, 226
Kennedy, Wg Cdr P.A. 322
Kenvyn, Flt Lt Ian 'Chunky' 241
Kenway, LAC F. 62, 75
Khan of Kalat 18
Kidney, Sqn Ldr Dick 200, 205,
    212
King, Fg Off 103
King, Flt Lt Dave 314
Kipling, Rudyard, author 11
Kirby, Flt Lt 39
Kirby, Lt 21
Kirk, Lt 13
Kirkland, Fg Off Terry 205
Kitson, Capt 14
Knight, FS L.B. 101
Knowlton, Cpl H. 51
Kupinsky, LAC Phil 303

Larsen, Fg Off J.E.L. 99, 104
Lazell, Sgt Vic 86
Lee, Gp Capt David (later ACM
    Sir David) 164
Leeder, FS 'Chiefie' (later Flt
    Lt) 81, 98, 101. 105
Leggett, LAC John 190, 192
Lester, Plt Off Hugh 130
Levin, Sgt Harold 'King' 95
Livermore, Cpl T. 51
Lloyd, Flt Lt Steve 279
Locke, LAC Walter 49
Long, Flt Lt Ian 'Ob' 261
Lord de l'Isle and Dudley 194, 195
Lord, Sgt (later Flt Lt) David
    'Lummie' 72, 75, 76, 77, 80, 84,
    87, 91, 93, 123
Loveridge, WO 178
Lovett, Fg Off Tony 207
Low, Wg Cdr Robbie 276, 277,
    279, 296, 298, 323
Low, WO 100
Luhman, Keith 44, 48, 49
Lynch, WO Colin 99, 101, 108, 119
Lynn, Vera, entertainer 115, 116,
    303, 304

Macdonald, Flt Lt 184
MacEwan, Brig 21
MacFarlane, Sqn Ldr R.M.C. 322
Mackie, Flt Lt K.F. (later Sqn
    Ldr) 81, 84, 85
MacLean, WO Duncan 100
Macnamara, Wg Cdr Brian 138,
    140, 146, 156, 171, 322
Major, Rt Hon John 258
Malone, WO Frank 141, 156, 158
Mann, Fg Off Bertie ii, 42, 46, 52,
    53, 54, 55, 58, 61, 63, 77, 312
Mann, Lt Leslie 6
Marks, Brig 105
Marshall, Flt Lt 184, 185
Martin, ACM Sir Mick 218
Marwood, Flt Lt Ross 277
Matthews, Sqn Ldr Roger 244
Maund, Sqn Ldr A.C. 322
Mavor, Fg Off 'Duke' (later AM
    Sir Leslie) 47, 60, 64, 65,
    248, 251
May, Sgt Charles 92
McClauchlan, WO 'Mac' 122, 123
McDade, SAC 225
McDonald, Capt Colin x, 1, 3, 4,
    7, 12
McDonald, Flt Lt 'Mac' 220, 228
McDougal, FS 141
McEwen, Flt Lt Alan 119, 128
McGill, AC1 W. 51
McGreevy, Sgt 99
McKee, Sgt 100
McLaren, FS E. 117
McMillan, Flt Lt Brian 62
Mee, Sqn Ldr Vince 264
Meehan, Sgt Paul 270
Millar, Maj E.L. 322
Miller, WO J.A. 131
Mills, LAC L.S. Taff 95, 101
Mills, Tubby 41
Mitchell, 'Mitch' 166
Moore, FS R. 131
Moore, WO Dusty 112, 308
Moreton, Fg Off Noel 30, 31, 42,
    43, 46
Morrell, Flt Lt Ben 290
Morris, Chris (reporter) 261
Mosely, LAC Donald 199
Moss, Sgt Laurie 139
Moudy, SAC 185
Mountbatten, Lord Louis 146,
    171, 173
Mulholland, Wg Cdr Jim 295,
    298, 313, 323
Murray, Maj R.G.H 322
Murray, Sgt Frank (later FS) 92, 99

Nash, Wg Cdr Terry 231, 233, 235, 236, 239, 323
Nattrass, Sqn Ldr Trevor 227
Neale, Flt Lt A.L. (temporary Sqn Ldr) 28, 322
Neale, FS Eric 1, 5, 7, 8
Neil, Flt Lt Frank 252
Newman, Cpl 183
Newton, Sqn Ldr Bertie 257, 258, 267
Nichol, Flt Lt John 261
Nicholls, LAC B. 51
Nicholls, Mark, journalisr 287
Nicholls, Wg Cdr W.T.H. 322
Nunn, Sqn Ldr John 227

Oddie, Lt G.S. 20
Odlin, FS 104
Offord, Wg Cdr R.J. 323
Ogden, Flt Lt Lloyd 139, 168, 169
O'Halloran, Cpl Terry (later Sgt) 200, 209, 210, 306
Olivier, Wg Cdr H.A. 108, 322
Orwell, George, author 216
Osama bin Laden 309, 310
Overton, Eve 169
Overton, FS John 140, 168, 169, 301

Parkinson, Fg Off George 89,
Parkinson, Wg Cdr Steve 274, 298, 323, plate 5
Parry, Cpl R. 101
Paxton, Flt Lt Tony 195
Paxton, Helena 195
Peace, Flt Lt Chris 258, 260
Peach, Flt Lt Stu (later ACM Sir Stuart) 248, 318, plate 16
Pearcy, Arthur (author) 71
Pearson, Sgt Jack 194
Pearson, Sqn Ldr 'Fatty' 85
Pearston, Sgt Pete 256, 264
Pedley, Flt Lt Stan 119
Pegg, Sgt 184, 185
Pelly, AVM 193
Penman, Sqn Ldr David 179, 182, 183, 184, 185
Penn, Fg Off Tim 244
Penwarden, LAC T. 51
Perry, Jimmy (author) 183
Perry, Sgt 87
Pescott, Sqn Ldr Kiley 312
Peters, Flt Lt John 261
Petrie, Sgt Bob 263
Pilley, Flt Lt Ray 225
Piper, Flt Lt Nigel 139
Pitchfork, Plt Off Graham 206, 209

Platt, Fg Off Chris 271
Playford, Fg Off 32
Plumbe, Flt Lt David 244
Pollington, Flt Lt Dave 217
Poulton, Fg Off E.A. 'Gene' 135
Powell, FS L. 51
Powell, Sqn Ldr H.S. 322
Price, Wg Cdr Bob 207, 211, 212, 213, 323
Prince Bernhardt of the Netherlands 205
Prince of Wales 30, 33

Q'ayum, Sir Abdul 11

Randles, Sqn Ldr Steve (later Wg Cdr) 255, 257, 323
Rankin, Lt 15
Raschid Ali 67
Rawlinson, Field Marshal Lord 28
Ray, Cpl Brian 198, 201, 202, 203, 206, 212, 215
Read, Flt Lt Bill 249, 282, 292
Read, Wg Cdr G.J.L 58, 59, 62, 322
Rees-Forman, Flt Lt Geoff 251
Reeves, Sgt Jack (Pappy) 92, 95
Reid, LAC John 158
Richards, FS R.I.M. 99, 100
Ridgway, Wg Cdr R.E. 322
Ridley, Fg Off 11
Ridoutt, Flt Lt Dick 119, 120, 125, 130, 132, 134, 281
Robb, ACM Sir James 192
Roberts, FS Ray 183
Roberts, Sgt Robbie 210
Roberts, Sqn Ldr Geoff 217
Roberts, WO D. 118
Robertson, Capt 103
Robertson, Sqn Ldr George 218, 220, 222, 224, 228
Robinson, Lt E. 14, 15, 16
Robinson, Fg Off 32
Robinson, Cpl Darryl plate 5
Robinson, WO 105
Robson, Cpl Alan 177, 183
Rock, LAC Jack 112
Rogers, Chf Tech 231
Rogers, Fg Off Gary 239
Rondot, Flt Lt Mike 233, plate 3
Roos-Keppel, Sir George 12
Ross, Sgt 158
Rouse, Flt Lt Ed 205
Rowbotham, AC1 G.E. 156
Rutherford, WO 301
Rycroft, Sqn Ldr Pete 259

Salmond, AVM Sir John 12, 30
Salmond, Gen Sir Geoffrey 12, 224
Salveson, Peter 87
Sargent, Flt Lt Rob 218, 229
Saunders, FS L.R. 131
Saxby, Paul plate 9
Scholtens, Sqn Ldr John 273
Schur, WO C.D. 131
Scott, Maj Walter 92
Scott, Wg Cdr P.H.L. 208, 209, 323
Scrafton, LAC G. 51
Selves, Flt Lt Martin 220, 228
Seymour, Cpl C. 51
Sharman, WO Derek 158
Sharpe, Plt Off Howard 'Howie' 117, 120, 122, 124, 128, 134
Shaw, WO Dugald 'Dougie' 159, 302
Sheard, Flt Lt Sasha ix, 319
Shepard, C/T 'Pip' 264
Sheppard, FS C.A. 106
Sherwood, Cpl 38
Shores, Christopher, author 73, 76
Simpson, FS George 107
Simpson, John, reporter 291
Singleton, LAC Len 156
Skilton, Cpl 'Skilly' 63
Slessor, Wg Cdr 50
Slim, Gen 117, 127
Slinger, Jack 114, 115
Smart, Cpl Bill 218
Smeaton, Plt Off Gordon M. 87, 88
Smethurst, FS N.W. 104
Smith, Chf Tech 190
Smith, Fg Off T.K.B. 'Keith' 156, 157
Smith, Flt Lt 'AJ' 250, 256, 265
Smith, Flt Lt Tony 173, 184
Smith, FS 22
Smith, LAC T. 51
Smith, Ramsey (reporter) 261
Smith, SAC Danny 248
Smith, Sgt J.H. 94, 98
Smith, Sgt 131
Smith, Sqn Ldr Ed 252, 273
Smith, Sqn Ldr Paul 291
Snaith, Flt Lt 'Snakey' 275, 282
Snow, Peter (reporter) 260
Soekarno, Doctor 148, 153
Soerabaya Sue 165
Soldinski, Zygmund, author 89
Somerford, AC1 T. 51
Spink, Gp Capt Cliff 259

Sprent, Wg Cdr Chris 217, 218, 226, 227, 323

Stanbridge, Fg Off, later AVM Sir Brian 106, 117, 118, 126, 158, 301

Stannard, FS 158

Stead, Sqn Ldr John 196, 322

Stephenson, Fg Off Clifton 54

Stevens, C/T Mark 281

Stevens, Sgt J. 131

Stilwell, Gen 117

Stockings, Fg Off John 271

Stone, Sgt 184, 185

Stonor, Wg Cdr T. 227, 323

Storrie, Sgt 112

Stubbins, SAC 225

Subidio, Gen 165

Sumption, LAC Leslie 72, 80, 83, 88, 91, 304

Sutcliffe, Sgt Ralph 201

Sykes, Ian plate 11

Tarrant, Cpl Ady 279

Taylor, Fg Off Phil 203, 204, 205

Taylor, Flt Lt Keith plate 8

Taylor, Flt Lt Max 86, 87

Taylor, Lt 4, 8

Taylor, LAC 156

Taylor, Plt Off J.M. 117

Teakle, Sonia 291

Teakle, Wg Cdr Paddy, later Air Cdre 284, 286, 288, 290, 291, 295, 310, 323, plate 12

Thatcher, Rt Hon Margaret 266, plate 8

Thesiger, Hon Joan 13

Thomas, Cpl Bert 95

Thomas, Fg Off 203

Thomas, Lt 13

Thomas, Sqn Ldr Nikki 311

Thompson, Flt Lt Mark 311

Thompson, WO 101

Thorpe, FS George 198, 199

Threadgould, Wg Cdr Al 258

Tilley, Lt H. 5

Timmis, Maj Martin 248

Toal, Flt Lt Kevin 225

Todhunter,Flt Lt Phil 'Tod' 293, 294

Tomkins, Mark, journalist 11

Toomer, Flt Lt Bryan 188, 192, 285

Topolski, Feliks, artist 87

Torpy, Wg Cdr Glenn 258

Townley, Fg Off Tom 'Chota' 101

Travers, Lt Paddy 7

Travis, Lt G.R. 12

Treffry, FS Eric 'Treff' 196

Trenchard AM Sir Hugh (later MRAF Lord) 3, 4, 23, 27, 28, 30, 125

Tricker, Flt Lt Gordon 175, 183, 184, 186

Trinder, Tommy, entertainer 116

Turner, LAC 'Titch' 135

Turner, Flt Lt Dennis 208

Tunstall, LAC Alf 176

Tweedie, Lt 4

Twiston-Davis, Plt Off 132

Ubee, Wg Cdr S.E. 60, 73, 322

van Zyl, Libby 159

Varden, Jack 113

Verey, AC1 R.. 51

Villiers, Lt F.E.E.'Ted' 20, 22

Vincent, Lt C. 21, 27

Vlasto, Sgt Mike (later Flt Lt) 62, 75, 86, 89, 92, 93, 94, 102

Vosper, Fg Off R.A. 32

Walker, Flt Lt Johnnie 104

Walker, FS Fred 140

Walker, Gp Capt John ('Whisky' or 'JR') 231, 233

Walker, Cpl Peter 128, 134, 142

Walker, LAC Stan 134

Walker, Sqn Ldr Ivor 279

Wall, LAC J. 69

Waller, Fg Off 38

Wallis, FS A.J. 101

Wallis, Wg Cdr Ken 195

Walpole, Gp Capt Nigel 219

Walser, Sqn Ldr A.A. 322

Walters, Plt Off 38

Ward, Plt Off Howard 117, 118

Wark, WO Sam 279

Watson, Flt Lt Nick 266

Watts, Cpl A.C. 'Benny' 45, 72, 88, 95, 113, 120, 122, 124, 129, 137, 143, 150, 185

Watts, Flt Lt 32

Webb, Plt Off George 112

Webster, Bob 126, 143

Webster, Cpl Jack 307

Weeks, Sgt 156

Welham, Cpl Horace 88, 94, 106, 113, 114, 116, 124, 125, 135, 248, 264

Wells, Lt 25

Wenning, Fg Off G.A. 131

Wetherburn, WEM George 69, 72

Wheeler,WO Johnny 283

Whelpdale, Flt Lt 140

White, Fg Off M.R. 'Blanco' 51

White, Sqn Ldr John 236, 237

Whiting, Sqn Ldr Spencer 140, 149, 152, 169

Whittingham, Sqn Ldr Jerry 256

Wicks, Sqn Ldr F.F. 322

Wiles, Sgt Andy 257, 265

Wilkinson, Flt Lt Steve 266

Williams, Flt Lt Douglas 'Chota' 85

Williams, FS R.B. 156

Williams, Plt Off 84, 85

Williams, Sgt 171

Williamson, Sqn Ldr.N. 322

Wilson, WO 105

Wilson-Dick, AM1 Ian ii, vii, 183, plates 1, 2 & 3

Wingate, Brig 91, 93, 96, 105

Winstanley, Lt G. 25, 26

Withers, Sqn Ldr D.W. 84, 85

Witts, Wg Cdr Jerry (later Gp Capt) 253, 258, 259, 263, 267, 268, 275, 298, plate 8

Worral, Charlie 115

Wratten, AVM Bill 258

Wright, Flt Lt Chris 294

Wright, Flt Lt 'Dicky' 280

Wright, Sgt 45

Wynn, Lawrie 95

Yates, Flt Lt Rich (later Wg Cdr) 281, 313, 314, 318, 323, plates 12, 14

Yates, Sgt 100

Young, Flt Lt 'Shifty' 256

Young, WO A. 104